HANDGUN HUNTING

How to Travel the World in Pursuit of Wild Game!

Mark Hampton

© 2002 by Mark Hampton

All rights reserved. No portion of this publication may be reproduced or transmitted
in any form or by any means, electronic or mechanical, including photocopy, recording,
or any information storage and retrieval system, without permission in writing from the publisher,
except by a reviewer who may quote brief passages in a critical article or review to be
printed in a magazine or newspaper, or electronically transmitted on radio or television.

Published by

700 E. State Street • Iola, WI 54990-0001
Telephone: 715/445-2214
Web: www.krause.com

Please call or write for our free catalog of publications.
Our toll-free number to place an order or obtain a free catalog is 800-258-0929
or please use our regular business telephone 715-445-2214.

Library of Congress Catalog Number: 2002105089
ISBN: 0-87349-364-8

Printed in the United States of America

About Our Covers

On the front:

The Taurus Model 455 "Stellar Tracker" was introduced in 2002 along with a new line of Taurus ammunition.

The new "Taurus Copper Bullets™" design utilizes the "Taurus HEX Bullet™" and is the result of extensive testing by the Taurus research and development engineers in collaboration with Randy Brooks of Barnes Bullets, Inc., and handgun ammunition expert Dick Metcalf.

"Taurus Copper Bullets™" ammunition employs non-polluting bullets, propellant, and primers, and will be produced by a strategic alliance among four major companies in the firearms industry:

- Taurus International Mfg., Inc., world leader in handgun manufacturing and metallurgical technologies, will direct the manufacture, marketing and international distribution of the new ammunition under the Taurus label.
- Barnes Bullets, Inc., will utilize its renowned X-Bullet technology to produce the new "Taurus HEX Bullet™" of pure Copper to meticulous performance standards.
- Hodgdon Powder, Inc., will provide a derivative of its environmentally friendly TITEGROUP® brand propellant, matched to the ballistic criteria for this project. This fast, clean-burning propellant delivers optimum accuracy and efficiency with lead-free projectiles.
- PMC Ammunition will assemble the "Taurus Copper Bullets™" cartridges using its highest quality solid brass casings and mercury-free primers.

The new Stellar Tracker specifications include:
Caliber: .45 ACP
Barrel: 2, 4 or 6 inches
Weight: 28/33/38.4 oz
Stocks: Taurus Ribber™ Grip
Sights: Adjustable
Features: Double action, matte stainless steel, comes with five "Stellar" Full-Moon Clips, integral key lock, five-shot.
Price: $525

On the back:

Both ends of the line of Taurus hunting revolvers are presented with the Model 17 Tracker and the Raging Bull. Specifications are below:

Taurus Model 17 Tracker - New For 2002

Caliber: .17HMR
Barrel: 6 inches
Weight: 45.8 oz
Stocks: Taurus Ribber™ Grip
Sights: Adjustable
Features: Double action, matte stainless steel, integral key lock, seven-shot.
Price: $391

Taurus Raging Bull Series Model 444/454/480

Caliber: .44 Magnum/.45 Long Colt/ .454 Casull/.480 Ruger
Barrel: 5, 6-1/2, 8-3/8
Weight: 53 to 63 ounces
Stocks: Rubber with cushion insert
Sights: Patridge front, rear adjustable.
Features: Double action, ported, heavy barrel w/vented rib, blue or matte stainless, integral key lock, .44 Mag. six-shot, 454 Casull and .480 Ruger five-shot.
Price: $575-$855.

Contents

Dedication 5

Foreword 6

Foreword 7

Chapter 1   Picking Up A Pistol 8

Chapter 2   Handloading: Your Chance To Learn More 16

Chapter 3   Handguns: A Great Choice For Hunting 19

Chapter 4   Long Seasons Make Small Game Hunting Great 24

Chapter 5   Break The Bonds Of Winter With Varmint Hunting 31

Chapter 6   The Most Popular Game In The Land 39

Chapter 7   Where The Deer And The Antelope Play 51

Chapter 8   Close-Range Action 60

Chapter 9   Handgunning On The Last Frontier 76

Chapter 10 Hunting Exotic Species: An Off-Season Challenge 88

Chapter 11 Hunting "Small" On the Dark Continent 96

Chapter 12 Mid-Sized African Game 105

Chapter 13 Playing A Dangerous Game 126

Chapter 14 Hunting Down Under 142

Chapter 15 Asia: High Mountain Action 152

Chapter 16 Culture and Custom: Hunting in Europe 166

Chapter 17 South America: Adventure South Of The Equator 173

Chapter 18 The Et Cetera Of Handgun Hunting 180

Arms Library 186

Index 212

Dedication

I'm thankful for good parents and a family who cherished hunting and fishing adventues. I am also grateful for a wife who understands and tolerates me chasing game all over God's great creation. I sincerely hope you enjoy this book half as much as I did gaining the experience to write it.

Foreword

It's not just a figure of speech when I say that the Honorable Mr. Mark Hampton, Representative of Missouri's 147th District, and I go back a long ways. Fully 35 years ago — maybe a wee bit more — Mark Hampton and I were Sub-Juniors and later Junior shooters on the Midwest trapshooting circuit. Mark was from central Missouri and I was from eastern Kansas. We seemed to meet up, occasionally shooting together but always competing against each other, at every major trap shoot in that part of the world.

As teenagers, we traded local, regional, and state titles back and forth, and we both made the *Sports Afield* "All-American" trap team together. Other than a couple of trapshooting and quail hunting mentors, there is nobody involved in the shooting sports that I have known as long as I've known Mark Hampton

After college, I put some time in the Marines, and then started writing. Mark has had a more varied — and in many ways more productive — career. He farmed, taught school, and established a successful commercial hunting operation in Missouri. Always involved in his community, with a winning smile and a slight Missouri twang to his speech, in time he was elected to the Missouri House of Representatives, and he's represented his district well at the State Capitol for many years now.

We ran into each other at a Safari Club convention many years ago, and have stayed in touch ever since. We have never hunted together, which is something I regret and hope we can fix one of these days. But we've compared notes on dozens of hunts, and over the years we have hunted in many of the same places. Actually, our hunting resumes are quite similar. Mark has hunted big game on all the continents, from the high mountains of central Asia to the tundras of Alaska and back again. He has hunted Africa a great deal, and is the only other living writer I can think of who has taken Africa's Big Five. But there's a big difference: For many years now Mark Hampton has done all of his big-game hunting with a handgun.

This challenge adds to immeasurably to the enjoyment. Mark Hampton accepts this challenge all of the time, and for this I respect him immensely. Hampton has hunted successfully with his handgun huge beasts such as cape buffalo, rhino, elephant, water buffalo, and banteng. He has taken lion and leopard. These animals are not only incredibly dangerous, but also are usually taken in difficult shooting situations, with the difficulty greatly magnified by the use of a handgun.

There are many "casual" handgun hunters who, like me, occasionally turn to the handgun. There are also many dedicated handgun hunters like Mark Hampton, who use the handgun almost exclusively. While there are few among us who will stalk elephant through the thickets of Africa or ibex in the mountains of Mongolia with handguns in our fists, we can all learn from a man who has "been there and done that!"

It's been a long time since Mark Hampton and I stood on a trap range together, tied for score and shooting off for some piece of silver or gaudy trophy that, in those days, meant all the world to each of us. Our paths diverged, and yet came back together as we have had the good fortune to hunt the game fields of the world. He knows his handguns and his handgun hunting, and in this book he shares not only a lifetime of adventures, but also his knowledge of the pistols, cartridges, bullets, and hunting techniques that make it all work. You'll learn from this book, and you'll enjoy it. And if you don't know him, you'll enjoy meeting Mark Hampton, the unassuming man from Missouri whose quiet smile comes through on every page. He's a man that I am very proud to have known all these years.

Who knows what the future might hold? Perhaps someday I'll have the great privilege to vote for him.

Craig Boddington
September, 2001

Foreword

Handgun hunting is pure unadulterated fun. No facet of our great sport is more exciting and challenging than pursuing game with a handgun. Show me a hunter who uses a "short arm" and I'll show you a hunter who understands the necessity of getting reasonably close to game, one who has a great understanding of an animal's habits and anatomy, and knows his hunting gun's capabilities as well as his own. Despite my use of the pronoun, handgun hunting is not just restricted to "him." Thankfully, an increasing number of women are getting into the sport.

Every sport needs heroes. Since I came down with handgun-hunting fever I've had several personal heroes including such greats as Elmer Keith, J.D. Jones, Larry Kelly, and Hal Swiggett. These men of vision essentially created the sport of handgun hunting in the mid-1950s with the introduction of the .44 Remington Magnum cartridge. Then in the 1960s Warren Center designed the Thompson/Center Contender, a single-shot handgun with interchangeable barrels. The Contender truly got people interested in hunting with handguns. At about the same time gun companies such as Ruger, Remington and others started producing true hunting handguns.

In recent years I've added another personal handgun hunting hero, Mark Hampton. The following pages will provide you some insight into his philosophies on handgun hunting and review of some of his exploits in the field. I first became aware of Mark Hampton quite a few years ago, when other writers would talk about a serious handgun hunter from Missouri. Missouri of all places! I was sure my next handgun hero would come from my home state of Texas or at least someplace farther west. The more I heard and on rare occasions read about Mark Hampton's exploits, the more I became enthralled and interested in his experiences and his opinions on the various facets of hunting with handguns. Hampton relatively quietly went about the world hunting with a handgun, in most instances a T/C Contender using barrels and cartridges designed by J.D. Jones of SSK Industries.

After finally meeting Mark, I had the opportunity to sit in on a couple of his seminars given at Safari Club International Conventions. This guy knows whereof he speaks.

Over the past few years Mark and I have continued to correspond. I have also visited with him at his hunting operation in Missouri. Mark is very personable and his knowledge is backed up by experience, not just theories. He is also passionate about hunting.

Now too, he thankfully serves as a State Representative in the Missouri legislature, where he can make a great impact on polices regarding wildlife and hunting.

After thinking about it for quite some time, Mark has finally decided to write a book. It is written for anyone who enjoys hunting, and especially those hunters who choose to use handguns. I know you will be impressed. Sit back, enjoy and learn!

Larry Weishuhn
2001

Chapter 1

Picking Up A Pistol

Why hunt with a handgun? I guess everyone who participates in this great sport has his or her own reasons. Most include some reference to the challenges involved. Hunting with a rifle lost its appeal to me many years ago (I truly hate cleaning smokepoles) and bowhunting just wasn't my cup of tea. Whatever reason you find to hunt with a handgun, I'm sure you will experience many rewards, memories, and much enjoyment.

Today's handgun hunters have never had it so good. We are blessed with an array of paraphernalia including quality handguns, optics, and bullets. Choosing a handgun for hunting can be a mind-boggling process. What a delightful dilemma! I am often asked which is the best choice for a hunting handgun, revolver or single-shot? Let me pause for a moment and say that most dyed-in-the-wool handgun hunters do not really consider automatics suitable for hunting. I do realize that certain autos are capable of handling deer, hogs, and perhaps a few other critters at short range, but I do not feel they are true hunting handguns by any stretch

Handgun hunting is a very challenging endeavor. Shooting offhand is extremely difficult with a scope and requires a lot of practice.

Handgunners should use every type of rest available including your own body. Here, the knees provide a valuable rest enabling the hunter to steady the crosshairs.

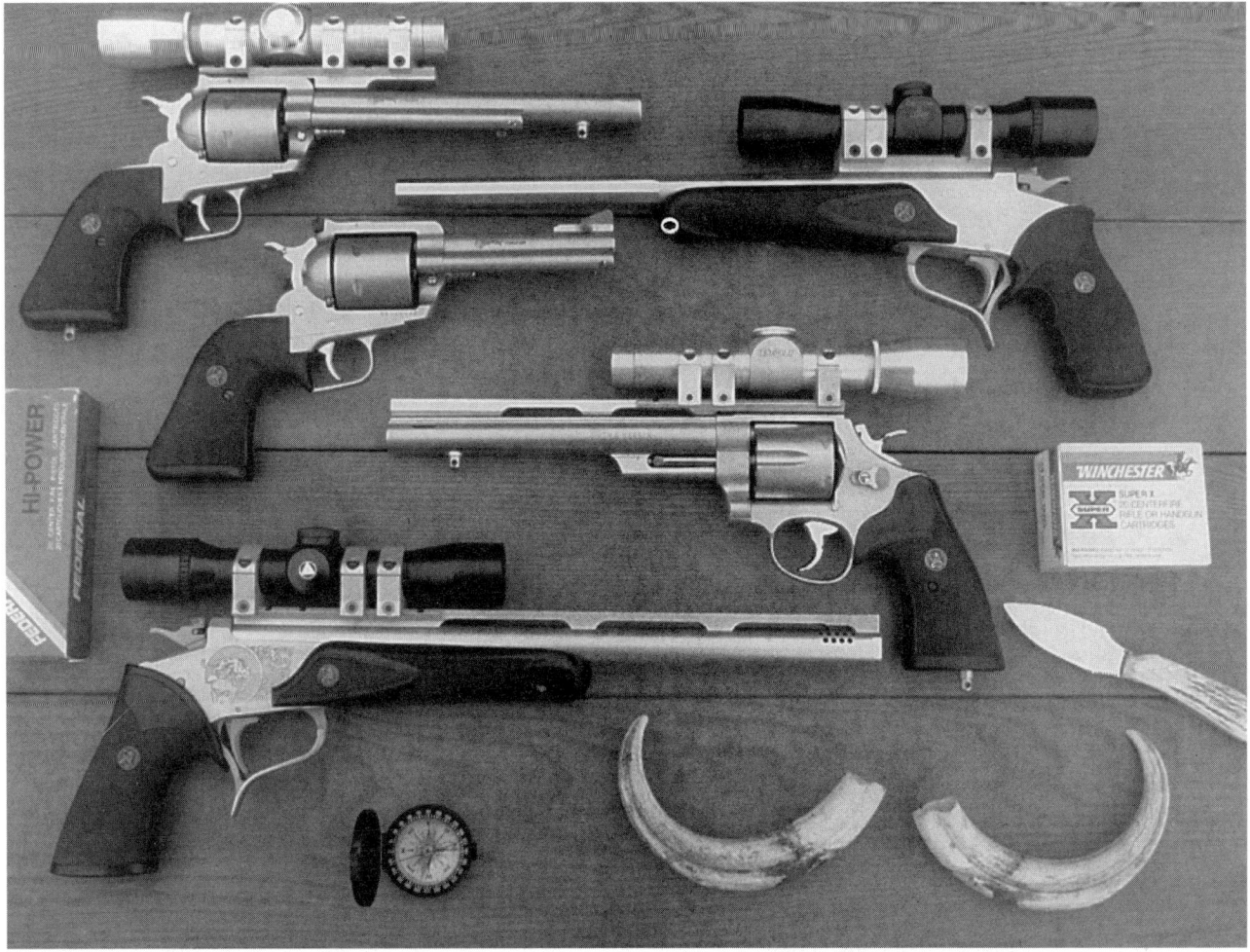

Hunting handguns come in a variety of packages from revolvers to single-shots. The handguns shown here are capable of handling a wide range of applications.

of the imagination. In general, they lack the power and accuracy so necessary for a rewarding experience in the field.

That leaves us considering only revolvers and single-shot handguns as our tools of choice. You should objectively evaluate several factors including circumstances of the hunt, calibers, and plain old personal preference. If you plan on hunting whitetails in the woods, stalking game in heavy cover, or chasing a pack of hounds around the country for hogs, bear, or cougar, a revolver becomes a logical choice. If your hunts take you into open country for antelope and mule deer, or into the mountains for species usually taken at long range such as sheep and ibex, the single-shot handgun capable of accurately delivering a bullet at 250 yards or more makes a lot of sense. I know serious handgun hunters who choose to hunt with a revolver exclusively. Then there are those who only hunt with a single-shot regardless what game is pursued. That's one of the factors that make this sport so appealing. You can hunt with whatever type of firearm and caliber you prefer and the challenge remains regardless of your choice.

First, let's look at suitable revolver calibers. One very important factor the hunter must consider is matching the ammunition to the game.

The .357 Magnum: This well-known cartridge has been around for many years and has taken much game. I've killed a few whitetails and hogs with the cartridge myself, but do not consider the .357 Magnum the best choice for medium-sized game. It is certainly inadequate for big game hunting. If you are an excellent shot, have the patience of Job, wait for the perfect broadside shot, never shoot at a running animal, and take your shots inside 60 yards the cartridge may suffice if you limit its use to game in the 150- to 200-pound range. It should be clear from these statements that I'm not real crazy about using the .357 Magnum as a big game hunting tool. My personal experience with the caliber leads

Revolvers are popular with many hunters— especially those who hunt in close cover. Even when the range is less than 75 yards, handgun hunters should always look for a way to steady their aim.

me to believe the .357 is marginal on any 150- to 200-pound animal unless shot placement is perfect.

The .41 Magnum: This "middle magnum" is the starting point for the serious handgun hunter. I have two very close friends who have a love affair with the .41 Magnum. Both of them have harvested quite a few whitetails with the .41 Magnum and are satisfied with it for their tree-stand, close-range woods hunting. This caliber has never received the popularity of other revolver cartridges normally considered as adequate hunting rounds. I suppose the reason for this is simply because the .44 Magnum does everything better than the .41.

The .44 Magnum: Simply stated, the .44 Magnum (officially, the .44 Remington Magnum) is a better choice than either of the two rounds listed above and has been used effectively all over the world. The sheer amount of factory ammo available for this round, plus the liberal bullet options, give the hunter an excellent selection for a multitude of tasks. I consider the .44 Magnum a 75-yard deer cartridge when fired with iron sights. It can be effective at 125 yards if a scope is used, under excellent conditions with someone that knows how to shoot. I realize a lot of silhouette shooters can knock down steel rams at 200 yards all day with the .44 Magnum. However, silhouette matches are held in broad daylight, the unobstructed target is in plain sight against a contrasting background and is standing perfectly still. Best of all, the exact yardage is known. That's a far cry from actual field conditions and certainly not equivalent to most hunting situations. Most hunters are seldom offered the perfect broadside shot at a known distance, in perfect lighting conditions. Also, the steel shooter can hit a ram in the guts, horn, or tail — anywhere — as long as the target falls. Make a similar hit on a big game animal and you will have a wounded animal on your hands, something we want to avoid at all cost.

It never ceases to amaze me that some believe magnum pistol rounds possess some kind of magical power. There is a lot of misconception about the ability of certain cartridges, including the .44 Magnum. Many shooters I have spoken with over the years believe this cartridge can unleash almighty power and whatever it touches turns into meat in the pot. That is simply not the case. "Magnum" does not mean "Magic." The plain truth is that any caliber has its limitations. The limitations of handguns are generally greater than those of high-powered rifles. Handguns require more skill to shoot, have shorter barrel lengths, lower velocity, lower energy levels, and less inherent accuracy. Magnum is simply marketing. The sooner this fact is accepted, the sooner shooters will become realistic with their expectations. The .44 Magnum is a great hunting cartridge

The whitetail deer is the most sought after big game animal in North America. Handgun hunters look forward to deer season so they can head to the woods with their favorite sidearm.

indeed, but like everything else in life, it too has confines and needs to be used within its capabilities.

The .454 Casull: This relatively new round gives added punch to the revolver shooter, providing with sufficient power to harvest the largest game North America has to offer, including moose and the big bears. It has even proven itself in Africa and elsewhere. The paper ballistics of the .454 Casull are mighty impressive, as are its recoil and muzzle blast. Still, it remains a close-range revolver cartridge even though it is unmatched by other revolver loads when it comes to power. With companies like Freedom Arms, Ruger and Taurus producing revolvers chambered for this round, I believe we will see a greater variety of factory ammunition become available. Several quality .45 caliber bullets designed specifically for hunting are making handloaders happier than ever with the .454 Casull. Hunters sometimes ignore bullet choice and focus only on the caliber of the projectile. The best, most expensive handgun and equipment in the world is worthless if the bullet isn't capable of the job it's expected to perform. More on that later.

A good shoulder holster like this one from Michaels of Oregon not only frees both hands but also protects your investment.

The .480 Ruger: This is the newest of the big-bore revolver rounds on the market. The big round first appeared in combination with a beefy Ruger Super Redhawk frame and a couple other manufacturers are now making revolvers to fire this powerhouse.

Black powder enthusiasts will find the T/C Scout as an answer to their handgun hunting needs. The Scout proved effective on African game such as this warthog.

Hunters looking for adventure and excitement may find handgun hunting just the ticket. If and when you get bored with rifle hunting, the handgun will provide a satisfying challenge.

The power of the .480 Ruger is impressive but the recoil is stout. Still, factory ammo is available and there seems to be a segment of the market leaning toward this round. Like the .454 Casull, the .480 Ruger is big enough to take any North American game and should prove suitable for some African game as well. Once again, it must be used within its limitations to be most effective.

Other Revolver Rounds: It seems there is virtually no end to the rounds available for use in revolvers. Talented custom gunsmiths can create just about anything. Get into a conversation with any bona fide gun enthusiast and you'll hear things like .475 and .500 Linebaugh, .50 AE and others. I've limited the discussion here to the more common calibers simply because they are the most readily available and information on them is widely distributed among hunters. This is not to say that the calibers listed here are the only ones that should be used. The key, as I stated before, is to match the load to the game you seek.

Single-Shots Mean More Power

Single-shot pistols can trade quantity of projectiles for velocity, sometimes to great benefit to the shooter. Typically, a single-shot, long-barreled pistol will give added range and more power. Pistols like the Thompson/Center Contender or Encore, H-S Precision, XP-100, Magnum Research's Lone Eagle, RPM's XL, Savage Striker, and a few others work extremely well for the hunter looking to extend the range of the hunting handgun by using rifle ammunition. These handguns safely launch high-intensity, flat-shooting cartridges that are ideal for hunting antelope and deer in open country while maintaining superiority in killing power in the woods.

The Thompson/Center Contender: This break-action pistol is the most popular single-shot handgun on the market. With easily interchangeable barrels, the Contender can offer great versatility in a very affordable package. A few of my favorite cartridges include the .223 Winchester, 7X30 Waters, .30-30 Winchester, and the old .45-70. Each one of these cartridges has a special place reserved in my arsenal. If you consider custom barrels from SSK Industries, the list can be almost endless. Some of my favorite custom barrels include the .250 Savage, 6.5 JDJ, .309 JDJ, and the .375 JDJ. It is almost unbelievable how accurate some of these guns are when set up correctly. At this writing, Thompson/Center has ceased production of the Contender to replace it with a newer model, the G-2, which will incorporate some updates to the classic design of the Contender.

The Thompson/Center Encore: At first glance, the Encore looks a lot like the Contender. But it is much stronger. The Encore is a strong break-action single-shot handgun capable of handling most of the "standard" belted magnum cartridges as well as cartridges of much greater diameter if pressures are lowered accord-

The Thompson Contender is the most versatile handgun on the market. With one frame, hunters can add many other barrels to their battery. Barrels come in different lengths, configurations, and finishes. This interchangeable system is unique and helpful to hunters.

ingly. Currently the Encore is enjoying popularity with handgun hunters in .243 Winchester, .270 Winchester, 7mm-08, .308 Winchester, 30-06, and a host of other rifle cartridges. The cartridge list for the Encore is lengthy and growing every day but I really like the .308 Winchester as a long-range hunting round. For really big game, SSK Industries makes the 375/06 JDJ, a wildcat that launches a 270-grain bullet at 2,450 fps. This kind of power is capable of bringing down anything in the world. Wildcat cartridges in the Encore are quite

There are many quality handguns available for a variety of hunting tasks. From the top is T/C's Contender with a custom barrel in .375 JDJ, a Ruger Super Blackhawk that has been transformed into a Predator by Mag-Na-Port International, and the MOA chambered in 250 Savage.

Handgun Hunting

numerous and hunters have never had so many good choices for any hunting application. For obvious reasons, the barrels from Encore and Contender pistols will not interchange.

Remington XP-100: This classic is now out of production, but there are still plenty of them in service and available in calibers such as the 7mmBR, 7mm-08 Remington, .308 Winchester, and the .35 Remington. These are all designed for hunters and are extremely accurate. I have a .284 Winchester chambered in a custom XP-100, with a McMillan stock that is truly a 300-yard gun if you have a good rest. This is not your typical garden-variety handgun by any means, but the ballistics and performance are not ordinary either.

H-S Precision: This bolt gun is very accurate and comes in 11 different calibers. My own H-S Pro-Series 2000 is chambered in .308 Winchester, and makes for an ideal handgun when sitting in a deer blind overlooking one of those big wheat fields.

The Savage Striker: Clearly identifiable with the bolt handle on the left side of a right-handed pistol, the Striker is yet another bolt-action handgun available in some fine hunting calibers. Recently I was shooting a Striker in .22-250 and was surprised by its out-of-the-box performance.

The Lone Eagle: Magnum Research offers an interesting single-shot that uses a rotating breechblock action. The lightweight polymer frame is very tough and the gun is available in several different calibers. While it may not look traditional, perhaps look shouldn't matter as much as performance when it comes to handgun hunting.

It's The Bullet That Counts

Penetration is my first priority for a hunting bullet and expansion secondary. It is critical for a bullet to reach and penetrate the vitals of an animal. The hand-

Any animal that can be taken with a rifle can certainly be taken with a handgun— provided the right cartridge and bullet selection is chosen for the job. This giant brown bear was taken with a single-shot Encore using a custom barrel in .375/06.

gun hunter using a .44 Magnum or .454 Casull shouldn't choose a bullet that gives drastic expansion at the expense of inadequate penetration. A balance of the two factors is necessary. The functions of penetration and expansion both rely on velocity and bullet design. This combination of four elements must come together to produce an effective bullet. From my experience, and information gathered from experienced revolver shooters, a hole all the way through an animal with an expanding, jacketed bullet that causes considerable tissue damage is preferred. This leaves an exit wound that makes for easier blood trailing and quicker kills. Let me point out that big cast bullets in revolvers essentially leave half-inch diameter holes in animals but in most cases they do not kill quickly. I have seen more than 100 head of medium-sized game shot multiple times, in the right spot, with these big, hard cast bullets, in both .44 and .45 caliber revolvers, and it never ceases to amaze me by how far the game will go afterward. Unless the shoulder or spine is broken, or a brain shot is made, the chase will be on. Honestly, a good broadhead from an arrow will kill game more quickly. All of you guys who are emotionally attached to your cast bullets for hunting, please save the phone calls, e-mail, and letters. A good expanding jacketed bullet such as the Hornady XTP and Winchester's Partition Gold causes more damage to vital organs and simply kills faster.

Combine a top-quality bullet with a powerful cartridge and put it in the right place from a reasonable range and you will be a successful handgun hunter. But all that is easier said than done. The pages of this book will give you the information you need. The rest is up to you.

Chapter 2

Handloading: Your Chance To Learn More

I began reloading ammunition many years ago and still do so today. For many, the decision to handload is based on a financial consideration. When I started handloading, I figured if I could load my own ammo, I could shoot twice as much for the same amount of money it cost to purchase factory rounds. It was a pretty simple decision to make when I was much younger, broke, and wanted to shoot a great deal. An RCBS Rock Chucker got me started. It's still going today.

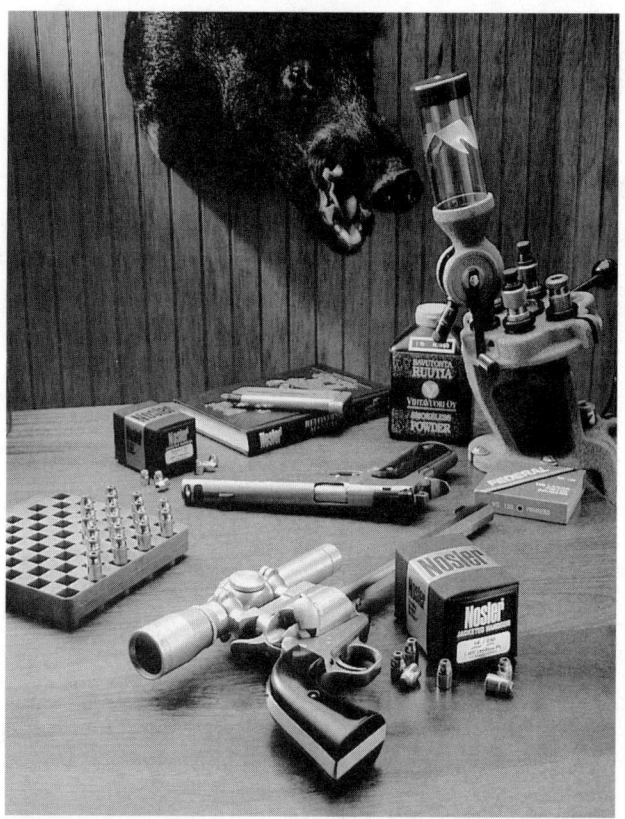

Getting started in handloading is relatively easy. Make sure you get up-to-date reloading manuals and use them carefully. There is plenty of information to get you headed in the right direction. Take your time and think about what you want, then look for the information that fills your need.

The versatility provided by handloading is one of its strong points. With that old Rock Chucker I could (still can) reload the bullet and powder combination I wanted, not just what was available commercially. Thirty years ago the selection of ammunition loaded commercially, and even the bullets available to the handloader, was not all that great by today's standards. I often loaded a cheap cast bullet for practice sessions, a thin-jacketed soft-point bullet for whitetail deer, and a solid to penetrate a buffalo should the occasion arise. By handloading I could also improve accuracy, in some cases by quite a bit. I also had control over the velocity.

Let me state right here and tell you this chapter is by no means intended to "reinvent the wheel" when it comes to handloading. Numerous authorities have written countless pages on the subject. If handloading is of interest to you I strongly suggest purchasing their wisdom. There are many books and manuals on reloading. If you don't like to read, many excellent videos are also available to show you how to safely enjoy this hobby. The National Rifle Association offers a basic reloading course designed with the beginner in mind. Of course there is a ton of information on the Internet. A great deal of it is inaccurate, and much of it dangerous, so don't believe everything out there. Personally, I wouldn't use any loading data that did not come from a creditable source such as is found in reloading manuals from Hornady, Nosler, Sierra, Speer, and others. Read and study this information thoroughly before handloading any ammunition.

Today, with so much quality ammunition being manufactured by a number of companies, I have to question why anyone would want to reload, unless of course the shooter finds it enjoyable. I'll have to admit, if you don't like the thought of handloading your own ammo, you certainly do not have to. Today, we have a wide variety of premium ammunition that is being produced by major ammunition companies. These days you can buy factory ammo intended for a variety of special hunting purposes, from prairie dogs to whitetail deer even up to Cape buffalo. Today's factory ammo is also extremely accurate. Oftentimes it is difficult for a handloader to duplicate the accuracy of today's factory ammo. So, why should anyone reload?

The personal satisfaction of developing and crafting exactly the ammunition wanted for a particular job and doing the job successfully remains one of the responses avid handloaders give. Exploring the fascinating field of internal and external ballistics is an enjoyable hobby for many of us. The ability to change a cartridge case from one caliber to another, and even a major change in case body and capacity in some instances, is an interesting process.

I own and shoot several different "wildcats." A wildcat is a cartridge that is not commercially available. In other words, I cannot go to the local sporting goods store and purchase ammo for these guns. If I want the benefits and experience of shooting a wildcat, I must load the ammo myself, or have one of my friends load the cartridges for me. Regularly I hunt with a 6.5 JDJ, .309 JDJ, .375 JDJ, or 375/06. These are just some of the many wildcat offerings that must be handloaded. Even today with such a variety of commercial ammo available, these wildcat cartridges offer ballistic advantages over the standard factory fare. Even factory cartridges can be greatly enhanced by handloading.

Another reason shooters handload their ammo is the satisfaction of making ammunition. Some hunters feel a sense of gratification by actually taking game with ammunition they designed and constructed. It's challenging, fun, and educational to develop and experiment with different loads and bullets. By shooting, testing, and evaluating handloads all summer, I can develop the most accurate load possible, using a specific bullet weight and design. And I can be totally confident when the autumn big game seasons roll around.

One of the primary reasons I handload is because I am fanatical when it comes to bullet selection. You can purchase the most expensive gun on the market and top it with the most expensive scope, but if you choose the wrong bullet for a particular hunting situation, everything else is irrelevant! Regardless what game you pursue, choose your bullet wisely. If you are not sure what bullet to use for a particular animal or situation, consult some of the major bullet manufacturers. They will steer you in the right direction.

Everyone has his or her favorite bullet design for different hunting applications. For single-shot handguns, I prefer boat-tail bullets when circumstances allow. These long, slender, pointed bullets have good ballistic coefficients (BC), and aerodynamic efficiency. They are generally more accurate than flat-nosed bullets. The higher BC of a bullet, the more easily it flies through the air, deflecting the wind. Boat-tail bullets differ from stan-

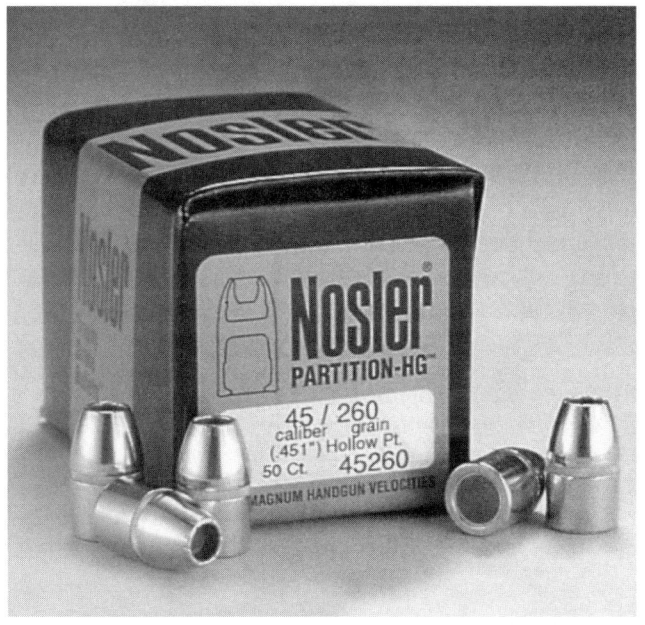

Handloaders have access to many great hunting bullets like those manufactured by Nosler. Reloading is not only a fun hobby but hunters can build their own loads to fit any hunting application. Quality bullets are important ingredients when handloading.

Hornady Manufacturing provides the handloader many top-quality hunting bullets. The author has used Hornady bullets on everything from prairie dogs to elephant. To put it simply, they work exceptionally well.

dard bullets in that their heel or base is slightly tapered. As a general rule, boat-tail bullets will retain more velocity resulting in flatter trajectory. In hunting situations, most of us will not see significant benefits from boat-tail bullets unless we are shooting beyond 300 yards. I want to point out that some of the highest BC ratings belong to match-grade bullets designed only for accuracy. They should not be used for hunting. Accuracy is important, but unless the bullet is designed to perform well on game, all the accuracy in the world doesn't mean squat.

Velocity is another factor that sometimes gets blown out of proportion. Just because a bullet goes 100 fps faster than another doesn't mean much unless there are some improvements in the accuracy or terminal performance departments.

Another advantage the handloader achieves is the ability to seat the bullet where it functions as efficiently as possible in the firearm. Let's take the .308 Winchester for example. There are many fine choices when it comes to factory ammo and there are a multitude of bullets loaded for a wide variety of tasks. But all that factory ammo is manufactured to fit and function in every gun chambered for the .308 Winchester. Do you know how many .308 Winchester firearms are floating around? Neither do I, but it's got to be a bundle or two. One of the easiest things for a handloader to do is find the overall length of the cartridge to make it shoot more accurately. Seating the bullet so it is closer to the rifling almost always improves performance. This is especially true with a single-shot handgun, because you don't have to worry about the length of the cartridge functioning in a magazine. If you are using a magazine-fed pistol, like the Savage Striker, you'll have to also pay attention to overall length as it relates to ammunition fitting as it cycles through the magazine. Revolver ammunition also has definite length limitations, for obvious reasons.

Factory ammo or handloads? It is your decision entirely. If you do decide to reload, pick up several different manuals or videos and follow the directions carefully. It can be a lot of fun and very satisfying. Then again, if you don't want to, the selection of great factory ammo means you don't really need to.

Single-shot handguns are very accurate— especially when the right bullet and load are used. Handloading allows you to tailor the round to your specific needs.

Chapter 3

Handguns: A Great Choice For Hunting

With few exceptions you can use a handgun to hunt almost anywhere hunting is legal in the United States. Local laws are clearly spelled out and adequately posted. The same isn't always true in other countries. When it comes to international hunting, the governments involved always seem to require some sort of special permit. Many Third World governments prohibit the private ownership of handguns and others, as a matter of national security, allow civilians to own firearms that chamber only non-military ammunition. When you say handgun, some foreign officials see only 9mm, .38 Special, .45 ACP. They may not equate "handgun" and "hunting" the way we in the United States do.

I am somewhat reluctant to put in print the names of the countries currently open to handgun hunting. Political climates can change overnight. Handguns may be forbidden today where they were legal several years ago. Places that prohibit handguns now could change policies before this ink dries. For example, places like

Single-shot handguns are winning the hearts of serious handgun hunters. They can handle bottleneck cartridges capable of handling most any hunting chore. Some of these handguns will outshoot many rifles.

To properly sight-in a handgun, a rock-solid rest should be used. Hearing and eye protection should be worn at all times. Hunters should spend as much time on the range as possible. Getting familiar with your handgun will pay big dividends come hunting season.

When long-range shooting is encountered, hunters should find the best possible rest available. The author likes to use his backpack as a rest while hunting in the mountains.

China, Azerbaijan, Mongolia, Tajikistan, Ethiopia, Botswana, Turkey, and Spain are now open to handgun hunters if you follow proper procedures.

The best thing a hunter can do if there is a question about using a handgun on an upcoming hunting trip is to enlist the help of a reputable outfitter or hunting consultant. Outfitters can help their clients obtain permission by giving the host country specific data relative to the handgun. Using words like "stockless" or "hand-held," on an application can prevent red flags from being raised over words like "pistol." It is also very important to detail the caliber of the round you'll be using, to make it perfectly clear the firearm is obviously not a military-style weapon. This provides some reference the bureaucracy can relate to and may increase the chance of getting the handgun into the country. Most Third World countries like to see rifle-type calibers, because they are familiar with

Here are two handguns capable of tackling big game anywhere on earth. The T/C Contender with an SSK Industries .375 JDJ barrel topped with a 4X Bausch & Lomb scope and a Predator conversion from Mag-Na-Port International in .44 Magnum. The variety of handguns currently available from several different manufacturers is nothing short of amazing.

For many hunters, the handgun is a ticket to adventure. Regardless of what type of handgun you choose or where you go, handgun hunting is challenging and just plain fun.

them. It's not a sure-fire method by any means, but it can make things easier.

One of my handgun hunting friends, Ray Young, has taken his handguns into Botswana, China, Mexico, Azerbaijan, Mongolia, Russia, Cameroon, Turkmenistan, and the C.A.R., all within the last five years. Each time, people would tell him it was impossible. But Ray was relentless and succeeded in legally getting his handguns in every country in which he wanted to hunt. He did so by doing his homework and obtaining the proper documentation. Ray also books his hunts through a major hunting consultant. He looks at it this way: If they want his business, they will do everything possible to get his handguns into the area he wishes to hunt. After all, these major hunting agencies have been booking hunts for years and they have plenty of government contacts.

On the other side of the coin there may actually be some outfitters that do not want to take you hunting because you intend to use a handgun. Some of these guys feel it will be much more work for them. They'd rather not bother or put forth the extra effort. Stay away from such outfitters. They are misguided and misinformed. Don't let anyone, especially a guide or outfitter, tell you a particular animal is impossible to take with a handgun. I have been told that this animal or that could not be taken with a handgun because of the sheer size of the beast, or the guide thought the shooting distance would be too great, or the terrain would not allow it. It's all nonsense. Any animal that can be taken with a rifle can be taken with a handgun. You are paying the bill. Hunt with the weapon of your choice. You might come up empty handed once in a while. But that's part of the challenge of hunting with a handgun. We accept that challenge every time we go hunting, whether it's in our backyard for whitetail, or Azerbaijan for Eastern tur.

I tell you all this not to discourage you from hunting with a handgun, but to show you that, if you are diligent, it can be done. Handgun hunting has made great strides in the past. I would like to see this trend continue. To keep handgun hunting growing, we all need to get involved with hunting organizations that promote our sport. I highly recommend joining the National Rifle Association, Safari Club International, and Handgun Hunters International. Don't just join, become an active participant. It just may be the only way we can count on hunting with the firearm of our choice for years to come.

	Handgun Hunting: Deer	**Handgun Hunting: Other Game**
Alabama	Allowed	turkey, bobcat, groundhog, fox, coyote, feral swine
Alaska	Allowed	
Arizona	Allowed	
Arkansas	Allowed	bear
California	Allowed	bear, wild boar, elk, bighorn sheep
Colorado	Allowed	elk, antelope, bear
Connecticut	Allowed	no animals restricted
Delaware		raccoons, opossums
Florida	Allowed	all game but migratory birds
Georgia	Allowed	bear, hog, small game
Hawaii		
Idaho	Allowed	all big game
Illinois	Allowed	
Indiana	Allowed	
Iowa	Allowed	
Kansas	Allowed	
Kentucky	Allowed	
Louisiana	Allowed	
Maine	Allowed	
Maryland	Allowed	upland game and forest game
Massachusetts		
Michigan	Allowed	
Minnesota	Allowed	no animals restricted
Mississippi	Allowed	no animals restricted
Missouri	Allowed	all big game
Montana	Allowed	no animals restricted
Nebraska	Allowed	

	Handgun Hunting: Deer	**Handgun Hunting: Other Game**
Nevada	Allowed	all big game and small game
Hew Hampshire	Allowed	
New Jersey		
New Mexico	Allowed	
New York	Allowed	
North Carolina	Allowed	bear, wild boar, small game
North Dakota	Allowed	all big game
Ohio	Allowed	no animals restricted
Oklahoma	Allowed	
Oregon	Allowed	all big game and squirrel
Pennsylvania	Allowed	bear, turkey, small game
Rhode Island		
South Carolina	Allowed	
South Dakota	Allowed	
Tennessee	Allowed	
Texas	Allowed	
Utah	Allowed	
Vermont	Allowed	
Virginia	Allowed	bear and small game
Washington	Allowed	big game
West Virginia	Allowed	bear, boar
Wisconsin	Allowed	small game, bear
Wyoming	Allowed	

Source: State Hunting Regulation Guide Books

Chapter 4

Long Seasons Make Small Game Hunting Great

As a kid growing up in Texas County, Mo. I did not have computers, e-mail, the Internet, video games, four-wheelers, or any other type of entertainment that is so prevalent today. Most boys played baseball and basketball during school, the rest of the time we were either hunting or fishing. Looking back, it really was a great life and I feel, in no way, deprived of anything. I can remember my father taking me squirrel hunting on weekends with an old, three-legged hound. We would hunt with two brothers who lived alone, down by Current River. Both men were real characters, to say the least, and could teach you more about the outdoors than you thought possible. They had the dog since he was a pup and trained him early to tree squirrels. Obviously the dog wasn't the fastest I've seen in action, but I do remember him as being the best around in those days.

Dad and his friends taught me a lot during those squirrel hunts, including how to properly handle a firearm and how to treat the land with a great deal of respect. Dad also taught me how to clean and care for the game we took after a successful day in the woods. There are many lessons that a young hunter can learn from these delightful small game hunting trips. I came away with a lifelong love of the sport.

To bring this chapter around to the business of handgun hunting, I'll point out what should be obvious to a lot of people: Small game hunting offers a prime opportunity to hone your handgun skills.

Think about the variety of game and the length of the seasons available in most areas of the country. Here in Missouri we have a squirrel season that lasts seven months with a daily limit of six bushy-tails. That gives you plenty of chances to tote your .22 into the woods and perfect your shot selection skills. Rabbit season doesn't last quite that long but it is another way to get out of the house and enjoy some time in the field while you concentrate on trigger control and sight picture.

In many cases you don't have to travel very far to enjoy the hunt. Most of my small game pursuits are within 10 miles of my house. Secondly, unlike a brown bear or guided elk hunt, it doesn't cost an arm and a leg to pursue small game. The majority of landowners will grant permission to hunt small game even when they may not be willing to let you go deer hunting. Squirrel or rabbit hunting doesn't demand a lot of expensive

A squirrel's head is a very small target. Hunters will need to find any rest possible to help steady the crosshairs. Getting the game to stay still is another matter.

A good .22 rimfire handgun is a pleasure to own and shoot. These .22 autos are capable of handling small game hunting pursuits with ease.

equipment or ammunition either. If you have any kind of .22 handgun you can participate.

Depending on where you reside, there are different techniques and methods employed to bag these critters. Both squirrels and rabbits can be hunted over dogs. It's very exciting to see and hear the canines in pursuit, but hitting a running rabbit with a .22 pistol is a test most shooters will not pass. Still-hunting is a very effective method and the way I do most of my small game hunting these days. It can be especially good in the early morning hours for both squirrels and rabbits. Remember all those squirrels rustling through the oak leaves as you sat in your treestand last year? Try slipping quietly through the forest early in the day and catching some of them on the ground; it's quite a challenge. The same is true of rabbits, which are most active right at dawn. Move quietly along a brushy fencerow and peer into the cover. Chances are good you'll see some cottontails and those bunnies will make you work for a good clear shot.

When choosing a handgun suitable for squirrel or rabbit hunting, keep in mind your target area (the animal's head) is about the size of a golf ball or just a tad larger. Believe me, there is a lot more space outside that target area than inside. Since I consider squirrels and rabbits both table fare, I never like to shoot them in the body where a bullet will damage the meat. Under most circumstances shots on small game occur at distances of less than 50 yards, so you will need a handgun capable of putting most of a 10-shot group inside a quarter from that distance. Luckily for us, there are many .22 rimfire handguns capable of fulfilling that requirement including single-shots, autoloaders, and revolvers. Pick a gun that feels good in your hand and turns in the kind of groups you require.

One of my favorite small game handguns is a T/C Contender with a 10-inch match barrel. This particular gun is topped with a T/C 2 1/2X to 7X scope, with the magnification left on 3X most of the time. This is the

If you're looking for an added challenge, pick up a .22 handgun and head to the woods. Those wild gray squirrels will keep you plenty busy.

Squirrel hunting is a demanding sport. This lady hunter is using a tree to steady her aim on a tree-hopping gray squirrel.

Handgun Hunting 25

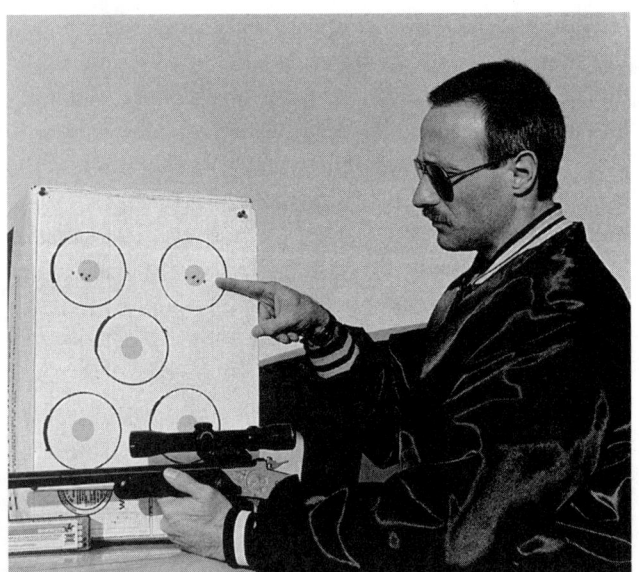

The small game hunter is wise to shoot several brands of ammunition to determine the one delivering the best accuracy. Shooting five-shot groups at 25 and 50 yards will help distinguish which brand of ammo shoots best from your gun.

handgun I head to the squirrel woods with whenever I want to bring home supper or practice for upcoming big game hunts. It is very accurate with Winchester fodder and if I can utilize a rest when hunting small game, the gun will always do its part. Another single-shot I enjoyed hunting with was the super-accurate Anschutz Exemplar. This bolt-action has one of the best triggers I ever pulled. The trigger came from the factory set at 9.85 ounces. The shooter needs to make certain the crosshairs are where you want them before applying any pressure to the trigger. The gun I was using carried a 7X Burris and was unbelievably accurate with CCI ammo. One bolt action I haven't yet used is the Savage Striker chambered for .22 rimfire. Savage also produces a .22 Magnum in this version and both are clip-fed. These guns should provide handgun hunters the tools necessary to enjoy many trips to the field. I've never considered it to be a handicap hunting with a single-shot contrary to what you may have heard in the past. Accuracy is much more important than firepower and these single-shots can certainly deliver.

If you prefer a semi-auto you have many fine choices. Ruger's Mark II pistols come in more than a dozen different models with barrel lengths varying from 4-3/4 to 10 inches, in a variety of configurations. This fine handgun comes in stainless or blue finishes, with a 10-round magazine. The Rugers are accurate and very dependable. I have always favored the 5-1/2-inch bull barrel, as it just seemed to balance well in my hands. There is definitely nothing wrong with the longer barrels especially when you top them with a scope. Another accurate and dependable .22 pistol is Smith & Wesson's Model 41. This gun has a great trigger, right out of the box, and comes in two different barrel lengths, 5-1/2 inches and 7 inches. I really fell in love with this gun when shooting the Sportsman Team Challenge competition. Using this handgun on the falling plates action event was a pure joy. The gun was topped with a Leupold/Gilmore red dot system and made for an excellent handgun for small game hunting. Smith & Wesson also provides the handgunner with other .22 rimfire offerings. The Model 41 just happens to be my personal favorite. Browning's Buckmark is another fine choice for the hunter looking for a quality semiautomatic. I have been very pleased with the performance of the Buckmark over the years. There are many other semiautomatic handguns available today that would work equally as well as the guns mentioned above. I'm not omitting any on purpose and certainly suggest that you try several to find the one that meets your needs

If you are a traditional revolver fan, the Ruger Blackhawk has been around for a long time. My first hunting revolver was a Blackhawk that belonged to my father. The gun came with interchangeable cylinders, one for .22 rimfire and the other chambered for .22 Magnum. If memory serves me correctly, the barrel was 4-7/8 inches. I used the gun mostly to dispatch fur-bearing

The Browning Buckmark, Ruger Single Six, or Ruger auto are all fine handguns for hunting small game. Just find the ammo that your gun prefers and have fun.

game that had been trapped, but it did serve well as a squirrel and rabbit gun when called to do so. Talk about dependable, that Ruger revolver always performed without fail. Freedom Arms manufactures a high-quality .22 rimfire revolver, the Model 83, that has proven to be extremely accurate and an excellent choice for the small game enthusiast. This revolver also offers interchangeable cylinders as an option. The handgun is not cheap, but its is a very fine revolver.

There is nothing wrong with shooting open sights while chasing small game, but early morning, cloudy, overcast days, or late evening pursuits could be a strain on the eyes when using iron sights. Trying to align the sights against a dark background can be challenging, at least for my eyes it's a real stretch. If you're like me and want to use a scope, purchase the best you can afford. Quality optics abound for .22 rimfire handguns. Manufacturers such as Simmons, Bausch & Lomb, Tasco, Burris, Leupold, and Nikon, all have optics that will work fine on most rimfire handguns.

There are several ongoing debates any hunter can join in when it comes to scopes. One of the most popular is the question of whether fixed-power models are superior to variable-power scopes. This pretty much depends on the shooter's individual taste. Twenty years ago, I never owned a variable scope and grew accustomed to fixed-power versions. Today there are many good variable scopes around and I find the shooter has a bit more flexibility with these models. I will admit that most of the time when hunting small game, my scope seldom leaves the 3X setting. However, it is nice to be able to crank up the magnification when trying to determine which brand of ammunition is the most accurate. As with most optics, and other things in life, you normally get exactly what you pay for. If I were trying to cut corners and save money, it sure wouldn't be on optics.

Speaking of accuracy and ammunition, hunters will need to figure out which particular brand of ammunition shoots best in their handgun. This may sound easy but with the huge selection of .22 rimfire ammunition currently on the market, this task could take a while. Simply purchase as many different brands as possible and plan on spending some time on the range. Normally I sight-in at 25 yards, then move out to 50 yards, shooting 10-shot groups with each brand of ammo. This shooting should be conducted from a good solid rest using sandbags or a commercially available rifle rest. You must eliminate as much human error as possible, allowing the gun and ammunition to do all the work. During this procedure, I do not want my shooting ability to be involved. What you are attempting to find out is what ammunition your handgun likes best. If you haven't conducted this type of test before you may be surprised to see the variations in group sizes from a dozen or more different brands of ammo. Every gun and barrel will be different; some changes will be more drastic than others. Even the ammunition can vary from different lots, and with changes in temperature. Your gun may prefer one specific brand of ammunition to all others, or it may shoot two or more equally accurately. My 10-

A squirrel's head is a very small target. Hunters will need to find any rest possible to help steady the crosshairs. Getting the game to stay still is another matter.

Shooting offhand is extremely difficult. In most cases the squirrel wins. However, there are times when it's the only option.

acorns, or cutting limbs. Even the slightest sound might give me an edge. While squirrel hunting, I'm always alert; looking in all directions, up and down, for the slightest movement. The demanding shooting requirements force me to work all the harder. Finding a good rest is mandatory while squirrel hunting and the activity sometime forces me to look for something new and different. I've used many of these ideas while hunting big game. Squirrel hunting also helps me keep my edge while stalking or still-hunting. I'm always sneaking through the woods as quietly as possible. When I want

inch T/C barrel likes Winchester's high-velocity Power Points. Another barrel on a different frame may digest these Winchesters totally differently, preferring another brand of ammo instead. It just takes some time on the range to determine things but that's why small game hunting is so great in the first place. It provides the hunter more time for hunting and the extra hours on the range shooting your handgun is time well spent.

Camouflage hunting clothing is, for some people, an important part of small game hunting. For others it is an afterthought. There is a third group that swears by wearing orange at all times. My hunting buddies and I have spent too much time arguing whether or not camouflage clothing is necessary. The deer hunters in our group claim they see more bushytails while wearing fluorescent orange. Personally, if I am not wearing some kind of camo, at the very least olive drab threads, I just don't feel right. I realize it may be only psychological, but I feel sneakier.

I consider squirrel hunting one of the best ways to prepare for the upcoming big game hunts. It gets me ready mentally. My eyes and ears are always working overtime as I listen for squirrels barking, chewing on

Yes, this T/C Contender chambered in .410 accounted for these pheasants. It's a different ballgame when your quarry flies. The author used 3-inch shells loaded with No. 6 shot to bag these birds.

to get myself ready for the fall hunting seasons, I know it's time to head for the squirrel woods.

Rabbit hunting simply extends my handgun-hunting season. I like to walk around the family farm, packing a sidearm, searching around brush piles or old fence lines for cottontails. Again, there are few things as tough as hitting a moving rabbit with a pistol, except trying to get a moving rabbit to stop so you can get a better shot with your pistol.

In an effort to put a different twist on small game pursuits, I fitted a Contender with a 16-inch .410 barrel, grabbed some 3-inch, 6 shot, and headed to the fields in an effort to bag a pheasant. One of my friends has a pheasant hunting preserve and invited me out for a day's hunt. You should have seen the look on his face when he saw the gun. I would be tagging along with two other hunters and during the course of the day, we all got plenty of shooting. I didn't bag as many birds as my buddies, but I was somewhat surprised that the T/C .410 was perfectly capable of knocking a pheasant out of the sky. It was quite the challenge and made the trip interesting and fun. After all, if we can't have fun handgun hunting, we might as well sell all of our guns and pick up golf.

If you will take along a .410 barrel during your big game hunts, you might be surprised when it will come in handy. This hunter tagged out early on a bear hunt and enjoyed the rest of his trip by bagging a few grouse with his extra barrel.

Perhaps one of the best things about small game hunting with a handgun is the opportunity for increased camaraderie. A few years ago, before my older brother passed away, we would hit the woods along with another buddy of ours before daylight searching for a limit of squirrels. One morning we split up and went in three different directions. I was the only one carrying a handgun and had taken a little ribbing about the short arm, but I had handguns long enough to be accustomed to such. Both gray and fox squirrels inhabit our woods, grays being the most challenging. The nervous little critters never seem to stay in one spot for very long. This particular morning was still, no wind blowing, making it a perfect time to be in the woods. As I was sneaking down an old logging road I made sure the Contender was loaded and the scope set on 3X. After hearing the barking and chattering of two squirrels fussing between themselves, I slowly eased my way toward the ruckus, trying not to make any noise in the dry leaves. Finally, I got in position to see one of the little grays sitting on a limb, now staring at me. I tried to hold the crosshairs steady from the offhand position, to no avail. So I inched my way next to a tree to rest the handgun. The squirrel got nervous and ran onto another limb, still staring at me, trying to figure out why I was disturbing his early morning ritual. I got the crosshairs settled and squeezed the trigger slowly, putting my first squirrel on the ground. The morning continued to yield opportunities with the squirrels winning more times than I did. We all met back at the truck later in the morning, having bagged four squirrels each, and called it another successful hunt. There was nothing special about that hunt, except that it was just great being out in the woods, enjoying nature with family and good friends. Later that year, I managed to get both of my squirrel hunting partners to take a handgun to the woods. That outing could be classified as a humbling experience because those gray squirrels delighted in frustrating us at every turn. The reward is just that the hunting allows us to be in the woods when nature wakes up in the morning. There is also a platter of fried squirrel with biscuits and gravy! Top those benefits with getting a little extra practice for the big game season and you have real reason to take up small game hunting with a handgun.

Chapter 5

Break The Bonds Of Winter With Varmint Hunting

During the winter months, a person can watch just so many movies, football games, and fishing shows. Heck, even the Outdoor Channel gets old after a while. It never fails: I usually get struck with a bad case of cabin fever long before winter is officially over. After the shortened hours of daylight, inactivity associated with winter doldrums, and a mild state of depression that is normally associated with these elements, it is no wonder I am ready to get of the house and start shooting at the first hint of spring weather.

Springtime varmints really give handgun hunters something to look forward to. Actually, varmint hunting can and does, take place throughout most of the year depending upon where you live and what varmints

Varmint hunting is popular in many states. The author took this coyote during a mule deer hunt in Montana. The Contender he is holding is a .309 JDJ using Nosler 165-grain BT.

Handgun Hunting

Accuracy is the key word on prairie dog shoots. The T/C Contender in .223 is an ideal handgun for this type of precision shooting. Black Hills ammo worked great on the Montana varmint hunt.

inhabit your area, and hunting these critters is another great way to stay sharp and prepare yourself for the fall big game season. Whether you like to sneak up on groundhogs, tackle a prairie dog town, or attempt to get a crow to stay still long enough to bust him, you will enhance your hunting skills. You will also become much more familiar with your handgun, scope, and ammunition. Varmint hunting also improves your skill estimating distance, learning to deal with crosswinds, and helps you to know your personal shooting limitations. I only wish I lived closer to prairie dog country. In my area, we had groundhogs to hunt a few years back, but our coyote population has expanded to the point that it is difficult to see a groundhog in the clover fields. So, we hunt coyotes.

Let's examine a few cartridges that will suffice as varmint medicine. The .22 rimfire is easy on the shooter and tough to beat for close-range opportunities. As stated earlier, ammunition is very economical and can be found most anywhere. Once you find a factory round your gun likes, accuracy for small targets such as prairie dogs should be no problem. Out to 50 yards or so, the .22 rimfire is a fine choice, and not being as loud as many of the centerfire cartridges, it will not spook the game as badly. The .22 Magnum is a step up on the ladder. It is a bit more expensive to shoot, but still offers the varmint hunter a decent close-range option.

The .22 Hornet, developed back in 1920, is another good round for varmints. The Hornet performs best from handguns with 40- to 45-grain bullets and excellent accuracy can be found with both bullet weights. Although not as powerful as the .218 Bee, the Hornet still makes a superb round out to 100 or 150 yards, with little recoil. I have had the pleasure of hammering a few groundhogs with this little cartridge, using factory Winchester ammo, fired from an Anschutz Exemplar. The combination performed very well.

It's not the most popular round for varmints but the .221 Remington Fireball is still going strong. Introduced back in 1962, and chambered in Remington's XP-100, this cartridge is amazingly accurate. This inherent accuracy has attracted many custom gunsmiths to build guns chambering this round. Loads pushing 40- to 50-grain bullets seem to perform the best. This cartridge is an absolute pleasure to shoot, easy on the pocketbook, and in the hands of a skilled handgunner capable of taking prairie dogs out to 200 yards.

Initially developed as a military round, the .223 Remington is probably the most popular varmint cartridge for handgun hunters. With a wide variety of .22 caliber bullets at its disposal, the cartridge is quite versatile, pleasant to shoot, and accurate. Quality bullets in .22 caliber come in almost limitless variety, and handloaders are able to buy brass, especially military surplus, in large quantities. The .223 is not only dynamite on prairie dogs and woodchucks, but it can also tackle larger predators such as bobcat and coyote. I have a custom barrel from SSK Industries fitted on a T/C frame and using either Nosler Ballistic Tips or Hornady's V-Max, the accuracy is astounding. It makes for a great varmint-hunting handgun.

This XP-100 has been rechambered to .22-250 and makes for an ideal varmint rig. The gun is highly accurate and recoil is almost non-existent.

This XP-100 came from Remington's Custom Shop. The gun is chambered for 7mm-08 and is very accurate. Mounted with a 4X Leupold scope, this handgun can handle coyotes with ease. Unfortunately, the XP-100 is now out of production.

The .250 Savage will serve double duty as a varmint and deer cartridge. Originally dubbed the 250-3000, because it pushed a .25 caliber bullet at 3,000 fps, it is now simply called the .250 Savage, since other velocity figures have been introduced. With its light recoil, the old cartridge is very pleasant to shoot and makes for an ideal coyote and deer round.

Wildcatters looking for a little more punch from their .25 caliber can step up to the .257 JDJ, which is based on the strong .225 Winchester case. The .257 JDJ can push a 75-grain bullet at more than 2,800 fps, which translates into a terminator on varmints. This is another one of those dual-purpose cartridges capable of tackling deer or antelope from long range, especially when using Nosler's 100-grain Partition bullet. I know of a couple avid handgun hunters who shoot this round all the time, both for varmints and whitetail. They cannot say enough about the accuracy and effectiveness. Because it has virtually no recoil, many hunters can shoot this round with phenomenal accuracy.

Another wildcat that I have had the pleasure of shooting a lot is the 6.5 JDJ, again based on the .225 Winchester brass. Pushing 85-grain bullets along at a sizzling 2,800 fps, it makes for a dandy varmint/deer cartridge. I prefer shooting Nosler's 120-grain Solid Base with this round. My gun shoots this bullet very well and, if I do my part, not many varmints get away. After shooting this handgun all year at varmints, I know exactly what to expect when deer or antelope season rolls around. This is one of those wildcats that require fire-forming of the cases, but that just gives you a good reason to practice more.

These are just a few of the cartridges that can suffice as varmint hunting medicine. There are many others capable of getting the job done and I may have left out your favorite cartridge. Others I did not mention but would work well in the varmint-hunting arena include, just to name a few, the .22 BR, 6mm TCU, 6mm BR, 6.5mm BR, 7mm TCU, and 7mm BR. Heck, who's to say you can't bust a groundhog with your pet load from a 45-70?

Now, that we've talked about ammunition, let's look at a few of the handguns suitable for the pinpoint accuracy involved in varmint hunting. Introduced back in 1963, Remington's XP-100 generated a lot of curiosity. During the years to follow, the single-shot bolt action evolved into a superb long-range handgun. The standard production XP was available in .223, 7mm BR, and the .35 Remington. Remington's Custom Shop offered the gun in a few more calibers, in left- or right-handed versions, standard or heavy barrel. It is a shame Remington dropped this fine long-range handgun. It is no longer in production. You can still find used guns in good condition. Whenever an XP-100 was set up properly, with the right loads, it could outshoot 90 percent of factory rifles on the market. The XP-100 is a varmint hunter's dream, and a groundhog's worst nightmare.

The Savage Striker is available in several different chamberings including this .22-250. The Striker makes a good handgun for varmint shooting especially when you top it with a quality scope like this variable Bausch & Lomb.

While we're addressing bolt actions, the Savage Striker, at this time, comes in three different models, chambered for several of the short-action calibers including .223, .22-250, .243, 7mm-08, and the .308 Win. This handgun is making its way into the hands of many hunters, perhaps in part because of its affordable price tag. The bolt of the Striker is on the left side. Depending on who you talk with about this feature, you will receive different reactions. Some shooters love the left-handed bolt; others cuss the very nature of its existence. Either way, the Striker is getting plenty of people talking. The gun is based on the popular Model 110 rifle action and with the bolt handle on the left, the shooter should, in theory, be able to work the action with the left hand while maintaining something of a shooting grip. A bipod or a sturdy rest makes the Striker a true long-range pistol.

Another fine bolt-action handgun currently in production is H-S Precision's Pro-Series 2000. The Pro-Series comes in two different models, varmint and silhouette, and is chambered in 11 calibers including 17 Remington, .223, .22-250, 7mm BR, and 7mm-08 Remington. The trigger is fully adjustable from 2.5 to 3.5 pounds, and the folks at H-S Precision guarantee 1/2 minute of angle accuracy at 100 yards. I purchased a varmint model in .308 Winchester and the gun tips the scales at a little over 5 pounds, without a scope. This is the type of handgun that is at its best from a good, solid, sandbag rest.

The M.O.A. Maximum is a unique single-shot incorporating a falling-block design, with a free-floating barrel that maintains consistent accuracy through a variety of temperatures. With a list of 30 standard calibers and the ability to create barrels for nearly any wildcat round, this handgun sees quite a bit of action in the silhouette games. I shot one chambered in .250 Savage one winter, bagging a number of coyotes.

The falling block is operated with an underlever bow on the front of the grip, making the pistol appear much like a lever-action rifle. The operation of the pistol requires that you swing the lever to extract spent rounds and reload. You then manually cock the hammer and engage the transfer bar safety in order to fire. The description is more complicated than the actions

The author downed this coyote with an MOA in .250 Savage. The Burris 3X-9X scope is a fine piece of optics for the varmint hunter. Varmint hunting provides the handgun hunter a lot of off-season enjoyment.

required to load and fire. It's really very easy. Once I got familiar with the loading and unloading procedure, the gun was quite fun to shoot.

With standard barrel lengths of 8-3/4, 10-1/2 and 14 inches and calibers from .22 rimfire up to .375 H&H Magnum, the Maximum can be quite a versatile pistol. And it gives away nothing in the area of accuracy.

Another single-shot handgun incorporating a bit of a non-traditional design is the Lone Eagle from Magnum Research. These pistols incorporate a very strong rotary, cannon-type breech, capable of digesting many bottleneck rifle cartridges including .22 Hornet, .22-250, .243, and 7mm-08, any of which will work well for the varmint-hunting enthusiast. Barrel length is 14 inches and complete barreled actions are interchangeable in the polymer stock. Loading and unloading the Lone Eagle is somewhat different. Rotating its breech ring clockwise, as far as possible, opens the action of the Lone Eagle. At this point a cartridge can be inserted. To close the action, simply rotate that breech ring counter-clockwise to its locked position. Yes, you will see part of the cartridge rim, but don't panic. Now you are ready to cock the firing pin, disengage the safety, and fire. It took some doing but I did finally get the hang of the operation. The gun is very strong and it won't cost you the farm.

The T/C Contender is one of the most versatile handguns ever to hit the market. The interchangeable barrels allow the shooter many options of calibers, all of which can fit the same frame. Factory Contenders are available in several barrel lengths, but I have always been a fan of the 14-inch models. I can't keep up with just how many different calibers are available, but I do know that the .223 is one of the company's best sellers. The break-action design is simple to use and just about every gun enthusiast has seen a Contender in operation.

When the folks at T/C decided they needed something a little stronger to handle higher pressures, they

Single-shot handguns like this Lone Eagle get called to duty for many varmint-hunting excursions. This particular loading design is super-strong and capable of handling a long list of calibers.

came out with the Encore. It looks a lot like a Contender, but the details give away the beefier nature of its construction. The Encore can fire rounds like the .22-250 as well as many others. This round is great on varmints but even with a 15-inch barrel, you do have some muzzle blast to contend with. For hunters looking for

When all other seasons closed, coyotes extend a hunter's time in the field. These varmints are smart and you will not get away with many mistakes. This coyote was taken with an Encore chambered for .308 Winchester.

something a bit different, companies like SSK Industries offer custom barrels for both the Contender and Encore, with more than 100 different options in a variety of barrel configurations. After shooting many of these barrels for almost 25 years, I can assure you of the accuracy and dependability behind them. For obvious reasons, the barrels of the Contender and Encore cannot be swapped between the two frames.

New on the horizon for T/C is the G-2 Contender. This second generation of the venerable Contender utilizes some of the design changes found in the Encore, but insures complete interchangeability with all original Contender barrels. All of T/C guns have proven reliable and accurate and the new G-2 should be no different. A varmint hunter would be well served with either model in an appropriate caliber.

See What You Are Shooting At

Before you can hit a target, you've got to be able to see it. To help aid in precise bullet placement so critical with varmint hunting, the shooter must be able to see the target at ranges out to 300 yards. That requires a good scope. Burris manufactures a straight 7X and 10X scope but most varmint hunters I run with use variables of some description. Burris makes a 3X-9X model that is a good choice, however, many varmint hunters, myself included, have switched to the company's 3X-12X model. I do not use the 12X setting unless there is a rock-solid rest available and I'm shooting at a varmint way out there. Leupold's 2-1/2X-8X is another good choice. I have two of these models on different hunting guns. Simmons makes a 2-1/2X-7X handgun scope that works very well. Bausch & Lomb makes a really fine 2X-6X long-eye-relief scope, with the newly established Rain Guard process.

These are just a few of the myriad scopes available today. If you pressed me to give you a straight answer on which one to buy, I'd tell you to get the best you can afford. Now, I know that's not giving you much to go on, but you've got to consider your hunting style, the game you are after, the region of the world you will be hunting and the options available with the scope.

First and foremost, consider your hunting style. Will you be still-hunting through the woods in search of whitetails? If so you'll likely want something with relatively low magnification and a big objective lens. That's because your shots will be short and you'll want to gather lots of light. On the other hand, if you are going into the high mountains in search of bighorn sheep or goats, you might want something with a bit more magnification. Your mountain scope might need to be a bit tougher, too, in order to deal with extremes in weather, altitude and abuse. In this chapter we are talking about varmint hunting. That means you'll typically be trying to hit a small target at moderate to long range from a

The Encore is available in several different calibers. These single-shot handguns are accurate and make a fine varmint-hunting rig.

very stable rest. You'll want a scope that will help you do that. That means a variable power unit that will take you up to at least 9X.

What about the reticle? Do you want simple crosshairs, a duplex reticle or something else? The choices in scopes today would fill a book. The long and short of it is this: Scopes help you aim. Anything you can do to put your bullet precisely on target will help you to be more successful. Do not look at scopes as an afterthought. If you are going to use one, consider it an integral part of your hunting weapon and acquire an intimate knowledge of its limitations.

Bullet selection can be very subjective and personal, but I believe it's safe to say that unless you do not want to ruin a pelt, highly frangible bullets are the way to go. But then again, even a .223 full metal jacket will put down a coyote in short order with a good hit. Varmint hunters, especially hunters seeking prairie dogs and woodchucks, typically like to see dramatic evidence of a hit. That means a hollow point (though you may give away a bit of accuracy) or something like Nosler's Ballistic Tips and Hornady's V-Max bullets are ideal choices for varmint hunting. They have the rapid expansion characteristics that many groundhog and prairie dog hunters expect. Many of your larger ammunition manufacturers are loading their ammo with these bullets today.

My brother and I, along with some friends, ordered 5,000 rounds of .223 ammo from Black Hills Ammunition for a recent prairie dog shoot in Montana. This ammo used 52-grain bullets from Hornady and boy were they accurate! Your bullet selection will change if you are attempting to sell bobcat, fox, or coyote pelts where you want minimal damage into the hide. Bullets designed for varmint shooting are usually very accurate. Buying in bulk will save you money and give you the chance to shoot until you are totally comfortable with the round and its performance.

Like small game hunting, varmint hunting allows the handgun hunter to spend many more hours in the field shooting a boatload of ammo, if you find the right spot. One serious handgun hunter I know keeps a journal of his woodchuck pursuits. For more than a decade he has maintained a detailed account of every groundhog he has taken, along with specifics on the handgun, bullet performance, scope, distance, and loading data. The amount of information this guy has at his fingertips is mind-boggling. This hunter can tell you accurate information concerning anything a varmint hunter will encounter, plus tidbits he has gained from actual field experience. When big game seasons roll around, this guy is more than ready and all those days he has spent stalking groundhogs have improved his shooting skills immensely.

Earlier, I mentioned a prairie dog shoot with my brother and some friends. This hunt took place on the Fort Belnap Indian Reservation in conjunction with a trophy antelope hunt. We must have hit the dog towns about right because there were more shooting opportunities in a few days' time than I would have experienced back home in 10 years. Most of the guys had custom rifles in .223 and .22-250. Me? I was packing a T/C, chambered for .223. Some days I got tired of shooting targets from 50 to 300 yards. That doesn't happen very often. I tried to discipline my distances to 250 yards and less, leaving the longer shots to the rifle-toting hunters. You can learn a lot about your gun, cartridge performance, and your own ability from this kind of shooting. It always surprised me to see how much the wind will push lighter bullets off course. The experience was not only enlightening, but also very valuable. Doping the wind is a skill that requires experience, and I am convinced that shooting an abundance of ammunition at varmints such as prairie dogs, crows, and groundhogs, is a great way to hone your shooting skills.

Prairie dogs and groundhogs are not the only quarry for the varmint hunter. Coyotes, bobcats, and the wily fox can provide great opportunities. The hunting method will be quite different than with prairie dogs or woodchucks. In the predator game, you are trying to bring the varmints to you, typically using a call imitating a rabbit in distress, woodpecker, or some other type of wounded critter in pain. These calls can be hand-held or pre-recorded. It all depends on your local laws and regulations.

Get yourself some good camouflage and set up in a position to observe a large area. I normally like to rest my back against something like a tree or bale of hay, in order to rest the handgun off my raised knees. Generally speaking, fox, providing one is in the area, will be the first to come in to see what the noise is all about. Coyotes and bobcats will take longer. I'm sure this varies in different parts of the country. Coyotes like to use the wind to their advantage, usually circling downwind before their final approach. Bobcats, my favorite varmint to hunt, usually come in slowly and cautiously. Hunters should be as still as possible while calling. Any movement could be enough to send a predator running the other way.

Predator calling tests just about all your stand-hunting skills, from site selection to range estimation to shot placement. Calling predators will certainly make you a better big game hunter.

The T/C Contender in .223 pushing 50- to 55-grain bullets is my favorite varmint rig. This handgun handles most of my varmint hunting needs. It is accurate and dependable and, if I can keep "pilot error" down to a minimum, a pesky coyote or a sneaky bobcat is in real trouble. Have you ever skinned a bobcat? If not, let me assure you that the target area is not real big. Without fail, one of my hunting buddies remarks about how small an area you've got to hit their vitals. That's why accuracy is so important and practice, especially practice in the field, is the best way to make you a better all-around hunter.

A bobcat should be considered a real trophy for the handgun hunter. This cat was taken with a T/C Encore chambered in .223 and topped with a Burris scope. Bobcats generally approach a call very cautiously.

Chapter 6

The Most Popular Game In The Land

If, God forbid, I could hunt only one big game animal for the rest of my life, it would be the white-tailed deer. The elegant whitetail is the most widely distributed big game animal in North America and also the most popular, with millions of sportsmen taking to the field each year seeking this worthy trophy. These beautiful creatures live in most every state in the lower 48 states and hunters chase deer using all different types of arms including rifles, bows, muzzleloaders, shotguns, and of course handguns. Deer provide delicious table fare, and it doesn't cost an arm and a leg to enjoy the challenge of pursuing them. And taking whitetail with a handgun is a challenge indeed; an absolute challenge.

Taking a mature buck with a handgun is no easy task, but having a record-book buck in your sights is not a requirement to enjoy hunting these smart, elusive critters. Some of my most memorable hunts have ended as I filled my tags with decent six- or eight-pointers. The survival instincts of a mature buck, as well as his senses of smell, hearing, and sight, are incredibly keen. It takes all your hunting skill to best a big deer and even then, you still have to make a good shot. It takes practice and

Any buck taken with a handgun can be considered a trophy. Hampton took this nice eight-pointer on the family farm with a T/C in .309 JDJ. Nosler 165-grain BT's were used to fill this tag.

skill. Luckily, I have the opportunity to observe these animals in their natural habitat all year long. I study their habits and behavior, record their movement patterns and make note of what they like to eat. Even after all that, I still get outsmarted from time to time on my own land here in Missouri.

Are you looking for a little more challenge from your next deer hunt? Then pick out a suitable handgun and get ready to have a rewarding deer season.

Becoming a good hunter takes a lot of time and a considerable amount of effort regardless what type of firearm you choose. If there is a difference with handgun hunting, it is that accurately shooting a handgun takes bit more skill and practice than does accurately shooting a rifle. Aside from that, no special equipment is required. I consider learning the skills required to become a good handgun hunter on par with what it takes to become an ethical and effective bowhunter. The degree of accuracy demanded from big game hunting is far less crucial than varmint hunting. For example, if you can keep your shots inside a 7- or 8-inch circle, this representing the vitals of a whitetail, you can harvest game cleanly and quickly, and that is what all true sportsmen want to accomplish.

At what distance can you keep the majority of your shots inside this 8-inch circle? Whatever that distance may be, that's the distance to which you should limit your shots in the field. If I cannot consistently hit a pie plate offhand at 100 yards, then I have no business shooting offhand at a whitetail at that distance. The same is true for you. Practice until you know your own limitations and those of your weapon.

Handgun hunters employ different methods for hunting whitetail deer depending on several factors; including terrain, personal likes and dislikes, and the habits of the quarry. Granted, the hunter living in Maine may use a different strategy than someone hunting deer in Colorado. And what works for the handgun hunter in Texas may be a total disaster in Minnesota. Be that as it may, there are some basic methods of hunting whitetails such as still-hunting (the art of moving very, very slowly through the woods trying to spot the deer before he spots you) that are challenging and rewarding. I'm not talking about blundering through the woods, hoping you run into a nice buck and drop the hammer on him. Still-hunting, or stalk hunting as some may refer to it, is an art that requires a tremendous amount of patience, skill, and self-discipline. To move the odds in favor of the hunter, one must move slowly and quietly, listening and watching much more than moving. To be effective you must maintain an awareness of the surroundings. This may sound easy, but, rest assured, in most areas of the country it is not.

The still-hunter must first ask the question, what am I trying to do? Will you be slipping around a buck's bedding area, trying to catch one coming or going to a feeding place? Or, will you perhaps be working your way through the woods hoping to intercept moving game? If you just go out in the woods and start walking down an old road, hoping you will see something and be able to get a shot, your success rate will not be very high. Doing so means you will be relying on luck. Of course there is nothing wrong with luck. Actually, I would rather be lucky than good any day, but I do like to have a game plan while hunting whitetail. Good still-hunters move like a snail, have eyes like a hawk, know what to look for, and are ready to shoot when opportunity knocks. A little pre-season scouting can pay big dividends and can give you some idea of where deer are feeding and possibly bedding. You'll need to find the trails that they may be using, and other important bits of information you can use to plan strategy.

Once you know the lay of the land, you'll need to pick the best time for the hunt. Still-hunting is easiest, but still not easy, just after a rain. Wet leaves on the forest floor silence your steps and let you slip through the woods silently. Wind can mask the sound of your movements but you'll have to deal with scent issues. Windy days also seem to put deer on edge. It's as if the deer know they can't hear approaching danger, so they are doubly watchful. Still-hunting in the snow can be either very effective or completely hopeless depending on the type and amount of snow. Dry crunchy snow means trouble with every step. An inch or two of heavy wet snow will be almost as quiet as leaves after a rain.

The pace of still-hunting is slow — painfully slow. How slow is a matter of opinion. Some say one step every minute. Some say one step every five minutes. There are two things you know for sure while still-hunting: While you are stopped you should be looking for any part of a deer and if all you see are white tails bouncing through the woods, you're going too fast.

There are several good choices when it comes to handguns suited for sneaking around the woods. I see revolvers topping the list. It doesn't really matter whether it's single-action or double-action, the average hunter will cock the hammer before each shot, even with a double action revolver. Caliber seems to be the

The Taurus .44 Magnum revolver makes a dandy whitetail gun for woods hunting. The .44 Magnum accounts for many whitetails every year.

Revolver fans have many quality handguns to choose from. Scoped or not, these handguns are ideal for close range deer hunting. The .454 Casull and .44 Magnum are both great cartridges for deer hunting.

real question. Cartridges such as .41, .44 Magnum, and .454 Casull are all good choices for whitetail.

Of the people I know who use the .41 Magnum, most fire 210-grain bullets. While not as popular as the .44 Magnum, the .41 Magnum is, nevertheless, a mighty fine deer cartridge. The .44 Magnum offers hunters plenty of options. Some hunters swear by 180-grain bullets, while others prefer bullets weighing 240 to 300 grains, claiming that regardless of the angle that presents itself, penetration is not a concern with these heavier slugs. As long as bullet placement is correct, I do not think it matters a great deal. I've taken several deer with .44 caliber bullets ranging from the lighter 180-grain offerings, to the heavier 300-grain slugs. I doubt the deer could tell any difference. The larger .454 Casull with bullet weights in the 250- to 260-grain range delivers more than enough power for any whitetail.

I love to carry a revolver while stalking whitetails and use several different models. The Predator from Mag-Na-Port International, which is a custom Ruger Super Blackhawk with a 4-5/8-inch barrel, is an ideal carry gun for hunting in the woods. It is easy to carry and packs a punch at the moment of truth. Another custom offering from Mag-Na-Port is their Stalker model. It, too, starts with a Super Blackhawk frame and, in addition to all the other Mag-Na-Port embellishments, the Stalker is equipped with a scope. Ruger's Redhawk and Super Redhawk are also great choices for this type of hunting. They too, come in barrel lengths ranging from 5-1/2 to 9-1/2 inches. Both of these strong, heavy-framed revolvers are capable of digesting a steady diet of full-power loads, should you have the desire or need to fire that many.

Smith & Wesson's new 629 Stealth Hunter is an ideal handgun for stalking whitetails, as are the company's many other offerings in famed Model 29 line. All of these .44 Magnum revolvers can be scoped or used with iron sights. When hunting whitetails in the early morning or late evening hours, especially in the woods, a scope can be a real asset to the hunter trying to get the drop on a buck. A 2X scope is usually suffi-

The Smith & Wesson 629 Stealth Hunter is a great deer gun.

cient for hunting in the timber; however, there is nothing wrong with any of the variable scopes that allow you to set your optics on the lowest possible setting while stalking. If a buck happens to be spotted in the distance, and you have remained undetected, you may have time to adjust the setting of the scope to a higher magnification.

Freedom Arms also makes some great revolvers in both .44 Magnum, and the increasingly popular .454 Casull. These high-quality handguns make an ideal choice while still-hunting through the woods. The big .454 Casull performs excellently on whitetails with any of the current factory ammunition. Bob Baker, the president of the company, took his first whitetail buck while hunting with me several years ago using a scoped .357 Magnum. He was hunting from a ladder stand and took a fine 10-point Missouri buck from less than 50 yards on opening morning.

Another gun I use frequently for stalking whitetails is a T/C Contender with a 10-inch, .44 Magnum barrel. This handgun is topped with a 2X scope. It is accurate with a variety of ammunition and easily carried during all-day hikes in the woods. I know what you're thinking, with a single-shot like the T/C, you only have one shot as opposed to the revolver's capability of quick follow-up shots. After hunting whitetails for more than 25 years, I have discovered that 99 times out of 100 the first shot you get will definitely be the best shot offered. I can't remember ever being at a disadvantage shooting a single-shot. If you make the first shot count, which is

Two of the author's favorite .44 Magnum handguns: A 10-inch T/C with 4X Bausch & Lomb scope, and a custom Ruger Super Redhawk with many refinements.

The Most Popular Game In The Land

what we are supposed to do anyway, you won't have to concern yourself with follow-up shots. The compact T/C has been a constant companion of mine for many still-hunting trips in the woods, and has been responsible for filling the freezer on more than one occasion.

It doesn't really matter which handgun you choose for stalking whitetails, just use the gun you feel most comfortable shooting. Keep in mind that successfully stalking a mature whitetail buck is a challenging endeavor, one that requires a lot of effort and persistence on your part. It's easy to get discouraged, but when you do score while still-hunting, you know you've accomplished something.

Tree Stands Mean Success

Hunting from an elevated stand is very likely the most popular of all deer hunting techniques. I hunt from a tree stand 90 percent of the time and feel this method is the best for consistent success. Most successful handgun hunters I know use tree stands instead of ground blinds. For years I hunted from 10-foot ladder-type stands, but today my stands are at least 15 feet off the ground. This keeps my scent away from the deer, and gives me a better view of the surroundings. It also conceals any movement a little better. The deer hunter who will climb and hunt from ladder stands, or any tree stand for that matter, should always use a safety device such as a harness, or safety belt attached to the tree. Each year, many hunters fall, sometimes fatally, for lack of a safety harness. Don't be one of them.

Just because you are up in a tree stand doesn't mean you can forget about pre-season scouting. Are you just putting up a tree stand and hoping a deer will pass by, or have you scouted the area and know firsthand that deer are using this area? Everything, right down to selecting the right tree, is important. Obviously you do not want to use a dead, crooked, or leaning tree to hang a stand. You also have to choose one that offers the right amount of cover, while providing you a good field of view. If you are using screw-in tree steps, you might want to avoid hard maple or similar trees. I like to take along a small saw so I can trim limbs or branches that might be in the way, once the stand is in place. There always seem to be a few that annoy me, even if they don't get in the way. Thanks to the noise associated with setting up a portable stand, I would much rather have the stand properly hung before I hunt, if that possibility exists. Such planning also allows me to check out the concealment provided by the stand location. Will I stand out

A ground blind can be deadly on whitetail when set up properly. Hunters should make sure they can get a steady rest for the firearm from inside the blind.

like a sore thumb or blend in with the environment? A background that conceals your presence is always an asset. Having the chance to review your location to make sure you get a quality shot at an undisturbed animal is nothing but a bonus.

A good stand site will obviously put you where the deer travel. The ideal location depends on several factors, including the route you must take to your stand when you are ready to hunt. You don't want to be spooking deer from bedding areas as you head to your stand. You'll also have to ask yourself if you want to hunt near feeding areas or escape cover. The best choice might be to set up between the two and intercept deer as they move from one to the other. Also remember that big bucks won't often use the "main" trails, but will follow secondary trails that give them more cover. You'll want a clear shooting path to those areas, too.

Pushing Deer Past The Shooters

Deer drives can be conducted by as many as 20 or more hunters, or as few as a couple of walkers working towards a single hunter on a stand. The idea is to push the deer out of hiding and past a waiting hunter. Sounds simple? Sometimes it can be, but it's not a sure bet by any stretch of the imagination. If you have a group of experienced hunters who are familiar with this method of hunting, it can be very effective, plus a heck of a lot of fun. In years past, our deer camp participated in making drives the better part of the day, only sitting on a stand in the early morning and late evening periods. We enjoyed a tremendous amount of success but probably just as important, boy did we have fun. There always seemed to be a lot of action, a lot of shooting, and the exercise was a bonus. The downside of this, for handgun hunters, is that running shots dominate. In my experience while making deer drives, regardless whether I was a walker or sitter, moving shots were the norm, not the exception. This is not good news for the handgunner. I do not like to shoot at running game unless everything is perfect; that includes range, shot angle and backstop. At times I've used a grunt tube to get a buck to stop momentarily. This works pretty good most of the time. The hunter must be ready to shoot the moment the deer stops to look. You certainly do not have all day to take this shot.

The best option for deer drives when hunting with a handgun might be to utilize one or two drivers pushing deer slowly toward no more than a pair of sitters. If the drivers move slowly through the woods, deer will hear them coming and sometimes get out of the way. In many cases, two drivers taking a leisurely stroll through the woods will prompt deer to leave the area on their regular trails, often at no more than a trot. This can create better shots for the sitters.

Permanent Elevated Stands Offer Comfort

If you have access to private land, perhaps you own or lease such property, the best method for handgun hunters is to sit in elevated deer blinds overlooking areas that deer frequent. On our family farm we have several of these blinds that extend 15 to 20 feet in the air, strategically situated in prime places. When I speak of prime places I am referring to food plots or areas that deer use when crossing from one patch of timber to another. A few of these elevated blinds are 4 feet long by 4 feet wide, 6 feet in height. They are ideal for one hunter. Others are 6 feet long by 5 feet wide, 6 feet in height. Two hunters can sit in these very comfortably. Blinds such as these can be equipped just about as lavishly as you like. All of the stands at our place are equipped with comfortable chairs, plexi-glass windows, shag carpet on the floor to muffle any noise, and of course sandbags to rest your firearm. They are comfortable blinds that enable a hunter to stay out longer, in any type of weather, putting the odds in the hunters favor.

Missouri's weather can be unpredictable. If it turns cold or rains for three days straight, we appreciate these blinds even more.

Again, stand placement is important. And, while the deer seem to ignore stands that have been in place for a while, hunters need to be acutely aware of how they enter and leave the stand. Deer know when hunters arrive and depart. If you don't make a careful approach, you can spook a trophy very easily.

Stay Put

The longer you can stay on your stand the better your chances of harvesting a deer will be. Patience is probably the deer hunter's best asset because it simply stacks the odds in your favor. Staying put in your

Elevated deer blinds, like the one shown here, can be a deer hunter's dream. Handgun hunters can increase their odds of filling a tag by exercising patience. You can sit in one of these blinds comfortably for hours, regardless of weather conditions, while waiting for that big buck to step out.

location at the end of a deer drive is also vitally important to safety. During a drive, the other hunters are basing their actions on what they assume to be your location.

Hunters should take along a few essentials while spending time in stands, waiting for Mr. Big to step out in the open. An empty milk jug for bladder relief is all-important. You don't want to mess up your chance at a big deer by spreading your scent all over the place. A couple of candy bars and something to drink will also be welcome additions, but remember, caffeine will make you need to "go" more often than plain water. If you are in a permanent elevated stand, a magazine or two will keep you occupied while sitting still hours on end.

Two other important items for the blind are quality binoculars and a rangefinder. Normally I take the rangefinder to the stand before season and by using reference points, determine distances to where the deer are likely to appear. I've even written those distances inside the blind, to remind me from year to year. It's helpful knowing the range of the old oak tree, corner post, big rock, or other such obstacles, so when the buck of a lifetime strolls out you will at least have an idea how far you're shooting. Likewise, I do not go deer hunting without binoculars. I use them almost constantly to spot and locate deer, as well as other wildlife. A good set of 10X50 Swarovski optics is always in the blind with me. My Swarovskis really shine in the early and late hours of the day when light gathering capabilities are needed. As the old saying goes, you get what you pay for; that could never be any more true when it comes to quality binoculars. I figure it this way, since I use the optics 20 times more often than my gun on any given hunt, surely I can justify spending a few bucks on a decent pair of glasses.

Choosing Your Weapon

Depending on the location of the deer blind, shooting opportunities can range from almost directly beneath the stand all the way out to 300 yards or more. The blind I use every season is situated on an old logging road with the longest possible shot being 125 yards. However when deer activity is greater on other parts of the farm, I often abandon ship and head for a different stand, which might allow for longer shots. The simple

Handguns for deer hunting vary widely. This nice buck was no match for the single-shot T/C Contender. Quality optics like the Bausch & Lomb 4X scope shown here, assist the hunter with proper shot placement.

rule is, revolvers can handle short shots, but the long shots often require something with more power; namely one of single-shots.

One of my hunting buddies has a T/C in 7-30 Waters with a 4X scope. He handloads using a 130-grain Hornady bullet, shoots the gun year-round, and knows exactly where the bullet will hit at different yardages. A couple of years ago he spotted a nice buck just inside the woods about 250 yards from his stand. Unfortunately, the buck never would come out into the field my friend was watching. Placing the sandbags on the edge of the blind, he prepared for his only opportunity. When the buck stepped into an opening inside the woods, the hammer fell and the 130-grain Hornady found its mark. That's what can happen when you choose a cartridge best suited for the type of hunting encountered, practice shooting all year long, and know where your bullet strikes at given ranges. To be perfectly honest, most hunters probably should never try a shot like that with a 7-30 Waters. My deer hunting buddy, however, knew exactly where the bullet would strike and had shot this combination many times, at this very distance. It was not a lucky shot by any means.

Another .284 caliber round that makes for an ideal whitetail cartridge is the 7mm-08. This cartridge can be found in T/C's Encore, older custom Remington's XP-100, Lone Eagle, H-S Precision, and other single-shot handguns. 140-grain bullets work exceptionally well in this round. It is a superb choice. I have a custom XP-100 chambered for .284 Winchester, bedded in a fiberglass McMillan stock, topped with a 3X-12X Burris scope. Now I know the .284 Win. wasn't popular and never did catch on with hunters. Initially it was made for the box-fed Winchester Model 88 and Model 100 rifles. But it is a fine cartridge regardless what you have been told. If I have ever owned an "honest-to-God", bean-field handgun, this baby will qualify. A Nosler 140–grain BT bullet leaves the 15-inch barrel just under 2,900 fps. That's pretty impressive out of a handgun.

Moving along, other popular deer cartridges include the quintessential 30-30 Winchester, .300 Savage, .308 Winchester, .35 Remington, and the old, but faithful 45-70. These are just a few of the many cartridges that suffice for stand hunting. Every deer hunter I know has a favorite deer cartridge and this makes some interesting campfire discussions that linger well into the night.

The H-S Precision Pro-Series 2000 bolt-action handgun is an ideal rig for use while sitting in a deer blind. This gun is chambered in .308 Winchester, wears a 2X-6X Bausch & Lomb scope, and is capable of sub minute-of-angle groups.

If I had to choose one factory round for use while hunting out of deer blinds, the .308 Winchester is my favorite. I have two handguns chambered for this great round, a T/C Encore and H-S Precision's Pro-Series 2000. Both guns are extremely accurate. If I will just do my part, the freezer will be filled with venison. Both of these guns shoot 150- and 165-grain bullets extremely well. I'm glad because these are the bullets I use the most while deer hunting. A .308 Winchester offers plenty of performance and is available in a wide variety of factory loads. You will be well equipped to bag just about any game animal in North America if you fire a .308.

There are many wildcats out there and I couldn't begin to list them all. But two of my favorite deer choices are the 6.5 JDJ, and the .309 JDJ. The 6.5 JDJ

The Savage Striker is another bolt-action handgun that works well for the deer hunter sitting in a blind. Both the 7mm-08 and .308 Winchester are fine rounds for whitetail hunting.

Bucks with a 20-inch inside spread are not found around every tree. The excitement of seeing a trophy buck can be overwhelming. That's one of the many reasons hunters continue to pursue this great game animal.

utilizes the very strong .225 Winchester brass, blown out and expanded to the larger diameter. The 120-grain Nosler Solid Base is my all-time favorite bullet for this round. It can be pushed approximately 2,350 fps. I've taken many whitetails with this little wildcat and have found the performance astounding. Throw in the fact that there is very little recoil and one can understand why so many hunters shoot this cartridge well.

The .309 JDJ is another wildcat that is dynamite on whitetail, and it too can be shot from a Contender. This cartridge is based on the .444 Marlin brass, necked down to .30 caliber and is capable of using a wide range of bullets. Ballistically speaking, it is almost identical in performance to the .308 Winchester. I frequently shoot Nosler's 150- or 165-grain Ballistic Tip bullets. They work great on deer-sized game. The 165-grain bullet can be pushed at around 2,450 fps. This is my favorite wildcat for hunting deer. I have a 2X-6X Bausch & Lomb scope mounted on my SSK Industries barrel, that is attached to a stainless T/C frame.

A couple of years ago I was using this gun on the third morning of deer season. I was hunting from a ladder stand overlooking some well-traveled paths when a deer stepped out into an old logging road just before sunrise. Grabbing the binoculars for a better look, I struggled to see how big his antlers were. He continued walking down this old road. Even though it was legal shooting time, with overcast skies in the early morning hours, visibility was poor. When the buck got within 70 yards, I rested the Contender on my knees and tried to steady the crosshairs. By now I could determine he wasn't a monster, but I was going to take him anyway. I was shaking like a train. Some people call this buck fever! I turned the scope setting up to 4X getting ready for my shot. When the buck turned broadside and started to step into the woods, leaving the road, I touched off with a shot I felt good about.

The buck flinched, jumped into the air and leaped forward, then disappeared into the woods. I waited a few minutes before climbing down. Heck, I even reached into my wallet for the deer tag and thought about taking pictures before the field-dressing chores. After checking the area where there should have been blood, then scrutinizing the entire area completely for the better part of an hour, I began talking to myself, actually cussing myself, for blowing what should have been an easy shot. That's deer hunting for you. It can be frustrating at times. I had taken nine bucks in previous years from that very ladder stand, not having one screw-up until then. Like I said, if I do my part any of the guns I shoot are accurate enough and powerful enough to bring down a deer.

The next morning I was hunting with my brother inside one of our larger blinds, overlooking a field where shots can be out to 300 yards. My brother commented that if I couldn't hit one at 70 yards, what made me think I could find the mark on something even farther out. I won't say what I told my older brother. We had been watching for a couple of hours before seven does came running out into the field. A nice eight-point buck was chasing them. Deer were running everywhere. I rested the T/C on a sandbag and turned the scope up to 6X. Michael, my brother, raised his rifle. I told him don't even think about it! Slowly I squeezed the trigger, remembering the blown shot, hoping not to repeat such a stunt. The buck had finally stopped. The loud muzzle blast broke the morning silence. At the shot, deer took off in every direction. We watched the buck enter the woods and expire. At 230 yards the Nosler BT punctured both lungs and I claimed the nice buck.

The handguns and cartridges mentioned here are by no means all of the excellent whitetail cartridges available. There are dozens of fine cartridges suitable for the handgun hunter looking to pursue whitetail deer, but, one important consideration should rise to the top: Regardless what handgun or caliber you choose, you must make the first shot count.

You should know right up front that when you squeeze off a round, the next shot will not be anywhere close to the quality of the first shot. This is all the more reason to make certain the first shot ends up exactly where you want it: in the vitals. If you do not know where the heart and lungs are located on a deer, find the resources and study the deer's anatomy. It's crucial that your bullet passes through the heart/lung area.

Making Those Shots Count

There are several things a hunter can do to help with this endeavor. First, sighting in your handgun properly is of paramount importance. Most of my deer hunting handguns are sighted-in around 2 or 3 inches high at 100 yards. This allows, depending on the cartridge being fired, the capability of taking a

This odd-looking eight-pointer fell to a T/C Contender in .309 JDJ. The distance was 230 yards across an open field. The buck was chasing does.

deer from 200 to 250 yards without holding over the body. Knowing where your gun shoots at 100, 150, 200, 250, even out to 300 yards is very beneficial. I practice nearly every week, from all different ranges. It helps judging distance in the field under actual hunting conditions.

America's most popular game animal is the whitetail deer. Thousands of handgun hunters take to the woods every fall hoping to fill their tags and freezers. Hunters do not need to hire a guide and invest in expensive equipment to enjoy this great fall tradition.

Practicing with a purpose means shooting from a variety of positions that you may encounter in the field. This is the second step in the process of helping make that all-important first shot really count. Once the gun is sighted-in correctly, you should avoid shooting from the bench. Once in a while during the off-season I'll even go to one of our blinds and shoot at targets placed in locations a whitetail might appear during the hunting season. I know this may sound a bit much but it does help prepare for that magic moment. Hunters should practice shooting from the sitting, kneeling, and standing positions, and should utilize different methods of resting the handgun. Look for a limb, rock, stump, fence post, or whatever else you might run across while hunting deer in your area. Shooting from the offhand position is not easy and that's all the more reason we should practice shooting in this manner. You never know when you will have to shoot this way. There is no substitute for practice. Becoming more acquainted with your equipment will only make you a better hunter, and increase your odds for success when hunting season rolls around.

I do realize that many of us have difficulty finding the time to practice as much as we like but we should avoid at all cost, waiting for the last minute to get prepared. It amazes me how many hunters wait to shoot their gun until the weekend before opening day, fire less than a box of ammo, then head to woods ready to harvest the yearly venison. As ethical hunters, we owe it to the game we pursue to make a clean, quick, humane, killing shot and not allow the animal to suffer for any length of time. If you have limited time to practice with live ammunition, you can always use "snap caps" to practice dry-fire training. Acquire the sight picture, hold the gun steady and keep the sights on target as you squeeze the trigger. This builds the muscle memory needed to maintain good shooting form.

More Than Just A Hunt

Deer hunting with a handgun is one of my most treasured pastimes in the outdoors. Being able to harvest America's most popular big game animal with a sidearm is a unique challenge. If you have experienced this thrill, you will know exactly what satisfaction I am talking about. If not, do yourself a favor, try bagging your next deer with a handgun and see what rewards you have been missing.

After chasing all kinds of game all over the world, the author enjoys hunting whitetail deer on his own farm about as much as anything.

For many of us, deer season is more of a ceremonial tradition than most of the other holidays on the calendar. When I was going to school, classes were dismissed during deer season. For those of you who have been involved with a deer camp, you'll know what I'm talking about when I say this is a very special place. Our family has had a deer camp since Missouri first opened a whitetail season. My Dad always invited all of his friends for the annual deer hunt. Sometimes we would have as many as 30 hunters in camp. It was back in the days when you could take off in any direction and hunt wherever you thought there might be a deer. I can't remember ever seeing a NO HUNTING sign. It was a time when hunters, at least in this camp, would shoot any deer regardless of gender or maturity. Dad was considered the patriarch of hunting camp and he would delegate me to conduct the deer drives, field-dress most of the game, and skin and quarter the harvest. The operation would sometimes last into the wee hours of the morning, that didn't include my duties playing part-time cook and bartender. That short nap before daylight the next morning wasn't much but seemed sufficient. Usually there was a poker game going on in one room of the cabin and a wild craps game going on in another. Smoke-filled rooms rang out with laughter and yelling, you didn't have to be in one of the games to know who was winning or losing. To say alcohol was prevalent would be the understatement of the year. Cooking meals for thirty hunters was always fun too. It was a special place, and a very special time of year, remaining so today. But a lot has changed in the past 30 years.

Presently, the camp has dwindled to about 10 or 12 hunters. Today, if you don't own or lease property, you will probably be hunting on state land and could find yourself sharing that property with many others. NO HUNTING signs are hanging on almost every tree. Diet coke and iced tea have replaced beer and the hard stuff. Nobody smokes anymore, unless it's a fine cigar. Most of the hunters fall asleep before the 10 o'clock news gets watched. Last year one of the old-timers requested baked food one evening instead of everything always fried, seems he was watching his cholesterol. Heck, maybe for dessert we should all enjoy some crème brulee. Poker and craps games are a thing of the past. Nobody knows how to play any more. Hunters no longer shoot at just any deer, they are selective and pass up immature bucks on occasion. Yes, like many things in life, deer camp has seen its share of changes. I can't help wonder what the next 30 years will bring. All I care about is that deer hunting, and deer camp, remain a special time and place.

Ken French of T/C Arms poses with a nice Texas whitetail. He is using a T/C, of course, in .300 Whisper with a 10-inch barrel. The shot was about 50 yards and the Nosler 150-grain BT performed well.

Chapter 7

Where The Deer And The Antelope Play

When I think of open-country handgun hunting, the first thing that pops into my mind is antelope. These animals represent, in my way of thinking, the real spirit of the American West. According to information from Safari Club International's record book, the pronghorn antelope, or "goat", as they are fondly referred to by many hunters, is really neither a goat nor an antelope. It is the surviving member of a family of fork-horned ungulates that inhabited North America millions of years ago. The pronghorn is both a grazer and a browser, and can be up moving or feeding at any time of day. Both the male and females have horns, which consist of a sheath with the same chemical composition as hoofs, hair, or nails. The female's horns do not grow as large as the males. Depending on what part of the country you are hunting, a buck with 12 inches or more of horn is decent. Anything more than 15 inches is more than respectable.

Antelope hunting on the open plains is a great opportunity for handgun hunters for several reasons. The weather is usually very pleasant during antelope season, making it an enjoyable time of year to be out in the great outdoors. If you have done a little scouting ahead of time, or you're hunting a good area, you can expect to see a lot of antelope during a hard day's hunt. It's also a great opportunity for a group of friends, or family members to share some time and enjoy the camaraderie of an enjoyable hunting experience. Anyway you look at it, antelope hunting offers a lot of challenge and fun, and many handgun hunters head to the plains every year in pursuit of this worthy trophy.

Many years ago I took a trip to Wyoming with a couple of buddies, Steve and Doyle. We all had gone from first grade through college together, yet this hunt proved to be the time of our lives, and not just because we all took nice bucks.

Our hunt together would be the first antelope hunt for both Steve and Doyle and they were quite excited about the Western experience. I was armed with a T/C in .358 JDJ. Steve and Doyle were each packing T/C's Contenders in .44 Magnum, using 180-grain bullets. None of us had what I consider ideal antelope medicine but that didn't slow us down any. Once we set foot in Wyoming, we begin seeing prairie dog towns everywhere. We obtained permission and decided this would be a great way to prepare for the long-range shooting so common with hunting antelope. After a few hours of busting varmints, missing many more than we touched, we drove toward Unit 71 and begin seeing antelope everywhere. When we arrived at the ranch, the landowner told us where we could set up camp, and gave us some ideas where the antelope would be moving come opening morning.

At the crack of dawn, I was watching seven does and fawns grazing past my position. I was halfway hidden by a group of large boulders that obliged me with a decent rest for the handgun. After the sun finally broke over the hill, a nice buck came following another group of does about a half-mile away. They were heading right towards me. Everything looked good until I saw a truck

This octagon-barreled T/C is topped with a 4X Bausch & Lomb scope. This particular gun is chambered for .375 JDJ.

These bolt-action handguns will deliver the necessary accuracy for open prairie hunting. From the top they are, Savage Striker in .308, H-S Precision also chambered for .308 Winchester, and a custom XP-100 in 6.5 x 284. With a solid rest, 300-yard shots are possible with these handguns.

stop just below the antelope. Three hunters jumped from the vehicle and the fireworks began. Even though I was wearing an orange coat, in plain sight, the hunters emptied their guns in my direction, never touching the antelope. The animals disappeared momentarily and the hunters drove off to another part of the ranch. Thirty minutes later the buck came back into my view as I placed a backpack on the large boulder for a rest. I had a perfect spot to hide and watched the buck come within 75 yards of the rock pile. The buck was walking slowly. Trying to keep the crosshairs on his shoulder, as he was moving, I squeezed the trigger and missed the antelope completely. I couldn't believe that I blew such a shot. Totally embarrassed and cussing at myself, I reloaded just in time to see the buck stop to look back for his female companions. The second shot, with the animal almost 200 yards away, was on the mark as the 13-inch buck dropped in his tracks.

While I was busy field-dressing the buck, I heard Steve shoot over the next ridge. Later I learned that a decent 12-inch buck had fallen victim to Steve's T/C .44 Magnum, with his shot being close to 150 yards. Later in the day, Doyle connected on a nice buck and we all got to go home feeling pretty good about the experience. After hunting antelope in several different states, I can see why some hunters want to go after these beautiful animals every fall.

Loading Up For Antelope

If you want to stalk the plains with an open-sighted revolver, by all means, knock yourself out. But the ideal antelope pistol is certainly some sort of single-shot handgun capable of shooting accurately out to 200 yards and beyond beginning. The smallest bullet diameter you should consider is .25-caliber. Connoisseurs of long-range accuracy love to pursue pronghorn because the hunting provides them opportunities to employ their skills and equipment at greater distances. An antelope is not a big animal. It is most often a bit smaller than your typical whitetail, and you need not be shooting a super-

Antelope hunting often requires long-range shooting. Hampton took this fine Montana buck with his .309 JDJ from over 150 yards.

magnum rhino-stopper to bring one down. Under normal circumstances, hunters will have to shoot accurately at longer ranges using a cartridge with a flatter trajectory than your run-of-the-mill revolver is capable. The .250 Savage would be considered a decent starting point. I feel the .257 JDJ is a better choice. In a Contender, the .257 JDJ using Nosler's 100-grain Ballistic Tip bullets is ideal antelope medicine. Working our way up the ladder is the 6.5 JDJ, again using a T/C frame as a launching vehicle, is a dynamite cartridge for long-range antelope hunting. It pushes a 120-grain bullet approximately 2,450 fps. The 7mm-08 is another ideal cartridge for this type of open-country hunting. The calibers mentioned thus far all recoil very little and are inherently accurate. There are many, many other cartridges that suffice as antelope hunting rounds. Throw in the wildcats currently available, most of which will work wonders in the right gun, and you have a nearly limitless selection.

My brother and I, along with some friends, got in on some Big Sky antelope hunting recently on the Fort Belnap Indian Reservation. I wasn't looking for just any antelope on this trip, but rather something over 15 inches. Prairie dog shooting dominated the first couple of days but then we concentrated on pronghorn. I was carrying a .309 JDJ loaded with 165-grain Nosler BT bullets, that sped through the chronograph at 2,450 fps. The T/C was topped with a 2X-6X Bausch & Lomb scope, and I carried a Bushnell rangefinder in my backpack. On a previous day of varmint hunting, we spotted a buck carrying horns we had estimated at more than 15 inches but were unable to get close enough for a good look. The day started in the area where we had seen the potential trophy, with us setting up a spotting scope to scan the plains.

After an hour or so of looking, we finally located the buck chasing some does and planned our stalk. The rut was in full swing as bucks were following does, trying to keep other bucks from interfering, and often fighting fierce battles. Our guide, Buz, had an antelope decoy in hand as we took off using a gully to conceal our presence. Sneaking along the gully for 45 minutes or so, we topped out over the edge for a look. No antelope. Not anywhere. Sliding back into the ravine, we quietly walked farther in the direction where we thought the buck and his herd of does might be located. Again, we eased over the edge to have a look and were puzzled by the complete lack of animal life. I glanced back to see how far we had actually walked down the gully and to my amazement, a herd of antelope was looking our direction from about 150 yards behind us.

Buz placed the decoy where the animals could see it. I rested the handgun on my backpack and waited. When the buck noticed the decoy, he took a few steps toward us, and then stopped. I assumed he thought it was an intruder, a possible threat to his dominance of the herd. At any rate, it gave me time to settle the crosshairs on his shoulder and squeeze the trigger. At the shot, the buck flinched and ran full throttle for about 75 yards before collapsing. That was my first experience using a decoy.

This was a fine Montana pronghorn with horns measuring more than 15 inches; I was very pleased with this fine buck. Later in the hunt, other hunters took some fine antelope, again using the decoy to perfection. With the rut well underway, the decoy worked like a charm. Proving to us that antelope hunting with a handgun is truly a fun, and usually successful adventure, with a lot of non-stop action.

A big mule deer is probably one of the most difficult trophies to obtain today. Pam Atwood took this monster with a Freedom Arms .454 Casull.

Noted writer and handgun hunter Larry Weishuhn took this fine mule deer with a T/C in .309 JDJ.

Open country hunting occasionally requires the hunter to shoot at long range. A good solid rest is paramount. The wise hunter is always looking for a steady rest.

The Whitetail's Larger Cousin

The mule deer is the other trophy of the plains. A big, and I mean a really big mule deer buck, is probably one of the most difficult trophies to now obtain in North America. Harsh winters, declining habitat, predation, over-hunting in some areas, and a host of other factors have put mule deer hunting, especially for trophy-class bucks, in a much different category than 20 years ago. Guided hunts for trophy mule deer, with a reasonable chance of taking a good buck, are getting more expensive every day. It's not terribly uncommon to see some of these hunts, conducted on private land with a reputable outfitter, priced at more than $5,000, and I have seen some hunts go for a lot more. Luckily, there are other options. These will be the do-it-yourself, non-guided hunts where you set up camp, scout for game, cook, skin and quarter your own game, and be responsible for getting your game out of the field.

My first mule deer hunt, which took place in Colorado, was something like the latter. A good friend of mine, Doyle Pitts, and I had set up camp, complete with an Army tent and cook stove and with sleeping bags on top of Army cots out in the national forest. It wasn't exactly Motel 6 but it was acceptable, at least for a few days. Conditions for deer hunting weren't favorable. It was fairly cool in the morning, but once the sun popped up, the temperature quickly rose into the 70s. We were hunting with a group of rifle hunters from Arkansas who had previously hunted the area. The day before the season opened, one of the boys fell and broke his leg in four places. We took him to the town of Delta, 40 miles away, and got instructions from the doctor to get him to his family physician as soon as we arrived back home. The doctor did put him in a cast. This unfortunate mishap cut our hunting time short.

Daybreak on opening morning found Doyle and I glassing a hillside with our binoculars. I was toting a .375 JDJ and Doyle was packing his T/C .44 Magnum. Both guns were wearing 4X Leupold scopes. Just as it became light enough to pick out objects through the binoculars, I spotted a buck feeding on a distant slope.

The Lone Eagle is available in a variety of calibers including .308 Winchester.

Dealing with the reality of a one-day hunt, Doyle and I had decided that any decent deer would suffice. We watched the buck feed until visibility improved. The buck, standing broadside now at approximately 200 yards, never knew we were there. I was on the ground trying to rest the Contender on my legs, while Doyle observed the buck with his binoculars. The roar of the hand-cannon broke the early morning silence and dropped the buck in his tracks, putting an end to my one-day mule deer hunt. Later in the morning, Doyle uused the .375 JDJ in place of his .44 Magnum, and brought down his first mule deer. It was a good shot from more than 200 yards, and two happy handgun hunters began the skinning chores.

Hunting mule deer out West, much like hunting antelope, demands a handgun and cartridge capable of shooting at least 200 yards. Yes, there are many mulies taken every year inside of 100 yards, and a revolver would work fine for that. But there are many places out

The XL can be chambered for a lot of different cartridges. The author is shooting this model, which is shown here with a muzzle brake, to test for accuracy from different shooting positions.

Handgun Hunting   57

West where close-range opportunities are difficult to come by. Cartridges like the 7mm-08 or .308 Winchester are good long-range mule deer fodder, and will take a buck cleanly beyond 200 yards if called to do so. I prefer the 140-grain bullets in the 7mm, and 150-grain in the .30 caliber, as these bullets perform sufficiently at long range. Some of the many single-shot handguns, that we have already discussed, capable of digesting bottle-neck rifle cartridges are really ideal for this type of hunting. Good optics are necessary for long-range hunting in open country. A fixed 4X will suffice but most of my handguns designed with long-range shooting in mind are mounted with a variable scope. I Frequently use one of three variables including the 2X-6X Bausch & Lomb, 2-1/2X-8X Leupold, and the 3X-12X Burris. When hunting in open country I leave the magnification set on about 4X and when time permits, crank the power up to whatever fits the hunting situation. I especially like the extra magnification when testing the accuracy of the handgun and bullet when shooting at the range. Higher magnification also helps when hunting open country.

Rocky Mountain mule deer are not the only subspecies of *odocoileus hemionus* pursued in open country. The desert mule deer is somewhat similar to the Rocky Mountain variety but slightly smaller, and with a smaller rump patch. Their antlers are not normally as heavy or as tall as those of the Rocky Mountain mule deer. Desert mule deer have adapted to a wide range of temperatures and the lack of vegetation and water. They are just as challenging to hunt as their larger kin as I

The XL by RPM is a very accurate single-shot handgun. This one is topped by a 3X-9X Burris scope.

found out during a trip to the Palo Duro Canyon near Amarillo, Texas.

There were eight hunters in camp. I was delighted to be in the company of Frank and Audrey Murtland, two avid handgun hunters from Michigan. We were hunting rough cedar- and juniper-filled canyons with remote river breaks. Some of the canyon walls in the Palo Duro area rise over 1,000 feet and make for some interesting hunting. Frank was carrying a .375 JDJ, Audrey held a T/C in .300 Savage, and I was packing a 6.5 JDJ loaded with 120-grain Nosler solid-base bullets. The first day of hunting, the wind gusted at more than 30 miles per hour, and had the deer holding tight in the cedar fortress the canyons provided.

The next morning we split up, each of us going to a different section of the 125,000-acre ranch. Our hunting methods were straightforward, walk around the rim of the canyon, glassing the area thoroughly, in an attempt to spot our quarry. We walked a lot of canyons and glassed a lot of Texas real estate on that hunt. It quickly became apparent a good pair of glasses was useful. Late in the day, after many miles of walking, I spotted a buck trying to destroy a cedar bush with his antlers. Being unable to judge the size of his antlers due to the thick brush, I decided to stay put and observe. After watching the show for 15 or 20 minutes, the buck finally lifted his head. He was a respectable, high-racked 5X5. I belly-crawled into an opening that offered a decent place from which to shoot. At about 100 yards, I stood up slowly behind a small cedar bush. Holding the crosshairs steady was difficult at best with the wind blowing, and the excitement starting to get the best of me. When the hammer fell, so did the buck! Much to my surprise, the buck got back on his feet as I reloaded. Unfortunately the buck disappeared without me being able to get off another shot. Anxiously I went to look for blood and fol-

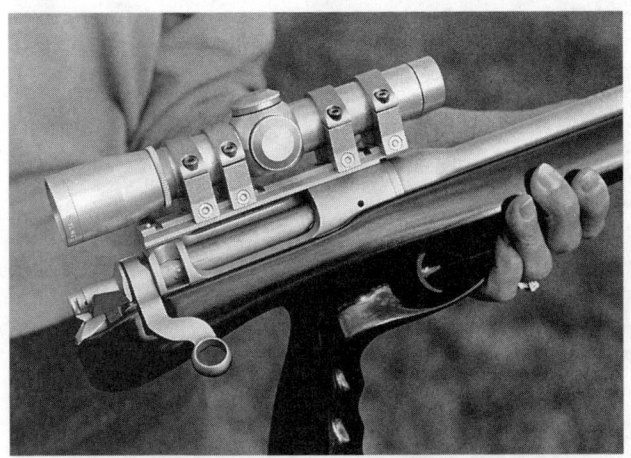

Even though the XP-100 is now out of production, the gun is used as a platform for a multitude of wildcat calibers. These single-shots are extremely accurate and capable of digesting just about anything you are man enough to handle.

Hunters expecting long-range shooting opportunities should spend time on the range to find out exactly where the bullet hits at various distances.

lowed the buck's trail to the rim of the canyon. There I was able to put a finisher in him. This time, the shot was 200 yards. Thankfully I had a good rest and was out of the wind. It does make a difference! It was too dark for any pictures. As we finished the field-dressing chores I just realized it was Thanksgiving Day. Once again, we had a lot to be thankful for, including the opportunity to hunt these beautiful creatures in the wide-open spaces.

Use Enough Gun

Regardless of what game you hunt in wide-open spaces, a good handgun and the right cartridge are critical. I have a few favorites for this type of hunting, starting with the 6.5 JDJ. This custom barrel from SSK Industries is mounted on a T/C frame, and the effectiveness of the 120-grain bullets is… let's just say it kills better than it should. Another favorite in my long-range battery is the Encore chambered for either 7mm-08 or .308 Winchester. My Encore supports a custom bull barrel from Fox Ridge Outfitters and wears a 2-1/2X-8X Leupold scope. It's chambered for the .308 because I have always been a fan of this cartridge. The wide variety of ammunition available makes it a versatile, long-range handgun. When a rock-solid rest is employed, 300-yard shots are not out of the question. No, I don't necessarily want to take those kinds of shots. Heck, I'd much rather get within 30 feet if possible. But reality tells me that's not always possible. If you don't like the Encore for some reason, and want to stick with a Contender, the .309 JDJ is, for all practical purposes, equivalent to the .308 in terms of ballistics. I have always sent Nosler's 165-grain BT bullets down the tube with the utmost confidence. Hunters who have experience with the .309 JDJ will tell you it is a very potent handgun cartridge. Because it is a wildcat, there is no factory ammo available. To shoot a .309 JDJ, you've also got to become a reloader.

Over the years I have noticed hunters tend to gravitate toward one type of firearm over another. Some handgun hunters use revolvers exclusively, others prefer some form of single-shot like the Contender, Lone Eagle, XL, Encore. After the T/C connection, my next choice for long-range hunting is the Remington XP-100, now unfortunately out of production. A few guys out there are emotionally attached to their XP-100s. Perhaps it is the accuracy these guns are capable of producing. My one and only XP-100 is a custom job chambered for .284 Winchester, with a McMillan stock, and a 3X-12X Burris scope. I like to refer to it as a 7mm-08 on steroids. The 140-grain BT bullet exits the muzzle at a shade under 2,900 fps. If you can rest this handgun, there is not a deer, antelope, or any other game animal of similar size that is safe while standing within 300 yards of the muzzle. Many are not safe beyond 300 yards. I'm not going to say how far beyond because some folks reading this will question my honesty. If you really want to push the envelope, the 6.5 X 284 is another barn-burner out of an XP-100. Basically, it is just a .264 caliber bullet fired from a necked-down .284 case. The ballistics on this round are astounding! It makes for a phenomenal long-range deer or antelope cartridge. Since the XP-100 is no longer in production, there is another bolt-action handgun available from H-S Precision dubbed the Pro-Series 2000. Mine is chambered for .308 Winchester. It will outshoot 90 percent of production rifles on the market.

Well, those are just a few of my favorite handguns and cartridges for open-country hunting. I'm sure you have your own choices as well. We can probably all agree on one thing, long-range handgun hunting out in the wide open spaces offers quite a challenge, and it's a lot of fun.

This is truly a "beanfield handgun" if there is such a thing. A custom XP-100 with McMillan stock chambered for .284 Winchester. The barrel wears a muzzle brake that definitely helps tame recoil. The scope is a Burris 3X-12X. Accuracy is phenomenal.

Chapter 8

Close-Range Action

It's true, hunting with a handgun is a challenge that pits the hunter's skill against what may appear to be enormous odds. Most of the time the odds would improve if you had a rifle. But there are certain types of hunting situations that lend themselves to a sidearm. Generally in these hunting situations the action is up close, and often, fast-paced. One of these situations is chasing game, either wild boar, black bear, or mountain lion, with dogs. If you haven't experienced this type of hunting, you may get the impression that running game with a pack of hounds is easy or even unethical, making the end result a sure thing. Rest assured it is never a sure bet and if you like to watch canines in action, and hear their music while in hot pursuit of game, you will enjoy the hunt and experience. Just be prepared to keep up with the dogs.

Many years ago a good friend of mine from New Zealand, Shane Quinn, came to the United States to

When the boar finally stops to fight the dogs, there is usually a heck of a fight. Hog hunting with dogs is a lot of fun and usually ends with a close-range shooting opportunity.

The author's friend, Shane Quinn from New Zealand, took this Texas boar after a long chase. Quinn is holding a .44 Magnum Predator that he used during the hunt.

visit some mutual friends in the Hill Country of Texas. We met in the Lone Star State to rekindle friendships and do a little hunting. At that time, few big game seasons were open so Shane decided he would like to go after a big hog with a handgun. I loaned him one of my .44 Magnums, a Predator conversion by Mag-Na-Port, supporting a 4-5/8-inch barrel. I carried a 7-1/2-inch Freedom Arms .454 Casull as we headed for a ranch that was loaded with wild hogs. Our guide turned three dogs loose early in the morning. They immediately jumped a wild hog near a waterhole. The race was on! We were determined to keep up with the hounds no matter what. At least that was the plan. Two hours into the pursuit, Shane and I were both soaked with sweat and our clothes ripped half-off from the brush. We looked as if we had been rode hard and put away wet. I was much younger then and thought I was in pretty good shape, but after following the hounds all over that ranch, my butt was beginning to drag. Occasionally the dogs bayed the big boar. Just about the time we could get close to the action, anticipating a possible shot, off to the other side of the ranch they'd go. Even though both of us were in our early 30s, this was getting physically demanding. Both of us were glad we didn't have to carry a rifle around in the brush. Our handguns rested in hip holsters. We finally did manage to catch up with the dogs, after three long hours, when the boar stopped to fight the three dogs. The guide told Shane to be darned careful and not accidentally shoot one of his dogs. Missing a boar and hitting a dog is fairly easy to do when the dogs are running around pumped with adrenalin, trying to grab the hog every chance they get. You never know what the dogs or hog will do from one second to the next. From somewhere around 15 steps, Shane carefully aimed the Predator and popped the big tusker with a factory 240-grain jacketed hollow-point. It was an exciting climax to a long, grueling chase. The handgun and hunter performed flawlessly.

After taking a well-deserved lunch break, we once again turned the dogs loose. Within an hour another race was in the making. Shane and I were both exhausted from the first episode, but took off again trying to keep up with the excited hounds. Even though blisters were killing my feet, I wasn't going to let them

This is the New Zealand way of packing out wild boar. It takes a strong back and a weak mind!

slow me down. After all, I had to convince my Kiwi friend that we Americans were 10 feet tall and bulletproof! This chase, like the first episode, lasted more than three hours. When the boar finally stood his ground to fight, he was in the middle of the thickest cover you can imagine. For 10 minutes I tried to get a shot through all of the undergrowth, being careful not get a dog in my sights, but it just was not going to work. The dogs were going crazy. The only option at this point was to climb a tree and gain a vantage point above all the commotion. Since the Freedom Arms was resting safely in a hip holster, I could use both hands and climb. Once I was about 10 or 12 feet off the ground, I could see what the dogs were fussing at in the middle of the brushy thicket. I was able to rest one foot on a limb and hang on the tree with one hand, leaving one hand for the gun. It wasn't exactly the way I had practiced or anticipated, but it could work. Pulling the .454 Casull from its home and leveling the sights in the middle of the boar's shoulder blades, I squeezed the trigger, dropping our second big hog of the day with a 300-grain slug. In both cases, our handguns were ideal firearms. I have had the pleasure of chasing boars with dogs in several states, and no matter where you hunt, it's always fun, the action is always fast and furious.

Handgunning for wild boar is a great challenge for any hunter. They can be hunted in many areas of the country. Prolific breeders, with a gestation period of three months, three weeks, and three days, sows drop piglets quite often. To put this into another perspective, in two years it wouldn't be uncommon for a sow to have five litters of piglets, with a litter ranging anywhere from two to 12. Obviously there are many variables that influence reproductive rates including nutrition, mortality rates, genetics, and other factors. I have never been accused of being a mathematician, but it doesn't take a rocket scientist to see that these porkers will not be placed on the endangered species list for a while.

Wild boar can be hunted year-round in many areas of the country. Landowners, who are often overrun with the porkers, generally welcome hunters. Too many hogs on a piece of property can devastate the landscape, tear

The author took this boar with a Freedom Arms .454 Casull. It was a long chase that ended with a short shot.

up the soil, leave holes in fences, and cause other unimaginable destruction.

How To Take A Hog

Wild hogs, sometimes called "the poor man's grizzly bear," can be hunted by using several different methods. Waiting on a stand, much like deer hunting, overlooking a feeding area can be productive. I prefer an elevated position, which improves visibility and confines scent. I have seldom observed a hog looking up into a tree. The best times to wait by a feeding area are early in the morning or very late in the evening, but hogs may be found feeding throughout the day during winter months or cooler weather. If hunting over bait is legal in your area, corn is a mighty strong magnet for hogs. Once the hogs find this corn they will keep coming back for more.

Wild boar hunting provides a lot of fun for handgun hunters. Boar can be hunted year-round by a variety of methods in many parts of the country.

The Mag-Na-Port Predator in .44 Magnum is a nice packing gun and packs a powerful punch for close-range shooting.

When hogs are working a bait pile, build a blind and wait in ambush.

For the handgun hunter who wants to get up close and personal with a big tusker, spot-and-stalk hunting is as challenging as it is exciting. Watch the wind, because hogs have exceptional noses and will vacate the area if they get a whiff of anything out of the ordinary.

Contrary to some opinions, wild hogs are not stupid. Put a lot of hunting pressure on the hog population and hogs turn nocturnal, moving only under the cover of darkness. They are quick and capable of covering a lot of ground in a short period of time when danger is present. Hogs rely primarily on their noses and ears to detect danger. If wild hogs have a weakness, it's their eyesight. They have problems determining anything clearly much beyond 75 yards or so. A wild boar is basically a four-legged garbage disposal capable of digesting just about anything. They do like grubs, ripe carrion, and acorns, but will eat a mouse, snake, or just about anything else. It is sometimes funny watching hogs go through the woods, with their noses on the ground, cleaning up acorns like a vacuum cleaner. This appetite makes it tough to establish a pattern, but if you can find a reliable food source, you can usually find hogs in the area.

Freedom Arms .454 Casull is a high quality revolver finding favor with many handgun hunters. This Mag-na-Ported model has a 7-1/2-inch barrel.

During the past decade, I have had the pleasure of guiding more than 2,500 hunters, with 25 percent of them using handguns. I have personally witnessed over 700 hogs taken with a handgun, not counting the ones that I have taken. While I may not be an expert on hog hunting, I have certainly observed enough actual field experience to gain a little understanding of these creatures and what it takes to bag one. First, there is a big difference between a 100-pound hog and a big, old boar that tips the scales at 300 pounds, or more. The body of a hog is dense and compact with fairly large bones that can be difficult to penetrate. Old males will often carry callous shields across their ribs that protect their vitals during fights with other males. In short they are tough to kill.

Hogs have been taken with a .357 Magnum using 180-grain bullets. This round works great on those 100-pound hogs but is not nearly as effective on the bigger boys. The bulk of the boars I have seen shot were taken with .44 Magnums. As with any hunting, shot placement is crucial. A lung shot offers the biggest target and the best opportunity for a quick, clean kill. A heart shot will do the job decisively but the target is smaller and most hunters are not sure of its exact location. If a boar

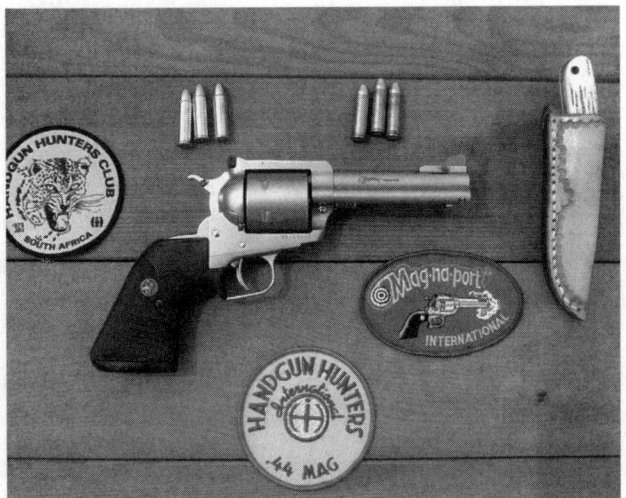

The Mag-Na-Port Predator is an ideal handgun for packing long distances. This gun can digest a steady diet of heavy loads, day after day.

64   Close-Range Action

The author, right, has guided many hog hunters. This 300-pound boar was taken at close range.

Ken French of Thompson/Center Arms took this big pig while hunting with the author. The handgun is a T/C, of course, chambered in .300 Whisper.

is hit in the right place, through the vitals, it doesn't seem to make a lot of difference concerning bullet weights. Most of the hunters I've guided were using 240- to 300-grain jacketed bullets. As I mentioned in an earlier chapter, hard cast bullets are not all they are cracked up to be, usually resulting in a hog that runs off, refusing to expire. This requires additional hits to make the kill. When a hog is not hit properly, which usually means the bullet struck too far behind the shoulders, missing the vitals, you can expect a lot of tracking and eventually more follow-up shots.

The .454 Casull offers more than enough punch to handle any hog hunting situation. I've watched big hogs taken with 260- to 300-grain bullets and cannot discern any difference in performance. Both bullet weights create an exit wound and mean very little extra work for the taxidermist. Other good hog hunting cartridges include, but are not limited to, the .308 Winchester, .35 Remington, .375 Winchester, .375 JDJ, and the .45-70.

For up-close action on a tough critter, hog hunting can generate plenty of excitement.

Big Cats And Black Bears

For other exciting action inside of fifty yards think about booking a mountain lion or black bear hunt. Revolver aficionados really appreciate the close-range hunting challenges that both provide.

Black bears are the most common bear in the world and are one of North America's most adaptable big

A big black bear can be tough to bring down. Proper shot placement and good bullet selection are important. Depending on location, black bears can come in different color phases such as this cinnamon-colored bear.

game animals. Black bear can be hunted behind dogs, over bait or by spotting and stalking and close-range shooting opportunities can usually be expected.

Fall bears tend to run heavier than those taken in the spring because of the extra weight they put on for hibernation. Be that as it may, bears taken in the spring often exceed 200 pounds, and some are much heavier. When following a pack of hounds chasing a bear, I like either the .44 Magnum or .454 Casull. Both cartridges keep gaining in popularity with hunters, especially with the increasing supply of quality, heavy bullets from a number of manufacturers like Cor-Bon, Garrett, Hornady, Nosler, Speer, and Sierra. During hunts where a lot of country may have to be covered, my revolvers can be found riding in a cross-draw holster. For me, it is the most comfortable way to carry the revolver and it doesn't get in my way when crawling around the brush, fighting my way through the thickets, or doing whatever else it takes to stay within hearing distance of the hounds.

Several years ago I followed a pack of dogs around the mountains of New Mexico for three days before an opportunity materialized. The chase, as usual, was grueling, long, and demanding before the bear decided to climb a tree. At that time a 10-1/2-inch barreled Ruger Super Blackhawk was on my side, loaded with factory

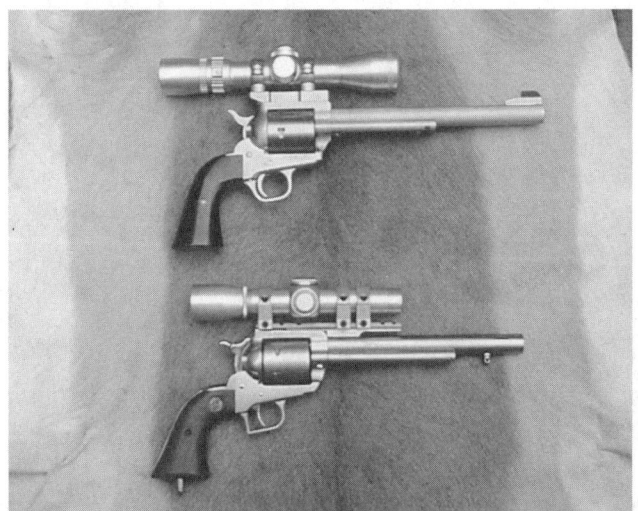

When scoped, Freedom Arms .454 Casull and Ruger's Super Blackhawk in .44 Magnum make excellent hunting revolvers.

This highly customized Super Redhawk has an octagon barrel with after-market grips.

Winchester 240-grain jacketed hollow points. The shot, somewhat anticlimactic, was 40 yards up into a huge pine tree.

The guides tell you right up front to make a good shot on the bear. The last thing they want is a wounded bear falling on the ground with their prized dogs. And I don't blame them one bit. At the shot, the 200-pound bear came crashing down, landing a few feet from the anxious, barking canines. Luckily he was stone dead as the .44 Magnum had, once again, done its job.

Handgun hunters who prefer hunting bear over bait are normally situated in a tree stand. To some, this may sound easy, perhaps unethical. It is not a guaranteed deal whatsoever. The hunters who choose this method must have patience, they must watch the wind and they must be very careful about leaving a scent trail when they approach the stand. There are a lot of cartridges that will suffice in this endeavor, as most shooting opportunities are well inside 50 yards. Realizing that I have made this statement more than once let me say again that shot placement is very important. No one likes the thought of trailing a wounded bear in the woods. The brush and undergrowth can be very thick and the job gets especially interesting after dark. The majority of handgun hunters waiting for bear are probably best served with a good quality, low-power scope, such as a 2X model. Open sights get more difficult to see when lighting conditions are not ideal.

As I mentioned, many handgun cartridges will handle this type of hunting chore including .44 Mag., .454 Casull, 7mm-08 Rem., .308 Win., 35 Rem., .375 Winchester, and the .45-70. My favorite cartridge, if there is such a thing, for close-range hunting is the .375 JDJ. Based on the strong .444 Marlin case, this

Ruger's .44 Magnum Redhawk can be scoped if the shooter prefers and makes a fine hunting revolver for close-range work.

Single-action revolvers in .44 Magnum are popular with a lot of handgun hunters.

Pamela Atwood took this fine bruin using a Freedom Arms .454 Casull. Pamela has hunted all over the world with handguns. She continues to pursue difficult challenges by hunting in remote parts of the planet.

wildcat was designed for the T/C Contender. Reloading for the cartridge is very straightforward, as you simply run a .444 case through a .375 JDJ full-length sizing die, insert the correct amount of your favorite powder, and you are ready for just about anything. One thing making the .375 JDJ so versatile is the selection of quality bullets available. The same bullets are used with any of the .375 caliber rifles. Several avid handgunners use the 220-grain bullets for game such as mule deer and black bear. Hornady's 270-grain spire-point bullet has always been my choice and makes for ideal medicine for big game. Pushing the big slug at approximately 2,050 fps, the round is capable of handling moose, bear, or elk, with ease. Speer's 285-grain Grand Slam is also quite good. Groups of 1-1/2 inches at 100 yards are common. This is pretty

The .45-70 is an ideal cartridge for close-range hunting regardless what game is intended.

Larry Kelly took this big mountain lion using his Stalker conversion. A 2X Leupold scope is mounted on this .44 Magnum.

Muzzle brakes come in a variety of configurations. The one shown here by SSK Industries is very effective.

phenomenal when you consider the size of bullet being launched. The .375 JDJ has taken game of all descriptions, including elephants, and was responsible for the last black bear I took while hunting over bait.

Mountain lions, or cougar as they are sometimes called, are also taken at close range, usually with the aid of dogs. Because of the cat's extreme shyness and extensive range, this is the only method that offers a reasonable chance of success. I have had the opportunity to chase lions over dry ground and snow. It was always exciting to watch the dogs work. Taking a mountain lion does not require a big, powerful cartridge. These creatures are thin-skinned and light boned. A big cat will weigh in the neighborhood of 160 pounds, sometimes a bit more. I know you've heard of monster lions that tip the scales at 200 pounds, but they are the exception, not the rule.

Cougars are normally taken from a tree or on a bluff, where the animal has stopped to fight the dogs. Shots are seldom more than 40 yards. Just like taking a bear that has been treed, a good first shot is imperative, as the guides do not want a wounded lion falling in the middle of their precious dogs. A heart/lung shot is best and there is usually enough time to aim carefully.

While it's been 25 years, I remember the strenuous lion hunt like it was yesterday. The hunt took place in Idaho with Gary Madsen who owned a pack of well-trained lion dogs. Our *modus operandi*, like most western lion hunting, entailed driving the truck as far as possible up canyon roads, then unloading the snow-mobile so we could scout for fresh tracks farther up the canyon. When the terrain no longer allowed for the snow machines, we walked the canyons with the dogs, hoping we would come across lion sign. I had waded in knee-deep snow for days and figured that I had finally been baptized into mountain lion hunting. We had been checking several different major canyons for several days, to no avail. On the fourth day of the hunt, Gary suddenly stopped the truck, "There's a lion track," he said.

My enthusiasm soared as I jumped out of the truck to take a closer look. That I was amazed would be an understatement of my reaction when I first laid eyes on the track. It was impressive. I wanted to turn the dogs loose at that very moment but the guide's experience

A mature bull elk is a trophy in anyone's book. Handgun hunters will find a worthy challenge pursuing elk.

Black bear can be hunted in several states including Alaska where this bruin was taken. A .375 JDJ with a 270-grain Hornady bullet proved successful.

told him to check farther down the road to make sure the lion hadn't crossed back to the other side. By the time we took this precaution, it was getting late in the afternoon. We drove back to where we had originally spotted the tracks and decided to release the dogs, hoping the cat was not too far away. Gary told me not to get my hopes up.

Up the mountain we climbed. After about an hour of trudging through the snow, Gary reluctantly told me the lion had backtracked and crossed the road, right in the middle of numerous elk and mule deer tracks. There were so many tracks in this one area you could hardly see the lion's paw print. After loading the dogs, we enjoyed elk steaks for dinner and planned our attack for the next day.

The next morning was great. It was a beautiful time to be in the snow covered Idaho Mountains. We observed several herds of antelope, eight bighorn rams, lots of mule deer and elk, plus coyotes and a ton of waterfowl. After going through our morning ritual, we drove back to the area where we had found the track. We unloaded the dogs and began the strenuous hike up the snow-covered hillside. My glasses fogged and then

The Ruger, top, and Smith & Wesson, below, are both fine revolvers. Many handgun hunters favor the .44 Magnum for close-range work.

Ruger's Super Blackhawk .44 Magnum helped Larry Weishuhn down this bull elk. Larry likes stalking as close as possible before shooting with his revolver.

immediately froze. The dogs started cold trailing and disappeared quickly. Keeping up with the hounds was impossible. Heck, if you could stay within hearing distance you should get a medal or something. If anyone tells you that hunting with dogs is easy, they have never been on a hunt like this. I was 25 years old at the time and taught physical education, jogged every day, and lifted weights three days a week. Trying to keep up with a pack of dogs in the thin mountain air, with knee-deep snow, can be extremely hard work.

Gary and I finally reached the top but whenever we would stop to listen for the dogs, both of us were breathing so hard we couldn't hear anything. We took a five-minute break and could faintly hear the dogs. They were far away. We took off in their direction and walked more than an hour. As we got closer to the action we could tell the dogs were excited about something. That gave me a little extra energy. Gary and I reached a knoll and stopped to catch our breath. Finally, we could see the dogs baying a lion at the edge of a cliff. "Get your gun ready right now," the Idaho cowboy barked. I jerked the Ruger from its holster. Peeking over the edge of the cliff, I came eye to eye with a mountain lion about 10 feet away. The hounds were going nuts! Gary was yelling at me to shoot! The lion was about to do something. I hadn't seen this much action since my last rodeo. I squeezed off a round and sent Winchester's 240-grain bullet into the magnificent cat. Even if I hadn't taken the cat, I learned that hunting behind a pack of hounds can be exhilarating, adventurous, and very rewarding.

While hogs, black bear, and mountain lion are three trophies normally taken at close range by handgun hunters, elk and bison would fall into this category. Elk are often encountered in dark timber, where long-range shooting is next to impossible. Getting a crack at a big bull elk in the heavy timber is a real challenge for the handgun hunter. I once found myself sneaking down an old road on the last day of a New Mexico elk hunt near the Chama region. It was raining lightly and the temperature was beginning to fall. Luckily, I spotted the group of elk before they laid eyes on me. Scrutinizing the small herd with my binoculars, I spotted a decent bull standing broadside

The Predator, from Mag-Na-Port International, is an ideal packing gun when close-range hunting opportunities are encountered. This handgun can digest a steady diet of heavy loads if called to do so.

Handgun Hunting 73

The author took this bison in South Dakota with a .44 Magnum Predator using Cor-Bon ammunition.

with his head down feeding. Slowly I sat on the ground to rest the Contender on my raised knees. Placing the crosshairs of the 4X Bausch & Lomb scope, I could barely make out the bull through the darkness inside the thick timber. When the gun broke the mid-morning silence, elk started running everywhere. The bull, however, made it only 60 yards before crashing to the ground. I was thankful for Hornady's 270-grain bullet, and a good scope that allowed me to see well enough to place the bullet where it belonged.

Another old, but still effective close-range elk cartridge is the .45-70. The old cartridge had many designations including 45/70/500. The number .45 represented the caliber, 70 as the amount of black powder loaded in the old Army load, and 500 was the weight of the bullet in grains. This cartridge was a military round back in the late 1800s and you would think its effectiveness and popularity would have diminished over the years. Actually, with the availability of better bullets, the aged .45-70 is still a great close-range hunting cartridge. I own and shoot an SSK barrel chambered for the .45-70 on a T/C frame, topped with a 2X Bausch & Lomb scope. It really is a fine hunting gun for opportunities under 150 yards.

Bison require a big, powerful cartridge because these animals can weigh up to a ton. The only bison I ever harvested was with a .44 Magnum Predator, using 305-grain Penetrator ammunition from Cor-Bon. I was doing some work with .44 Magnums at the time and wanted to see how the short-barreled Ruger would perform. One of the handiest holsters I've found for these revolvers is a cross-draw rig from Thad Rybka. The bison hunt took place in South Dakota over Christmas vacation and the weather was typical for that time of year; cold, windy, and spitting snow. We drove around the 50,000-acre ranch until we came across three bulls, one of which looked huge. The outfitter and I got as close as we could; within 60 yards. From there I sent one of the big slugs into the bull's neck. I wouldn't have placed the shot there but that's where the outfitter wanted me to shoot. Personally, I hate a neck shot on any game. Sure, you may

Proper eye and ear protection should always be worn when shooting. The author spends a lot of time on the farm burning up ammo during practice sessions and hearing protection means he won't be going deaf.

knock an animal off his feet with that shot, but if your bullet does not hit the spinal column, the animal will probably get back up and run away wounded. But the outfitter didn't want any meat damaged with a shoulder shot. It took a couple of more follow-up shots before the big bull went down. The bison weighed close to a ton and supported almost 18 inches of horn. Handgun hunters harvest many bulls every winter, either for their excellent meat, or as an addition to a trophy collection. The .44 Magnum might be on the small end of the effectiveness scale for bison. There are three very effective cartridges that stand out as bison medicine: the .454 Casull, .375 JDJ, and again, the faithful .45-70. Penetration is important because buffalo have thick hides, massive bones, and large muscles. Getting a bullet into the vitals requires a lot of penetration.

Close-range hunting opportunities come in many different forms but it all adds up to a lot of excitement and a chance for handgun hunters to get in the middle of the action. We simply have to choose the right cartridge and bullets to match the game we seek, and don't forget proper bullet placement.

Open sights are ideal for close-range work. These fine handguns work exceptionally well when you are following a pack of dogs in pursuit of bear or wild boar.

Handgun Hunting 75

Chapter 9
Handgunning On The Last Frontier

Alaska can truly be categorized as a sportsman's paradise. A land of immeasurable natural beauty, our 49th state is blessed with quite a diversity of terrain, and wildlife. If you could hunt in Alaska twice a year for the next 20 years, you would probably touch but a fraction of this wonderful land. The "Last Frontier" is immense, with mountain ranges where glaciers are still working their way to the sea and lower elevations of tundra and vast river valleys. Handgun hunters looking for excitement and adventure, and don't mind tough mountain climbs, or the frustration of losing days because of foul weather, don't have to look any farther than Alaska. The mere thought of handgun hunting in Alaska conjures up images of a true wilderness experience and abundant wildlife.

Two of the most popular targets of handgun hunters in Alaska are moose and caribou. These monarchs of the north are often taken in conjunction with one another. The Alaska-Yukon moose is the largest of all moose species. A big bull will weigh in the neighborhood of 1,800 pounds. Alaska law requires all meat must be packed out. This may take days if you shoot one in the wrong spot. The antlers of a big moose are one of the world's most impressive trophies.

Caribou too, develop some awesome antlers. The animals are somewhat unique in the deer family as both the bulls and cows commonly grow antlers. The barren ground species, which inhabits Alaska, is the most widely hunted of the caribou. If hunters hit a migration just right, it is an unbelievable sight! However, hunting can be very frustrating when you are in the wrong place. Always wanting to experience the thrill of hunting moose and caribou on a combination hunt, I booked a hunt with Bob Tracey and headed for Alaska. Bob came highly recommended from another handgun hunting buddy, George Faerber, who guides for black bear out of Trapper Creek. The moose and caribou hunt would take place out of Non Dalton, an Athabascan native village situated in the northern portion of Bristol Bay. Overlooking Six Mile Lake, this sleepy little village with a population of about 250, is home to the largest sockeye salmon run in the world. We would be hunting the Mulchatna caribou herd. The area also holds

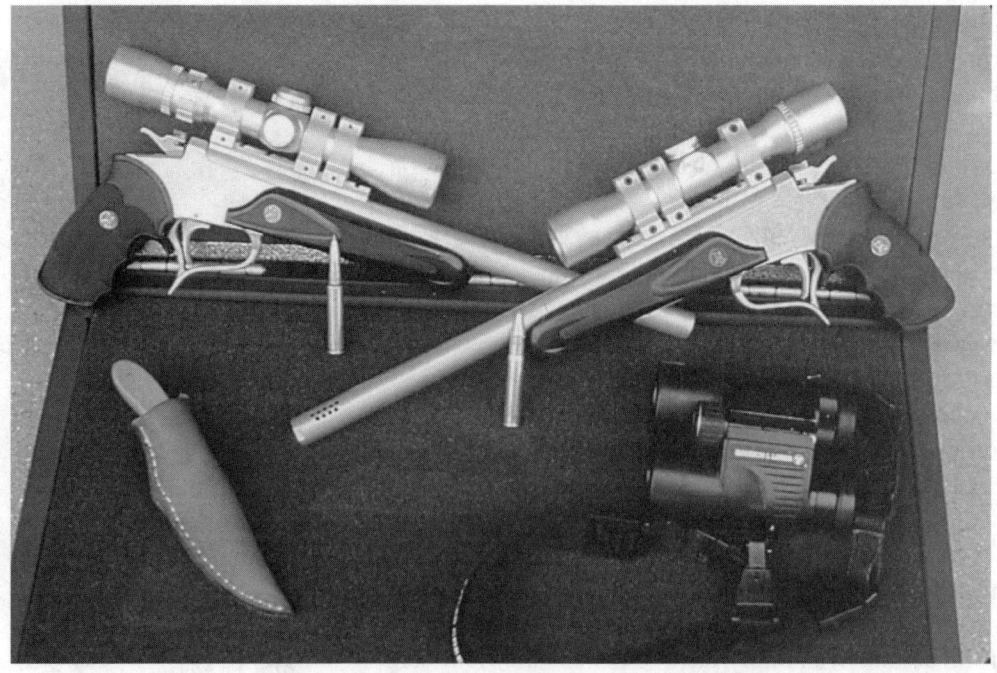
Alaskan weather can be tough on hunters and equipment. These stainless Contenders were used during the author's moose and caribou hunt.

Moose are the largest member of the deer family and their huge antlers are much sought-after by hunters. A big bull moose like the one shown here will tip the scales around 1,800 pounds. The 67-1/2-inch antlers are indeed impressive! Once a big moose is down, the fun is over and hard work begins.

some really big moose. The stage was set for an unforgettable experience.

Upon my arrival in Non Dalton, Bob suggested we concentrate on moose first, then after the really hard work was out of the way, begin looking for a trophy caribou. The weather kept us at bay for two days with the wind, rain, and fog working against us. When we finally did get a break, Bob's Super Cub was loaded and we took off for spike camp. For me, flying in the Super Cub over the Alaskan landscape is a treat in itself. During our flight out to camp we spotted several moose, herds of caribou, and even a brown bear. Nestled along the banks of the Nushagak River Drainage was a large tent draped around a wood floor. It would be home for the next few days. We were right in the middle of moose, caribou, and bear country. Every night when I fell asleep, a loaded .375 JDJ was right by my side.

I chose the .375 JDJ for moose, using the Hornady 270-grain spire point bullets. My other two choices for moose hunting would have been the .454 Casull with 300-grain bullets, or the .45-70 throwing 400-grains of lead. Both of the guns I took for this trip were stainless. Alaskan weather can be tough on equipment, and hunters alike. The weather played havoc with our hunting, which is fairly common in Alaska during these hunts. There were sporadic movements of passing caribou but nothing that warranted a second look. Luckily, I had brought enough reading material to keep my mind occupied.

It didn't take me long to figure out why Bob had strongly suggested quality, ankle-fit hip boots, and the best rain gear money can buy as the two most important pieces of equipment to bring. It was the fifth day of a scheduled 10-day hunt before we spotted a couple of huge bull moose. They were feeding out from a spruce thicket. We watched the two mature bulls through a spotting scope until dark, and then assembled a little two-man tent for the evening. Early the next morning after a cup of coffee and a handful of trail mix, we began the mile walk toward the thicket where the two bulls were last seen. When we got within approximately 200 yards, I couldn't believe my eyes. Two other hunters were closing in on our moose. I thought we were in the middle of nowhere. The other two hunters had emerged from the fog and beat us to the location where we anticipated the bulls would be hiding. We waited around for a while but never heard a shot and didn't see either the moose or the other hunters again.

The following day we located another good bull and watched him disappear into a spruce thicket. It was late in the morning and apparently the bull was going back into the timber to nap. Bob suggested we wait him out, which meant sitting all day long until the moose returned to feed in the evening. I wanted to go into the thicket and kill him, but Bob warned me about the risk. If we spooked him, our one chance at this bull would be history. We waited and watched all day long, glassing the landscape to kill time. We spotted a black bear feeding on berries. The occasional caribou came drifting past, but nothing worth going after. The gusting wind was cold and I became impatient. Late in the evening Bob told me to wake up and pay attention. The moose was expected to come out and feed anytime now. Eventually, I got a glimpse of something big and white. After looking through the binoculars I could see it was the huge antlers of our quarry. I couldn't believe my eyes. The rack seemed huge, and indeed it was! I started to get buck fever, or whatever you call it when a moose makes you nervous. I made certain the Contender was loaded. We managed to get within 60 yards of the big bull before I sent the 270-grain Hornady into his vitals. The bull stumbled and started trotting off as I quickly reloaded and sent another round into the bull's neck. This second shot dropped the bull in his tracks. Now I was really shaking!

A big, mature Alaskan-Yukon moose is an impressive animal, growing the largest set of antlers of all the deer species. This bull was no exception, weighing in the neighborhood of 1,800 pounds and supporting a 67-inch-wide rack. I can honestly tell you that all the fun is over at this point. Alaska law does not allow any meat left behind, so we had to pack all the meat and antlers up a hill to an area where Bob's Super Cub could land. Packing this amount of meat, uphill, is hard work. My back has not been the same since.

After all the work was complete, I switched guns and we began looking for a big caribou. Even a big caribou is not hard to bring down when hit properly. I carried the .309 JDJ for this leg of the hunt. Highly gregarious animals, caribou are nomadic creatures, mainly active during the daylight hours. They seem constantly on the move, searching the tundra for lichen, their favorite food.

We passed up several decent bulls hoping to run across a real monster of the Alaska-Yukon Barren Ground variety. I'm sure you have seen great migrations of caribou on the Discovery Channel. Unfortunately, we were nowhere near anything like that phenomena of nature. As a matter of fact, after traversing many, many miles, and glassing the tundra diligently, Bob commented that we were hunting awfully hard for a good caribou. Finding a big bull became a real challenge.

On day nine, we watched several small herds. But still no big bulls were anywhere to be found. The ankle-fit hip boots were rubbing blisters on my feet and growing more painful all the time. But what should you expect when covering 15 miles a day?

Breakfast on the tundra is not a full-blown meal. Normally a cup of coffee and handful of trail mix and it's time to go hunting.

This caribou was taken on the last day of a 10-day hunting trip. A stainless Contender in .309 JDJ was used to drop this respectable bull. Good walking boots, the best rain gear money can buy, and quality optics are essential for Alaska hunting trips.

We finally spotted a bull Bob described as "a real monster," right in the middle of 80 or more caribou. Bob informed me this bull would probably make the Boone & Crocket book, but getting a good, clean shot at him within this large of herd would be a real problem. We climbed a steep mountain, approaching the herd from the downwind side, and hopefully out of sight. It took a little more than an hour to finish the climb and by the time we made it to top, the caribou were gone. It was hard to believe that a herd of 80 animals could just disappear. It was even harder to believe, when we did spot them again, they were feeding in the area we had just come from at the bottom of the mountain! This was psychologically painful to watch. We made a valiant effort to catch up with them but it just wasn't possible. When we finally reached the tent after dark, tired and exhausted, I cherished a Baby Ruth candy bar, drank a diet 7-UP, crawled into the sleeping bag, ignoring the blisters and quickly drifted to sleep.

The last day of our hunt started with a hot cup of coffee and a cigar. We ran out of trail mix. Reluctantly, I forced on the hip boots and we took off, roaming the picturesque real estate in search of a trophy caribou. Somewhere around noon we located the herd, or at least we thought it was the same herd, and found the monster bull still present. We executed our stalk carefully, realizing this might be the last chance to take a caribou. The caribou were scattered all over the place. But we couldn't find the monster anywhere. The females eventually spotted us and now were alert, forcing us to

Hunting in Alaska can be a grand adventure providing you have the right equipment. Quality raingear and ankle-fit hip boots are two important items. Quality optics are also high on the list.

The interior grizzly bear do not grow as large as the coastal bears because of differences in food supply. This grizzly was taken with a .375 JDJ in fairly dense cover.

Alaska is home to a good population of black bear. Hunters looking for some top-notch bear hunting don't have to look beyond Alaska.

freeze in our tracks. They decided to make an exit and caribou began moving everywhere. There were antlers all over the place but we still couldn't make out our bull. Near the end of the herd were five good bulls and I got ready to shoot, trying to determine which one wore the biggest headgear. We decided I should go after the last bull so I tried to steady the crosshairs on the moving target. When the hammer fell I was surprised. The 165-grain Nosler found its mark and the bull didn't go 60 yards before collapsing. Even though he wasn't the monster bull we were hoping for, this caribou was a hard-earned trophy and one I'll never forget.

Loaded For Bear

I mentioned George Faerber's name earlier. I had the pleasure of hunting with him for both black and grizzly bear. George and I first met while hunting together on the famed Y.O. Ranch in Texas. That is where this entire bear hunting idea was hatched. George and I hunted for grizzly north of Trapper Creek, into the Alaska Range, in a more open tundra area. The landscape was typical Alaska, magnificent and beautiful, and seemed almost endless, with no houses, no buildings, nothing but more awesome country.

The first day we saw several moose and a few caribou, but no bears were present in the area. Camp that evening was the usual tented affair with dinner prepared on a Coleman stove. I am not much of the camping type, never have been. When George informed me the nearest motel was more than 100 miles away, I managed to endure.

The next morning we were greeted with rain. Despite the weather, we spent most of the day glassing. Good optics and fine raingear helped us get through the day. Again, we spotted a few moose, several caribou, but the grizzly bears could not be found. George had to pick up a couple of Swedish hunters back in Anchorage so we took a break from the weather and headed home. This was a spring hunt and I was in no hurry since vacation

A big brown bear is an impressive animal. In the fall, a big male can weigh more than 1,000 pounds. A trophy brown bear could be considered the ultimate test for the handgun hunter.

time wasn't being used up. The following day, while George drove into Anchorage to pick up the hunters, he had one of his assistant guides take me to a bait site so I could look for a big black bear. This would kill some time and allow George to get organized with his other clients. Then we could get back searching for grizzly. At the time I was packing the .375 JDJ loaded with my favorite 270-grain Hornady spire points. Before George departed for the airport, he told me to watch for a big black bear, have a good time, and not worry about any grizzly bears because there were none in this area.

Arriving at the site, I sat on the ground behind a few logs in what appeared to be a makeshift blind. It was around 4 p.m.. when the assistant guide left. He said it wouldn't get dark until midnight and that's when he would be back to pick me up. I thought for a moment and then realized, that was a long time to sit around and wait for a black bear, or anything else. The mosquitoes were swarming all over the place and I knew this had the making of a long evening. A moose caught my attention around 9 p.m., as he strolled through the area. At 10 o'clock I caught movement out of the corner of my eye, and quite frankly, my heart almost stopped when the grizzly came walking into view 60 yards away. I remembered George telling me not to worry; there were no grizzlies in the area. The bear was not coming to the bait, he was actually walking in the opposite direction as I slowly rested the Contender on my knees, which were now shaking. The grizzly looked big to me, of course I am no authority on grizzly bears and don't pretend to be one. I found the bear in the scope as he continued to walk through the woods, but too many obstructions kept me from shooting.

When the bear walked through the first opening, I touched the trigger and the big bruin dropped at the shot. As the bear began rolling down the hill slightly, I quickly reloaded. The bear was desperately trying to get back up on his feet. I jumped up and ran across the swamp in an attempt to get in a better position to shoot. The adrenaline rush at this particular moment was over-

Spike camps allow hunters to spend more time in game-rich country. This tent arrangement is common during extended hunts in Alaska.

whelming! I got in position to shoot and proceeded to put more 270-grain bullets into the beast. It's amazing how fast you can load a single-shot when you're scared. As the bear expired, I regained my composure.

With several more hours of daylight remaining, and nothing better to do, I walked back over to the blind and sat down. My ears were still ringing from the muzzle blast of the handgun as I seldom use plugs when hunting. It's no wonder I'm going deaf. Anyway, I know what I am about to say is hard to believe but at 10:50 p.m., less than an hour after shooting the grizzly bear, a black bear appeared on the bait. At seventy yards, I placed the crosshairs on the bear's shoulder and once again, the .375 JDJ broke the evening silence. I'm not positive but I think the muzzle blast took out six or seven mosquitoes. The bear ran about 40 steps and collapsed. When George and his assistant came to pick me up around midnight, they could not believe what had taken place. That's bear hunting for you. The grizzly was not the big bear I had imagined as he only squared 7-1/2 feet. Honestly, if he had gotten away, I would have sworn he was the biggest bear in Alaska. The black bear was a nice one, squaring a solid 6 feet.

The two exciting bear hunting experiences ended up costing me a lot of money, because they made me want to go after a big brown bear. For many, a brown bear is one of North America's most coveted big game trophies, especially for a handgun hunter. There is usually some confusion centered on the difference between a brown bear and a grizzly. It's the same species, except for record keeping purposes. Bears taken in Alaska Game Management Units 1-10 and 14-18 are classified as brown bears. These units cover the area from the saltwater coast to the first ridge of inland mountains where the bears have a better food source and grow larger. The calorie-rich salmon provide brown bears with plenty to eat and the coastal bears grow much larger than their inland buddies. All other bears taken from the interior of Alaska are considered grizzly bears. A Kodiak bear is simply a brown bear taken from Kodiak Island. Since 1

You need a big bullet to stop a big bear. The .375/06 dropped this bruin quickly, but shot placement was also important.

A big brown bear is an impressive animal. This huge bear squared 9 feet, 10 inches without any stretching. The hide is in perfect condition.

had enjoyed hunting with Bob Tracey for moose and caribou, and this same area supports a real good opportunity to take a big brown bear, we found ourselves back in the Super Cub flying out to spike camp.

Our first day of glassing for bear was enjoyable as the weather was great. We were hunting in Unit 17B, not too far from where I had taken both the moose and caribou. It was fun to watch the herds of caribou roaming around the tundra, and occasionally we would spot a moose. The caribou cows were dropping calves at this time of year and Bob informed me both the wolves and bears were preying on these newborns whenever the opportunity arose. There was still quite a bit of snow covering the landscape and the mountains were completely covered. The region was absolutely breathtaking and I was glad to be a part of it. We would glass for a while, cover more new territory, and then glass some more. Late in the afternoon we spotted a bear on the adjacent hillside and watched him for more than 30 minutes. I thought he was a beauty but Bob guessed him being about an 8-footer and told me it was too early in the hunt to go after him. Since it didn't get dark until 11:00 P.M., we were able to cover a lot of territory in a day's time. Right before dark, we located another bear walking down a little creek. Once again, I got excited but Bob didn't share my enthusiasm. Trusting the experienced guide, we passed up this bear and wandered back to camp in the dark. Camp was the usual two-man tent where we ate some freeze-dried treats before crawling into the sleeping bag. My loaded handgun was always in reach.

Two other experienced guides, Fred and Aaron, were helping us on this hunt and both commented on the handgun I was using for bear. Neither had witnessed a handgun in action and I could tell they were a bit apprehensive. I was carrying a T/C Encore with a custom barrel from SSK Industries chambered for a new wildcat dubbed the .375/06. This cartridge is based on a 30-06 case, with the neck expanded to accept a .375 caliber bullet. The round is capable of pushing a 270-grain bullet at 2,450 fps, and that is a handful coming out of a 15-inch barrel. A muzzle brake helps tame the recoil somewhat and I had installed rubber grips to help save my hands. It is still no pussycat. The stainless barrel wore a new Bausch & Lomb 2X-6X scope, with the revolutionary Rain Guard that proved to be a real asset when the weather turned sour. I felt this was an ideal rig for hunting dangerous game like a big brown bear in Alaska's unpredictable environment. I had a sneaky suspicion that all three of the guides, deep down, had reservations about a handgun for something as large and tough as brown bear.

The next morning we were up at first light, glassing more real estate. We worked our way along the river, negotiating muskeg swamps. Even though the day was pretty much uneventful, the weather cooperated, and we were able to see caribou and moose moving about the tundra. Later in the afternoon, Bob and Fred spotted a bear walking right along the banks of the river. The bear was probably two miles away but even at this distance he looked big to me. But then again, all the bears I had seen so far looked big to me. The big beast eventually wandered out of sight, but Bob and Fred wanted to have a closer look. I got the feeling this just might be the bear we were looking for. We began working our way closer to the Nushagak River, checking the wind periodically. Bear have a great sense of smell. Next to the river was a thick stand of pine that would conceal our presence. Walking through the timber was slow going as we tried to remain as quiet as possible among the pinecones. The gushing sounds of the river helped muffle some of the noise. Fred and Bob both kept checking the wind.

The guides suspected the bear to be close to the river, so we sneaked along the banks, watching and looking everywhere. We had been slowly working our way along the riverbank for about an hour when a raven landed on a huge mound of grass just ahead. About that time, a big bear walked to the top of the mound and scared the bird away. I don't know who was more scared, the bird, or me. I quickly placed my shooting sticks in position, sat down on the ground and steadied the handgun on my knees. Both of the guides whispered this is the bear we are after. They said he was more than 9 feet for sure. His hide appeared to be in perfect condition.

The bear lay down on top of the mound, facing directly at us, so I could not shoot. All we could do was sit and wait. For the most part, all we could see was the bear's massive head. His ears appeared tiny in comparison to his head. Fred whispered that he was probably lying on top of a kill, perhaps a moose or caribou, which he had covered to keep other critters from stealing his meal. The Bausch & Lomb range finder read 82 yards. Sitting there undetected, I actually had a chance to calm my nerves while we watched the big bruin drift off to sleep. It was an awesome sight. I was thankful for the opportunity to simply be there at this moment. Only about 30 minutes passed, but it seemed more like two weeks before the bear got up to stretch a bit. With the hammer already cocked, I rested the crosshairs on his

For some, a huge brown bear is the ultimate North American trophy. The author took this monster with a T/C Encore using a custom barrel from SSK Industries in .375/06. Hornady's 270-grain Spire Point performed exceptionally well.

shoulder and squeezed the trigger. At the shot, the bear dropped instantly. He wouldn't have dropped any quicker if he had been hit by a .577 Nitro Express. "Load up again!" Fred exclaimed. "Just in case he tries to get up." I loaded another round quickly and, sure enough, the bear tried to get back on his feet, only this time he gave me a better broadside shot. The second round caught him right behind the shoulder. The distinct sound of the bullet striking home was evident. The big bear rolled off of the grass-covered mound and disappeared. He made it 15 steps and fell motionless right in the middle of a little creek next to the river. Fred walked over to make certain the bear was dead. After giving us the thumbs-up sign, we all went over to inspect the trophy.

When I first laid eyes on the bear, he didn't look that big. What I didn't realize was that three-fourths of his body was underneath the water and I really couldn't see the big picture. It took all of us, giving everything we had, to roll the bear out of the water; then I saw how incredibly huge the bear really was. All three of the guides guessed him weighing in the neighborhood of 1,000 pounds. The hide was in perfect condition and at that moment I was the happiest handgun hunter in the world. Underneath the mound of grass was a dead moose, just as Fred thought. The next few hours were spent taking pictures and skinning out the bear, then packing everything back to camp. By the time we reached our sleeping bags that night, everyone was exhausted, but happy.

After fleshing the bear, we put a tape on him and found, without any stretching, he squared 9 feet, 10 inches. Fred and Bob told me if you want to stretch him out like everyone else does, he would go 10 foot easy. I didn't need any fancy stretching jobs, as it was obviously a-once-in-a-lifetime trophy.

More Alaskan Bounty

Dall's sheep and the majestic mountain goat are also available to the Alaskan handgun hunter. For many hunters, sheep hold some kind of fascination and are the ultimate trophy, usually taken in remote wilderness areas. The dedicated sheep hunter will climb mountains, go days without making a successful stalk, and sometimes go home empty handed without finding a suitable ram. But hunting in the beautiful mountains with a chance of taking an elegant sheep is what drives the serious mountain hunter. As to be expected, this type of mountain hunting requires being in good physical condition, and being able to shoot accurately at long ranges. The Alaskan Dall's sheep offers hunters the least difficult of the North American sheep to hunt. They also are probably less expensive hunts than any other of the wild sheep. Without a doubt, a Dall sheep taken with a handgun is a tremendous feat and a worthy challenge for any mountain-climbing handgun hunter.

The mountain goat is another highland dweller that is probably one of the most underrated trophies in North America. Perhaps it is because the horns only grow to 10 inches or so, and the horns are not nearly as impressive as sheep or antlered game. Anyone who has ever negotiated the mountains to get within range of these animals will have a much different perspective. The difficulty of the hunt lies with the amount of physical effort necessary to climb the steep mountains the goats call home. In most goat-hunt settings, the view borders on spectacular.

A big male might weigh as much as 300 pounds and will require a cartridge with sufficient energy to tackle such a tough animal. Because of the severity of the climbing involved, there have not been a lot of mountain goats taken with a handgun. I personally have not seen any mountain hunting in North America that rivals that of goat hunting in Alaska. If you want to experience this great hunting opportunity for an impressive animal that does not get the kind of respect it deserves, don't wait forever. The mountains can be very unforgiving.

Alaska also offers chances at the Sitka black-tailed deer, a few free-ranging bison, and some species and hunting locations open only by special drawings. Whatever inspires hunters to pursue game in wilderness areas, mountaintops, or wide-open tundra, Alaska can satisfy those desires. It is a fantastic place for handgun hunters looking for the ultimate challenge.

Chapter 10

Hunting Exotic Species: An Off-Season Challenge

If your desire to hunt big game doesn't fade away with the end of the traditional hunting seasons, you might be a candidate for hunting exotic species at a private ranch. Now, before you comment, as others sometimes do, about how easy it is to bag "captive" animals, you've got to realize that hunting free-roaming antelope and wild sheep is not an easy day on the shooting range. Whether you hunt on a ranch in the United States or an arid plateau in northern India, these animals still have keen senses and well-developed survival instincts. You will not be walking out in the pasture with a grain bucket to shoot some docile and semi-domestic animal.

Yes, I'm sure there are a few unscrupulous operations out there that have given this type of hunting a bad rap. But the truth is you never hear about the ethical operators because, simply, there is nothing bad to say about them, leaving the critics nothing at all to say.

Hunting exotics offers the sportsman the opportunity to hunt some unusual trophies without traveling abroad. It is a great way to introduce first-timers to the sport. It

Nilgai are challenging to hunt and make a worthy adversary. This big bull was taken from 228 steps with a .375 JDJ. It is a true trophy, don't be mislead by the shortness of horn.

A big aoudad, like this 34-inch ram, is one of the author's favorite exotics. Mature rams will exceed 250 pounds and require a handgun caliber capable of putting this stoutly built animal down for keeps. An H-S Precision Pro-Series 2000 chambered for .308 Winchester was used to bag this trophy. Black Hills 165-grain fodder performed well.

offers them good experience with firearms, safety issues, wildlife, and hunting related matters.

One of my favorite exotics and also one of the most challenging is the aoudad sheep, or Barbary sheep as it is sometimes called. Originally from North Africa, free-ranging aoudad can be found in some mountainous areas of north central and west Texas. In the Glass Mountains for example, they offer the sheep-hunting enthusiast a prime opportunity to hunt these challenging trophies when other hunting seasons are closed. A big male will go 250 pounds, maybe more. They are stoutly built and tough to bring down.

I was chasing these wild sheep around a large Texas ranch many years ago with Thompson Temple, who promoted exotic hunting a great deal. We spent an entire day on one ranch and after seeing one immature ram, changed locations. So much for driving out into the pasture and shooting the first one that appeared.

The guides thought I was nuts trying to get an aoudad with a handgun but I was bound and determined to prove them wrong. Shortly after daylight we were overlooking a different ranch he called Rocky Top, and I could see why the guides were snickering at the thought of me hunting for these sheep with a handgun. The ranch was mountainous with steep rocky canyons choked full of cedar, chin oak, and prickly pear. Visibility was minimal because of thick cedar and brush. Getting close enough to one of the wild, spooky aoudad that lived on the ranch was going to be interesting. When we had reached the very top I looked around and then asked the guide how many aoudad have been taken here with a handgun. "None," came his quick reply. I could understand why. Our method of hunting was glassing each canyon at least for an hour or so before moving on to the next one. We hunted hard all day and never laid eyes on a sheep. The guide assured me there was aoudad on this ranch.

The mouflon is the smallest of the world's wild sheep. They are wild and elusive, providing a challenging hunt. Janet Danuser took this fine ram with a T/C Contender in 6.5 JDJ. Since they do not lose their horns, mouflon can be hunted throughout the year.

The wind was gusting early the next morning as we began glassing the canyons for aoudad. It became obvious the weather had the game holding tight. We searched several canyons diligently, but to no avail. I looked at my watch, it was 3 p.m., and we still had not seen any sheep. Catching movement on top of the ridge, a quick look through the binoculars revealed three rams. The sheep had noticed us about the same time we'd noticed them and they started walking away. The rams were more than 200 yards away when I rested the T/C between my knees and got ready to shoot. One of the sheep stopped, partially hidden behind some cedar trees. I could see the shoulder of the ram and touched off a round from the .375 JDJ. The bullet struck home, the ram flinched, ran about 70 yards, and fell. He sure wasn't the biggest ram I have ever seen but he was trophy in my book.

As this book was being written I had the bug to go after another aoudad. My pursuit for a big ram, one with horns more than 30 inches long, found me on the Mexican border near the town of Del Rio, Texas. Aoudad sheep have lived in this particular area for decades. The ranch where we decided to hunt held a lot of mature rams and they were beginning to rut. I found them just as challenging to hunt as they were 20 years ago. This ranch was truly a paradise for big aoudad. During the course of the hunt I was passing up 30-inch rams looking for something bigger. When everything finally came together a big ram was spotted with several females high on a ridge working their way to my right. The big sheep stopped momentarily and offered a decent shot. Placing the crosshairs on his shoulder from a rock-solid rest, I launched the 165-grain Nosler BT from an H-S Precision Pro-Series 2000 bolt-action handgun. The shot was around 150 yards and the big ram dropped instantly when the bullet struck his shoulder. He was an old male with 34-inch horns. I was very pleased with this sheep but I know there are bigger ones on this ranch. As a matter of fact, the aoudad are dying of old age on Sycamore Creek.

The European mouflon is a beautiful sheep, although quite a bit smaller than the aoudad. He too, can be difficult to hunt. Mouflon are among the world's smallest sheep and can be found on private ranches in the U.S., and are free-ranging in Hawaii. Excessive crossbreeding among other types of sheep such as the barbados, means purebred mouflon are more and more difficult to find. Many years ago I went with a friend and chased sheep all over a private ranch in Texas. There was only one mouflon on this ranch. He was a big male with horns in excess of 30 inches. We arrived at the ranch and started hunting around noon on a Friday. I saw the little sheep a few times but he never offered a shot, always running away whenever he detected our presence. To make a long story short, late Sunday afternoon before we had to depart for home, I somehow managed to get one opportunity at this ram. With the help of a Contender in 6.5 JDJ, the wise old male got to ride back home with me. After hunting hard for two and one half days, I felt lucky to get a shot, and expected to go home unsuccessful. That is the type challenge you will get from some of these exotics under the right circumstance.

Another one of my favorite exotics is the nilgai, or blue bull. Nilgai are native to India and eastern Pakistan. They are somewhat odd in appearance, even supporting what appears to be a turkey beard on their neck. A large bull will weigh five-six hundred pounds. They have excellent eyesight, sense of smell, and can be extremely challenging to hunt. These large antelope are extremely hard to bring down. They remind me of the mountain goat. Their horns do not reach impressive lengths and the nilgai are a most underrated game animal.

This handgun hunting couple is all smiles after a successful nilgai hunt. The gun is a Freedom Arms .454 Casull.

The blue bull was the first exotic introduced into the Lone Star State. The animals were obtained from a bankrupt circus and released on the King Ranch sometime close to 1930. Later the animals were transplanted to other ranches in the southern part of the state. Today, populations are thriving and show no signs of decreasing.

When a handgun hunting friend of mine and I traveled to south Texas for some of this challenging action the guides, as usual, started laughing at us when we brought out the handguns. Both of us were using scoped Contenders in .375 JDJ. At this particular ranch, the nilgai were exceptionally wild and difficult to approach. Whatever the reason, getting within 200 yards of a decent bull was next to impossible. Rarely did you ever see one standing still. Most of the time a nilgai was seen in a flat-out run. Boy, are they running machines. I missed the first two shots I took because I misjudged the range. That gave me a good idea what the guide was thinking. My third opportunity came when we spotted three good bulls about a half-mile away. These dark-colored mature bulls were actually walking instead of running, which came as a pleasant surprise. After a short stalk, I took a rest on a mound of dirt and placed the crosshairs on the shoulder of the biggest bull. At the shot, the big Hornady spire point went through both lungs and made an exit on the opposite side. The distance was an honest 228 steps, which was my closest opportunity for a clean shot. We found the mature bull supporting 9-1/2-inch horns. They don't get a lot bigger.

Bob, a fellow handgunner from Virginia, also got to see just how challenging nilgai bulls were. It took three days before he scored. I believe previous hunting pressure contributed to their skittish nature during the hunt, but whatever the reason it was difficult to get within handgun range. I think Bob used up most of his luck on some of the hogs he took during this trip because the nilgai proved a humbling experience. Bob and I both walked away from this hunt with a great deal of respect for the old blue bull. If you have not hunted these critters because they are an exotic, or perhaps those short, stubby horns don't impress you much, you're really

The axis deer, originally from India, is one of the most beautiful deer in the world. The author took this 34-inch trophy in Texas with a 10-inch T/C Contender in .338 Woodswalker.

missing out on a challenging hunt. As an added bonus, the meat is wonderful.

Exotic Deer Provide Antlered Opportunity

One of the most beautiful deer in the world has to be the axis. Native to India, where they can no longer be hunted, the axis, or chital deer is one of the most numerous exotics in Texas, where many are now free-ranging. Their main beams can exceed 30 inches. The antlers are lyre-shaped and typically have three points per side. Axis deer are very popular with hunters not only as a trophy game animal, but also because of their wonderful meat.

Most bucks start in velvet sometime during December, and are rubbed out by June. They can however, shed their antlers anytime, so it is not terribly uncommon to see bucks with antlers, at the same time you observe others without any antlers. For this reason they can be hunted throughout the year.

During a trip to visit my brother in Texas, we decided to head into the Hill Country and look for a really big axis buck. I had hunted axis before in a couple of different states, but on this trip we would hold out for a monster. After calling several ranches, one manager agreed to take us on his property giving us the opportunity for something 34 inches or larger. It was good to spend time with family and be able to chase these beautiful creatures. As usual, many other different species of game could be seen while searching for a big axis buck. I was using a 10-inch T/C chambered for .338 Woodswalker, topped with a 4X scope. Firing from a bench rest, this rig could literally cut holes at 50 yards. When we eventually located an axis buck that looked huge, he ran off with a herd of does as we were trying to judge his antlers. Luckily, he stopped to look back just long enough for me to put a Nosler 210-grain bullet into his smoke room. He was a very impressive buck with beams measuring exactly 34 inches. If the opportunity comes around, I would gladly hunt them again tomorrow. Axis deer are magnificent animals with some of the most palatable meat of all the exotics.

Fallow or sika are also quite popular. Several years back I had hunted with Hal Swiggett; a grand storyteller, writer, editor, guide, handgun hunter extraordinaire, and a few other things I won't dare mention. Hal and I met at the famed Y.O. Ranch with a trophy sika deer as our quest. It was after Christmas but before New Year's Eve, so most of the other big-game seasons were closed. Before the hunt, Hal told me not to bring any guns because he had plenty I could borrow.

The first morning we drove to the shooting range and Hal started unpacking guns. Thirty minutes later he was still unpacking guns. The old boy had some mighty interesting handguns in the back of his trusty Ford pickup. We shot guns for the better part of the morning until my right hand was glad it was lunchtime. Since I had never shot a .300 Savage before, that's what we threw in the truck for the sika hunt. I believe Hal had 165-grain Nosler BT bullets loaded for this round.

Hunting with Hal Swiggett is an adventure by itself. This sika buck was taken at the Y.O. Ranch using Swiggett's .300 Savage. Nosler's 150-grain BT did the dirty work.

The Y.O. is a huge place and you can see a lot of different game running around during the course of a day. We enjoyed viewing the animals and telling hunting stories. Actually Hal did most of the talking. I just enjoyed listening to the many yarns. The first day we never bumped into a big sika but Hal had a plan that would sure knock them dead.

Early the next morning, Harvey Geoff, another guide and wildlife expert for the Y.O. joined Hal and me. Harvey would spend the day helping us locate a good deer. I couldn't have been in better company as we looked over a lot of game and covered a lot of the famous Texas ranch. We told more stories than you can imagine. Some might have even been true.

We didn't take much of a lunch break because the sika, at least the big ones, still eluded us. Later in the afternoon we searched another part of the ranch and bumped into a good buck with four points per side. The sika was standing broadside behind a clump of trees some 90 yards away, as the .300 Savage did its job. The trophy sika deer was really a bonus and paled in comparison to the companionship and camaraderie. I am quite certain there are a lot of non-hunters out there who will never understand this part. I have chased a lot of game around the Y.O. Ranch, just like a lot of other handgun hunters, and every hunt has been rewarding in more ways than one.

The blackbuck antelope is one of the most sought-after exotics. This fine trophy was taken in the Texas Hill Country.

Blackbuck: The Other Antelope

The blackbuck antelope is another very popular exotic that can be quite a challenge to hunt. This graceful little antelope is native to India and Pakistan, and thrives in Texas, where the climate and habitat is similar to that of their native land. Mature males are black on their upper parts with contrasting white around the underpants, chin, ears, and area around the eyes, making a very handsome game animal. I have weighed a number of field-dressed males and they typically tip the scales around 70 to 75 pounds. Needless to say a large caliber gun is not necessary, but long-range shooting is fairly common. Blackbuck males are very territorial, so once you find a big one in a certain area, he will usually be found not far away. These graceful antelope are very fast, skittish, and tough to hunt with a handgun. I have taken several blackbuck using a variety of handguns but I don't think I have ever had a shot under 150 yards. Thus, again proving my point that hunting exotics is by no means an easy outing.

The graceful blackbuck antelope is a fine trophy for the handgun hunter. They are difficult to hunt and provide the hunter with plenty of off-season excitement. The author took this fine buck in Texas using a T/C Contender with Simmons scope.

Some of the other exotics that can be hunted on private ranches in the United States include water buffalo, eland, scimitar-horned oryx, addax, ibex, corsican sheep, and red deer, to name just a few. With the exception of the deer species, most of these animals mentioned can be hunted year-round. These exotics can be a welcome alternative during the off season, providing the hunter a good reason to get out of the house and try that new handgun, scope, or accessory package.

My Personal Story

I hunted exotics fairly extensively before deciding to get into the game ranching business 10 years ago. Since then I've had the good fortune of meeting many hunters as I led them in pursuit of several different species. In that time I've learned something from hunters and I also think I have something to teach them.

I've found that about 10 percent of the hunters could be classified, if you had to categorize them, as experts. These individuals take hunting very serious, are familiar with their firearm, know exactly where their gun shoots at various ranges, make good judgment calls on when to shoot, or not to shoot, and overall are just plain good outdoorsmen. Another 10 percent of the hunters would likely be better off if they sold their firearms and took up golf, bowling, or some other activity. The remaining 80 percent fall somewhere in between these two extremes. I guess it's no secret that most of us would benefit by shooting more often. There is really no substitute for practicing with your handgun. We all should practice as much as time will allow. We owe that to ourselves, and more importantly to the game we hunt. Secondly, and I know a lot of people don't want to hear this, but getting and staying in good physical condition will allow us to enjoy the hunt more. I'm not talking about being able to run a marathon or swim the English Channel. I'd just like to see hunters not have to strain to finish a day in the woods.

A lot of hunters ask me how big an operation I run. I must tell you that the average guy cannot judge acreage. Unless you're someone in the real estate business, or a farmer, most people cannot determine 150 acres from 400 acres, or 640 acres from 1,280. As far as hunting exotics is concerned, size does matter, to a point, but so does the type of terrain and how much cover is involved. When you are selecting a game ranch for a hunt, what you know about the terrain is much more important than the number of acres you are going to be tramping across. Five hundred acres with heavy timber or brush mixed with some rolling hills can be much more difficult to hunt than 2,000 fairly open acres of flat land. For example, there are many whitetail deer hunters here in Missouri, who hunt on a piece of property that is 200 acres or less, because that's what their family or friends happen to own. Does that mean chasing an exotic on something less than 1,000 acres will be less of a challenge? I don't think so. The enjoyment comes from several different aspects of the hunt, not just from the size of the parcel on which the game is found.

A scoped handgun is difficult to shoot in the offhand position. Hunters should always look for a way to rest the handgun. We owe it to the game we hunt to make a clean, quick, and humane kill. One well-placed shot will avoid wounded game.

Hunting exotic species can extend your days in the field. By shooting frequently and knowing where your gun shoots, hunters can increase the odds of success. This handgun hunter is sighting-in before heading to the field.

Hunting the exotics may not be for everybody, but for many of us, it sure is a great opportunity to enjoy some off-season hunting. It is also a really good way to introduce younger hunters, women, or anyone having the desire to see what hunting is all about, and give them some experience in the field. I know that I can't be the only one who enjoys hunting this variety of non-indigenous animals. When I first started in the game ranching business, I was the third such operation to be licensed in Missouri. Today, there are 24 game ranches licensed by the Conservation Department. That's got to say something.

Chapter 11

Hunting "Small" On The Dark Continent

Many hunters still have the misconception that hunting in Africa is only for the very wealthy. Nothing could be further from the truth! There are many hunting packages that include seven to 10 days of hunting for seven or eight trophy animals for less than the cost of a guided Dall's sheep or bear hunt. In many cases, Africa provides the hunter more "bang for the buck," especially on a per animal basis, than most any other place in the world. Granted, if you wish to hunt lion, elephant, bongo, mountain nyala, or rhino, you can expect to reach deeper into your wallet. But Africa is blessed with an incredible array of wildlife, including some little critters that don't quite receive the status as larger, high profile glamour game like sable, kudu, Cape buffalo, Lord Derby eland, and the other animals mentioned above. These are Africa's hidden treasures. They provide a unique challenge, are great fun to pursue, and don't cost the hunter his or her retirement savings.

My first encounter with these little trophies occurred back in 1983. It was my very first safari and I planned on being an opportunist. In other words, I was going to take advantage of any game encountered during the 10-day trip. Like many first-timers to Africa, I thought this would be a once-in-a-lifetime hunt and I would never get the opportunity to return. So, as any trophy materialized, even if the animal wasn't on my "wish list," I was more than ready to pull the trigger.

During the first day of our safari, a little antelope, not much bigger than a jackrabbit, crossed in front of us and disappeared into the bush. Craig, my professional hunter, told me to take him if the chance presented itself. Heck, I didn't have a clue as to what it was. Craig quickly informed me that is was Sharpe grysbok, and we both scrutinized the area with our binos. One of the trackers spotted the little grysbok partially hidden next to a bush. Finally, I found the tiny creature and tried to rest my crosshairs on his shoulder. It was no easy task with a target that small!

Duikers are relatively small creatures and are taken as opportunity species on most safaris. A T/C Contender in .375 JDJ was used for this trophy duiker. The 270-grain Hornady bullet leaves two .375 caliber holes in the hide which is nothing for a taxidermist to repair.

When the .375 JDJ went off, so did the grysbok. He didn't go far. The trackers did what they do so well: follow game. Craig shook my hand and said, "Congratulations, that is the first grysbok we have ever taken on this ranch with a handgun." His horns measured a whole 2 inches, which is as long as they get. The grysbok truly was a record-book trophy. After that first encounter with

The .375 JDJ pictured here on the right is fine for taking smaller antelope. The big bullet simply passes through leaving two holes and doing virtually no damage to the hide. The .308 Winchester, shown here on the left, also works well on smaller antelope.

small antelope, I have always looked forward to the challenge these animals provide.

There are two schools of thought when it comes to putting a bullet into one of the smaller African game animals. Some claim that a .375 caliber is a fine choice because you just punch a hole through the hide, leaving minimal damage for the taxidermist to repair. Others argue that smaller calibers are by far a better choice. I've taken a fair number of such animals with both .223 caliber handguns, and bigger bores in .375 caliber. If hunting an area where other game might be found such as kudu or eland, it just makes good sense to carry the larger caliber because you never know what you might bump into. When hunting specifically for a little trophy, such as the blue duiker, knowing I was not going to take any other game in that particular area, I would opt for the smaller caliber. Regardless what caliber you prefer, from a .22 rimfire to a .454 Casull, shot placement is imperative, because you do not have much room for error on these small targets.

For my money, these little, and often overlooked pygmy antelope, do not receive the respect they deserve. Some of my most memorable hunts have involved chasing the smaller game in Africa. On one such hunt, the rolling hills of the Natal Midlands afforded my wife and me the chance to pursue oribi,

Common reedbuck are located in certain parts of southern Africa. This respectable male was taken from 300 yards using a .309 JDJ. A rock-solid rest was used to execute the shot.

Considered mountain game by some, the vaal rhebuck offers a challenging hunt. This buck was taken with a .309 JDJ from 200 yards.

common reedbuck, and vaal rhebuck for several days between some uneventful leopard hunts. Truthfully, we were so frustrated with the leopard hunting that we decided to take a well-deserved break and go hunting for some plains game.

One particular unfenced ranch reminded me of Wyoming as I watched a common reedbuck race across the plains. I loaded my Contender chambered for .309 JDJ, cranked the Bausch & Lomb scope up to 6X, found a rock-solid rest and waited for the nicest buck to stop. A Nosler 165-grain BT was on the launching pad. At about 300 yards distant, the buck stopped momentarily to see if his two female companions were with him. The guides, who had never witnessed the performance of a handgun, looked at each other kind of funny and asked me if I was going to shoot.

"Hold your ears!" I told them. The reedbuck dropped in his tracks making this shot a little more dramatic, and converting some non-believers. From that moment on, all of the guides and trackers were anxious to see the handgun in action.

Good binoculars are helpful when you are searching for smaller animals. This tracker has borrowed the author's Bausch & Lomb Elite optics and is glassing the African plains.

Mountain reedbuck are not as large as their counterparts, common reedbuck, but make a challenging endeavor for the handgun hunter. This trophy was taken from long range with a T/C Contender.

Hunting the elusive little vaal rhebuck involved a lot of walking and glassing. Many classify this little antelope as mountain game. It is most challenging to hunt. They are spooky and blend in well with their surroundings. The mountainous terrain we were hunting provided an ideal habitat for the vaal rhebuck, found nowhere else in the world. A flat-shooting caliber is necessary for hunting these shy, wary animals. Seldom are shots taken at ranges less than 200 yards.

While climbing a steep hillside early one morning, we jumped a nice ram out of his bed in the long grass. We had been glassing adjacent hillsides during our climb and this guy was enjoying a morning nap when we came along and disturbed his rest. After running flat out to the next ridge, he stopped to look back. I had already sat down, and was resting the T/C between my legs awaiting a possible shot. The wind was blowing and keeping the crosshairs steady was difficult, but God was smiling on me as the 165-grain BT somehow found its mark. Even though the scenery was beautiful

The klipspringer is a beautiful animal and makes a great addition to any trophy room. This fine male was taken with the .375 JDJ and a 270-grain Hornady bullet. As with any African safari, you never know what you will run into next.

Handgun Hunting 99

The steinbok is another beautiful animal that is primarily taken by chance. This fine male was taken with the .375 JDJ while the author was looking for other plains game.

and the hunt was very challenging, the shot saved me from climbing any more mountains. I really didn't mind all the climbing.

A few days later we were hunting the grassy plains looking for oribi, another small, graceful antelope. Again, very few people hunt these animals with a handgun. I can't really tell you why. Oribi, like many other small African antelope, provide a great amount of fun and unique challenge. And, one doesn't have to mortgage the farm to hunt them. We didn't see many oribi where we were hunting. Perhaps the grass was too high or the wind kept the animals from moving. Late in the evening, one of the trackers spotted a nice male hiding in a patch of grass 175 yards away. It was a tough shot, but if there happened to be any non-believers left in the hunting group, I silenced all the skeptics. The shot might have been lucky, but I wasn't about to admit it!

A couple of years later we made a quick trip to the Orange Free State for black springbuck, another species that is only found in South Africa. The vast plains of the area are nearly treeless but you can find an abundance of plains game. As a rule, shots here are long. After spending a considerable amount of time scouting, we happened upon three nice rams. More time behind the binoculars allowed me to pick out the ram with the largest horns. At 180 steps, the .309 JDJ did its job again.

There are three-color phases of springbuck and I wanted to collect all of them for the trophy room. The few days it took to find and bag these trophies were very enjoyable. I liked the challenge and got to see some interesting country and magnificent game. It certainly was a welcome leg of the trip after experiencing bad luck on the leopard hunt.

Years later I hunted the Orange Free State again, this time using the 6.5 JDJ. My favorite load sped a Nosler Solid Base through the chronograph at 2,350 fps. I love this round in a Contender. It is extremely accurate and recoils very little. The 6.5 JDJ is an ideal cartridge for hunting antelope in the open plains where shots can be long. My love affair with the round is a long, successful one.

J.D. Jones and I spent more than 30 days hunting in Africa on one trip, and I can't tell you how much game we took with this cartridge. J.D. was testing and evaluating the cartridge and naturally I had no choice but to assist. Luckily, my wife didn't file for divorce after my lengthy absence from home.

Peter Harris, the professional hunter, and I took several trophies, including a beautiful mountain reedbuck, in the O.F.S. during one safari. The smallest of the reedbucks, the mountain reedbuck has a very soft, almost wool-like, coat and prefers rocky hills. The largest horns recorded in the SCI Record Book measure a tad over 9 inches. But these delicate little antelope cannot be judged by their horns alone. They make a beautiful mount and will enhance any trophy collection. My only shot at a mountain reedbuck came late in the day. We spotted him at more than 300 yards and planned a stalk and tried to get closer. Because of the wide-open spaces we crept very slowly trying not to spook the ram. At about 169 yards, Peter advised we better not try to get too close for fear of spooking the reedbuck. I used a rock to rest my Contender and at the shot Peter slapped me on the back and I knew the bullet had found its target. For anyone who enjoys long-range shooting, the O.F.S. is a great place to experience Africa.

Klipspringer is yet another member of the pygmy antelope family. In the Afrikaan language, klipspringer means rock-jumper. These animals are normally taken as opportunity species while hunting for other game. With hooves shaped like miniature suction cups, klipspringer can bounce around the rocks with ease. They prefer rocky outcrops and normally can be seen in pairs. The klipspringer I have taken over the years have fallen victim to the .375 JDJ. Obviously two holes could be found in the skin but no damage occurred to the hide.

My best klipspringer came as we were hunting for kudu. We had covered a lot of the African veldt looking for a good bull, but to no avail. While on the lookout for kudu, I noticed something jumping around in the rocks above us and I pointed toward the movement and ask the professional hunter what it might be. A quick look through the binos revealed two klipspringers; one female and the other a really good male. I sat down, resting my back on a rock, and tried to find the animals through the scope. The pro hunter, still looking through his binos, informed me that if I wanted a big klipspringer, this one would suffice. Finally, I found the male in the scope and squeezed the trigger. The loud roar of the .375 JDJ echoed through the hills. The female took off running as the male stumbled and fell. It was a big male and I have him mounted life-size in the trophy room.

Springbuck are fairly common in parts of southern Africa. Shots are generally beyond 100 yards.

The Cape grysbok is a very shy, secretive creature coming out only during late evening hours. This male was taken with a T/C in .223.

Steenbok are also often encountered in the same territory as the klipspringer. These beautiful little antelope tip the scales at around 20 pounds. Mature males have straight horns measuring 4 or 5 inches. The last time I shot one, we were hunting in Zimbabwe and searching for other game at the time. I was packing the .375 JDJ walking down an old trail when something ran across in front of me. It was moving so fast neither the professional hunter nor I could tell what it was. One of the trackers eventually spotted the steenbok, hiding behind some brush, staring at us. About the time I located the animal, he turned broadside and acted like he was ready to take off. When the crosshairs found his shoulder I dropped the hammer. The 270-grain Hornady did not damage any of the hide. The larger calibers work fine on these smaller animals even though you may have to follow them a short distance after the shot.

I mentioned that many of these little antelope are taken while actually hunting for other game. There are hunters who plan safaris, normally after they have hunted Africa many times, specifically around the little antelope species. I took several of the small antelope while hunting the Eastern Cape of South Africa, looking to collect some of these trophy animals, along with other game. I don't know if I personally would organize a safari for suni and red duiker exclusively, but I understand why old Africa hands proceed with such plans. The hunting is fun and challenging. On my wish list were white springbuck, common springbuck, cape grysbok, southern bush duiker, as well as other larger game found only in this area.

While hunting the Eastern Cape, I used a Contender in .223 Winchester topped with a Bausch & Lomb variable scope. The first day we drove around an area that resembled the Wyoming plains, looking for white springbuck. The day reminded me of time spent hunting antelope out west. The springbuck were exceptionally wild and it was a real chore getting within 250 yards of the skittish little critters. After several unsuccessful stalks, a nice male finally made a mistake and stepped within range. The Winchester 55-grain bullet worked well on the springbuck. Late in the evening while hunting on another ranch, I was able to take a common springbuck with the same ammo. The shot was somewhere in the neighborhood of 200 yards. That is about what one can expect.

The next day we went to look for mountain reedbuck. Since I had taken a good one on a previous outing, I wanted my wife to try her hand. She declined, stating she was perfectly happy with her role as spotter and photographer. We spent the entire day looking for a decent male in terrain that looked like mule deer country. Despite the cooler temperatures and gusty wind, the .223 found action before dark. Yes, it does get cool, sometimes very cold, in the Eastern Cape.

Two small antelope I really wanted to take were the Cape grysbok and blue duiker, so we changed locations again in pursuit of Cape grysbok. These animals are predominantly nocturnal and because of this, they are most difficult to take, even in areas where they are common. I considered myself lucky when we finally scored. My only opportunity came at dark, when it was almost too dark to see through the scope. The distance was maybe 100 yards, but it seemed much farther in the fading light. We saw a few females but only one male. The little .223 provided all the accuracy and power I needed and the light recoil was a real asset when it came to shooting at smaller targets.

During our pursuit for the grysbok, we stumbled on to a monster of a bush duiker. The pro hunter almost insisted that I shoot it because he had never seen one any bigger. I had taken duikers before but nothing like this one. Not being a record book hunter, we never bothered measuring this trophy but our photos revealed a particular horn configuration with exceptional length. When I received my mount from the taxidermist after that trip, the bush duiker I shot was not the one in the crate. Apparently the old switch-a-roo had taken place at some point along the way. Somewhere, hanging on someone's a wall, is a record-class bush duiker taken by yours truly. Not that this is a big deal to me, but it's the principal of the matter. It is certainly not the first time something like this has happened, nor unfortunately will it be the last.

The average blue duiker weighs less than 10 pounds and is the smallest of the duiker family. It

The white springbok is found only in certain pockets of South Africa. The author used a .223 to take this buck.

The predator does not win every time. This photo shows the bat-eared fox came in second against a porcupine.

was nothing but luck that allowed me to take the blue duiker and the story doesn't make for a great hunting tale, so let's just say that I got one. The hunt was legal and ethical, but I won't take up the space here with the details.

These little antelope do not have the impressive horns that adorn other game, but they are sure enough challenging to hunt. They also make interesting and unique life-size mounts that enhance, and round out, any trophy room.

Africa is blessed with an abundance of wildlife and habitat. Some of the little trophies mentioned play an important part of the ecosystem. There are many others I have not listed such as the dik-dik, suni, and many species of forest duikers. Some are more difficult to hunt than others. Hunters take certain animals, like my blue duiker, because they are just lucky enough to see one. Others species are taken as targets of opportunity while chasing other game, yet some may have to be singled out and hunted specifically. Any way you stack it, the small antelope of Africa will test any handgun hunter.

There are other creatures that provide handgun hunters unique and challenging opportunities. I wouldn't really call them trophies and they are not the type of game to plan a safari around but varmints such as jackal and hyena are usually taken in addition to the more well known species. When I have experienced "down time" for various reasons on safari, and found myself sitting at a waterhole, I'm sometimes surprised by what appears. Various small cats such as the caracal, serval, civet, and genet, are quite common in certain areas. Many hunters have never seen some of these small nocturnal critters, even after numerous safaris. The majority of the encounters I have experienced with these shy animals have been while I was sitting in a leopard blind. With the exception of the hyena, all of these little varmints offer very little in terms of a target area. Obviously an accurate gun is necessary if you plan on taking any of these back home to the taxidermist.

Yes, Africa has more than its share of splendid wildlife. You may never see any of the little trophies gracing the front pages of your favorite sporting magazine, but that doesn't mean they are less challenging to hunt.

Chapter 12

Mid-Sized African Game

Moving up the ladder to larger African plains game, the animals vary drastically in weight from the whitetail-sized impala to the larger eland, which will tip the scales approximately the same as a big bull moose.

My baptism to hunting these larger species was an eye-opener. There were five of us, all first-timers to Africa, embarking on a handgun-only safari. The hunters included Larry Wise, J.D. Jones, Ray Guarisco, John Reinhart and me. We were hunting for a variety of game in Zimbabwe on a 10-day trip. Everyone carried a T/C Contender as a primary gun. The chamberings included .45-70, .375 JDJ, or .358 JDJ. Each one of the

This bushpig fell to the author's .358 JDJ during his first safari.

Impala are abundant in many parts of Africa. About the same size as the North American whitetail deer, the impala makes a nice mount for any trophy room.

hunters also carried a backup gun. All were iron-sighted .44 Magnums of various makes, loaded with 300-grain bullets. I was paired up with Larry, a chap from out East who packed a .45-70 Contenter.

Our first day of hunting found Larry and I teamed up with our professional hunter, Craig Hunt, and three of his trackers. We began hunting along a riverbed, on foot. Larry had won the coin toss for the first shot. After easing our way through the bush for some time, the first animal we encountered was a nice bushpig. Larry quickly dispatched it with his .45-70. It wasn't thirty minutes later I also scored on a bushpig using my .358 JDJ.

Because we were hunting in dense brush our shots were relatively close. Seems the drought in the area had taken a toll on the warthogs, as we found many dead during our safari. The bushpigs were dining on their carcasses. Warthogs must have water. During drought conditions, these animals are usually the first to bite the dust.

Bushpigs are basically nocturnal. Some hunters go on several safaris before even seeing one. We just happened to be in the right place at the right time for these porkers. Our walk down the riverbed continued and a little while later one of the trackers stopped and pointed. Four waterbuck females were looking at us from 100 yards away. It was Larry's turn to shoot but he wasn't interested in waterbuck. I was more than interested. I got ready by resting the Contender on an old stump. The cows got nervous and took off, disappearing into the veldt. Five seconds later the bull came out of the dense bush by the riverbed. He was a dandy. A mature waterbuck male will weigh around 350 pounds, maybe more. This bull was in a hurry to keep up with his girlfriends and never offered a good shot. The trackers followed the spoor immediately and I was

Blue wildebeest are common in many parts of Africa. This bull was taken with a 6.5 JDJ using 120-grain Nosler bullets.

right behind them. Craig reached down and grabbed a handful of dirt and sifted it through his fingers, checking the wind direction. It wasn't a factor at this time. We came to an opening and spotted the bull standing beside the four cows. He was broadside at 150 yards. I quickly dropped down and got in the Creedmore position and placed the crosshairs of the 4X Leupold on the bull's shoulder. I squeezed the trigger and the gun roared. All five waterbuck took off. We found blood where the bull was standing and began following his trail. It wasn't a good shot and I knew it. During the next two hours I learned how valuable good trackers are in these situations. Their intuitive skills are priceless. If it weren't for their tracking skills we never would have seen the animals again. Eventually I finished off the bull with the 6-inch customized Ruger .44 Magnum.

As we covered mile after mile, Larry and I spotted a lot of other game including steenbok, duiker, zebra, and warthogs. Neither of us could believe the amount of game we had seen, and it wasn't yet even noon.

Late in the day Larry popped a nice impala ram. There were lots of impala in the area and taking one wasn't terribly difficult. Right before dark, Craig and I stalked a herd of blue wildebeest using anthills to conceal our presence. After sneaking from one anthill to another, we managed to get within 60 yards of four bulls. Craig pointed out the largest one. I took a rest on top of an anthill we were hiding behind. When the bull stepped clear of the others, I touched off a round. The 250-grain slug hit solidly in the chest and that ended a great day of hunting.

Wildebeest are not that graceful, nor do they make a beautiful trophy, but a big bull will weigh more than

Cape eland are big animals requiring a big bullet to bring them down for keeps. This bull was taken with a .375 JDJ. Eland also provide some of the best game meat in Africa.

400 pounds. One had better hit him in the right spot. Wildebeest along with a lot of other African game can be very tough. Well-constructed bullets are crucial. To say that bullet selection is one of the most critical aspects of handgun hunting some of the medium-sized game in Africa would be a gross understatement. You want accuracy, penetration, expansion and weight retention. It's a lot to ask of a projectile, but ignoring even one of these can mean the difference between a quick kill and long, hot walk through the bush in search of a wounded animal.

The next day we started looking for sable. We followed tracks for a couple of miles but never did catch up with the animals. Larry and I both wanted one, but we also knew the area was not loaded with good bulls. Moving on to another area, we spotted a few sable but nothing worth a second look. The herds were made up of young bulls and females. Finding no sable, Larry took a nice wildebeest with a 400-grain Speer from his .45-70.

During the afternoon we searched for a big kudu bull. Larry and I both wanted a bull over 50 inches. We didn't find any on this day but when a herd of zebra appeared, I took one with a .375 JDJ using a 270-grain Hornady. If you have not hunted Africa, I can assure you that a zebra is not like a horse and they are certainly not tame. In areas where they have received hunting pressure, they are darned tough to hunt. By the end of the second day, Larry and I both were tired. We'd put on about 10 miles each day.

The Livingston eland is a huge animal. The author took this big bull with a .375 JDJ.

Tired but happy because this was Africa, and we were loving every minute of the experience.

Early the next morning we picked up fresh eland tracks and followed them for hours before catching up with the herd. The trackers were phenomenal. Craig spotted a good bull in the herd and a short stalk put us within 100 yards of the unsuspecting animals. The Livingstone eland are very big animals and in my opinion, eland meat is the best in all of Africa. I was using a .375 JDJ for this hunt so I made sure the first shot, taken from a sitting position while resting the gun between my knees, was right in the boiler room. Trying to get this animal, estimated to weigh between 1,800 and 2,000 pounds, into the Land Rover was quite a chore. We got the bright idea of hoisting him up from a tree limb in order to get the big animal in the back of the Land Rover. The trick was finding a limb strong enough. It must have been quite a spectacle.

On the way back to the ranch I shot an impala from 80 yards. It had been a good morning of hunting. Larry took a nice kudu bull early in the afternoon. His 400-grain Speer did a superb job. The horns were over 50 inches and Larry was delighted. I would imagine that kudu are the equivalent of our North American elk. They are absolutely beautiful animals and make a great trophy for any handgun hunter.

There were many warthogs in the area and due to the drought, our outfitter and professional hunter, Don Price, gave a huge discount on the ugly critters. If memory serves me correct, we could shoot warthogs for $30 a piece. Later in the evening, I took one of the ugly hogs running away from me with the .358 JDJ. This cartridge

Getting an eland bull into the back of the Land Rover is not an easy task. You can get a better idea of how big these animals really are when one is hanging from a tree.

is based on the .444 Marlin case necked down to .35 caliber. During the period of time this hunt took place there were not a lot of quality bullets available for this caliber, but the 250-grain Speer did a decent job on most of the African game.

Before the sun disappeared, Larry took the second eland of the day with his .45-70. One well-placed shot was all that was required. The 400-grain Speer bullet in the .45-70 worked well on all game encountered and would be a fine choice for any such hunting.

Kudu were elusive. At least for me they were. Everybody in camp had already taken nice bulls and had several chances for others. During the pursuit for kudu, I managed to take another bushpig. This one fell victim to the 44 Magnum. My wife also got in on the action and she too took a bushpig, with the open-sighted Ruger.

Warthogs are taken in many parts of Africa. Even though their appearance leaves a lot to be desired, they are great trophies for handgun hunters.

Obviously there were a lot of bushpigs in the area and we come upon them often. I have been on 10 different safaris and have never seen another one since this first hunt. Larry and I both took more warthogs during the course of the hunt as did other members of our party did the same. But, at least for a while, a kudu eluded me.

Finally, after walking our usual ten miles or more my chance finally came. The big bull was walking broadside just 75 yards away when I touched off a round. He stumbled and disappeared into the bush. The trackers did a fantastic job of trailing the wounded animal. But unfortunately, six hours later the blood trail vanished and the bull mixed in with another herd of kudu. Tracking that one animal became almost impossible. This was very frustrating for the hunter, guide, and trackers, not to mention the wounded game.

The next morning we made our last attempt to recover the wounded kudu but the search was in vain. I attributed the loss of that animal solely to poor shot placement, and shot selection, on my part. I had no one to blame except myself. After lunch we were sneaking through the thick bush next to a river when a nice bushbuck was spotted. I pulled the Ruger out of the holster. The Limpopo bushbuck was a mere 20 yards away when the 300-grain bullet found its mark. The bushbuck is a grand trophy often overlooked as hunters opt for the larger spiral-horned antelope. They love the thick stuff found on the riverbanks.

On the ninth day of our 10-day hunt, I still hadn't scored on a kudu. I could have easily taken a respectable bull with a rifle, but I was strictly hunting with a handgun, just like the rest of our group. I wanted a 50-inch or better kudu in the worst way. But the beautiful, spiral-horned antelope didn't seem to care how much my plane ticket cost, or how badly I wanted one. They just wouldn't cooperate with me. Our many stalks had turned sour. Craig knew how badly I wanted one of these elegant trophies and he suggested we drive to another area where kudu where known to frequent. We were hoping to spot a good bull before shooting light faded. Our plan succeeded and we spotted a good bull from the vehicle. The big bull and a female were up feeding. We quickly parked the Land Rover and began our stalk by circling downwind. We tried to slip quietly through a quarter mile of bush, in an attempt to intercept the animals. I checked one last time to make certain the .45-70 was loaded, and then looked through the scope to be sure the lens was not covered with dust. As we slowly approached an opening, with only a few minutes of shooting light left, the majestic kudu bull continued feeding just 60 yards away. They were totally unaware of our presence. I cocked the T/C and raised it slowly, lining the crosshairs just behind the shoulder. For a brief moment, I thought back at the last time I shot a kudu and the results were disastrous. I wasn't going to let that happen again. When the hammer dropped it sent the 400-grain Speer at 1,600 fps, through both lungs. He didn't run very far. Finally, I had taken the one trophy that had eluded us so many times. The kudu is such a great game animal providing memories that I'll never forget. I will always cherish the opportunity to hunt kudu.

Larry and I ended our hunt by taking some other game including more impala and warthogs. Those species were abundant and offered quite a bit of fun, plus we gained a lot of experience from them. We never did find a really good sable but there is always a reason to go back to Africa. At the conclusion of this group hunt we finished with 67 trophies to our credit. The vast majority of game was taken with our T/Cs. Less than 10 head were taken with the revolvers. We learned that Africa is truly a handgun hunter's paradise and the larger species of game

Hampton and his wife are shown here with a tremendous gemsbok bull taken with a 6.5 JDJ. This bull had horns over 42 inches in length.

112   Mid-Sized African Game

This bull elk fell to a .375 JDJ firing a 270-grain Hornady bullet. Note the third scope ring holding the scope to the mount. Big guns mean big recoil and scopes must remain in place to maintain accuracy.

If I had to hunt only one animal it would be white-tailed deer. This Missouri buck was dropped with a .308 Winchester round fired from a T/C Encore. The combination is great on deer.

Dall's sheep are found in the mountains of Alaska where weather and terrain demand a tough gun. Pamela Atwood took this trophy with a Freedom Arms .454 Casull, stainless, of course.

The author loves hunting in the American West. Not only are the shots long and challenging, but look at the scenery.

Cape buffalo are exciting to hunt, especially with a handgun. They are difficult to bring down and well-constructed bullets must be used.

Yes, I'm shooting over my hat. Anything that will hold the pistol steady is an asset. And I do mean anything.

If you have a choice between offhand and finding a steady rest always take the time to find a rest. Your bullet placement will improve greatly.

If you're looking for a truly fun handgun hunt, the pronghorn antelope fills the bill. This fine Montana buck was taken with a .309 JDJ using Nosler's 165-grain BT. Shots will often be long. This antelope was taken at over 150 yards.

Here's that cinnamon black bear in color. As with any animal, good shot placement on a black bear is paramount. You could hit the vitals from this angle, but slightly quartering away will present a better shot.

With a paw as big as my head and massive claws, I'd rather not have this brown bear take a swipe at me. Everything has to come together perfectly to tag a bear like this one. I'm thankful it all did.

A squirrel's head is a very small target. Hunters will need to find any rest possible to help steady the crosshairs. Getting the game to stay still is another matter.

If you will take along a .410 barrel during your big game hunts, you might be surprised when it will come in handy. This hunter tagged out early on a bear hunt and enjoyed the rest of his trip by bagging a few grouse with his extra barrel.

With a hat placed on an anthill, you can really steady the crosshairs. This set-up provided the author with a much-needed rest during one of his hunts.

←*Coyote hunting demands good camo and an accurate pistol. When all other hunting seasons are closed, you can still hone your skills by hunting coyotes.*

A spotting scope can be a valuable asset for handgun hunting. Using one allows you determine trophy quality before setting up a stalk. It could save you miles of walking.

The author and his guide, Brenton Hurt, covered a lot of miles in their quest for banteng. The hunting got tough and the temperature would always be hot and uncomfortable.

This white springbok really stands out. As you can see not all animals taken in Africa require huge bullets. This trophy fell to a .223.

Lacking in equestrian skills, the author tries to hang on while keeping up with the dogs. Shooting off the horse was another matter. This is not a scene out of the Wild West, just a part of the South American hunting experience.

Asia is all about mountain hunting and mountain hunting requires good binoculars and patience. Sometimes you can glass for hours before you find game.

Hunting the Gredos Mountains in Spain was a wonderful experience. The author's guide, Juan, is pointing out some ibex high on the mountain. ➜

A severe snowstorm in the Tien Shan Mountains made for a tough ibex hunt in Kyrgyzstan. Horses were used to get around. Note the pistol sling on my back.

The red hartebeest is an odd-looking critter, and makes an interesting addition to any trophy room.

The bontebok is very similar to the blesbok. Hampton took this specimen with his 6.5 JDJ using a 4X Leupold scope.

Larry Kelly took this big nyala bull with his Mag-Na-Ported Stalker.

offer a unique challenge. It had been everything we all had ever dreamed about, and more.

More To Come

After my first hunt, I went back to Africa the very next year looking for a big sable and some other game. A fully mature male sable will be coal-black in color and is a very impressive animal. Ray Guarisco and I were hunting together at the time and both of us wanted a bull over 40 inches. This 40-inch mark seems to be the Holy Grail for sable hunters. It took some time, and we had to look over several animals, but we finally found a good bull that offered a decent shot. For this hunt, Ray and I both were using the .375 JDJ with 270-grain Hornady bullets. My shot was only 75 yards or so. Using a good solid rest, the hand cannon roared and the big bull didn't go very far. I was glad he didn't. Later in the hunt we located another good bull for Ray. One well-placed shot with his T/C claimed our second sable bull over 40 inches. If we didn't take another animal on the trip, it would still be a success.

We had hit upon the right combination of caliber and bullet type for these tough animals and both of us had done our job with shot placement.

The gemsbok is another strikingly marked game animal that touches the hearts of many hunters. My first gemsbok hunt was back almost 20 years ago. We were hunting an area of South Africa that held several good bulls but getting within handgun range of these shy animals posed a problem. These members of the oryx family have excellent hearing, eyesight, and sense of smell. Their horns are long, straight, and very sharp on the tips. They can be difficult to judge in the field and I was willing to wait for a good bull. After several unsuccessful stalks I began to wonder if we could get close enough. When my shot did come, I had a good rest for the .375 JDJ and launched the 270-grain bullet into the gemsbok's ribcage. The bull flinched, ran about 70 yards or so, and piled up. We stepped off 278 paces from where the shot was taken. That's as close as we could get. I do not like shooting at those ranges with .375 caliber handguns but it was impossible to get closer. Several years later I shot a really good bull with

The author's wife, Karen, is enjoying the afternoon sun while waiting for the trackers. This little hut served as home for several days while hunting in South Africa.

horns measuring more than 42 inches. At that time the 6.5 JDJ claimed the magnificent trophy. I've witnessed other hunters take gemsbok with the 6.5 using 125-grain Nosler Partition bullets. Again, a combination of bullet performance and shot placement is paramount.

The odd-looking hartebeest is another animal I had to shoot from long distance. There are several species of hartebeest classified in the record books. We were hunting the Cape or red hartebeest of South Africa. J.D. and I were hunting together and using the 6.5 JDJ for a variety of game. The hartebeest spooked quite easily on the particular ranch we were hunting. Perhaps it was previous hunting pressure or the gusty wind blowing on this day. Whatever it was that made them nervous made it quite a chore for us to get within striking distance. We finally got our bulls at distances of 268 and 278 steps, respectively. Both animals fell with one shot each. At these ranges, any handgun hunter must be practiced and steady to make a good shot.

The black wildebeest, or white-tailed gnu as they are sometimes called, is another odd-looking beast and quite different in appearance when compared to the blue wildebeest. The early Dutch settlers regarded the animal as a wild ox. Wildebeest like the open plains and in areas where they have received hunting pressure, can be difficult to approach. When you see black wildebeest take off, they appear to have gone insane, racing across the plains, running in circles and doing all sorts of weird stunts. Long shots usually are necessary. A big male is a stout animal that may weigh as much as 400 pounds. J.D. and I both took good bulls in the Orange Free State but had to put on a display of long-distance shooting to do it. Our 6.5's with 125-grain Nosler Partition bullets did the trick.

Blesbok and impala are usually on the first safari "wish list." They are not that difficult to take when you are in the right area. Both animals are similar in size to our whitetail deer. Any cartridge that works on deer will suffice for these animals. The bontebok is very similar to the blesbok and if you have both of them in your trophy room, it will be difficult to tell them apart unless they are mounted life-size. The blesbok is a little smaller and sports longer horns than the bontebok. His rump patch is pale in comparison to the bontebok. The bontebok is much more richly colored with an iridescent purplish appearance, mixed with contrasting areas of pure white. Hunters looking for a pure bontebok these days should be well informed beforehand as there are many crossbreeds carrying a variety of characteristics.

One of the most beautiful spiral-horned antelope is the nyala. It is a very shy animal that loves the thick cover of the African bush. Mature males will have dark horns with ivory tips. Oddly enough, the female does not look anything like the male. They are best hunted either early in the morning or late evening. The only one I ever took was right at dark, during the last few minutes of shooting light. I could barely make out the bull's chest area in the 4X scope, but when I was certain, the hammer dropped on the T/C. In my opinion, a big nyala bull is one of the most impressive looking trophies in Africa.

The Cape bushbuck is still another spiral-horned antelope that is quite impressive. There are eight subspecies of bushbuck that are recognized in the various record books. On my last safari, my wife and I had an interesting experience with a Cape bushbuck one evening. We had positioned ourselves at the edge of the thick bush, overlooking a clearing. The plan was for us to sit and wait, hoping a bushbuck would come by on the way to a nearby river. Apparently the bushbuck, which came along just about dark, got wind of us and began barking. Seems he was a bit aggravated by our scent and presence. The closer he got, the more he barked. His barking became more intense and louder. My wife looked at me in disbelief and I could tell from the look on her face that she was getting concerned. It was just about dark and this animal was barking at us from a few yards away, yet we couldn't see him. It was clearly evident that this bushbuck was very upset with us being in his domain. Roy, our PH, placed some shooting sticks down and motioned for me to get ready. I rested the Encore on the sticks and got ready. Fortunately, the bushbuck could not

The black wildebeest is an unusual animal. The author took this big male with a T/C Contender in .375 JDJ.

locate us even though he knew something was up. Just minutes before shooting light evaporated, the bushbuck stepped into the opening and looked for the strange creatures invading his turf. I had the variable scope set on 4X and quickly placed the crosshairs on his shoulder. The .308 Winchester broke the evening silence as the 168-grain bullet reached its intended destination. My wife couldn't believe the bushbuck was capable of making all of those barking sounds.

During that same trip in the Eastern Cape I had the opportunity to take a Cape kudu on the last day of a scheduled 10-day hunt. We had taken other game during this hunt as we searched for a monster kudu. The Cape variety is a different sub-species than the Southern Greater kudu, and will not be quite as big. Our last day found us desperately searching for a better-than-average bull. With literally minutes of shooting light left, Karen and I were sneaking up on three decent bulls in the acacia bush. We were using binoculars trying to determine the bull with the longest horns, when all three animals came walking past our position at 50 yards. They never knew we were around. I eased the Encore onto the shooting sticks and waited for the biggest bull, which was bringing up the rear, to walk out in the clearing. The bullet caught him just behind the shoulder as he flinched, and ran about 75 yards before crashing. It was a perfect ending to another great safari experience.

We could continue to discuss other African game that could fit in the larger antelope category for a long time. There is the tsessebe, bongo, Lord Derby eland, sitatunga, roan, and a multitude of other game that offer the hunter enough reasons to hunt Africa for years to come. As far as cartridges are concerned, I have my favorites just like everybody else. Excluding really big game like the eland, one cannot go wrong with rounds such as the .308 Winchester. There are plenty of quality bullets in the 165- to 180-grain class to take almost any game mentioned. With the right bullet, the 7mm-08 is another fine cartridge for medium-sized game. If someone were to force me to hunt with a revolver, I would have to choose the .454 Casull or .480 Ruger with 260- or 300-grain bullets. Whatever you decide to hunt in Africa one thing is certain, you will never regret taking an unforgettable safari. And regardless how many times you go, there will always be a reason to return.

Chapter 13

Playing A Dangerous Game

Most hunters heading to Africa dream about hunting the "Big Five." Lion, leopard, Cape buffalo, rhino, and elephant are considered dangerous game and are the stuff of safari legends.

I, too, thought about stalking Cape buffalo or following lion spoor, but never imagined it would ever happen.

I guess life is full of surprises. I decided to go for it — with a handgun.

But there was some resistance to my plan. It wasn't outright resistance, but there seemed to be an undercurrent of discussion focusing on the drawbacks of using a handgun for such an outing. On sev-

Audrey Murtland poses with a good Cape buffalo from Mozambique. A T/C chambered for .358 JDJ with 225-grain Swift bullets did the trick.

The author shows off his cape buffalo taken with a .375 JDJ using 300-grain Hornady solids. The cape buffalo is a worthy adversary for any handgun hunter.

eral occasions, I have heard people talk negatively about hunting dangerous game with a handgun. Some of these comments even come from outdoor writers and folks within the firearms industry. But hunting dangerous game with a handgun is no stunt like some would have you to believe.

A few bow hunters go after a Cape buffalo or some other member of the big five each year, and you never hear anything negative about these situations. Well, the right bullet and load, pushed from the proper handgun, is a hell of a lot more effective on big game than a broadhead! Tackling any game with a handgun is a challenge and it's no different when your sights are leveled on a bull elephant. Yes, the elephant can, given an opportunity, kill you. I guess you take your chances when skydiving, racing cars and boats, motorcycles, or climbing mountains. The most I have ever feared for my life in Africa was during rush hour traffic in Johannesburg. Now that was scary!

But let's get back to hunting the big five with a pistol. It can be done, if you do it correctly. My first opportunity to stalk Cape buffalo was an exciting experience. But then, all experiences with Cape buffalo are exciting. Hunting an area in southern Zimbabwe, we left camp before daylight for the sole purpose of hunting buffalo. I carried a Contender, chambered for the old .45-70. The round was loaded to the maximum, pushing a 500-grain Hornady bullet. I had just checked to make sure the lens of the scope was clear, when the professional hunter pointed at fresh buffalo tracks. The trackers took over and we followed them for quite some time. Eventually we caught up with the herd. It included somewhere around 20 animals and they had changed directions and were angling toward us. Everybody froze! I was sitting down at the time and watched as the herd kept coming closer. We all were afraid to move. At 40 yards, the lead buffalo stopped and looked me directly in the eye. I felt like I owed him money and he had come to collect! As I placed the crosshairs on his shoulder, I tried hard to quit shaking. It was impossible. When the gun roared the buffalo stumbled and ran away with the rest of the herd. We took off after the buffalo and immediately found a good blood trail. The animals were about 200 yards from a park boundary. If he crossed the park line, we could go no further and I would have to pay the trophy fee anyway. I quickly moved into shooting position and proceeded to dump more 500-grain slugs into his chest cavity. It is simply amazing how much lead these animals can take. He didn't make it to the National Park boundary line and I had my first buffalo with the .45-70. Incidentally, the 500-grain bullets over a stiff charge of powder are not fun to shoot, and there will be no doubt in your mind when the gun goes off.

While I only mention a few here, there are a lot of handgun cartridges suitable for hunting dangerous game. The .45-70 has already been mentioned and it is a sledgehammer with those huge slugs. Most dangerous game will be taken at under 75 yards with many shots less than 50 yards, making the .45-70 well suited for this type of hunting. The .375 JDJ has probably accounted for more big game than most any other cartridge. The Hornady, 300-grain FMJ is what most handgunners use when big, tough game is the quarry. Custom gun makers have been building hand cannons for years and with a well-designed muzzle brake there are very few rounds that can't be used in an Encore frame. The limits are on the shooter's ability to control the gun and deal with the recoil. Most custom gun makers can put something together to meet your needs. If you want to hit something hard, a custom gun maker can give you what you need.

A case in point is the .375/06 JDJ. It's relatively new to the scene and with time, the cartridge may find favor with hunters seeking truly big game. This cartridge is based on the .30-06 case, with the neck expanded to .375 caliber. It must be used on an Encore frame and will not work on a Contender. The cartridge pushes a 270-grain bullet at 2450 fps. It burns up over 60 grains of powder in the process and is a handful. A muzzle brake is mandatory. Rubber grips also make things bearable. I haven't yet used the round in Africa, but the next chance I get to stalk buffalo, this is the round I will use.

Revolver fans will find the .454 Casull a good choice with the heavier bullets. Those who want even more power can step up to the Linebaugh group of cartridges. The .475 and .500 Linebaugh rounds will certainly suffice for dangerous game. As will the longer versions the

The black rhino, like the one pictured here, are no longer hunted because rampant poaching has decreased their numbers substantially.

.475 and .500 Maximum. Those who opt for the 475 Linebaugh also have the option to fire .480 Ruger rounds as "light" loads on smaller game. Several custom gun makers are turning out revolvers that use these rounds and Hornady offers factory ammunition for both. If you need something even bigger, Magnum Research offers a .45-70 revolver. That's firepower.

I have seen buffalo herds varying in size from three or four old bulls to herds of 100 or more. It is always much easier to sneak close to a buffalo with only a few eyes watching. I was hunting the large bovines in the famous Zambezi Valley once and several attempts to get within range of a big bull failed. We were foiled at every turn. Either the wind would change direction or, if we did manage to get close, the herd was made up of cows and calves. But it was special just being there. Whether I was watching elephants feeding from a distance or sneaking up on a black rhino to take a picture, it was all a part of my African hunting experience.

The Zambezi Valley is a huge valley north of the Zambezi escarpment, extending from Lake Kariba on the Zambezi River eastward to the Mozambique border. Human presence is virtually nonexistent and the area is not only beautiful but it serves as a sanctuary for wildlife. Plains game like kudu, bushbuck, warthog, impala, and sable roam around in the area but the valley is most famous for its dangerous game. I stalked and photographed several black rhino and was even charged by one. One day we played a little of game of cat and mouse and I was the mouse. That was back in the days when I could run fast. Black rhinos do not have a sense of humor.

Early one morning my professional hunter and I were walking down an old trail looking for buffalo tracks. We both looked up and spotted two old bulls at the same time. They were feeding directly ahead of us. The bulls were by themselves, facing us. I dropped to the ground and followed the cat-like sneak of M'koni, the pro hunter. Easing up to the base of an old tree, I braced my back on the trunk, raised my knees and rested the T/C between the kneecaps. I was using the .375 JDJ at the time. The largest bull looked up and stared right at me. I don't think he realized I was a threat, perhaps I just appeared out of place. There, less than 60 yards away was 1,600 pounds of bad attitude. I leveled the crosshairs on the bull's heart and squeezed. The bullet struck home and old bull took off with his buddy. M'koni and I tried to keep up. About 150 yards later the bull stopped and turned broadside. Before he could charge, I put three more rounds in him expeditiously. Hunting buffalo is always a heart-pounding experience. This was no exception! He was a good bull and a great trophy for this country boy.

The Cape buffalo is definitely a tenacious creature. They can absorb a lot of lead even when hit in the right place. Today, several package deals are available, in more than one country; with trophy fees included for less money than a brown bear hunt. If you want to experience Africa and have a crack at one of the big five, this is a good way to get your feet wet.

Hunting The Monsters

Our primary goal while we were hunting in the Zambezi Valley was elephant hunting. Nights around the campfire were spent discussing elephant cartridges and shot placement. Camp was the old-style tented affair and you could hear lions and hyenas after dark. Guns were always loaded and ready under the cot during the night. One night we had hyenas just outside our tent. We were awakened by horrible sounds of howling, hollering, screaming, and other dreadful sounds. For a

Elephant hunting can entail a lot of walking while searching for the right animal and the ideal opportunity.

J.D. Jones bagged this elephant with a .375 JDJ from a range of about 20 steps as the animal charged.

while, it felt as if we were in a horror movie. The hyenas were probably looking for a free meal, but eventually left us alone. It wasn't always the toothy critters we had to worry about. The area was infested with the dreaded tetse fly but we refused to allow them to jeopardize our pursuit of jumbo.

Our game plan called for Ray Guarisco to hunt a different area with his pro hunter, and J.D. Jones and I would tag along with M'koni. J.D. and I flipped a coin to see who would shoot first. I lost. If you think elephant hunting entails just walking out there and shooting one of the big, dumb critters, you are badly mistaken. Elephants are not stupid. The first few days Jones and I came back to camp with only blisters on our feet for our efforts. We walked a lot of miles and saw some elephants, but nothing we were looking for. But again, just being in the valley was an experience I'll never forget.

J.D. finally got his chance when we spotted a herd of about 25 animals one afternoon. I was armed primarily with a Nikon motor-driven camera and would attempt to get this event on film. I also carried a custom Ruger Super Blackhawk that had been customized by Mag-Na-Port International. It rested in a cross-draw holster and was loaded with 310-grain hard-cast bullets. It's a great carry gun for emergency situations.

M'koni constantly checked the wind as we moved in. As we got within 50 yards of the herd one of the females detected our presence, alarmed the rest of the

The author took this bull with one well-placed brain shot with his .375 JDJ. The elephant dropped instantly.

herd, and took off. We followed their tracks and 30 minutes later, the same scenario was repeated. Our third attempt at stalking the herd was a little too much for one of the old females. She came charging at us frantically flapping her ears, trumpeting loudly. I wasn't an expert on elephants but it didn't appear to be a false charge by any means. It was an awesome sight indeed. The charging elephant closed the gap at an alarming rate. Six tons of fury came toward us like a freight train. At 40 yards, all I could do was try to focus the camera. At 30 yards, it didn't take a rocket scientist to see this was definitely not a fake charge. When the elephant was inside the 20-yard-line I took off running and I was running was for keeps. Hey, even rats leave a sinking ship! The last thing on my mind was good photography. I heard the gun roar and stopped to look back. The elephant lay stone dead 16 paces from the end of J.D.'s .375 JDJ barrel. The frontal brain shot was quick and humane. J.D. had the nerve to ask me if I got everything on camera!!

When we arrived back at camp, we learned of Ray's good fortune. He too, had taken a bull with one well-placed 300-grain solid. Ray was also using a .375 JDJ. As we celebrated the day's hunt we could hear lions roar in the distance. And some people wonder what keeps drawing hunters back to Africa.

Early the next morning we searched for elephant tracks at a nearby waterhole and spotted five animals feeding at a leisurely rate. There was one bull in the herd that we would take if possible. M'koni checked the wind by sifting sand through his fingers. It was deadly calm. Cautiously, we worked our way in front

Hampton took this white rhino with 300-grain Hornady solids from his .375 JDJ. The shot was taken from 60 yards with the bullet passing almost through the large beast, lodging in the skin on the opposite shoulder.

Playing A Dangerous Game

These black rhino enjoyed charging the author and forcing him to run faster than he liked.

of the herd, hoping a stray current of wind wouldn't take our scent the wrong direction. Thirty minutes later we were in a position to intercept the feeding animals. Actually, I could hear the elephants before I could see them. Sounds of limbs being ripped from trees were obvious. I stood in front of a mopani tree, trying to break my outline. My heart was beating so fast I thought I was having a heart attack. The anticipation was getting the best of me. The sounds of elephants coming toward you when you can't see them, is a bit unnerving to most of us. When the five animals appeared, the bull was in the lead. They were totally unaware of us and that's just what we wanted. We watched them continue to feed, steadily working closer to our position. At 30 yards we watched the bull yank a limb off a mopani tree and stuff it in his mouth. The bull continued walking directly at me, and I do mean directly. I tried to align the crosshairs between the bull's eyes. We were too close to get a full field of view and I needed a 2X scope in this situation. The 4X scope did not have a large enough field of view at this distance. I had to place the crosshairs on one eye, and adjust accordingly. When the tusker stepped inside the 20-yard-line, I squeezed the trigger. It was a classic frontal brain shot. The bull dropped so fast I failed to see it fall. That's how quickly they drop when things go right. It was quick, humane, and painless.

Today, we live in an era where it is sometimes not politically correct to talk about hunting, especially elephant hunting. It might come as a surprise to some that elephants are not an endangered species! In some areas they are overpopulated. Where elephant hunting is allowed and there is the financial incentive to manage them properly, the animals do quite well. Countries that do not allow elephant hunting, and where there is no economic incentive to manage the animals often find that poaching runs rampant and the pachyderms are threatened. Sport hunters have never decimated elephant populations. Also, I have never seen any meat go to waste in Africa and my elephant was a prime example. There were at least 75 or more natives participating in the butchering process. A few hours later nothing was left but a few bones

I hope to spend more time with these giants someday. Elephants are magnificent animals and I hold a tremendous amount of respect for them. This could possibly be the ultimate challenge for a handgun hunter.

I know firsthand of approximately 20 head of elephant that have been taken with handguns. The overwhelming majority of the ones I am aware of have been taken with the .375 JDJ. The 45-70 and .454 Casull and a few other rounds have also been used to drop a few pachyderms. For bullets, you have to use solids, or FMJ, as penetration is of paramount importance.

Taking On The Rhino

Of all the wonderful creatures that we have the opportunity to hunt, I find none more bizarre than the rhinoceros. This creature is a relic from the days of the dinosaur. The rhino is big, and tough, with hide like an armor plate. It is almost impossible to penetrate. The rhino has poor eyesight but makes up for that with acute hearing and a great sense of smell. He is ungainly and slow, for the most part, but can swing that pointed horn in a manner that will get your attention. The black rhino has been on the endangered species list for quite some time because of poaching and habitat destruction. Sport hunting had nothing to do with this decline in population. The value of the rhino horn for making dagger handles in northern Yemen was and is a contributing factor. Rhinos have also been poached because some use their horn as an aphrodisiac and for its supposed medicinal effects. As far as color is concerned, there is no difference between the black and white rhino. The black rhino has a pointed lip and is somewhat smaller in size than the square-lipped white rhino. Thanks to quality conservation efforts, the white rhino is no longer in danger of extinction. Healthy populations can be found in South Africa where their numbers are increasing and considered safe. That's where I headed for a piece of the action.

The weather was hot during the November hunt. I was with Angus Brown of Elliras for some plains game and hopefully a rhino. With the unforgiving heat, the hunting was a little slow but we did take some nice trophies. I scored on a nice nyala late one evening before dark. That was icing on the cake.

This .44 Magnum Ruger Super Blackhawk has been customized by Mag-Na-Port and was responsible for taking a once-in-a-lifetime trophy lion.

On the fourth day of our hunt we ran across two big rhino bulls. Since I had been hunting other game, I took the 270-grain load out of the .375 JDJ and replaced it with a 300-grain solid. Sneaking up on a rhino is not that difficult but getting into a position to make a clean shot seemed impossible. I wanted to put one good shot in this beast and not have to chase him all over creation, or have him chase me. The bull I wanted always seemed to be behind the other. It was like they knew what I was up to. After 30 minutes or so, a broadside shot presented itself. The crosshairs were bouncing around all over the place as I tried to relax. When the hammer fell, both rhinos took off running. I could see the bullet had struck him in the lung area but I was really trying for a heart shot. We began tracking the animals and about a half-mile later found the big bull. The bullet had penetrated through the lungs and was lodged on the opposite side, just under the thick hide of the massive beast. The white rhino is the largest land mammal after the elephant. A big bull will tip the scales around 6,000 pounds. I do not have the desire to hunt another one but this big rhino provided enough memories to last a lifetime.

To make your hunt successful, you need power, penetration and a steady hand. Rhinos are tough, so practice your shooting and be prepared to pass on less than ideal shooting opportunities.

In Search Of The King

My encounter with lions came about by accident more than anything else. I was hunting with Frank McCort when we took a reconnaissance mission to the Matake Hills area, in order to search for buffalo tracks. The weather was cold, windy, with misty rain. It sure didn't seem like Africa. During our outing, we observed some lion tracks in a sandy roadbed. Frank informed me that lions were raiding cattle on a nearby ranch and making enemies of the folks who owned the livestock. The lions were also hammering away at game in Matake Hills, where they were hiding.

The big cats had come to this area originally to feed on the drought-killed buffalo from the Gona Re Zhon Game Reserve, which was not too far away. When the easy pickings from the buffalo had been devoured, the lions turned to cattle and game. I was not booked for a lion hunt and didn't think much more about the situation. We headed back to camp after assessing the buffalo spoor and got ready for the next day.

Early the next morning we were discussing the game plan over a cup of hot tea. We all loaded in the Land Rover and headed back to the area where we had found buffalo tracks. Along the way, one of the trackers knocked on the top of the Land Rover, signaling for Frank to stop the vehicle. John, the tracker, was a bit excited as he told Frank of the lion tracks that he had spotted in the road. Everybody got out of the vehicle to look at fresh shumba tracks that had been made the night before. Both trackers told Frank it was the spoor of a male lion. Frank looked at me and said, "You do realize these tracks were made sometime between the time we were up here yesterday evening, and right now. Would you mind spending some time following the tracks?"

Frank didn't have to twist my arm. We all loaded our guns and began following the two trackers. Frank and Keith, another professional hunter, loaded their rifles, and I dropped a 270-grain Hornady in the spout of my T/C.

As the two trackers followed the lion tracks, the rest of us walked behind, constantly looking ahead. Frank was hoping the lion hadn't gone too far before laying down for his afternoon siesta. Depending on the time when the lion left those tracks in the road, we might be 10 hours behind him, or 10 minutes. Frank and Keith both advised me to be ready. They didn't have to say anything because I was already wound tight.

Before noon, another lion joined the lion we were following. Judging from the tracks, the two lions were almost identical in size. Two sets of tracks would be easier to follow than one. With no food or water, we pressed on. But at that point, food and water was the last thing on my mind.

Watching the trackers follow lion spoor for hours was worth the price of admission. They were unbelievable. We found where the cats had stopped for a drink of water. Frank, Keith, and both the trackers thought they would head for a place to rest afterward. The tracks continued down an old path where a herd of eland crossed in front of them. You could see that one of the lions followed the eland while the other one got in front of the herd. Their attacked proved unsuccessful as evident from the story told by the tracks. A short while later the same type of approach was tried on a kudu. Again, the lions came up short. After two unsuccessful attempts on plains game, the lions headed for the thick stuff; the natives call it ironwood. As we approached, everyone got ready. It was like walking up behind a bird dog on point, anticipating a quail to flush at any moment. My adrenaline was in flood stage. Visibility was poor in the

A male lion is a trophy for any handgun hunter. Hampton took this one with his .375 JDJ as it trotted along about 35 yards away.

tangled vegetation, and I just knew something was going to happen at any minute...but it didn't. It was tense going through the thick stuff and you could see that the trackers were very apprehensive about the whole scene. We worked our way through the dense cover and came out into an opening on the other side. The lion tracks continued up a hillside. It was getting to be around 3 p.m. and everyone needed some water. We had left the vehicle just after daylight and hadn't stopped to rest once. It was beginning to show.

Slowly we continued to work our way up the hill. Luckily the sun was at our backs. Once on top, the trackers were looking around as they had lost sign of the tracks. Keith and Frank wandered off to my left, also looking for the tracks. Nobody had said a word. We were just looking around while the trackers were figuring out what to do next. BOOM! Frank's rifle roared and startled the daylights out of me. I caught a glimpse of a tawny shape emerge. One of the lions got up directly in front of me and started trotting to my right. At 35 yards the crosshairs came across the area behind his shoulder as I dropped the hammer. Frank and Keith were unable to shoot this lion because I was standing directly in the path between them. I reloaded quickly. When the lion had run far enough, Frank fired a round at him. I shot again and the lion stumbled, and fell, about 40 yards away. This cat was down for good. I turned to the other lion, which at this time, was trying to get on his feet. I touched off a round into him, Frank followed suit. It was all over in a matter of about six seconds. Three shots had been fired at each lion. Frank had shot the first cat as he raised his head during naptime. That was the first shot. I just happened to be standing in a position to take the second lion as he jumped up to run away. Handshakes and backslapping went on for

15 minutes or more. Everyone, including the trackers, was jubilant.

When I stopped and thought about this whole episode, I realized that John and Chi Butu, the two trackers, were the ones who needed congratulating. There are very few people in the world that could have followed those tracks for nine hours on this type of ground. We are not talking about a sandy soil or loose dirt. It was difficult tracking conditions for most of the way. Much of that skill is instinctive. If you have watched good trackers in action, you will know exactly what I'm talking about.

Both lions were males and weighed in the neighborhood of 400 pounds. By the time we found the vehicle and loaded the lions, we were ready to head back to camp. The lions filled the back of the Land Rover completely. They were impressive looking to say the least. Most lions today are taken over bait, perhaps a zebra, part of buffalo or hippo. There are places where tracking is involved and it can be very exciting. I know this is one day of cat hunting that I'll never forget as long as I live.

Spotted Death

It doesn't take a .375 to tackle a leopard. However, there is nothing wrong with using a .375 for old "spot." The leopard is a thin-skinned animal with light bone structure. I know you have heard all about those 200-pound leopards, but in reality, anything around 140 to 150 pounds is probably more realistic for a male cat, and that is considered a good trophy. So, you don't need a .458 Winchester Magnum with solids to handle your leopard hunting pursuits. What you do need is a good light-gathering scope because in most circumstances, shots will occur very late in the evening, or even after dark under a light where legal. Unfortunately, handgun scopes do not compare with riflescopes in the light-gathering category.

You also want a gun you can shoot accurately. The last thing a professional hunter wants to do is follow a wounded leopard. These cats are extremely dangerous when wounded. They are lightning-quick and seldom will you ever have the good fortune to hear one coming. You will hear the other members of the big five, charging toward you, but old "spot" will be in your face while you're wondering where he came from.

The classic method of hunting the cats is over bait. Tracking is used in some areas where the terrain will allow and those that have done it say it's a blood-pumping experience. Dogs are also being used today, just like mountain lion hunting in North America. This is the ticket if you object to sitting in a blind.

I consider myself an expert at sitting in a leopard blind. No, I am not proud of this distinction. I didn't say I was an expert leopard hunter. Just the opposite is true. Actually, I am probably the worst leopard hunter in history, or maybe just the unluckiest.

It all started back in the early 1980s when we were walking across the African veldt looking for eland tracks. I had borrowed a .375 JDJ topped with a 2X scope. We came to a riverbed to look for tracks when the professional hunter grabbed my arm and whispered "Leopard!" It is not unheard of but it is uncommon to see a leopard in broad daylight. There, in the riverbed

Leopard hunting can be very time-consuming. Here bait is being hung in hopes that a cat will start feeding sometime soon.

150 yards away, was a leopard walking nonchalantly. I sat on the ground and rested the T/C between my knees. Through the 2X scope, the leopard appeared as small as a house cat. I squeezed the trigger and the .375 broke the evening silence. The cat jumped and ran off into a reed patch. The PH thought we had him. I wasn't sure. We walked up to the reeds and found they were much too thick to be looking for the spotted buzz saw during the fading light.

Early the next morning we walked up the riverbed to look for the leopard. I was wearing a revolver on my hip in preparation for the search in thick cover. My wife was carrying the TCR 83 rifle, which was new at this time. Our hunting party consisted of Craig, the professional hunter, and three of his trackers. Craig was packing a shotgun. Before we made it to the spot in the reeds where the leopard disappeared, another leopard crossed the sand 100 yards in front of us, much to our surprise. I jerked the rifle from my wife and jerked the trigger too, seeing the bullet hit the sand in front of the leopard. The cat ran off. I was sick, ticked off, frustrated, and disgusted with myself. Somehow I had managed to miss two leopards, in broad daylight, in less than 24 hours. This was quite a feat indeed. Sometimes I even amaze myself. Little did I realize that the trials and tribulations of leopard hunting had just begun.

In the years ahead I had the good fortune to visit Africa several times and, for the most part, everything fell into place. I would always get a good selection of plains game, including some real nice trophies. But never did I get chance to miss another leopard.

Cat hunting usually takes time so I booked a two-week safari where we concentrated entirely on leopard. This would put an end to my leopard-hunting career once and for all.

Like most leopard hunts, we hung bait in several different locations. Impala seemed to be the bait most PH's prefer but we would use warthogs or baboons occasionally. The following days you make your rounds, checking to see if any of the baits had been hit. The plan is

After spending more than 50 nights in a blind, the author finally connected with this cat. One shot from the .375 JDJ was all that was necessary.

Although not an official member of the big five, hippos probably kill more people in Africa every year than all other animals combined.

pretty basic. When you find the bait where the leopard had eaten the night before, construct a blind a short distance away, then wait for the leopard to return. Everyone who hasn't hunted leopard thinks this is a piece of cake. It certainly sounds simple enough. I know a few hunters have taken a leopard the first night in a blind. Lucky bastards!! When a leopard doesn't visit one of the baits, you wait. The next day you get up and check all the baits. This may go on for several days. It is very time-consuming. If you are really serious about cat hunting, all other game becomes secondary.

Finally we got a hit on one of our baits. We constructed the blind and about 4 p.m., got into position and anxiously awaited the return of our quarry. I made the perfect rest for the Contender. Now if the leopard would just cooperate. Once it got dark, you can only listen for the sounds of chewing, or crunching of bone.

A leopard blind is a unique place. You cannot talk, move, read, smoke, make any noise, or go to the bathroom. You can breathe, if you do so quietly. You can enjoy the stinging sensation from the insect bites on the back of your neck. When it is cloudy or overcast, the darkness becomes pitch-black and you cannot see your hand in front of your face. You can count the stars, if there are any. The stars did come out that first night. Unfortunately the leopard did not. We had sat there for six hours.

The next day we checked all of our baits again. None of the others had been disturbed. With nothing better to do, we were back in the grass-covered blind at 4 p.m., sitting quietly and patiently for another six hours. This scenario went on for 17 days with the end result always the same. I finally had to head home and go back to work. Boy, was I glad to go back to work.

Being a little hard headed, I booked another 14-day safari and once again hunted exclusively for leopard. Wouldn't you know, another two weeks of sitting in a blind and not one time did a leopard show. Once again, it was nice going back to work.

As you can imagine, I really wanted to kill a leopard. Now it was getting personal. I called my good friend and professional hunter, Peter Harris, and asked him how many days I should book for a leopard? He paused for a moment before he told me two weeks would be

Not an official member of the big five, the crocodile is certainly considered dangerous game.

plenty. Considering my luck with leopard, I booked a 19-day safari.

To get a jump on things, bait had already been placed before my arrival on this trip. The trip started off on the wrong foot when my gun case was stolen at the airport. Three very specialized handguns were inside that case. Luckily, I had some friends in South Africa that were kind enough to loan me a Contender in .375 JDJ.

The first night we got into a blind overlooking an impala that a big male leopard had partially eaten. The pro hunter had a small microphone, (listening device) placed near the bait and was wearing a set of headphones so he could listen for the cat chewing. Yes, modern technology had even hit the African bush. This particular night turned out like all the others.

The following evening we were back in the blind. This time we had hand signals worked out, so if the leopard showed up, we will know what to do. One tap on my leg meant the cat was on the bait. Two taps on the leg signaled get ready to shoot because the light was coming on. A brisk slap in the face would indicate, wake up you're snoring! After dark the baboons were barking and I couldn't help wonder if they were yelling at the leopard. An hour passed by and a tap on the leg made my heart start racing. The T/C was resting on a sandbag with the crosshairs placed perfectly on the bait. I eased my hand on the grip and slowly cocked the hammer. About that time two taps on the leg almost gave me a heart attack. The anticipation was killing me. The spotlight turned on and cut through the darkness. I placed the crosshairs on the animal feeding at the bait and started squeezing the trigger. Peter grabbed me and said don't shoot! It was a civet cat. My heart sank. My hopes were not far behind.

The leopard hunting saga continued. We changed locations when different bait had been hit, but the outcome was always the same. The cats were not consistently coming back on a regular basis. In one instance, we left the blind around 10 p.m., as usual, and returned to camp. The next afternoon when we returned to the blind, and found the leopard had hit the bait sometime after we left! This put us spending the entire night in the blind, just in case the cat would return after midnight. I sat in a chair, covered with blankets, for 14 hours. And I did this more than once. Damn, that was fun.

At the end of this 19-day safari with exactly 100 hours logged in the blinds, I still went home without a leopard. And to think, if I hadn't missed those two opportunities at old "spot" back in 1983, I wouldn't have to pay good money to enjoy these captivating experiences.

At this point in my leopard hunting career, I couldn't give up. Yes, I planned another safari for leopard. Before I finally did put a bullet in a leopard, I had spent more than 50 nights in a blind. This may be some kind of record. I'm not proud of this by any means. Now you see why I consider myself an expert when it comes to sitting in a leopard blind.

My shot, only about 40 yards or so, went through both shoulders and killed the cat instantly. The 270-grain spire point from the .375 JDJ took out both lungs and made an exit. It wasn't a big cat but at this stage of the game, what could I say? If enough time will pass, I might want to go back and try for a really big male someday. But for right now, I'll just enjoy hunting something else for a change.

Other Dangerous Game

While not officially members of the big five, the hippo and crocodile can certainly be classified as dangerous game. Truthfully, I would bet more people are killed every year from hippo and crocs than all the big five put together. And they both provide unique hunting opportunities. I have not taken a hippo yet but I have hammered a croc. They are not easy to kill. But for anyone looking to add a bit of adventure and excitement to the safari experience, as if there is not enough already, hunting for these two worthy adversaries is a good way to start.

Chapter 14

Hunting Down Under

Hunters looking for adventure and the chance to tackle big game in exotic places can find plenty of opportunities in the land "Down Under". Australia is not a large continent, but it is a great place for tropical vacations and hunting adventures. For most hunters, the Top End, or northern Australia, is of interest because that is where water buffalo, banteng, sambar, and plentiful numbers of wild boar can be found. The large bovines are usually what attract hunters to the island continent.

Water buffalo are huge animals, often weighing more than 1,600 pounds, making them larger than many Cape buffalo. Although they are not as dangerous as the Cape buffalo in Africa, they can be difficult to bring down, sometimes aggressive, and are always exciting to hunt!

Banteng are not quite as big but they will still weigh in excess of 1,000 pounds. Very few have been taken with handguns. It should go without saying that large calibers and big bullets are necessary. I consider the .375 JDJ caliber or something very similar to be the

Hunting buffalo with a handgun is extremely challenging. The author passed on the bull in the background looking for a much bigger one.

minimum for these big animals. Since most shooting opportunities at these hollow-horned ruminants are inside the length of a football field, both the .454 Casull and handloaded .45-70, or the .475 or .500 Linebaugh are also good choices. A few years ago my wife and I had the pleasure of hunting the South Pacific with another couple, Frank and Audrey Murtland of Michigan. Frank and Audrey were both avid handgun hunters using Contenders chambered for a wildcat in .35 caliber. The cartridge they were both using was basically a .35 caliber bullet seated in a .444 Marlin case. Today we call this the .358 JDJ. I was packing the .375 JDJ. We were all anxious to stalk buffalo in Australia's Northern Territories.

En route to camp we enjoyed a scenic helicopter flight over some of the continent's most rugged terrain before landing between the trees near our camp on the Mann River. It was a picturesque setting situated in the middle of buffalo country. At the time, this area hadn't

Water buffalo remain the major calling card for hunters wishing to travel to Australia. They are big, tough to bring down, and challenging to hunt. What more could you ask for?

Audrey Murtland is shown here with the magnificent bull she took with her T/C Contender. If you didn't already know, handgun hunting is not just for men.

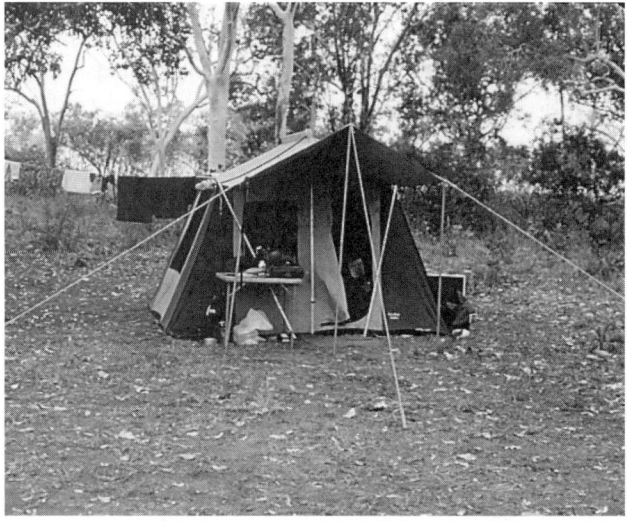

Camp in the Outback is often a tented affair and hunters are able to spend quality time in the bush where buffalo live.

The "water-in-the-bag" routine provided showers during the hunt in Australia. Five gallons is all you get so don't take too long. Don't expect Motel 6 in the Australian bush.

suffered from the government's buffalo eradication campaign, which had diminished buffalo numbers drastically in certain areas. Our area had plenty of buffalo and we were all looking forward to some top-notch hunting. After lunch we took a little stroll and soon spotted three nice bulls but it was too early in the hunt for anyone to get truly excited. I had plenty of time and decided to assist Frank and Audrey score on buffalo first before I started hunting.

The Australian environment and surroundings reminded me a lot of Africa. The area was desolate! No doubt we were in a remote part of the Outback. On our first morning of actual hunting we found a herd of buffalo with some really good bulls. After making sure her Contender was loaded with a 225-grain Swift bullet, Audrey proceeded to sneak up on the biggest bull. Being careful not to alarm the others, she stalked to within 70 yards of the big buffalo. Then calmly placed the Swift bullet squarely through its lungs. It was a well-placed shot and the big bull did not go far. After a finishing shot, it was all over but the picture taking and congratulations.

Our tent camp was always a welcome sight after a hard day's hunt. Interestingly we had a vegetarian camp cook. To my surprise he did a fine job, even with the meat dishes. Showers were provided by the ol' "hang-a-bag-of-water-in-a-tree" trick. When the bag of water was empty, your shower was over! If you preferred a bath, the Mann River obliged, that is if you didn't mind a few freshwater crocodiles. These little "freshies," as they are called, don't bother humans too often; it's the saltwater variety that gives cause for concern. Saltwater crocs in Australia are the largest in the world and can be very dangerous. Taking a dip in the moonlight was always refreshing at our camp, even if a few crocs were nearby. Dingos sang every night and they took the place of the radio. There was no electricity available.

Frank was looking for a monster buffalo and passed up several "shooters" during the next few days. We constantly searched for buffalo around water, hoping to catch them coming to or leaving their wallows or creek beds. Often we would encounter small herds of females and their calves with an occasional young bull mixed in. After several days of passing up smaller bulls, we finally managed to locate a really good one for Frank. It was late in the evening when we spotted an old solitary bull in some tall grass. After sneaking around in front of the old male, Frank and I intercepted him as he was making his way toward the river.

At 50 yards the big fellow turned toward us. He realized something was out of order. We didn't dare go any closer. Using the side of a tree for a rest, Frank put a bullet into the big bull's side. The buffalo jumped and stumbled toward the river. Follow-up shots on these big animals always seem to be in order. Frank expeditiously administered the *coup de grace*. The old bull's horns showed a lot of character from years of fighting. Frank had every reason to be happy.

I never did find a monster buffalo in that area but I did take care of some big wild hogs. I used 280-grain Cor-Bon ammo in my custom .375 JDJ, which handled just about everything on this hunt including several 250-pound boars.

Frank and Audrey both took good bulls and were ready to change scenery, so we flew to Smith Port on the beautiful Cobourg Peninsula. There we would search for banteng. The Cobourg is a wilderness area, rich in Aboriginal culture, and the only place in the world where banteng can be legally hunted. The banteng harvest is tightly controlled. Only a few permits are offered every year with a portion of the proceeds going directly to the Aborigines.

It is thought Banteng were imported to Australia sometime around 1830. But the first documented release was in 1845 at Victoria Settlement in the Northern Territory. Closely related to the gaur, the banteng is an ox-like creature living in thick, jungle-like environments. Many who have seen my trophy room have commented that this animal looks like a cow. It may resemble an ox but believe me, the banteng is a worthy adversary, both rare and elusive. Their sense of smell is excellent! The area they inhabit is unique. I considered it a privilege to hunt their kind in such a fantastic ecosystem. The area was alive with exceptional bird and animal life, but we didn't travel halfway around the world to bird watch.

The first afternoon we went on a reconnaissance mission from the new camp and spotted the first banteng any of us had ever seen in the wild. It was an old, solitary bull that anyone would be happy to hang on the wall.

We were only an hour or so away from camp but Audrey and I didn't even have our guns loaded. After all, we were just going to look around for a bit before seriously hunting? Frank was quite a bit smarter, had his gun loaded, and took advantage of the situation. It didn't take Frank long to get into position for a good shot. The big bull was standing behind some brush, partially hidden, and took Frank's first and only shot at

Follow-up shots are common with big animals like water buffalo. Heavy, well-constructed bullets should be used on tough game.

the base of the neck. It was a well-placed shot from 75 yards away and it ended Frank's banteng hunt almost as soon as it began. Looking at the smile on Frank's face, I don't think he was offended the least bit by ending his hunt the first afternoon.

I thought my hunt might be a piece of cake after seeing how Frank scored so quickly. Audrey and I were ready. Little did we realize that our good fortune was about to take an abrupt turn and getting our banteng was not going to be a "walk in the park." We hunted together for the next few days, leaving camp well before daylight and hunting all day before returning after dark.

The white, sandy beaches of the Arafura Sea were absolutely gorgeous and the breeze from the ocean was always refreshing. There was plenty of fauna and flora to keep us entertained. Many species of parrots, doves, and other unique birds call the peninsula home. There are also the buffalo, kangaroo, dingo, goanna, and the huge saltwater crocs. We also got to see a lot of real estate. It wasn't unusual to cover 12 to 15 miles per day even with the temperature heating up around mid-morning.

The banteng proved highly elusive. When we did spot a good bull, the wind would change directions during our stalk, sending the animal running away into the jungle-like cover. This routine was repeated to the point where it began to get frustrating. Earlier I mentioned that the banteng's sense of smell was superb, but they can also see and hear well. The harder we tried, the worse things became. The days kept passing. In spite of the setbacks, Audrey was bound and determined to get a banteng. Nobody could have hunted any harder. I just kept my fingers crossed.

Toward the end of our hunt we spotted a herd of banteng with three good bulls in the mix. It was right

As a bonus, several wild boar were encountered during the Australia hunt. Most of these pigs weighed over 200 pounds.

before dark and I was hoping Audrey could get a shot before light failed. Audrey managed to get within 50 yards of the biggest bull. It was a well-executed stalk and I was quite impressed. Totally undetected, the lady handgunner placed her first shot in the boiler room. The 225-grain Swift bullet performed well. At that time, Audrey was probably the only female hunter to harvest a banteng with a handgun. We were all ecstatic! Persistence had paid off. That night everyone congratulated the Murtlands on their successful hunt.

I still hadn't scored. On the last day of the hunt, I began to get somewhat concerned. The banteng weren't playing fair. As always, we left camp before daylight and drove to a different area to look for a bull. The game plan was simple: find a banteng, put a bullet in his lungs. Unfortunately up to this point it had not been that simple. Covering more miles than expected, we eventually ran into a herd with one good bull in the bunch. After glassing the area thoroughly, we executed a stalk from about 300 yards away.

Australia has green ants that will bite the heck out of you, and, they always seemed to do this right in the middle of a stalk. I cussed them under my breath and brushed them off as we tried to quietly approach the herd. About the time we were reaching the halfway point on the stalk, the wind changed direction, causing the herd to make an unceremonious departure. It was nothing new but it sure was making things difficult. We really didn't have anything better to do at that point, so we followed their trail hoping to run across them again. About an hour later we stopped to discuss our options. Did we want to continue and hope we would catch up with the herd again or should we start looking for another bunch before sunset? After all, it was the last day of the hunt and wasting daylight wasn't in our best interest. I happen to notice a white patch of something in the thick vegetation ahead and took a quick look through the binoculars. It was a stroke of luck! It was the bull we had seen earlier, along with four females. I was surprised one of the cows hadn't seen us or caught our scent. It wasn't a good shot but it was the only one I had. I placed the crosshairs on the big bull from an offhand position and squeezed the trigger. When the .375 JDJ roared, banteng left in all directions. I kept my eyes on the bull while reloading quickly. I took off running as fast as my legs would go trying to keep up with the bull, knowing a follow-up shot was necessary. Two more 280-grain Cor-Bon bullets were needed to put the bull down for keeps. I couldn't believe it! Finally it all came together! I was one happy camper. The big bull will always be a special part of handgun hunting Down Under. Now if I can just find the guy who said hunting a banteng was like shooting a cow!

After the banteng hunt, Frank and Audrey went home leaving Karen and me to hunt the last few days of our stay with Mike Barrett, another outfitter who specialized in water buffalo. Mike had access to some private land south of Darwin that held some big buffalo. As you may have guessed, I truly enjoy buffalo hunting. Big bulls are hard to bring down. Their sheer size makes for a challenging handgun hunting endeavor. Our first afternoon in Mike's area provided sufficient action to keep us entertained and occupied. We walked up a riverbed to an area the buffalo used for wallowing. A wallow is simply a large mud hole. The buffalo wade into this mud to cool themselves and the layer of mud on their bodies also helps to keep the insects from biting.

Frank Murtland took this old bull during the Australian hunt. This bull was well past his prime with signs of age and years of fighting.

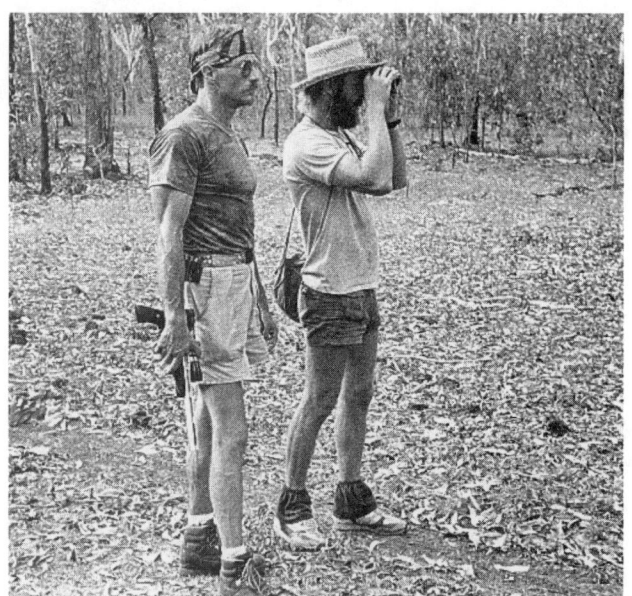

The author and his faithful guide, Brenton Hurt, covered endless miles for days looking for banteng. The five-days of hunt was almost not enough time.

We spotted some small herds comprised mainly of cows and young ones. All were laying down in the shade when we saw them. I told Mike that I preferred to hold out for a monster. There were seven animals off to one side but we couldn't determine the size of their horns. Since we had a great vantage point and the animals never knew we were around, Mike and I watched the buffalo through the binoculars for an hour or more. When they got up it was clear that one in the group was a real ancient bull with wide horns. He definitely stood out from all the rest. We tried desperately to get a shot, but it wasn't going to happen. Before we could get in position to shoot, some of the females detected our presence and alerted the others. As the herd spooked and ran away, I was particularly impressed with the width of this bull's horns. Running away from us he looked like an airplane trying to take off. Mike thought the bull would return to this area for water. I hoped he was right.

Looking for a really big buffalo takes time and effort. Here the hunting party takes a break to rest. The Outback is vast and one can expect to walk a great deal while hunting.

The author took this bull on the last afternoon of his scheduled hunt. Only a few permits are available every year for banteng, making this trophy all the more sweet.

We scouted a different area late that evening and came across another very good bull. Mike informed me this new male would score close to 110 SCI points, which is a darn good bull for this day and time. The old bull was massive and anybody in his or her right mind should have taken him. Reluctantly, I passed on this bull because I just couldn't get that wide bull we had seen earlier out of my mind. I wasn't interested in how much this animal would score or how well he might fare in the record books. I just wanted another chance at those wide horns.

Early the next morning we crawled down the creek bottom in the area of the big wallow where we had spotted our quarry the day before. We found a place to hide and waited to see if he would come back. Sure enough, around 10 a.m. all seven of the buffalo, including the bull with the wide horns, came out of the bush toward the wallow. Much to our surprise, the animals went past the wallow and kept on walking. I was so shocked I didn't even attempt a shot even though at one time they were less than 80 yards away. We crawled for 100 yards and hid behind a termite mound to see where the animals were going. Apparently there was another wallow we didn't know about. The buffalo were now over 200 yards away when they gave us another surprise. They turned around, for no apparent reason, and headed right back toward us. Thankfully we had a good hiding spot behind the termite mound. It seemed like we were playing peek-a-boo with the buffalo, peeking around the mound to see what they were up to. They kept walking closer and closer. For a while I thought they might even walk right beside the mound we were hiding behind. It was a grand spot for an ambush. When the wide-horned bull turned broadside at 50 yards, it was more than I could take. I had a great rest with the mound and when the crosshairs settled, the Contender launched a round, which landed in the bull's football-sized heart. Before the bull went down, I put several more 270-grain Hornady Spire Points into him. They surely can absorb a lot of lead!

His horns measured 82-inches from tip to tip. I was thrilled to see this guy again. A good stalk thrown in with a little luck resulted in a storybook ending.

Mike and I spent the next few days hunting for wild hogs and other critters. The Outback was a wonderful place to spend time with a handgun. The hogs proved to be smarter than expected, giving us some enjoyable and challenging hunts. I carried a .338 Woodswalker and a 7 JDJ in a Contender for the other varmints.

Deer Down Under

Several deer species thrive in Australia. The sambar deer is regarded by many as the most difficult and prestigious trophy animal in all of Australia. It is a worthy adversary for the handgun hunter. The sambar is rather large and will weigh 400 pounds or so. These big-bodied deer normally have three points per side with thick bases and main beams that can measure up to 10 inches in circumference. Sambars usually stay close to thick scrub and swampy areas, which makes them difficult to hunt. The only one I ever took was by a stroke of luck. After spending 10 weeks, over a period of three years, hunting in the South Pacific I have only seen one decent trophy. An offhand shot from 100 yards in pouring rain somehow found its mark. Like I said, it was a stroke of luck.

Any of the guns and loads suitable for mid-sized African game will work fine for sambar deer.

Another deer species worthy of interest is the rusa deer. It is not quite as large as the sambar but still tips the scales at more than 250 pounds. They also usually have three points per side. The rusa is an interesting animal. Probably the best rusa deer hunting remains in

The guide is examining a wallow where buffalo frequent. The mud helps keep insects from biting so much. Sometimes the buffalo will visit these places daily.

A big water buffalo is impressive to say the least. These horns measure almost 7 feet from tip to tip.

New Caledonia but unfortunately handguns are not allowed on that island. There are some pockets in Australia that hold rusa and I have been fortunate enough to take one of these animals.

The smallest deer in Australia is the hog deer. It is about the size of a big dog. Its face looks like it ran into a brick wall and they run around with their head down like a hog, which is probably how they acquired their name. Like the sambar and rusa, these little deer also have racks with three points per side. They prefer swamps and dense cover and spend most of their time in thickets. You can spend a good deal of time in this type of cover hoping to get a shot at a trophy. The different species of deer are not generally what brings hunters to Australia, but they surely can spice things up while you are hunting the "land down under".

Australia was not only a great hunting experience, the people were most friendly and helpful. Australians are easy going and their warm hospitality was truly appreciated. Handgun hunters can find a lot of possibilities in Australia. It's just a shame that handguns are not allowed in New Zealand and New Caledonia. There are a lot of fantastic game animals that would make hunting the South Pacific truly a handgunners' paradise.

Chapter 15

Asia: High Mountain Action

Asia was, at one time, home to an abundance of big game. The world's largest continent has held or holds more dangerous game than Africa, including elephant, rhino, gaur, tiger, snow leopard, bear, and water buffalo to name just a few of the species. But in the face of years of military action and tremendous political chaos, the wildlife has suffered drastically.

Still, the adventurous hunter, can find ample opportunities awaiting. This huge land mass is a mountain hunter's Mecca. Asia has the distinction of having more species of goats and sheep than all other continents combined, but is usually not the first destination the traveling hunter wishes to visit. Most hunters, myself included, hit the Dark Continent as their first destination outside of North America. But sooner or later, thoughts turn to Asia and a stop truly is a must for the international, adventurous hunter.

The ride to camp was provided by a Russian-made jeep. It was a great vehicle, but after eight hours the camp was a welcome sight.

The Mongolian camps consisted of the traditional ger, basically a round tent. It was a welcome sight after a hard day of mountain climbing.

Most of my Asian hunts were booked through a hunting consultant, Bob Kern of the Hunting Consortium. (540-955-0090) Kern has a lot of experience and has been sending hunters to Asia for many years. It is a definite asset to have this knowledge at one's disposal. I have always felt comfortable going through a reputable booking firm especially to Third World countries. They deal with complex travel arrangements and hunting programs on a daily basis. It costs no more to use Kern's vast experience and contacts than booking directly with an outfitter. If problems occur I have someone to help sort out such matters. Selecting a hunting consultant should be the first step in planning your trip to Asia.

If you are the type individual that likes everything to run smoothly, on time, without surprises or mishaps, you might want to think twice about hunting Asia. Not that everything gets screwed up all the time, but you can usually count on travel complexities and inconveniences when you head to Asia. Take my first trip to Mongolia for example. I caught a flight out of St. Louis to Chicago, and it was there that problems began. The airline officials had me removed from the aircraft in Chicago, enroute to Beijing. They informed me they wouldn't take my gun and ammunition into China even though I had the proper documents. I was then flown to Frankfort, and from there, on to Beijing. Unfortunately my luggage, including the gun and ammunition, never arrived. It was quite disturbing to say the least. I did get to walk on the Great Wall, visit the Ming Tombs, and see other historic sights before departing to the U.S. a few days later. My first trip to Asia was more of a sightseeing excursion and not exactly what I had in mind.

The next year I finally made it all the way to Mongolia, with my gun and ammo. Along with some other hunters, I was met in Hovd by a team of Mongolians who took us on an eight-hour jeep ride to a camp nestled in the Altai Mountain range. It was quite an undertaking just getting to camp. The long ride in a Russian-made jeep, over dirt roads with no fast-food places anywhere, let me know I was certainly out of the U.S. Once in camp I found the surrounding mountains picturesque and magnificent.

Most mountain hunting entails long-range shooting. Ibex, sometimes overlooked by sheep hunting enthusiasts, are tough animals. Precise long-range shooting and proper shot placement are paramount. These factors in mind, I chose a T/C Encore chambered in .308 Winchester, topped with a 2-1/2X to 8X Leupold scope. Winchester's Supreme 168-grain ammunition got the call for Siberian ibex. Practice sessions involved a lot of time shooting at targets from 200 to 300 yards, which is what I realistically expected to encounter on the hunt.

The Altai mountain range is Mongolia's largest, with many summits reaching elevations of 12,000 feet above sea level. Composed mainly of rocky mountain ranges, the Altai is home to the snow leopard, wolves, the magnificent argali sheep, and Siberian ibex. A hunter must be in good physical condition to enjoy, and endure these rugged mountains.

We started the hunt after a quick breakfast of eggs, rice, and tongue, then drove over more dirt roads for an hour or so before we stopped in a riverbed that was swallowed up by the surrounding mountains. I looked up at both sides and wondered how we were going to get up to the top. I should have known!

After the first 100 yards my lungs were trying to acquire as much oxygen as possible. We were somewhere around 10,000 feet in elevation and the air was a little thin. After we had climbed 200 yards, I stopped to catch my breath. As I went about gasping for air, the guides fired up a cigarette. There was something psychologically demeaning about that picture! A short while later we spotted our first ibex. They were females and young ones but it was a wonderful sight.

Our climb up the mountains took more than three, heart-pounding hours. The guides wanted to get on top the mountain in order for us to be in a better position, looking down on the ibex. Periodically glassing the area, we continued to work our way toward the top. We located a herd of a dozen or more ibex and tried to get closer for a better look. Peeking over a group of boulders, we spotted one big billy. At 320 yards all we could do is look. I definitely didn't want to attempt a shot at that range if we could cut the distance. While trying to

In the High Altai Mountains of Mongolia, the author placed his Encore on a backpack for a rest. The first ibex taken was 221 yards away.

The Siberian ibex of Mongolia provides a true mountain hunting experience. This one fell victim to an Encore in .308 Winchester. Long-range shooting is expected, so hunters will need to be familiar with the gun and bullet trajectory.

figure out a way of getting closer, the ibex jumped up and took off running for no apparent reason. Looking around a little bit, we noticed another man and his dog on our mountain. The guides said he was a local hunter looking for marmots. Deep inside I suspected a poacher was trying to get an ibex. At any rate, what are the odds of another hunter on the same mountain? The Altai mountain range is vast and this guy happened to be on the same mountain, spooking our ibex! I am sure the local hunter had the same thoughts about us being on "his" mountain.

With the presence of another man on the mountain, our hunting strategy changed drastically. My enthusiasm was shattered! We began to work our way down the mountain in a different direction. Our descent took us into an isolated valley. There we spotted a bachelor group of ibex males. We crawled around on our hands and knees for five minutes looking for a decent place from which I could shoot. Finally, one of the guides motioned me to put my backpack on a rock ledge. I checked to make certain the Encore was loaded and the scope setting was on 4X. Peeking over the ledge I found an awesome sight! Eight big ibex males were situated across the canyon. My Bushnell rangefinder flashed 221 yards. I tried to determine the largest male but they were all about the same size. Resting the handgun on the backpack, I placed the crosshairs on what I thought to be the biggest ibex and touched a

Chamois are mountain-loving animals usually taken at long range. Hunters who enjoy the high-country adventure will cherish time spent stalking these wonderful game animals.

round off. The ibex immediately dropped in his tracks and began rolling down the rocky hillside. I prayed his horns would not shatter.

My interpreter asked if I wanted to fill my second license since visiting hunters have the option of taking two ibex. Quickly I reloaded thinking that would surely answer his question. The second ram had run toward us and was now standing 121 yards, looking around to see where all of his buddies had gone. Just then the 168-grain bullet caught the ibex behind the shoulder. The guides started slapping my back and congratulating me and shaking hands with each other. They had never before witnessed a handgun in action. I may have been the happiest man in all of Asia. According to all of my research, that was the first Siberian ibex ever taken with a handgun. It was the beginning of many more Asian adventures to come.

The key was, of course, good shot placement and a steady rest. I can't emphasis enough the importance of realistic practice at distant targets as you prepare for an Asian hunt.

For a long time I refrained from going after Bezoar ibex in Turkey because of hunting reports that reflected local poaching, over-hunting in most areas, and a decline in trophy quality. But when Craig Boddington returned from hunting a new area and spoke very highly of his experience I had several conversations with Kaan Karakaya of Shikar Safaris and organized a March hunt for ibex.

During one of our conversations Kaan advised there would be a lot of snow in the Taurus Mountains. Hopefully this would drive the ibex to somewhat more accessible, lower elevations. The Bezoar ibex thrive in steep, rocky, rugged mountain terrain, and precipitous cliffs. They often stay in areas that are impossible for humans to reach. When predators of any type put pressure on the ibex, it's not uncommon for them to live in caves by day, only coming out after dark to feed. The Bezoar ibex is a very elusive animal and makes for a challenging mountain experience for the handgun hunter. Before this hunt, I know of only one ibex that had been taken with a handgun. This caused my determination to rise to its highest level.

I chose to use the same T/C Encore chambered in .308 Winchester for this hunt that I had taken to Mongolia. The only difference was the ammunition. I switched to 150-grain Winchester Supreme factory loads. My handgun was sighted in at 200 yards and I was hoping to get within that range.

The two local guides that would be helping during my hunt were actually reformed poachers. Communication was awkward, but Bekir, the interpreter, assisted with language barriers. I could tell they didn't think much of my handgun; distain for such weapons was common in the past.

On the first morning we glassed a snow-covered mountainside that I really didn't believe any animal could inhabit. It was cold and there was lots of snow on

Rarely do you see a hunter with a Bezoar ibex taken with a handgun. The author took this billy in Turkey. The shot was 168 yards taken with an Encore in .308 Winchester.

Handgun Hunting

the ground. We hadn't glassed long before I spotted a lone billy lying on the edge of a rock halfway up the almost vertical mountain. Murat, one of the local guides, and Bekir took turns using my 10X-50 Swarovski binoculars to scrutinize the male.

Several minutes passed before Bekir said he thought the ibex would go around 105 centimeters, which is somewhere in the neighborhood of 42 inches. That's a very respectable ibex indeed! We decided to go after this billy so we loaded our backpacks and took off up the mountain. Unfortunately I failed to bring along any mountain climbing gear.

The partially frozen snow made the long climb most difficult. We would walk a few steps then break through the frozen crust. Sometimes I would sink in up to my waist. After a while this became physically demanding. We could not be quiet in this situation, so we had to plan our stalk accordingly.

Halfway up the mountain we spooked two females. Somehow we managed to miss them in our glassing efforts. It was a costly mistake as they took off with the billy following behind. With nothing better to do at this point, Bekir and I continued to climb hoping we might find them again. I had to remind Bekir, the 24 year-old mountain trekker, that I didn't get my gray hair by accident and a brief rest periodically would be most welcome. We finally reached the top of the mountain but never saw the ibex again. As we slowly crawled back down off of the mountain it was a miracle that we didn't start an avalanche.

When we finally reached the bottom I could tell Murat was upset about something. He had been watching us from the bottom of the mountain and could also see the ibex. Once we climbed to the top, the ibex were only about 200 yards away, but we couldn't see them. Now, looking through a spotting scope, I could see the male lying down on a rock. As it was early in the afternoon, we made a plan to go back up the mountain again.

Good binoculars are essential for glassing for extended periods of time. The guides borrowed the author's 10X50 Swarvoski binos while looking for tur.

158 Asia: High Mountain Action

The climb back up the mountain was both physically and psychologically painful. Murat was leading the charge this time and Bekir stayed at the base of the mountain watching the show. Through the spotting scope we could see the ibex, still bedded down. We had designated a reference point we could recognize once we were on top. Our plan was to get back on the top of the mountain and shoot down at the bedded ibex. It sounded good to me.

It took almost three hours to reach the top. We caught our wind and slowly eased along the mountaintop. Finally, I spotted our reference point and motioned for Murat to be quiet. When Murat peeked over the edge, he grabbed my backpack and laid it down on some rocks. I carefully eased over to the ledge, not being crazy about falling off the mountain, and spotted the ibex a mere 80 yards below. The billy never knew we were there. Just as I rested the Encore on the backpack, Murat spoke something in Turkish. I didn't understand a word of it, but the billy must have heard it clearly. Immediately the ibex was up and running. He vanished in the blink of an eye.

The thought of spending the rest of my life in a Turkish prison was the only thing that kept me from killing Murat. I just couldn't imagine an old poacher, someone who has killed a lot of ibex in the past, would do something to alert the animal and blow our chance. The hike back down the mountain was a long one to say the least.

The next morning a park ranger, Sadettin, agreed to give us a hand. He knew the area well and understood ibex. If he knew how to be quiet, I was glad to gain his assistance.

We started out hunting in the same basic area as the day before. Late in the morning we spotted what looked like the same male. Our quarry was lying down among some giant rocks halfway hidden in a mountain crevice. I was impressed the guides located him through the spotting scope. Sadettin, who also didn't speak a word of English, laid out a plan that would have us on one side of the mountain, shooting across to where the ibex was bedded. This time I made certain that Sadettin understood not to make any sound that might alert the ibex.

Even though my wife accuses me of having boots for every occasion, I did not have the appropriate foot-

Mountain camps on some Asian hunts can be very primitive. Basic shelter is all you need until the weather turns sour.

This old Russian Army transport truck took the hunting team far into the mountains. It was unbelievable where the vehicle could go.

wear for this climb. I had to step in the same tracks Sadettin left in the frozen snow. On such a steep mountainside, one slip of the foot and I would have fallen 600 yards below. We finally reached an outcrop of huge boulders. Sadettin peeked over the edge and took a reading with my rangefinder. He motioned 168 yards. I eased the Encore on top of the backpack and peeked over the rocks. By that time my glasses were fogged over and my heart was still pounding from the invigorating climb. I believe the ibex knew something was up. He stood up, alert and facing directly at us, when I picked him up in the scope. I was wishing my glasses would clear up a little so I could see clearly. Placing the crosshairs on the ibex, trying desperately to see through my fogged over glasses, I squeezed off a round. The ibex dropped immediately. Sadettin had a strange look on his face, as he had never seen a handgun in action before. We shook hands and enjoyed the moment over a fine cigar. It was a moment made possible by pursuing the game to the limits of endurance, then counting on an accurate handgun and a proven round to bring down the game.

I thought the Taurus Mountains were difficult to climb until I hunted for Eastern tur in the Caucasus Mountains of Azerbaijan. That limits of endurance statement from the ibex hunt certainly applied in Azerbaijan. The Caucasus is a narrow range of high, extremely rugged mountains that divide Europe and Asia. Tur, which is a Russian name for these mountain dwellers, favor higher elevations, precipitous terrain and make for an elusive adversary. At the time of my hunt I could not find any references of a tur taken with a handgun.

The Caucasus is not the ideal place to take your "better half," but my wife wanted to come along. The first morning we were up at 4 a.m. eating breakfast. We were in the saddle shortly thereafter for an hour ride into country too steep to ride the horses. Then we began to climb on foot. The horses were used for packing our supplies and the climb to the top was unmerciful! At one point, Mehman, our local guide, instructed me to grab the horse's tail. It really did help having the horse pull me up the mountain. Six long hours later we reached a spike camp up in the mountains. After a bite of lunch and a well-deserved break, we hit the trail again.

Mehmen used my binoculars to spot a large herd of tur on an adjacent mountain. Boy! Tur really blend in with their surroundings. The local guides wanted to make a push or drive, in an attempt to move the game near our position. Looking over the terrain, I didn't think it was possible. This hunt was booked as a stalking hunt but after seeing the abrupt, near vertical terrain, I decided to give the drive a chance. To be perfectly honest, I do not know how one could get close to a tur in some of these areas. Bekir, the same English-speaking guide from the hunt in Turkey, and I set up on a stand, much like deer hunting, and waited patiently. About an hour later we heard the guides yelling. I looked down the mountain and saw animals running way beyond shooting range. Bekir jumped up and started running downhill. I tried to keep up. My little legs were going as fast as they could but my body, gaining unwanted momentum, was going much faster and I soon found myself rolling downhill, end over end. It was an Olympic-class tumble! When my body finally came to a rest I felt lucky there were no broken bones. My glasses and scope were also intact. I was still dazed and dumbfounded from the spill, but Bekir was shouting, "Shoot!" I looked down the mountain several hundred yards and saw tur running like

The Caucasus Mountains of Azerbaijan are steep, with sliding shale making climbing conditions most difficult. The Eastern tur or Dagestan tur, as they are sometimes called, prefer precipitous terrain and are extremely challenging to hunt.

crazy. It would have been a heck of a shot for an avid rifleman. I didn't even attempt a shot. When the local guides arrived, they seemed disappointed I hadn't whacked one of the tur they had driven past. It was then I knew we had better stalk these creatures. When we made it back to camp, it was after dark and I was more than ready for the sleeping bag.

Before daylight the next morning, we enjoyed a cup of coffee and a handful of trail mix, and then once again begin climbing. Hiking over loose shale on steep inclines proved challenging and physically demanding. Negotiating abrupt, rocky pinnacles, climbing over and around cliffs, and being in a couple of places where I shouldn't have been, became a psychological factor as well as a physical challenge. Some of the climbs were downright treacherous. I made the mistake of looking down a couple of times. One slip of the foot and, well, it wasn't a pleasant thought. I was glad Karen remained in camp. We looked over a lot of country during the day and decided to head back to base camp to reorganize. After climbing mountains all day long, the 8-mile hike back to camp was refreshing!

Before daybreak the next morning we loaded our gear in an old Russian Army transport truck and drove for two hours up a riverbed where I couldn't believe a bulldozer could travel. It was an amazing ride! After some "diplomatic relations" with a local family, we began our six-hour climb to the top of the mountain. At 3,500 meters we encountered snow. The scenery was absolutely breathtaking. Mehman and Bekir spotted a large group of bedded tur. But when we couldn't determine horn size, we tried to get closer. On the way, nine more tur appeared from nowhere including one really big male. We were 400 yards away and had to lie motionless and hope they didn't notice us. Finally they disappeared over the ridge in the same direction the other animals were spotted. Climbing over and around three different shale-covered pinnacles, it took us over an hour to get in position for a better look. It was impossible to walk quietly on the shale. We all peeked over a ridge and glassed a herd of approximately 25 tur. It was a magnificent sight.

The tur were taking their afternoon nap in a rocky basin. Mehman would whisper to Bekir, then Bekir

Lunch in the Tien Shan Mountains. It was beautiful country but the ibex were impossible to reach.

A severe snowstorm in the Tien Shan Mountains made for a tough ibex hunt in Kyrgyzstan. Horses were used to get around.

would translate to me, and for several minutes we debated on which one had the largest horns. We finally reached a conclusion. It was a difficult decision. There were several worthy candidates in the group. The rangefinder read 257 yards. I had a great handgun rest on the backpack, holding the crosshairs on the top of the big male's back as he lay on the rocks. Slowly I squeezed off a round.

Bekir shouted, "You missed!"

I couldn't believe it. I refused to believe it. Panic sunk in as I tried to fumble another round into the chamber. All the animals took off running and momentarily disappeared behind a ridge. When the herd appeared again, they were running across the face of the adjacent mountainside. I asked Bekir if he was sure I missed? He was all too confident about the miss although he admitted never seeing the bullet hit.

The Eastern tur is most difficult to hunt. Few if any have ever been taken with a handgun. This big male was taken from 257 yards with an Encore in .308 using Winchester 150-grain factory ammo.

Handgun Hunting 163

This respectable mid-Asian ibex is the first of its kind to be taken with a handgun. Hampton used an Encore in .308 Winchester with 150-grain factory Winchester ammunition to bag this mountain climber from 373 yards.

I felt good about the shot and asked Mehman to search diligently behind the ridge where the animals had disappeared for a few seconds. The 39-year old Russian, who could out-walk 99 percent of the world's population, hiked over and disappeared into the gorge. He was gone 15 minutes when I heard him yell. I can't tell you how quickly that changed my disposition. Bekir and I hurried to see what Mehman was yelling about. When we reached the top of the ridge and looked down, Mehman was standing over a large reddish-brown creature with cylindrical horns that curved way behind the neck. The 150-grain bullet had passed through the top portion of his heart, claiming a huge East Caucasian tur. I'm mighty glad Bekir was mistaken!

The Caucasus Mountains are full of beauty and grandeur, offering the ultimate challenge, grueling adventure and elusive game. This is definitely one experience I'll never forget. I would have to put this one high on the list for any mountain hunting enthusiast looking to push the envelope on adventure.

My luck with mountain hunts had been pretty good until I went to Krygyzstan for Tien Shan or mid-Asian ibex. Mike Adams, Jere Burnette, and I hunted hard for six days and never had the opportunity to fire a shot. A freak snowstorm dumped three feet of snow and left us planning a hunt for the next year.

True to our word, all three of us met up in Krygyzstan the following year. It was an adventure just getting to camp.

After several days of travel, including seven hours in a six-wheeled Russian military truck, we found ourselves saddled up for a ride into the snow-covered mountains. The scenery was beautiful! Marco Polo sheep were everywhere. We saw more ibex the first day than we had the previous trip combined. I almost got my shot late in the afternoon after we climbed a mountain and found a herd of ibex, including one nice male, feeding on the adjacent ridge. At 320-yards, the big ibex looked impressive. The herd was walking away from us and a decent shot never materialized. It

The Marco Polo sheep is a magnificent trophy for any handgun hunter. Pamela Atwood took this fine ram in Tajikistan with an XL single-shot handgun. Quite an accomplishment!

didn't matter as I would have hated to finish this hunt on the first day.

The next morning we were back on the horses. After a couple of hours of riding up the creek, we then climbed up the mountains and located more ibex. There were several males in a herd of about 45 animals but nothing worth a second look. Later that morning my opportunity finally struck. Two good males were spotted near the top of a mountain. I quickly took a reading with my rangefinder. The display said 373 yards separated us. Perhaps it was the altitude affecting my judgment or perhaps the excitement from the guides. Maybe I just got caught up in the moment. Whatever it was, I found myself resting the Encore on a huge boulder. The crosshairs were perfectly still above the shoulders of the ibex. There was no wind blowing. The ibex was standing broadside. I felt confident I could make this shot. When the hammer fell sending a Nosler 150-grain bullet up the mountainside, the big ibex dropped immediately. The guides were astonished! All those practice sessions had paid off. I had used the right bullet, the right load and made the shot count. After eight hard days of hunting mid-Asian ibex on two different trips, I finally got the crosshairs on one. This had been a fantastic experience and an unforgettable hunting adventure.

Will I return to hunt in Asia? Something tells me many more adventures are awaiting. Let's see there are blue sheep in China, sind ibex in Pakistan, and if I win the lottery, Marco Polo sheep in Tajikistan. Yes, there are plenty more Asian adventures in the works.

Chapter 16

Culture and Custom: Hunting in Europe

It's not uncommon to find yourself shooting uphill or downhill in the mountains. Either way, a good rest, like a backpack, will help steady the crosshairs.

European hunting has a history of deep-rooted traditions. In many cases hunting was the exclusive right of the nobility or the landed aristocracy. Even though the privilege of hunting is no longer restricted to the royal families and their designees, the sport still enjoys tremendous prestige in much of Europe,. The hunting culture and customs are much more complex in Europe than in the rest of the hunting world. There are often elaborate rituals and displays of respect for the trophy taken. All of this makes for an interesting cultural experience while hunting in this beautiful, yet somewhat sophisticated hunting theater.

My wife and I first experienced Europe during our 20th wedding anniversary. I explained to Karen that Europe would be a great place to enjoy the occasion and she agreed. That was until she saw my gun case and ammunition being packed for the trip. In addition to celebrating our 20 years together, I had my eye on an Alpine ibex. This magnificent animal is one of Europe's most desirable and sought-after trophies. Like other species of ibex, the Alpine variety thrives in precipitous terrain and offers the mountain hunter a challenging and most rewarding experience. I didn't tell Karen but if an alpine chamois happened to materialize during the hunt, I certainly wouldn't pass up an opportunity.

The first day of celebrating our anniversary found us climbing the mountains long before daylight. As luck would have it, a front moved into the mountains and

The author's wife, Karen, is holding a chamois taken in Europe. Her smile lasted only moments, because she was freezing in the foul weather.

with it came gusty winds, colder temperature, and rain. My wife asked previously if we needed raingear, unfortunately with my infinite wisdom, I had advised her we would in no circumstance need raingear. The higher we climbed, the steeper the mountains became, and the weather more inclement and my wife more miserable. Before we got close to the top of the mountain it really started raining. The weather was deteriorating rapidly and so was my wife's pleasant disposition. It wasn't long before Karen asked, "What are we doing for our 25th anniversary?"

I thought about that for a moment and before I had a chance to reply, she informed me that it wasn't important, and really didn't want to know. I did begin to wonder if there would be a 25th.

Several hours into the climb, we still hadn't spotted any game. It wasn't exactly the type of day I imagined. The weather had turned terribly sour! The altitude became a factor and it was much more difficult to breathe. Turning back to see if Karen was still following, I found her soaking wet and shivering, appearing as if she were having the time of her life. About that time the guide got my attention. He had spotted movement up the mountain. You couldn't see much beyond 100 yards due to the fog, so we stopped and glassed the area as best we could. A gust of wind blew some fog out of the way and I could see a chamois standing on a rock some 120 yards away. I placed my backpack on a rock and rested the Encore on top, waiting for the guide to give the go-ahead. The beautiful Alpine chamois was alone, standing there looking around in all his glory. When I saw the thumbs-up sign, I leveled the crosshairs on the shoulders and sent a 168-grain Winchester Ballistic Supreme up the mountain to claim our first European trophy.

The Alpine ibex is an incredible and prestigious mountain game animal and I couldn't wait to see one in the wild. One of my hunting companions had informed me it wouldn't be a problem getting within 100 yards of the ibex so I didn't worry about bringing a rangefinder. Murphy's Law would unfortunately prevail once again.

Our ibex hunt started, like most Alpine hunts do, after a grueling climb up a steep mountain. The time spent getting in decent physical condition before this hunt was an excellent investment.

After glassing a lot of beautiful country for several hours, we still hadn't found any ibex. During the day we continued to climb more mountains and glassed more

The Alpine ibex is an impressive animal and a coveted trophy. This fine specimen was taken at long range using an Encore chambered for .308 Winchester.

real estate and by late in the afternoon we spotted nine ibex bedded down on an adjacent mountainside. They were enjoying the warm sunshine taking an afternoon nap. We could see three nice males in the small group, but couldn't get any closer than about 300 yards.

Communication was made awkward due to the fact my guide couldn't speak a word of English and my foreign language skills left a lot to be desired. I picked some daisies and placed them on a flat rock in the formation the ibex were situated on the slope. With hand gestures I desperately tried to communicate with the local guide that the daisies were ibex. Now if I could only ascertain which ibex he wanted me to shoot. After several frustrating minutes of unproductive communication, I finally came to the conclusion that the guide wanted me to take the third one from the left. At least that's the best I could determine. This should be the oldest, most mature male in the herd, but not necessarily the male with the longest horns. In much of Europe the hunter pays for the animal on a graduated scale and in many cases, you shoot what the gamekeeper chooses for you.

Like most hunters here in North America, I want to know the financial consequences "BEFORE" pulling the trigger, not after. I wasn't thrilled about making a $10,000 mistake with this ibex decision. I turned the scope setting up to 6X and rested the Encore on the backpack. It was a good rest. I needed all the help possible, because the range was every bit of 300 yards. At the shot, all the ibex took off running except the big billy.

He was 12 years old, the one I was supposed to shoot, and a magnificent trophy that will always be remembered. I felt honored and privileged to have experienced part of the European hunting tradition.

Since that hunt I have acquired an ibex "obsession." For whatever the reason, I decided to pursue the four different species of Spanish ibex. Like most other sheep and wild goats, the ibex in Spain are hunted in rough terrain, at higher elevations. Long shots are to be expected. But, it was a challenge I was ready to accept.

During an SCI Convention I met a young outfitter, Juan Toquero, and booked a hunt with him for a Gredos ibex. On several occasions, I had been told that handguns were forbidden in Spain. Juan was kind enough to fax me the paperwork concerning the legality of handguns, so I was certain to stay within the confines of the Spanish regulations. Apparently some

Hunting the Gredos Mountains in Spain was a wonderful experience. The author's guide, Juan, is pointing out some ibex high on the mountain.

of the other outfitters either did not know the law or they just didn't want to take a handgun hunter. Currently, as long as the barrel is 12 inches or longer, handguns are permitted in Spain.

My wife and I arrived in Madrid the day after Christmas and Juan immediately drove us to the Gredos Mountains. Going through customs with a handgun was relatively painless.

Rain was pouring down as we drove into the mountains. Juan was concerned about crossing the many valleys and rivers that lay between our hunting area and us. The heavy rainfall meant snow at higher elevations. This turned out to be helpful, forcing the ibex down to lower elevations.

The first morning the local gamekeeper met us shortly after daylight. He had been keeping an eye on the ibex as well as the rising water conditions. At first light we climbed toward the top of a snow-covered mountain. Heavy fog deterred our glassing attempts but it was enjoyable just being in the mountains. At least it wasn't raining!

Periodically, the fog diminished and we could glass the beautiful real estate looking for ibex. We watched a few females feeding in the early morning light on the rim of a canyon. Before we had a good opportunity to glass the area thoroughly, the fog rolled back in, halting our efforts. We simply sat down and waited

Gredos ibex are challenging to hunt in the mountains of Spain. The author took this good male with his .309 JDJ from around 80 yards.

Handgun Hunting

patiently. A few minutes later the fog lifted again and we noticed a big male keeping company with the females. A quick check on the rangefinder found 187 yards separated us. The big male jumped up on a chunk of rock and turned perfectly broadside. I steadied shooting sticks and placed the Contender in position. Through the scope I could see obstructions in the bullet path and before I could establish a clear shot, the fog rolled back in. All we could do was wait. Patience never has been one of my strong points. I sat there like a kid waiting for the rain to stop so we could play baseball, wondering how long it would take. Minutes seemed like hours. When the fog disappeared, so had the ibex. We glassed the area completely but the ibex obviously had moved on.

As quietly as possible, we climbed around the rocks and over other obstacles to get a better view. After scrutinizing the area for over an hour without seeing our quarry, we continued climbing very slowly. Both Juan and the gamekeeper focused their attention on the opposite side of the mountain. For some unknown reason, I glanced over at the gigantic boulders to our right. There I spotted horns barely visible between some rocks. I grabbed the back of Juan's coat and then told him to put his backpack on the ledge beside us. The gamekeeper took a quick look through his binoculars and told me to shoot. As soon as the crosshairs settled, I squeezed the trigger, sending the Nosler 165-grain BT 80 yards to its intended target.

The ibex flinched then jumped over a couple of boulders. He tried to stay on his feet as I needlessly sent a second round claiming our first Spanish trophy. The 10-year-old male was a great representative of the Gredos Mountains.

But I didn't go all the way to Spain to hunt just one ibex. Another outfitter, Tomas Hertz Garcia, had also organized a hunt for Ronda ibex the smallest of the Spanish ibex. During the drive south, toward the Mediterranean Sea, my wife and I enjoyed the many historic, artistic, and cultural treasures for which Spain is so famous.

The next morning at first light we climbed again and glassed again. Most of this new territory overlooked the Mediterranean Sea. It was breathtakingly beautiful! Once we reached the top, our search for ibex continued. We glassed for game on both sides of the mountain and by late in the morning we had located a small herd. There was one real good male in the bunch. He was feeding below us almost 300 yards away. We hid quickly behind some rocks and watched the ibex feed their way toward us ever so slowly. They were at 220 yards when I placed the backpack on the edge of a rock, I made certain the .309 JDJ was loaded, cranked the scope up to 6X, and got ready. I had the crosshairs on the ibex for a while but there was always some brush, a female, or a bad angle to contend with. I waited for the right opportunity. It never materialized. The wind had been gusting all morning and finally blew in a hard rain. Like mountains anywhere, weather conditions can change quickly in the higher elevations of Spain. The animals disappeared into a valley and we never saw them again.

We were greeted with sunshine the next morning and, after a brisk climb up the mountain, we began glassing again. Many of the ibex we spotted early on were females with their young. So we decided to keep moving, looking for a big billy.

We took a break around noon and enjoyed lunch while glassing the canyon spreading below us. It was then that Tomas spotted a herd of ibex in a ravine. After watching the group for over an hour, we planned our stalk. Karen decided she would stay put while Tomas and I snaked our way through bushes and boulders. I crawled the last several yards to get in position behind a huge boulder. It was there I rested the Contender on my backpack and peeked over the edge. There below, approximately 220 yards away were 10 ibex. I did not believe the distance recorded on the rangefinder so I asked Tomas to take another look and be certain of the range. Again, the rangefinder read 218 yards. To me it seemed like 300 or more yards. Judging distance in mountainous terrain can be very deceiving, but with an excellent rest and great familiarity with my gun, I knew the shot would be no problem.

The author and his wife, Karen, take a lunch break in the mountains during an ibex hunt. Mountain hunters are encouraged to drink plenty of water so dehydration doesn't become a factor during the hunt.

There are four different species of Spanish ibex. The smallest of the group is the Ronda, like this one taken on a December hunt.

The shot should have been no problem, so I was astounded when my shot missed! The echo must have confused the ibex. They did not know which way to run. I quickly reloaded and cussed myself for missing the shot. Tomas told me to relax. The ibex were now running up the mountain toward us. I was anxious to shoot again but Tomas convinced me to be patient. It seemed like three hours but was only about five minutes. The ibex cut the distance to 137 yards. Thankfully I had regained my composure. When the male jumped up on a rock I was ready. The crosshairs settled perfectly on the shoulder. I gently pulled the trigger. The Nosler 165-grain bullet struck home as the ibex immediately fell from the rock where he was standing. The 9 year-old Ronda ibex was a beautiful representative of the species. I could not have been more pleased.

The trick to hunting in Europe, if there is one, is to book your hunts with a reputable outfitter, get a handle on the laws and regulations concerning your handgun and thoroughly understand the customs and costs before you pull the trigger.

The following year my wife and I returned to finish the Spanish Slam of ibex. There is something about mountain hunting that gets into a persons system. I love the mountains and really enjoy stalking the game that inhabits these majestic places. Juan Toquero picked us up in Madrid and we immediately headed north to look for Beceite ibex. The mountains were partially covered what snow and it was cold. The wind was gusting up to 30 miles per hour. Conditions were not ideal, but that didn't deter our enthusiasm.

The fist morning we started glassing the mountains looking for big ibex. The cold wind made glassing difficul. I couldn't keep my eyes from watering. When I spotted the first group of ibex there was one male with six female companions. It was a decent male but Juan said he wasn't near big enough for the first morning of the hunt. We continued our efforts by looking in areas that were partially out of the wind. During the course of the morning we covered a lot of area but didn't locate many ibex. The strong wind was not our friend.

Late in the day as we were about ready to call it quits a group of ibex were spotted just below the top of a steep mountain. It was an ideal place for the animals to escape from the gusting wind. Looking through the binoculars I could see two males and six females. One of the males was a youngster but the other one was impressive. Juan excitedly told me this guy was a keeper. The ibex were about 600 yards away. We tried to conceal ourselves as best we could in an attempt to cut the distance. Once we made it behind some big boulders I asked Juan to check the distance with my range finder. Juan said they were still too far. I asked him again for the distance. He looked at me funny and replied "245 yards." I told him to put the backpack on the rock and make sure I'm shooting the right one!

I was carrying the XP-100 in .284 Winchester topped with a Burris 3X-12X scope. I knew where the Nosler 140-grain BT would land at that distance. Once I got a good rest on the backpack and wiped the water from my eyes, I felt confident about taking the shot. The scope was cranked up to 6X. The big ibex was following one of his girlfriends along the side of the mountain. I kept the crosshairs on the animal and waited for him to stop. When he finally stopped for a brief second the Nosler bullet struck home. Juan slapped me on the back and shook my hand. I don't know who was happier.

Earlier in the day Juan had told me we would be looking for an ibex with a horn length of at least 70 cm. This animal was 12 years old and wore headgear 76 cm in length. I think Juan was the happiest.

With three of the Spanish ibex taken only one remained, the Sierra Nevada variety. We drove to the city of Granada and spent the night. Early the next morning we were consumed by the grandeur of the Sierra Nevada Mountains. At sunrise there was not an ounce of wind blowing and that was a pleasant change from the day before. It was still cold but the mountains were empty of snow.

As with most mountain hunting, a considerable amount of time involves glassing. It wasn't long until we were seeing ibex. Many of the males were still hanging close to females but Juan informed me the rut was almost over. After climbing a short distance we encountered a nice male feeding along with several other females. The ibex were across the canyon approximately 300 yards away. Juan and one of the other guides studied the ibex through spotting scopes for almost 30 minutes before passing. The day was going to be ideal for hunting and there was absolutely no reason to get in a hurry. Juan wanted to get a Sierra Nevada ibex with horns that exceeded 60 cm. I was just enjoying the opportunity to bee ibes in such a beautiful setting. Later in the morning we located a group of 15 bachelors feeding on an adjacent mountain slope. Three of the males in this group were definitely shooters. Unfortunately they were in the wide open, about one-half mile away, with no possible way to approach them without being detected. Juan suggested we drive around to the backside of the mountain and approach from behind. This would take some time and hopefully they would still be in the area.

It took over an hour to get around the mountain. We parked the truck and filled our backpacks with gear, guns, and spotting scopes. The climb up the mountain took over an hour and it sure got your lungs working and circulation flowing. Once on top we began searching for the ibex. It's a funny thing how the landscape looks different from another part of the mountain. No ibex were in sight. Surely they didn't just disappear. Proceeding a little further around the mountainside we finally spotted four of the 15 ibex. Luckily, three of the big males were in the group. They were too far away for any possibility of a shot, leisurely working their way toward us, feeding and just wandering about. Juan suggested we try to close the distance some by sneaking up to another group of boulders. Doing so put us within 300 yards of the ibex. I placed the backpack on one of the rocks and waited. It seemed like an eternity but the animals finally walked inside the 250-yard mark. Unfortunately there was just enough brush to make shooting impossible. They were not spooked so we waited patiently. As the animals eventually got around the brush I took the XP off safety and tried to locate the biggest male. Juan informed me the distance was 205 yards. After scrutinizing trophy quality through the spotting scope we both agreed on which one was the largest. I steadied the crosshairs and the loud .284 broke the afternoon silence on the mountain. The others took off running but our ibex couldn't go anywhere. Juan was impressed with the XP. I was happy to add another ibex hunt to the memory bank! The Sierra Nevada ibex supported sweeping horns that measured 68 cm and was 10 years old.

It had been another wonderful hunting experience in the European climate. Heck, I already want to go back for one of those big red stags, or perhaps a roe deer, maybe a mouflon, or one of those huge fallow bucks. Hunting in Europe is a special treat. The food is fantastic, the people are friendly, and the wine isn't too bad either. The hunting? Well, you owe it to yourself to experience the enormous variety of opportunities Europe has to offer. The challenging and satisfying hunting rewards are a special part of European traditions.

Chapter 17

South America: Adventure South Of The Equator

You don't hear much about big game hunting in South America. This fascinating continent is home to the largest rain forest in the world. Argentina is known for its fantastic bird shooting. But big-game species that thrive in specialized habitats have declined as South America clears it forests and opens new areas for agriculture. While the continent is one of the last frontiers for big-game hunters, much of the pristine wilderness has been destroyed. The problem stems from the absence of sound conservation programs. With the absence of revenue generated from the sale of licenses or tags to help finance management practices, wildlife management is non-existent. In developing countries, an animal with no economic value is considered worthless.

I can't say those exact topics were on my mind as I was walking down the aisles looking at all the hunting booths during an SCI Convention. I just thought heading to South America would be an interesting experience.

After I got to talking with Paco, an outfitter from Argentina, I settled on a water buffalo and puma hunt. The water buffalo in Argentina do not have horns as big as the Australian variety, but they are just as large in body. The puma, or cougar as we call them, do not grow to the size as the ones found in North America, but are a challenge to hunt nevertheless. Both animals provide a good excuse to hunt South America, not that I needed an excuse.

Argentina is taking steps to overcome some of the problems associated with its wildlife management. Several species of game, including water buffalo, red stag, pigs, puma, brocket deer, and others, can be hunted. The landowners are beginning to realize the economic benefits of wildlife and are getting involved in conservation. It's not too late and I honestly believe the country will have a bright future of good hunting opportunities.

Going through customs in Buenos Aires was painless. I was packing two handguns for this hunt. My favorite .375 JDJ for the buffalo, and the Encore chambered in .308 Winchester for everything else. The handguns were packed inside a Bear Track gun case and never changed point of impact with all the travel requirements. A good gun case is money well spent no matter where you are headed.

Our hunt took us to the northern portion of Argentina, where we tried to stalk buffalo in the extremely tall weeds and thick vegetation. I really couldn't believe we were trying to sneak up to anything in the thick underbrush. Every time we bumped into a herd of buffalo, they would catch our scent and take off running. Most of the time I simply heard them running off, or saw the tops of the tall weeds move as buffalo left the area. I couldn't begin to determine a shootable bull in the dense, jungle-like growth and was hoping to catch one in one of the few clearings we found, but that was just wishful thinking. Shot placement was also a concern. If you can't see very well, how do you place your shot correctly? The last thing I wanted was to be following a wounded buffalo in this jungle. Both Carlos, our guide, and I had, in the past, been gored by wounded buffalo. I can't speak for Carlos, but I wasn't looking for another trip to the hospital with a punctured backside.

After many frustrating attempts, we finally got lucky. A herd of eight animals turned broadside about 45 yards away, finally giving me a decent shot. The largest bull was in the back of the herd and I had to wait for the cows to walk past as sweat popped out all over me. Seconds seemed like hours. When the big bull walked out, I held the crosshairs on his shoulder and squeezed the

Argentina is home to trophy-class red stags. Although smaller than elk, the red deer is challenging and fun to hunt. This bull was taken with a T/C in .375 JDJ from 150 yards using Hornady's 270-grain spire point.

This South American water buffalo provided a most challenging hunt in dense cover. A T/C Contender, in .375 JDJ using Hornady 270-grain spire points, did the job.

trigger. The 270-grain Hornady punched a hole in the bull's ribcage as we could see the dust fly. I reloaded quickly and put more lead in the big bull as he tried to keep up with the others. A few minutes later we were taking pictures of my first South American trophy.

With the big buffalo behind us now, I switched guns and carried the Encore for the remainder of the week. A Leupold 2-1/2X-8X scope was mounted on the .308 barrel. The gun liked Winchester's 168-grain Ballistic Supreme ammo. The Encore was fairly new at this time and I was anxious to give it a good workout. After shooting a few rounds at the range, we were ready to go hunting.

Even though I had booked a puma hunt along with the buffalo, I also wanted to hunt the little brocket found in this area. The gray-brown brocket deer is a relatively small deer weighing only 35 to 40 pounds. Their horns are only 3 to 5 inches long.

Several days of hunting from daylight until dark, turned up no male brocket deer. We tried everything and

While they do not grow impressive antlers like many deer species, the brocket deer can be very challenging to hunt. The author and his wife, Karen, traveled to Argentina for a chance to pursue these diminutive deer. An Encore in .308 with Winchester's 150-grain Ballistic Supreme bullets proved themselves on this South American hunt.

still no brocket deer. The roads were few and far between, just like the clearings. The thick undergrowth did not help matters any as the little deer could hide almost anywhere. Their dull brown color blended perfectly with the surroundings. A few females were seen but never a male. Late one evening we finally spotted a male feeding in one of the few clearings. I wasted no time getting a rest and placing the 168-grain factory fodder in the buck's vitals. The shot, not difficult at all, was only 45 yards away. It was the only male spotted during the entire trip. I was lucky! There have been very few brocket deer taken with a handgun. Even though an average coyote will outweigh most brocket deer, I was still very pleased with this South American trophy.

The South American cougar is somewhat smaller and lighter in color than those found in North America. As with most mammals, cougars found nearest to the equator tend to be smaller in size. However, that does not lessen the amount of excitement experienced when chasing these cats. The puma hunt was behind dogs and anytime you mix a bunch of dogs with a feline, the action tends to get heated.

The two gauchos, Chinco and Raoul, turned loose a pack of mix-breed dogs and a race was shortly underway. Just trying to keep up with a chase like this is exhilarating and tiring. It was late in the afternoon before we finally caught up with the dogs. Instead of climbing a tree as usual, the cougar was fighting the dogs on the ground and it was a hell of a battle. I tried to talk Karen into shooting this cat. She declined and informed me that I had better do something fast. Quickly I got into position and tried to put a stop to all this nonsense before the cat hurt one of the dogs. For a moment, I thought the puma might even jump on one of us. My wife was concerned and kept telling me to shoot. It was difficult to get a clean shot because the cat was always moving. At times, we were extremely close to the action. Perhaps too close! I wanted to end things quickly without anyone getting hurt, or accidentally shooting one of the dogs, which was certainly

Although not as large as the cats in North America, the South American puma is still exciting to hunt. Under most circumstances dogs are used, and this cat stopped to fight on the ground.

The white-lipped peccary is an aggressive pig that often attacks, and is capable of killing the dogs. These are vicious pigs that are exciting to hunt, especially with a handgun.

possible during all the commotion. When the cat finally gave me the opportunity, I put my first shot right behind his shoulder. The cat jumped toward one of the dogs, just missing with a swipe from his razor-sharp claws and quickly died. It was a heart-pounding moment that lasted just a few seconds, but will be remembered forever.

Back at camp we enjoyed the day's hunt with good wine and fine steaks. Camp consisted of a Spanish-style hacienda with a roaring fireplace. It was a perfect place to relax after a hard day's hunt. The Spanish-style cuisine was always delicious. Carlos, who was a bit of a world traveler himself, and I would discuss firearms and ballistics every evening around the fire. Hunting stories always lasted until midnight or after. Tall tales just seemed appropriate for the occasion.

We still had a few days left on the hunt and decided we would go after a white-lipped peccary. They are considerably larger than the collared peccary and a mature male will tip the scales between 60 and 80 pounds. The hunt gave us another opportunity to use the dogs again. These pigs are very aggressive and can rip a dog into pieces with absolutely no trouble.

An unusual aspect of this hunt is that I would have to ride, and shoot, from a horse. Now, I am not much of a horseman. Honestly, I don't even like horses and I do believe they can sense this. From the horse's perspective, I am certain the feeling is mutual.

The hunt went something like this: When the dogs jumped a pig they would chase it from one thicket to another as I rode in a feeble attempt to keep up. In the dense vegetation I would seldom see the pig, except when the porker would turn to attack the dogs. It was clear the dogs had played this game before, because they knew just when to retreat.

I wasn't thrilled with the idea of shooting from horseback, even though John Wayne made it look easy. Several times I asked Paco, "Are you sure this horse will one shot and didn't get thrown. Unbelievable! As I rode off into the sunset, smoking a cigar, I could hear the gauchos laughing at my equestrian skills, but the memories of the hunt will never fade.

The last day of our hunt found us sitting in a windmill blind waiting for a collared peccary, or javelina as they are sometimes called. Paco had talked me into trying for one of the pigs and I couldn't say no. About 15 feet or so up the windmill was a platform built with boards wired to the side. It was a rather primitive setup that resembled some of our old deer blinds. We were watching one of the only sources of water on the property. It seemed like a good place for a blind. I was actually hoping for a fairly long shot with the Encore in order to gain a little more experience with this handgun. It was late afternoon and the shadows began to cover the nearby hay field. Paco and I had glassed diligently for any sign of movement, but nothing showed. It had already been a good hunt and I wasn't expecting, or hoping, that a javelina would appear in order to make this hunt a success. As I sat there, waiting patiently, knocking a few biting insects away, Paco punched me on the leg. With only a few minutes of shooting light, a big javelina walked into the field we were watching. I checked the scope to see that it was on the 4X setting and placed the Encore on the side rail. I used my glove as a sandbag. After looking through his binos, Paco told me to take him right behind the shoulder. The pig was standing perfectly broadside with his head down feeding. When the hammer fell and sent Winchester's 168-grain Supreme bullet to its intended target, it ended a great South American hunting trip. The shot measured

Javelina, or collared peccary, provide handgun hunters with a lot of enjoyment. They are fun to hunt and can be pursued most any time of the year. This big pig was taken with an Encore in .308 Winchester.

not throw me when I shoot?" His reply was consistent, "Mark, trust me." Well, I didn't trust Paco and couldn't help anticipating the horse going crazy at the shot.

I was using a .44 Magnum Ruger Redhawk that Carlos wanted me to shoot. Trying to steady the revolver with one hand while holding the reins with the other, as the dogs were barking frantically, was quite the Argentina-style hunting experience. Of course the white-lipped peccary never stays in one place for very long. Just about the time I would get in a position to shoot, the vicious little porker would take off and I would try to keep up. Finally the aggressive pig came out of the bush to attack the dogs and I happened to be in the right place. Somehow I managed to make the first shot count. I couldn't believe it myself. The horse didn't seem to mind the loud noise and I had actually hit the pig with

Winchester 150-grain Ballistic Silvertip ammunition was used successfully during part of the South American hunting trip. The .308 Winchester is one cartridge that works well in an Encore and makes for an ideal handgun hunting round.

110 paces. It was not that difficult but, due to the approaching darkness, was all I wanted. I'm glad Paco talked me into hunting for a collared peccary.

Other South American Game

Argentina is also home to the red stag. These large-bodied deer are just a bit smaller than elk, but larger than a big mule deer. Mature stags can support heavy antlers with many points per side, commonly forming a crown at the top of the main beam. Red stag are popular with hunters as they are challenging to hunt and their venison is delicious. The red stags I have taken were with 7mm, .30, and .375 caliber handguns. A well-placed shot with a bullet that will perform on these big-bodied deer is necessary. When stags go into rut, they roar, which is similar to the elk's bugle. Even though I have never had the pleasure of hunting them in the rut, they have always provided a great experience and challenging stalks.

Other species commonly pursued by hunters in South America include feral goat, mouflon sheep, blackbuck antelope, axis deer, and feral hogs. Some of these are hunted on large, private estates. There is plenty of game to keep a person busy while enjoying the warm hospitality of the South American people. And you don't have to speak Spanish to enjoy the country. Plenty of adventuresome hunters overlook Argentina. They shouldn't. The people are friendly, handgun hunters are welcome, and there is a diversity of game to be hunted. What else could you want?

Chapter 18

The Et Cetera Of Handgun Hunting

There is certainly no shortage of things to talk about with regard to handgun hunting. Guns, accessories, tactics, locations, you name it and someone will have an opinion or two on the topic. Throughout this book I've made reference to using guns and ammo from SSK. The JDJ calibers have served me well over the years, but they are by no means the only ones available or suitable for handgun hunting. J.D. Jones makes some great guns and has developed ammunition that brings outstanding performance to the shooting bench and the field. So have some other custom gun makers. A few who come to mind include John Linebaugh in Cody, Wyo., Hamilton Bowen in Tennessee, Jack Huntington in Grass Valley, Cal., and Gary Reeder in Flagstaff, Ariz. Reeder alone has developed several different wildcat cartridges and a great muzzle brake. And, as I said before, the Linebaugh rounds are now commercially manufactured. That's a testament to not only the quality of the guns, but their popularity as well. The long and short

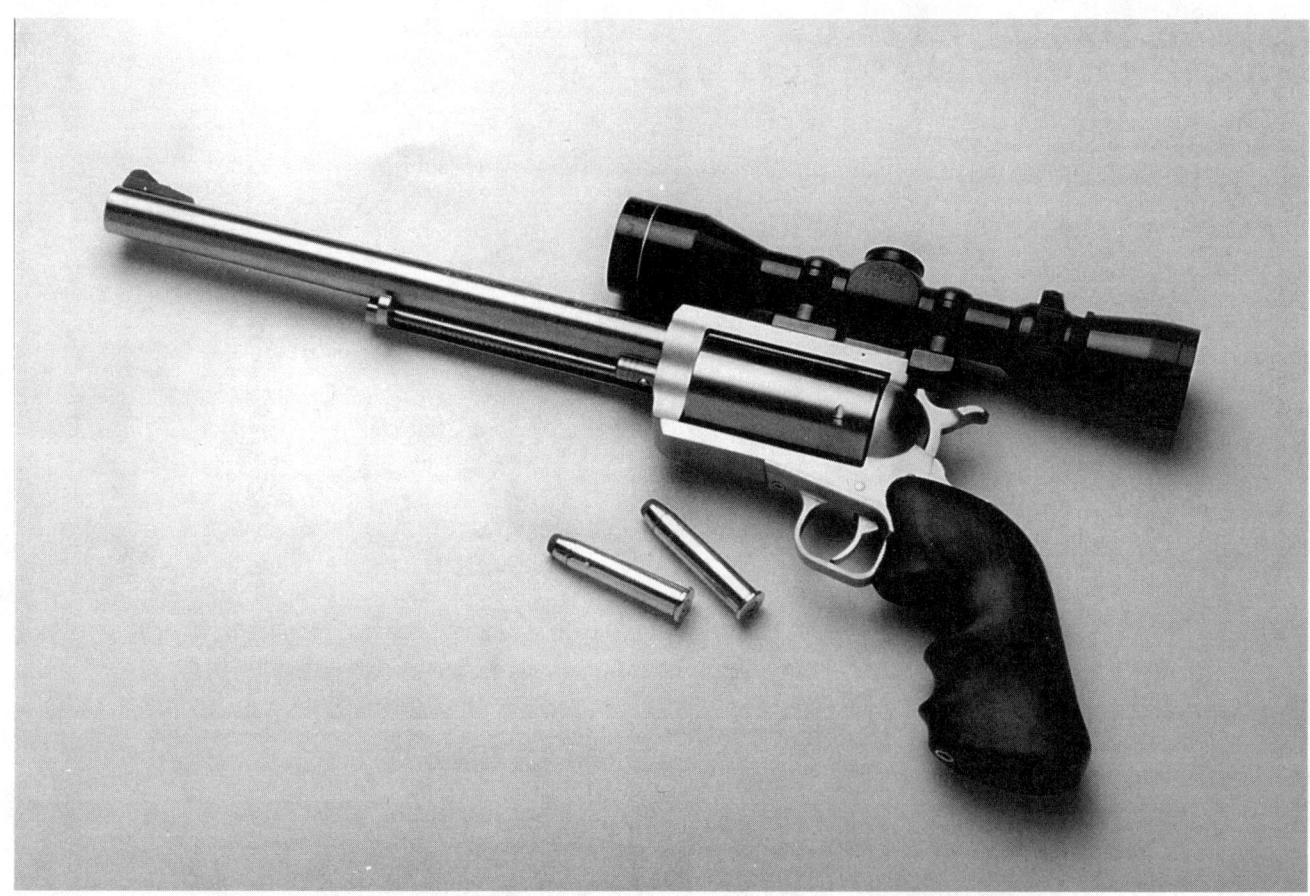

The new BFR revolver from Magnum Research is available in .45-70, .444 Marlin, .454 Casull, .22 Hornet, and .45 Long Colt. The company plans to add .480 Ruger and .450 Marlin to the line in the near future.

A spotting scope can be a valuable asset for handgun hunting. Using one allows you determine trophy quality before setting up a stalk. It could save you miles of walking.

of it is this: If you want to find a hunting handgun, there are plenty of places to look.

On the commercial side Ruger and Hornady have teamed up on the new .480 Ruger. This round was developed by Steve Hornady and ballistically speaking, lies in between the two other cartridges. Unfortunately, I have been unable to use this new cartridge on game but it should make an excellent round for the whitetail, black bear, or hog hunting enthusiast. It should be able to take game every bit as effectively as the other two revolver rounds. I seriously doubt if it will take the place of either the .44 Mag. or the .454 Casull, and only time will tell if makes a permanent place into the handgun hunter's battery. I do think that Ruger and Hornady have come up with a good concept within this new offering.

Previously, I also mentioned that Magnum Research has introduced a five-shot revolver with a 10-inch barrel the company dubs as their BFR. I know what you're thinking and no, the company says that stands for the "Biggest Finest Revolver." For those of you out there wishing for a .45-70 revolver, this just may be what you have been looking for. This major-league revolver is also available in .450 Marlin. If you are one of those shooters looking for abrupt recoil, this is just what the doctor ordered. It will bring down just about anything you can get close enough to shoot.

And that brings us to recoil. Some of these calibers produce a considerable amount of recoil. How do you cope with recoil? You do your best to tame it. Most of my guns are Mag-Na-Ported or are fitted with an SSK Arrestor brake on the muzzle. Again, there are as many different muzzle brakes as there are custom gunsmiths. Porting or a muzzle brake will redirect some of the propellant gas to reduce the recoil and control the muzzle.

Good grips will not only help tame recoil, they can improve your accuracy. Just about every gun on the market can be fitted with aftermarket grips. And you can have your choice of materials from molded rubber to exotic woods. The key is to get something that feels good. The choice is completely personal, but very important because trouble with recoil can lead to a flinch. That means you'll miss more often and no one wants that.

Most of us flinch at some time in our shooting career. This is a terrible habit that is very hard to break. I have found most flinching occurs as a result of excessive noise from the muzzle blast or anticipating heavy recoil. Without proper ear protection, flinching will only get worse. It is strongly recommended that you always wear ear protection when shooting, and that includes .22 rimfire. Some shooters wear both plugs and muffs to give added protection.

Another way to overcome a flinch is to practice regularly with small-caliber pistols or low-power handloads. The system allows you to practice with the idea of eliminating your flinch, then moving up to the full-power loads.

The right mind-set is also an important aspect when shooting a large handgun. Even though this sounds simplistic, just before the shot I tell myself the gun is not going to hurt me. Most of the time I am right. Confidence gained through a lot of shooting is another key to good shot placement. If you know what your gun is going to do when the hammer falls, you'll be less likely to flinch and pull the shot off target.

What You See Is What You Get

Many beginning handgun hunters often ask about the best sights for a particular handgun. I have always let the circumstance decide this question for me. If I am following a pack of dogs and plan on the action being fast and up close, or stalking game in heavy cover where the shot will be inside 50 yards, open sights are the natural choice. Sight styles are almost unlimited, but I would strongly suggest adjustable sights, especially for anyone who reloads. Changes in ballistics will change point of impact and it is far better to adjust your sights than to change your load.

The down side of open sights is that as you age, the sights get harder to see and use. Aging eyes will enjoy quality optics. For close-range work, use one of the red-

A range finder is an important item for many hunts. It takes the guesswork out of the game. Still, hunters must know where the bullet hits at various yardages or the optical tool is of little value.

dot systems. These don't provide any magnification, and make for excellent close-range aiming. In the past, red-dot systems were often made specifically for competitive action shooting. Today, there are many fine red-dot sights that will work great for hunting.

When it comes to scopes, most beginning handgun hunters will benefit by choosing a 2X scope. Shooting a scoped handgun can be tough to get used to, so start with low power and a small caliber weapon and gain experience by shooting a lot. A good .22 rimfire is a great way to get started, and the ammo is not so hard on the pocketbook. It takes time and experience to get accustomed to the critical eye relief situation with handgun scopes, and target acquisition can be slow at first. Once the hunter gets familiar with the ins and outs, many other scope options are available including a straight 3X or 4X, or one of the many variables available. I currently use the 2X-6X from Bausch and Lomb, 2-1/2X-8X Leupold, and 3X-12X Burris. There are many other quality optics available today including those from Simmons, Tasco, Nikon, and others. Even though I seldom hunt with the scope set on its highest setting, I like to have that power at my fingertips when testing a gun and ammo for accuracy. In general, the scope also allows the hunter a better view of when to shoot, or not to shoot. With traditional iron sights you seldom see obstructions like limbs or brush that could deflect a bullet. Using a good scope, I have on several occasions been able to hold off after seeing a limb in the bullet path, thus waiting for a good, clear shot. The older I get, the more I rely on quality optics.

In order to give the shooter years of enjoyment, the scope must be mounted properly. That means a good base mount secured properly on the gun is crucial. I have used the T'SOB base mount from SSK Industries for years and have never had a problem to date. There are several manufacturers of top-quality scope mounts and your goal is to get one that fits your gun, your needs and your pocketbook. Most of my guns, especially those with considerable recoil, utilize three rings for added insurance. If you do not feel confident mounting a scope by yourself, make certain a reputable gunsmith does it for you. Once you have secured the scope with a good base mount and rings, you can be assured the gun will perform at its best as far as optics are concerned.

While we are on the subject of optics, one piece of equipment I never leave home without is a range finder. I have never considered myself a lover of gadgets, but this is one item that comes in handy on many excursions. The first range finders to hit the market several years ago were fairly large. Today, I use a Bushnell Pro Scout that weighs less than 7 ounces and fits easily into a shirt pocket. There is really no reason for not having one of these items in your pack or coat during any hunt. When shooting game at extended ranges, judging distance becomes critical for any handgun hunter, and the range finder eliminates the

A good holster allows the hunter to use both hands freely. It also can help protect your handgun from the elements.

guesswork. When I am sitting in a deer blind, I like to have reference points such as an old tree, fence post, big rock, or any other object, and know exactly how far they are away from the stand. When a deer shows up near one of these objects, I have a pretty good idea of how far away he is and can hold accordingly. I may not know the exact distance, but I will be close. When time permits, it is really nice to be able to get a reading

Handgun hunters travel all over the world. They also hunt in their backyards. Wherever you decide to hunt, tackling game with a handgun will be full of challenges and rewards.

Shooting sticks come in all sorts of shapes and sizes. They sure do help hunters place shots accurately.

on the animal you are about to harvest, then you know exactly how far you will be shooting.

Knowing the distance is important for long range shooting but it's really only half the equation. If you do not know where your bullet will strike at different ranges, 100, 150, 200, 250, or 300 yards, you are still playing a guessing game. It is crucial that you become familiar with the trajectory of your bullet, and where your gun shoots at various ranges. The key word in that last sentence is "your" gun. It pays big dividends to know where "your" gun shoots, and not go by what some book says, or what your buddy tells you. Once you know the approximate distance at which you will be shooting, and know where your gun and load shoot at this range, you have eliminated the guesswork. The chances of making a clean, one-shot kill are thereby enhanced.

Ammunition Is Key

There has never been as much high-quality ammunition, utilizing premium bullets, available for the handgun hunter as there is today. Ammunition manufacturers are providing shooters with an array of different bullet weights, in a variety of shapes and configurations, for wildly diverse applications. The big ammo makers are producing ammunition for everything from varmints to elephants. Years ago if you wanted a specific load, with a particular bullet in mind for that special hunt, you were forced to reload the ammo yourself. Today, the handloader is hard-pressed to duplicate many of factory rounds currently available. Handloaders can only dream about some of the powders that ammunition manufacturers use every day. So, if you don't reload, and don't want to get started making your own ammo, don't despair. I have a room full of factory ammo from Winchester, Black Hills Ammunition, Federal, and Hornady Custom Ammo. They all produce quality ammunition for hunters.

Packing Heat

What's the best way to carry your favorite hunting handgun? I'm somewhat reluctant to say because over the years I have probably spent in excess of $1,000 on different holsters and I'm still searching today for the right one. For revolvers that are not scoped, I do appreciate the cross-draw style. Wearing one of these models I find that bending over, sneaking around the woods in thick brush, or getting in and out of the vehicle is very easy, and non-binding. There are a ton of options out there, from expensive hand-tooled leather to the less expensive synthetic models, and everyone will have a different opinion on what works best. For larger handguns, especially those scoped single-shots, some variety of shoulder rig with the weight distributed as evenly as possible is usually best. I've often carried my handgun in my hand, or placed it in a gun case with a sling attached to the case. By all means, use whatever works best for you and the manner in which you intend to hunt.

Take A Rest

Experienced handgun hunters are constantly looking for a means to rest their firearm and steady the sights for precise bullet placement. I don't like to shoot offhand unless there is no other option. When the opportunity and time allows, I am certainly looking for a rest. Handgun hunters can come up with array of possibilities and

Yes, handguns are more difficult to shoot accurately than rifles. Look for ways to rest your handgun and make the first shot count.

This 9-inch square steel target is an asset for practice sessions. If you can place your bullet in the 9-inch area, from various ranges, you can hit the vitals of a big game animal.

they all serve the same purpose, to ensure a quick, humane kill. When the terrain allows, my favorite way to rest the handgun is off my backpack. This makes for a steady rest especially in mountain terrain where there is little if any brush. There are times when tall grass or vegetation will obstruct your line of sight. It is then that other alternatives come into action. Shooting sticks are a great asset in this type of environment. I normally carry a pair of shooting sticks when I'm faced with a situation that does not permit the use of the backpack. Other good choices that include anything available; be it a stump, fence post, termite mound, tree limb, or anything else you can use to aid in the quest of keeping your sights steady.

Accurate pistol shooting also requires breath control. Have you ever watched someone who really knows how to shoot a rifle? Watch a dedicated varmint shooter or bench rest enthusiast; someone who is a better-than-average rifle shot. Notice his breathing. Accuracy is improved when most of the air is exhaled from the lungs, leaving just a bit of air, and the breath is held while squeezing the trigger. Personally, I exhale somewhere between three-fourths to seven-eights of the air in my lungs, then hold my breath while squeezing the trigger. Depending on your age, physical condition, and other factors, you may have somewhere around six or seven seconds to get the shot off before we begin to feel uncomfortable. This is more than enough time to steady the crosshairs and squeeze off a round. If you haven't taken the shot within six to eight seconds, you probably need to catch your breath and start all over again. Practicing good breathing techniques will help you become a better handgun shooter.

Mechanically Speaking

A gritty, hard-to-pull trigger makes shooting accurately a real challenge. I have witnessed world-class handgun shooters struggle when shooting a handgun with a horrible trigger, so you can imagine what the rest of us have to overcome. We are living in a time when excessive litigation has prompted manufacturers to make trigger pull heavier than is desirable for accuracy. They do this with the idea of reducing accidents and protecting themselves from lawsuits. This could be considered good news for the gunsmithing business because it is next to impossible to obtain an acceptable trigger from the factory these days.

For the shooter, this means you should have a reputable gunsmith work on the trigger, not some shade-tree mechanic. I prefer the trigger pull on most of my hunting handguns to be less than three pounds, with a clean, consistent, crisp break. If I hunted strictly in warm weather, which I do not, I would have the trigger pull set at about two pounds. Unfortunately, a light trigger pull in cold weather is not safe and could lead to an accidental discharge.

If you are genuinely interested in becoming a better handgun shooter, and want to get serious about handgun hunting, there is absolutely no substitute for practice. Shooting is a physical skill and the only way to get more proficient is by practicing, correctly, over and over again. The best way to start is by choosing a good .22 rimfire. You can shoot all day long and you won't have to take out a loan to pay for the ammunition. Also, I enjoy shooting from actual field positions that will be used in real-life hunting situations. I often practice with my backpack as a rest or use the shooting sticks I carry in the field. To build your skills, you have to practice with a purpose. Shoot from several different positions and sometimes choose targets that accurately represent the game you seek. When was the last time you had a big black bull's-eye to shoot at while hunting? Shooting builds confidence. Confidence, in turn, makes you a better shot.

Finally, I want to stress the important role we as hunters play in wildlife conservation. It is hunters who actually pay for conservation. The anti-hunting fraternity will put on a "dog and pony show" but in reality do little to promote the well-being of sustainable wildlife practices. Don't ever be ashamed of being called a hunter!

THE ARMS LIBRARY

Books listed here may be bought from Ray Riling Arms Books Co., 6844 Gorsten St., P.O. Box 18925, Philadelphia, PA 19119, Phone 215/438-2456; FAX: 215-438-5395. E-Mail: sales@rayrilingarmsbooks.com. Joe Riling is the researcher and compiler of "The Arms Library" and a seller of gun books for over 32 years. The Riling stock includes books classic and modern, many hard-to-find items, and many not obtainable elsewhere. These pages list a portion of the current stock. They offer prompt, complete service, with delayed shipments occurring only on out-of-print or out-of-stock books.

Visit our web site at **www.rayrilingarmsbooks.com** and order all of your favorite titles on line from our secure site.

NOTICE FOR ALL CUSTOMERS: Remittance in U.S. funds must accompany all orders. For your convenience we now accept VISA, MasterCard & American Express. For shipments in the U.S. add $7.00 for the 1st book and $2.00 for each additional book for postage and insurance. Minimum order $10.00. International Orders add $13.00 for the 1st book and $5.00 for each additional book. All International orders are shipped at the buyer's risk unless an additional $5 for insurance is included. USPS does not offer insurance to all countries unless shipped Air-Mail please e-mail or call for pricing.

Payments in excess of order or for "Backorders" are credited or fully refunded at request. Books "As-Ordered" are not returnable except by permission and a handling charge on these of 10% or $2.00 per book which ever is greater is deducted from refund or credit. Only Pennsylvania customers must include current sales tax.

A full variety of arms books also available from Rutgers Book Center, 127 Raritan Ave., Highland Park, NJ 08904/908-545-4344; FAX: 908-545-6686 or I.D.S.A. Books, 1324 Stratford Drive, Piqua, OH 45356/937-773-4203; FAX: 937-778-1922.

HANDGUNS

Advanced Master Handgunning, by Charles Stephens, Paladin Press, Boulder, CO., 1994. 72 pp., illus. Paper covers. $14.00.
Secrets and surefire techniques for winning handgun competitions.

American Beauty: The Prewar Colt National Match Government Model Pistol, by Timothy Mullin, Collector Grade Publications, Canada, 1999. 72 pp., 69 illus. $34.95
69 illustrations, 20 in full color photos of factory engraved guns and other authenticated upgrades, including rare 'double-carved' ivory grips.

Axis Pistols: WORLD WAR TWO 50 YEARS COMMEMORATIVE ISSUE, by Jan C. Stills, Walsworth Publishing, 1989. 360 pages, illus. $59.95

The Ayoob Files: The Book, by Massad Ayoob, Police Bookshelf, Concord, NH, 1995. 223 pp., illus. Paper covers. $14.95.
The best of Massad Ayoob's acclaimed series in American Handgunner magazine.

Big Bore Sixguns, by John Taffin, Krause Publications, Iola, WI, 1997. 336 pp., illus. $39.95.
The author takes aim on the entire range of big bores from .357 Magnums to .500 Maximums, single actions and cap-and-ball sixguns to custom touches for big bores..

The Browning High Power Automatic Pistol (Expanded Edition), by Blake R. Stevens, Collector Grade Publications, Canada, 1996. 310 pages, with 313 illus. $49.95
An in-depth chronicle of seventy years of High Power history, from John M Browning's original 16-shot prototypes to the present. Profusely illustrated with rare original photos and drawings from the FN Archive to describe virtually every sporting and military version of the High Power. The numerous modifications made to the basic design over the years are, for the first time, accurately arranged in chronological order, thus permitting the dating of any High Power to within a few years of its production. Full details on the WWII Canadian-made Inglis Browning High Power pistol. The Expanded Edition contains 30 new pages on the interesting Argentine full-auto High Power, the latest FN 'MK3' and BDA9 pistols, plus FN's revolutionary P90 5.7x28mm Personal Defence Weapon, and more!

Browning Hi-Power Pistols, Desert Publications, Cornville, AZ, 1982. 20 pp., illus. Paper covers. $11.95.
Covers all facets of the various military and civilian models of the Browning Hi-Power pistol.

Canadian Military Handguns 1855-1985, by Clive M. Law, Museum Restoration Service, Bloomfield, Ont. Canada, 1994. 130pp., illus. $40.00.
A long-awaited and important history for arms historians and pistol collectors.

The Colt .45 Auto Pistol, compiled from U.S. War Dept. Technical Manuals, and reprinted by Desert Publications, Cornville, AZ, 1978. 80 pp., illus. Paper covers. $11.95.
Covers every facet of this famous pistol from mechanical training, manual of arms, disassembly, repair and replacement of parts.

Colt Automatic Pistols, by Donald B. Bady, Pioneer Press, Union City, TN, 1999. 368 pp., illustrated. Softcover. $19.95.
A revised and enlarged edition of a key work on a fascinating subject. Complete information on every Colt automatic pistol.

Combat Handgunnery, 4th Edition, by Chuck Taylor, DBI Books, a division of Krause Publications, Iola, WI, 1997. 256 pp., illus. Paper covers. $18.95.
This all-new edition looks at real world combat handgunnery from three different perspectives—military, police and civilian. Available, October, 1996.

Combat Revolvers, by Duncan Long, Paladin Press, Boulder, CO, 1999, 8 1/2 x 11, soft cover, 115 photos, 152 pp. $21.95
This is an uncompromising look at modern combat revolvers. All the major foreign and domestic guns are covered: the Colt Python, S&W Model 29, Ruger GP 100 and hundreds more. Know the gun that you may one day stake your life on.

The Complete Book of Combat Handgunning, by Chuck Taylor, Desert Publications, Cornville, AZ, 1982. 168 pp., illus. Paper covers. $20.00.
Covers virtually every aspect of combat handgunning.

Complete Guide to Compact Handguns, by Gene Gangarosa, Jr., Stoeger Publishing Co., Wayne, NJ, 1997. 228 pp., illus. Paper covers. $22.95.
Includes hundreds of compact firearms, along with text results conducted by the author.

Complete Guide to Service Handguns, by Gene Gangarosa, Jr., Stoeger Publishing Co., Wayne, NJ, 1998. 320 pp., illus. Paper covers. $22.95.
The author explores the revolvers and pistols that are used around the globe by military, law enforcement and civilians.

The Custom Government Model Pistol, by Layne Simpson, Wolfe Publishing Co., Prescott, AZ, 1994. 639 pp., illus. Paper covers. $24.50.
The book about one of the world's greatest firearms and the things pistolsmiths do to make it even greater.

The CZ-75 Family: The Ultimate Combat Handgun, by J.M. Ramos, Paladin Press, Boulder, CO, 1990. 100 pp., illus. Soft covers. $25.00.
An in-depth discussion of the early-and-late model CZ-75s, as well as the many newest additions to the Czech pistol family.

Encyclopedia of Pistols & Revolvers, by A.E. Hartnik, Knickerbocker Press, New York, NY, 1997. 272 pp., illus. $19.95.
A comprehensive encyclopedia specially written for collectors and owners of pistols and revolvers.

Experiments of a Handgunner, by Walter Roper, Wolfe Publishing Co., Prescott, AZ, 1989. 202 pp., illus. $37.00.
A limited edition reprint. A listing of experiments with functioning parts of handguns, with targets, stocks, rests, handloading, etc.

The Farnam Method of Defensive Handgunning, by John S. Farnam, Police Bookshelf, 1999. 191 pp., illus. Paper covers. $25.00
A book intended to not only educate the new shooter, but also to serve as a guide and textbook for his and his instructor's training courses.

Fast and Fancy Revolver Shooting, by Ed. McGivern, Anniversary Edition, Winchester Press, Piscataway, NJ, 1984. 484 pp., illus. $18.95.
A fascinating volume, packed with handgun lore and solid information by the acknowledged dean of revolver shooters.

.45 ACP Super Guns, by J.M. Ramos, Paladin Press, Boulder, CO, 1991. 144 pp., illus. Paper covers. $24.00.
Modified .45 automatic pistols for competition, hunting and personal defense.

The .45, The Gun Digest Book of, by Dean A. Grennell, DBI Books, a division of Krause Publications, Iola, WI, 1989. 256 pp., illus. Paper covers. $17.95.
Definitive work on one of America's favorite calibers.

Glock: The New Wave in Combat Handguns, by Peter Alan Kasler, Paladin Press, Boulder, CO, 1993. 304 pp., illus. $27.00.
Kasler debunks the myths that surround what is the most innovative handgun to be introduced in some time.

THE ARMS LIBRARY

Glock's Handguns, by Duncan Long, Desert Publications, El Dorado, AR, 1996. 180 pp., illus. Paper covers. $18.95.
An outstanding volume on one of the world's newest and most successful firearms of the century.

Hand Cannons: The World's Most Powerful Handguns, by Duncan Long, Paladin Press, Boulder, CO, 1995. 208 pp., illus. Paper covers. $22.00.
Long describes and evaluates each powerful gun according to their features.

The Handgun, by Geoffrey Boothroyd, Safari Press, Inc., Huntington Beach, CA, 1999. 566 pp., illustrated. $50.00.
A very detailed history of the handgun. Now revised and a completely new chapter written to take account of developments since the 1970 edition.

Handguns 2002, 13th Edition, edited by Harold A. Murtz, DBI Books a division of Krause Publications, Iola, WI, 1999. 352 pp., illustrated. Paper covers. $22.95.
Top writers in the handgun industry give you a complete report on new handgun developments, testfire reports on the newest introductions and previews on what's ahead.

Handgun Digest, 3rd Edition, edited by Chris Christian, DBI Books, a division of Krause Publications, Iola, WI, 1995. 256 pp., illus. Paper covers. $18.95.
Full coverage of all aspects of handguns and handgunning from a highly readable and knowledgeable author.

Handgun Reloading, The Gun Digest Book of, by Dean A. Grennell and Wiley M. Clapp, DBI Books, a division of Krause Publications, Iola, WI, 1987. 256 pp., illus. Paper covers. $16.95.
Detailed discussions of all aspects of reloading for handguns, from basic to complex. New loading data.

Handgun Stopping Power "The Definitive Study", by Evan P. Marshall & Edwin J. Sanow, Paladin Press, Boulder, CO, 1997, soft cover, photos, 240 pp. $45.00
Dramatic first-hand accounts of the results of handgun rounds fired into criminals by cops, storeowners, cabbies and others are the heart and soul of this long-awaited book. This is the definitive methodology for predicting the stopping power of handgun loads, the first to take into account what really happens when a bullet meets a man.

Heckler & Koch's Handguns, by Duncan Long, Desert Publications, El Dorado, AR, 1996. 142 pp., illus. Paper covers. $19.95.
Traces the history and the evolution of H&K's pistols from the company's beginning at the end of WWII to the present.

Hidden in Plain Sight, by Trey Bloodworth & Mike Raley, Professional Press, Chapel Hill, NC, 1995. Paper covers. $19.95.
A practical guide to concealed handgun carry.

High Standard Automatic Pistols 1932-1950, by Charles E. Petty, The Gunroom Press, Highland Park, NJ, 1989. 124 pp., illus. $19.95.
A definitive source of information for the collector of High Standard arms.

Hi-Standard Pistols and Revolvers, 1951-1984, by James Spacek, James Spacek, Chesire, CT, 1998. 128 pp., illustrated. Paper covers. $12.50.
Technical details, marketing features and instruction/parts manual of every model High Standard pistol and revolver made between 1951 and 1984. Most accurate serial number information available.

The Hi-Standard Pistol Guide, by Burr Leyson, Duckett's Sporting Books, Tempe AZ, 1995. 128 pp., illus. Paper covers. $22.00.
Complete information on selection, care and repair, ammunition, parts, and accessories.

How to Become a Master Handgunner: The Mechanics of X-Count Shooting, by Charles Stephens, Paladin Press, Boulder, CO, 1993. 64 pp., illus. Paper covers. $14.00.
Offers a simple formula for success to the handgunner who strives to master the technique of shooting accurately.

Hunting for Handgunners, by Larry Kelly and J.D. Jones, DBI Books, a division of Krause Publications, Iola, WI, 1990. 256 pp., illus. Paper covers. $16.95.
Covers the entire spectrum of hunting with handguns in an amusing, easy-flowing manner that combines entertainment with solid information.

Illustrated Encyclopedia of Handguns, by A.B. Zhuk, Stackpole Books, Mechanicsburg, PA, 1994. 256 pp., illus. Cloth cover, $49.95
Identifies more than 2,000 military and commercial pistols and revolvers with details of more than 100 popular handgun cartridges.

The Inglis Diamond: The Canadian High Power Pistol, by Clive M. Law, Collector Grade Publications, Canada, 2001. 312 pp., illustrated. $49.95
This definitive work on Canada's first and indeed only mass produced handgun, in production for a very brief span of time and consequently made in relatively few numbers, the venerable Inglis-made Browning High Power covers the pistol's initial history, the story of Chinese and British adoption, use post-war by Holland, Australia, Greece, Belgium, New Zealand, Peru, Brasil and other countries. All new information on the famous light-weights and the Inglis Diamond variations. Completely researched through official archives in a dozen countries. Many of the bewildering variety of markings have never been satisfactorily explained until now. Also included are many photos of holsters and accessories.

Instinct Combat Shooting, by Chuck Klein, The Goose Creek, IN, 1989. 49 pp., illus. Paper covers. $12.00.
Defensive handgunning for police.

Know Your Czechoslovakian Pistols, by R.J. Berger, Blacksmith Corp., Chino Valley, AZ, 1989. 96 pp., illus. Soft covers. $12.95.
A comprehensive reference which presents the fascinating story of Czech pistols.

Know Your 45 Auto Pistols—Models 1911 & A1, by E.J. Hoffschmidt, Blacksmith Corp., Southport, CT, 1974. 58 pp., illus. Paper covers. $12.95.
A concise history of the gun with a wide variety of types and copies.

Know Your Walther P38 Pistols, by E.J. Hoffschmidt, Blacksmith Corp., Southport, CT, 1974. 77 pp., illus. Paper covers. $12.95.
Covers the Walther models Armee, M.P., H.P., P.38—history and variations.

Know Your Walther PP & PPK Pistols, by E.J. Hoffschmidt, Blacksmith Corp., Southport, CT, 1975. 87 pp., illus. Paper covers. $12.95.
A concise history of the guns with a guide to the variety and types.

La Connaissance du Luger, Tome 1, by Gerard Henrotin, H & L Publishing, Belguim, 1996. 144 pages, illustrated. $45.00.
(The Knowledge of Luger, Volume 1, translated.) B&W and Color photo's. French text.

The Luger Handbook, by Aarron Davis, Krause Publications, Iola, WI, 1997. 112 pp., illus. Paper covers. $9.95.
Now you can identify any of the legendary Luger variations using a simple decision tree. Each model and variation includes pricing information, proof marks and detailed attributes in a handy, user-friendly format. Plus, it's fully indexed. Instantly identify that Luger!

Lugers of Ralph Shattuck, by Ralph Shattuck, Peoria, AZ, 2000. 49 pages, illus. Hardcover. $29.95.
49 pages, illustrated with maps and full color photos of here to now never before shown photos of some of the rarest lugers ever. Written by one of the world's renowned collectors. A MUST have book for any Luger collector.

Lugers at Random (Revised Format Edition), by Charles Kenyon, Jr., Handgun Press, Glenview, IL, 2000. 420 pp., illus. $59.95.
A new printing of this classic, comprehensive reference for all Luger collectors.

The Luger Story, by John Walter, Stackpole Books, Mechanicsburg, PA, 2001. 256 pp., illus. Paper Covers. $29.95.
The standard history of the world's most famous handgun.

The Mauser Self-Loading Pistol, by Belford & Dunlap, Borden Publ. Co., Alhambra, CA. Over 200 pp., 300 illus., large format. $29.95.
The long-awaited book on the "Broom Handles," covering their inception in 1894 to the end of production. Complete and in detail: pocket pistols, Chinese and Spanish copies, etc.

9mm Handguns, 2nd Edition, The Gun Digest Book of, edited by Steve Comus, DBI Books, a division of Krause Publications, Iola, WI, 1993. 256 pp., illus. Paper covers. $18.95.
Covers the 9mm cartridge and the guns that have been made for it in greater depth than any other work available.

9mm Parabellum; The History & Development of the World's 9mm Pistols & Ammunition, by Klaus-Peter Konig and Martin Hugo, Schiffer Publishing Ltd., Atglen, PA, 1993. 304 pp., illus. $39.95.
Detailed history of 9mm weapons from Belguim, Italy, Germany, Israel, France, USA, Czechoslovakia, Hungary, Poland, Brazil, Finland and Spain.

The Official 9mm Markarov Pistol Manual, translated into English by Major James Gebhardt, U.S. Army (Ret.), Desert Publications, El Dorado, AR, 1996. 84 pp., illus. Paper covers. $12.95.
The information found in this book will be of enormous benefit and interest to the owner or a prospective owner of one of these pistols.

The Official Soviet 7.62mm Handgun Manual, by Translation by Maj. James F. Gebhardt Ret.), Paladin Press, Boulder, CO, 1997, soft cover, illus. 104 pp. $20.00
This Soviet military manual, now available in English for the first time, covers instructions for use and maintenance of two side arms, the Nagant 7.62mm revolver, used by the Russian tsarist armed forces and later the Soviet armed forces, and the Tokarev7.62mm semi-auto pistol, which replaced the Nagant.

P-38 Automatic Pistol, by Gene Gangarosa, Jr., Stoeger Publishing Co., S. Hackensack, NJ, 1993. 272 pp., illus. Paper covers. $16.95
This book traces the origins and development of the P-38, including the momentous political forces of the World War II era that caused its near demise and, later, its rebirth.

The P-38 Pistol: The Walther Pistols, 1930-1945. Volume 1. by Warren Buxton, Ucross Books, Los Alamos, MN 1999. $68.50
A limited run reprint of this scarce and sought-after work on the P-38 Pistol. 328 pp. with 160 illustrations.

The P-38 Pistol: The Contract Pistols, 1940-1945. Volume 2. by Warren Buxton, Ucross Books, Los Alamos, MN 1999. 256 pp. with 237 illustrations. $68.50

The Arms Library

The P-38 Pistol: Postwar Distributions, 1945-1990. Volume 3. by Warren Buxton, Ucross Books, Los Alamos, MN 1999. $68.50
Plus an addendum to Volumes 1 & 2. 272 pp. with 342 illustrations.

PARABELLUM - A Technical History of Swiss Lugers, by V. Bobba, Italy.1998. 224pp, profuse color photos, large format. $100.00.
The is the most beautifully illustrated and well-documented book on the Swiss Lugers yet produced. This splendidly produced book features magnificent images while giving an incredible amount of detail on the Swiss Luger. In-depth coverage of key issues include: the production process, pistol accessories, charts with serial numbers, production figures, variations, markings, patent drawings, etc. Covers the Swiss Luger story from 1894 when the first Bergmann-Schmeisser models were tested till the commercial model 1965. Shows every imaginable production variation in amazing detail and full color! A must for all Luger collectors. This work has been produced in an extremely attractive package using quality materials throughout and housed in a protective slipcase.

Pistols and Revolvers, by Jean-Noel Mouret, Barns and Noble, Rockleigh, N.J., 1999. 141 pp., illustrated. $12.98.
Here in glorious display is the master guidebook to flintlocks, minatures, the Sig P-210 limited edition, the Springfield Trophy Master with Aimpoint 5000 telescopic sight, every major classic and contemporary handgun, complete with their technical data.

Report of Board on Tests of Revolvers and Automatic Pistols, From the Annual Report of the Chief of Ordnance, 1907. Reprinted by J.C. Tillinghast, Marlow, NH, 1969. 34 pp., 7 plates, paper covers. $9.95.
A comparison of handguns, including Luger, Savage, Colt, Webley-Fosbery and other makes.

Ruger Automatic Pistols and Single Action Revolvers, by Hugo A. Lueders, edited by Don Findley, Blacksmith Corp., Chino Valley, AZ, 1993. 79 pp., illus. Paper covers. $14.95.
The definitive work on Ruger automatic pistols and single action revolvers.

The Ruger "P" Family of Handguns, by Duncan Long, Desert Publications, El Dorado, AZ, 1993. 128 pp., illus. Paper covers. $14.95.
A full-fledged documentary on a remarkable series of Sturm Ruger handguns.

The Ruger .22 Automatic Pistol, Standard/Mark I/Mark II Series, by Duncan Long, Paladin Press, Boulder, CO, 1989. 168 pp., illus. Paper covers. $16.00.
The definitive book about the pistol that has served more than 1 million owners so well.

The Semiautomatic Pistols in Police Service and Self Defense, by Massad Ayoob, Police Bookshelf, Concord, NH, 1990. 25 pp., illus. Soft covers. $9.95.
First quantitative, documented look at actual police experience with 9mm and 45 police service automatics.

The Sharpshooter—How to Stand and Shoot Handgun Metallic Silhouettes, by Charles Stephens, Yucca Tree Press, Las Cruces, NM, 1993. 86 pp., illus. Paper covers. $10.00.
A narration of some of the author's early experiences in silhouette shooting, plus how-to information.

Shooting Colt Single Actions, by Mike Venturino, Livingston, MT, 1997. 205 pp., illus. Paper covers. $25.00
A definitive work on the famous Colt SAA and the ammunition it shoots.

Sig/Sauer Handguns, by Duncan Long, Desert Publications, El Dorado, AZ, 1995. 150 pp., illus. Paper covers. $16.95.
The history of Sig/Sauer handguns, including Sig, Sig-Hammerli and Sig/Sauer variants.

Sixgun Cartridges and Loads, by Elmer Keith, reprint edition by The Gun Room Press, Highland Park, NJ, 1984. 151 pp., illus. $24.95.
A manual covering the selection, use and loading of the most suitable and popular revolver cartridges.

Sixguns, by Elmer Keith, Wolfe Publishing Company, Prescott, AZ, 1992. 336 pp. Paper covers. $29.95. Hardcover $35.00
The history, selection, repair, care, loading, and use of this historic frontiersman's friend—the one-hand firearm.

Smith & Wesson's Automatics, by Larry Combs, Desert Publications, El Dorado, AZ, 1994. 143 pp., illus. Paper covers. $19.95.
A must for every S&W auto owner or prospective owner.

Spanish Handguns: The History of Spanish Pistols and Revolvers, by Gene Gangarosa, Jr., Stoeger Publishing Co., Accokeek, MD, 2001. 320 pp., illustrated. B & W photos. Paper covers. $21.95

Street Stoppers: The Latest Handgun Stopping Power Street Results, by Evan P. Marshall & Edwin J. Sandow, Paladin Press, Boulder, CO, 1997. 392 pp., illus. Paper covers. $42.95.
Compilation of the results of real-life shooting incidents involving every major handgun caliber.

The Tactical 1911, by Dave Lauck, Paladin Press, Boulder, CO, 1999. 152 pp., illustrated. Paper covers. $22.00.
The cop's and SWAT operator's guide to employment and maintenance.

The Tactical Pistol, by Gabriel Suarez with a foreword by Jeff Cooper, Paladin Press, Boulder, CO, 1996. 216 pp., illus. Paper covers. $25.00.
Advanced gunfighting concepts and techniques.

The Thompson/Center Contender Pistol, by Charles Tephens, Paladin Press, Boulder, CO, 1997. 58 pp., illus. Paper covers. $14.00.
How to tune and time, load and shoot accurately with the Contender pistol.

The .380 Enfield No. 2 Revolver, by Mark Stamps and Ian Skennerton, I.D.S.A. Books, Piqua, OH, 1993. 124 pp., 80 illus. Paper covers. $19.95.

The Truth AboUt Handguns, by Duane Thomas, Paladin Press, Boulder, CO, 1997. 136 pp., illus. Paper covers. $18.00.
Exploding the myths, hype, and misinformation about handguns.

Walther Pistols: Models 1 Through P99, Factory Variations and Copies, by Dieter H. Marschall, Ucross Books, Los Alamos, NM. 2000. 140 pages, with 140 b & w illustrations, index. Paper Covers. $19.95.
This is the English translation, revised and updated, of the highly successful and widely acclaimed German language edition. This book provides the collector with a reference guide and overview of the entire line of the Walther military, police, and self-defense pistols from the very first to the very latest. Models 1-9, PP, PPK, MP, AP, HP, P.38, P1, P4, P38K, P5, P88, P99 and the Manurhin models. Variations, where issued, serial ranges, calibers, marks, proofs, logos, and design aspects in an astonishing quantity and variety are crammed into this very well researched and highly regarded work.

U.S. Handguns of World War 2, The Secondary Pistols and Revolvers, by Charles W. Pate, Mowbray Publishers, Lincoln, RI, 1997. 368 pp., illus. $39.00.
This indispensable new book covers all of the American military handguns of W.W.2 except for the M1911A1.

Ballistics And Handloading

ABC's of Reloading, 6th Edition, by C. Rodney James and the editors of Handloader's Digest, DBI Books, a division of Krause Publications, Iola, WI, 1997. 288 pp., illus. Paper covers. $21.95
The definitive guide to every facet of cartridge and shotshell reloading.

Accurate Arms Loading Guide Number 2, by Accurate Arms. McEwen, TN: Accurate Arms Company, Inc., 2000. Paper Covers. $18.95
Includes new data on smokeless powders XMR4064 and XMP5744 as well as a special section on Cowboy Action Shooting. The new manual includes 50 new pages of data. An appendix includes nominal rotor charge weights, bullet diameters.

The American Cartridge, by Charles Suydam, Borden Publishing Co. Alhambra, CA, 1986. 184 pp., illus. $24.95
An illustrated study of the rimfire cartridge in the United States.

Ammo and Ballistics, by Robert W. Forker, Safari Press, Inc., Huntington Beach, CA., 1999. 252 pp., illustrated. Paper covers. $18.95
Ballistic data on 125 calibers and 1,400 loads out to 500 yards.

Ammunition: Grenades and Projectile Munitions, by Ian V. Hogg, Stackpole Books, Mechanicsburg, PA, 1998. 144 pp., illus. $22.95
Concise guide to modern ammunition. International coverage with detailed specifications and illustrations.

Barnes Reloading Manual #2, Barnes Bullets, American Fork, UT, 1999. 668 pp., illus. $24.95
Features data and trajectories on the new weight X, XBT and Solids in calibers from .22 to .50 BMG.

Big Bore Rifles And Cartridges, Wolfe Publishing Co., Prescott, AZ, 1991. Paper covers. $26.00
This book covers cartridges from 8mm to .600 Nitro with loading tables.

Black Powder Guide, 2nd Edition, by George C. Nonte, Jr., Stoeger Publishing Co., So. Hackensack, NJ, 1991. 288 pp., illus. Paper covers. $14.95
How-to instructions for selection, repair and maintenance of muzzleloaders, making your own bullets, restoring and refinishing, shooting techniques.

Blackpowder Loading Manual, 3rd Edition, by Sam Fadala, DBI Books, a division of Krause Publications, Iola, WI, 1995. 368 pp., illus. Paper covers. $20.95
Revised and expanded edition of this landmark blackpowder loading book. Covers hundreds of loads for most of the popular blackpowder rifles, handguns and shotguns.

Cartridges of the World, 9th Edition, by Frank Barnes, Krause Publications, Iola, WI, 2000. 512 pp., illus. Paper covers. $27.95
Completely revised edition of the general purpose reference work for which collectors, police, scientists and laymen reach first for answers to cartridge identification questions.

Cartridge Reloading Tools of the Past, by R.H. Chamberlain and Tom Quigley, Tom Quigley, Castle Rock, WA, 1998. 167 pp., illustrated. Paper covers. $25.00
A detailed treatment of the extensive Winchester and Ideal line of handloading tools and bullet molds, plus Remington, Marlin, Ballard, Browning, Maynard, and many others.

THE ARMS LIBRARY

Cast Bullets for the Black Powder Rifle, by Paul A. Matthews, Wolfe Publishing Co., Prescott, AZ, 1996. 133 pp., illus. Paper covers. $22.50
   The tools and techniques used to make your cast bullet shooting a success.

Complete Blackpowder Handbook, 3rd Edition, by Sam Fadala, DBI Books, a division of Krause Publications, Iola, WI, 1997. 400 pp., illus. Paper covers. $21.95
   Expanded and completely rewritten edition of the definitive book on the subject of blackpowder.

Complete Reloading Guide, by Robert & John Traister, Stoeger Publishing Co., Wayne, NJ, 1997. 608 pp., illus. Paper covers. $34.95
   Perhaps the finest, most comprehensive work ever published on the subject of reloading.

Complete Reloading Manual, One Book / One Caliber. California: Load Books USA, 2000. $7.95 Each
   Containing unabridged information from U. S. Bullet and Powder Makers. With thousands of proven and tested loads, plus dozens of various bullet designs and different powders. Spiral bound. Available in all Calibers.

Early Loading Tools & Bullet Molds, Pioneer Press, 1988. 88 pages, illustrated. Softcover. $7.50

European Sporting Cartridges: Volume 1, by Brad Dixon, Seattle, WA: Armory Publications, 1997. 1st edition. 250 pp., Illus. $60.00
   Photographs and drawings of over 550 centerfire cartridge case types in 1,300 illustrations produced in Germany and Austria from 1875-1995.

European Sporting Cartridges: Volume 2, by Brad Dixon, Seattle, WA: Armory Publications, 2000. 1st edition. 240 pages. $60.00
   An illustrated history of centerfire hunting and target cartridges produced in Czechoslovakia, Switzerland, Norway, Sweden, Finland, Russia, Italy, Denmark, Belguim from 1875 to 1998. Adds 50 specimens to volume 1, Germany-Austria. Also, illustrates 40 small arms magazine experiments during the late 19th Century, and includes the English-Language export ammunition catalogue of Kovo (Povaszke Strojarne), Prague, Czeck. from the 1930's.

Game Loads and Practical Ballistics for the American Hunter, by Bob Hagel, Wolfe Publishing Co., Prescott, AZ, 1992. 310 pp., illus. $27.90
   Hagel's knowledge gained as a hunter, guide and gun enthusiast is gathered in this informative text.

German 7.9MM Military Ammunition 1888-1945, by Daniel Kent, Ann Arbor, MI: Kent, 1990. 153 pp., plus appendix. illus., b&w photos. $35.00

Handbook for Shooters and Reloaders, by P.O. Ackley, Salt Lake City, UT, 1998, (Vol. I), 567 pp., illus. Includes a separate exterior ballistics chart. $21.95
   (Vol. II), a new printing with specific new material. 495 pp., illus. $20.95

Handgun Muzzle Flash Tests: How Police Cartridges Compare, by Robert Olsen, Paladin Press, Boulder, CO.Fully illustrated. 133 pages. Softcover. $20.00
   Tests dozens of pistols and revolvers for the brightness of muzzle flash, a critical factor in the safety of law enforcement personnel.

Handgun Stopping Power; The Definitive Study, by Marshall & Sandow. Boulder, CO: Paladin Press, 1992. 240 pages. $45.00
   Offers accurate predictions of the stopping power of specific loads in calibers from .380 Auto to .45 ACP, as well as such specialty rounds as the Glaser Safety Slug, Federal Hydra-Shok, MagSafe, etc. This is the definitive methodology for predicting the stopping power of handgun loads, the first to take into account what really happens when a bullet meets a man.

Handloader's Digest, 17th Edition, edited by Bob Bell. DBI Books, a division of Krause Publications, Iola, WI, 1997. 480 pp., illustrated. Paper covers. $27.95
   Top writers in the field contribute helpful information on techniques and components. Greatly expanded and fully indexed catalog of all currently available tools, accessories and components for metallic, blackpowder cartridge, shotgun reloading and swaging.

Handloader's Manual of Cartridge Conversions, by John J. Donnelly, Stoeger Publishing Co., So. Hackensack, NJ, 1986. Unpaginated. $39.95
   From 14 Jones to 70-150 Winchester in English and American cartridges, and from 4.85 U.K. to 15.2x28R Gevelot in metric cartridges. Over 900 cartridges described in detail.

Hatcher's Notebook, by S. Julian Hatcher, Stackpole Books, Harrisburg, PA, 1992. 488 pp., illus. $39.95
   A reference work for shooters, gunsmiths, ballisticians, historians, hunters and collectors.

History and Development of Small Arms Ammunition; Volume 2 Centerfire: Primitive, and Martial Long Arms. by George A. Hoyem. Oceanside, CA: Armory Publications, 1991. 303 pages, illustrated. $60.00
   Covers the blackpowder military centerfire rifle, carbine, machine gun and volley gun ammunition used in 28 nations and dominions, together with the firearms that chambered them.

History and Development of Small Arms Ammunition; Volume 4, American Military Rifle Cartridges. Oceanside, CA: Armory Publications, 1998. 244pp., illus. $60.00
   Carries on what Vol. 2 began with American military rifle cartridges. Now the sporting rifle cartridges are at last organized by their originators-235 individual case types designed by eight makers of single shot rifles and four of magazine rifles from .50-140 Winchester Express to .22-15-60 Stevens. plus experimentals from .70-150 to .32-80. American Civil War enthusiasts and European collectors will find over 150 primitives in Appendix A to add to those in Volumes One and Two. There are 16 pages in full color of 54 box labels for Sharps, Remington and Ballard cartridges. There are large photographs with descriptions of 15 Maynard, Sharps, Winchester, Browning, Freund, Remington-Hepburn, Farrow and other single shot rifles, some of them rare one of a kind specimens.

Hodgdon Powder Data Manual #27, Hodgdon Powder Co., Shawnee Mission, KS, 1999. 800 pp. $27.95
   Reloading data for rifle and pistol loads.

Hodgdon Shotshell Data Manual, Hodgdon Powder Co., Shawnee Mission, KS, 1999. 208 pp. $19.95
   Contains hundreds of loads for lead shot, buck shot, slugs, bismuth shot and steel shot plus articles on ballistics, patterning, special reloads and much more.

Home Guide to Cartridge Conversions, by Maj. George C. Nonte Jr., The Gun Room Press, Highland Park, NJ, 1976. 404 pp., illus. $24.95
   Revised and updated version of Nonte's definitive work on the alteration of cartridge cases for use in guns for which they were not intended.

Hornady Handbook of Cartridge Reloading, 5th Edition, Vol. I and II, Edited by Larry Steadman, Hornady Mfg. Co., Grand Island, NE, 2000., illus. $49.95
   2 Volumes; Volume 1, 773 pp.; Volume 2, 717 pp. New edition of this famous reloading handbook covers rifle and handgun reloading data and ballistic tables.
   Latest loads, ballistic information, etc.

How-To's for the Black Powder Cartridge Rifle Shooter, by Paul A. Matthews, Wolfe Publishing Co., Prescott, AZ, 1995. 45 pp. Paper covers. $22.50
   Covers lube recipes, good bore cleaners and over-powder wads. Tips include compressing powder charges, combating wind resistance, improving ignition and much more.

The Illustrated Reference of Cartridge Dimensions, edited by Dave Scovill, Wolfe Publishing Co., Prescott, AZ, 1994. 343 pp., illus. Paper covers. $19.00
   A comprehensive volume with over 300 cartridges. Standard and metric dimensions have been taken from SAAMI drawings and/or fired cartridges.

Kynock, by Dale J. Hedlund, Armory Publications, Seattle, WA, 2000. 130 pages, illus. 9" x 12" with four color dust jacket. $59.95
   A comprehensive review of Kynoch shotgun cartridges covering over 50 brand names and case types, and over 250 Kynoch shotgun cartridge headstamps. Additional information on Kynoch metallic ammunition including the identity of the mysterious .434 Seelun.

Lee Modern Reloading, by Richard Lee, 350 pp. of charts and data and 85 illustrations. 512 pp. $24.95
   Bullet casting, lubricating and author's formula for calculating proper charges for cast bullets. Includes virtually all current load data published by the powder suppliers. Exclusive source of volume measured loads.

Loading the Black Powder Rifle Cartridge, by Paul A Matthews, Wolfe Publishing Co., Prescott, AZ, 1993. 121 pp., illus. Paper covers. $22.50
   Author Matthews brings the blackpowder cartridge shooter valuable information on the basics, including cartridge care, lubes and moulds, powder charges and developing and testing loads in his usual authoritative style.

Loading the Peacemaker—Colt's Model P, by Dave Scovill, Wolfe Publishing Co., Prescott, AZ, 1996. 227 pp., illus. $24.95
   A comprehensive work about the history, maintenance and repair of the most famous revolver ever made, including the most extensive load data ever published.

Lyman Cast Bullet Handbook, 3rd Edition, edited by C. Kenneth Ramage, Lyman Publications, Middlefield, CT, 1980. 416 pp., illus. Paper covers. $19.95
   Information on more than 5000 tested cast bullet loads and 19 pages of trajectory and wind drift tables for cast bullets.

Lyman Black Powder Handbook, edited by C. Kenneth Ramage, Lyman Products for Shooters, Middlefield, CT, 1975. 239 pp., illus. Paper covers. $14.95
   Comprehensive load information for the modern blackpowder shooter.

Lyman Pistol & Revolver Handbook, 2nd Edition, edited by Thomas J. Griffin, Lyman Products Co., Middlefield, CT, 1996. 287 pp., illus. Paper covers. $18.95
   The most up-to-date loading data available including the hottest new calibers, like 40 S&W, 9x21, 9mm Makarov, 9x25 Dillon and 454 Casull.

Lyman Reloading Handbook No. 47, edited by Edward A. Matunas, Lyman Publications, Middlefield, CT, 1992. 480 pp., illus. Paper covers. $24.95
   A comprehensive reloading manual complete with "How to Reload" information. Expanded data section with all the newest rifle and pistol calibers.

THE ARMS LIBRARY

Lyman Shotshell Handbook, 4th Edition, edited by Edward A. Matunas, Lyman Products Co., Middlefield, CT, 1996. 330 pp., illus. Paper covers. $24.95
  Has 9000 loads, including slugs and buckshot, plus feature articles and a full color I.D. section.

Lyman's Guide to Big Game Cartridges & Rifles, by Edward Matunas, Lyman Publishing Corporation, Middlefield, CT, 1994. 287 pp., illus. Paper covers. $17.95
  A selection guide to cartridges and rifles for big game—antelope to elephant.

Making Loading Dies and Bullet Molds, by Harold Hoffman, H & P Publishing, San Angelo, TX, 1993. 230 pp., illus. Paper covers. $24.95
  A good book for learning tool and die making.

Metallic Cartridge Reloading, 3rd Edition, by M.L. McPherson, DBI Books, a division of Krause Publications, Iola, WI., 1996. 352 pp., illus. Paper covers. $21.95
  A true reloading manual with over 10,000 loads for all popular metallic cartridges and a wealth of invaluable technical data provided by a recognized expert.

Military Rifle and Machine Gun Cartridges, by Jean Huon, Alexandria, VA: Ironside International, 1995. 1st edition. 378 pages, over 1,000 photos. $34.95
  Superb reference text.

Modern Combat Ammunition, by Duncan Long, Paladin Press, Boulder, CO, 1997, soft cover, photos, illus., 216 pp. $34.00
  Now, Paladin's leading weapons author presents his exhaustive evaluation of the stopping power of modern rifle, pistol, shotgun and machine gun rounds based on actual case studies of shooting incidents. He looks at the hot new cartridges that promise to dominate well into the next century .40 S&W, 10mm auto, sub-sonic 9mm's - as well as the trusted standbys. Find out how to make your own exotic tracers, fléchette and sabot rounds, caseless ammo and fragmenting bullets.

Modern Exterior Ballistics, by Robert L. McCoy, Schiffer Publishing Co., Atglen, PA, 1999. 128 pp. $95.00
  Advanced students of exterior ballistics and flight dynamics will find this comprehensive textbook on the subject a useful addition to their libraries.

Modern Handloading, by Maj. Geo. C. Nonte, Winchester Press, Piscataway, NJ, 1972. 416 pp., illus. $15.00
  Covers all aspects of metallic and shotshell ammunition loading, plus more loads than any book in print.

Modern Reloading, by Richard Lee, Inland Press, 1996. 510 pp., illus. $24.98
  The how-to's of rifle, pistol and shotgun reloading plus load data for rifle and pistol calibers.

Modern Sporting Rifle Cartridges, by Wayne van Zwoll, Stoeger Publishing Co., Wayne, NJ, 1998. 310 pp., illustrated. Paper covers. $21.95
  Illustrated with hundreds of photos and backed up by dozens of tables and schematic drawings, this four-part book tells the story of how rifle bullets and cartridges were developed and, in some cases, discarded.

Modern Practical Ballistics, by Art Pejsa, Pejsa Ballistics, Minneapolis, MN, 1990. 150 pp., illus. $29.95
  Covers all aspects of ballistics and new, simplified methods. Clear examples illustrate new, easy but very accurate formulas.

Mr. Single Shot's Cartridge Handbook, by Frank de Haas, Mark de Haas, Orange City, IA, 1996. 116 pp., illus. Paper covers. $21.50
  This book covers most of the cartridges, both commercial and wildcat, that the author has known and used.

Nick Harvey's Practical Reloading Manual, by Nick Harvey, Australian Print Group, Maryborough, Victoria, Australia, 1995. 235 pp., illus. Paper covers. $24.95
  Contains data for rifle and handgun including many popular wildcat and improved cartridges. Tools, powders, components and techniques for assembling optimum reloads with particular application to North America.

Nosler Reloading Manual #4, edited by Gail Root, Nosler Bullets, Inc., Bend, OR, 1996. 516 pp., illus. $26.99
  Combines information on their Ballistic Tip, Partition and Handgun bullets with traditional powders and new powders never before used, plus trajectory information from 100 to 500 yards.

The Paper Jacket, by Paul Matthews, Wolfe Publishing Co., Prescott, AZ, 1991. Paper covers. $13.50
  Up-to-date and accurate information about paper-patched bullets.

Reloading Tools, Sights and Telescopes for S/S Rifles, by Gerald O. Kelver, Brighton, CO, 1982. 163 pp., illus. Softcover. $15.00
  A listing of most of the famous makers of reloading tools, sights and telescopes with a brief description of the products they manufactured.

Reloading for Shotgunners, 4th Edition, by Kurt D. Fackler and M.L. McPherson, DBI Books, a division of Krause Publications, Iola, WI 1997. 320 pp., illus. Paper covers. $19.95
  Expanded reloading tables with over 11,000 loads. Bushing charts for every major press and component maker. All new presentation on all aspects of shotshell reloading by two of the top experts in the field.

The Rimfire Cartridge in the United States and Canada, Illustrated history of rimfire cartridges, manufacturers, and the products made from 1857-1984. by John L. Barber, Thomas Publications, Gettysburg, PA 2000. 1st edition. Profusely illustrated. 221 pages. $50.00
  The author has written an encyclopedia of rimfire cartridges from the .22 to the massive 1.00 in. Gatling. Fourteen chapters, six appendices and an excellent bibliography make up a reference volume that all cartridge collectors should aquire.

Sierra 50th Anniversary, 4th Edition Rifle Manual, edited by Ken Ramage, Sierra Bullets, Santa Fe Springs, CA, 1997. 800 pp., illus. $26.99
  New cartridge introductions, etc.

Sierra 50th Anniversary, 4th Edition Handgun Manual, edited by Ken Ramage, Sierra Bullets, Santa Fe, CA, 1997. 700 pp., illus. $21.99
  Histories, reloading recommendations, bullets, powders and sections on the reloading process, etc.

Sixgun Cartridges and Loads, by Elmer Keith, The Gun Room Press, Highland Park, NJ, 1986. 151 pp., illus. $24.95
  A manual covering the selection, uses and loading of the most suitable and popular revolver cartridges. Originally published in 1936. Reprint.

Speer Reloading Manual No. 13, edited by members of the Speer research staff, Omark Industries, Lewiston, ID, 1999. 621 pp., illustrated. $24.95
  With thirteen new sections containing the latest technical information and reloading trends for both novice and expert in this latest edition. More than 9,300 loads are listed, including new propellant powders from Accurate Arms, Alliant, Hodgdon and Vihtavuori.

Street Stoppers, The Latest Handgun Stopping Power Street Results, by Marshall & Lanow. Boulder, CO, Paladin Press, 1996. 374 pages, illus. Softcover. $42.95
  Street Stoppers is the long-awaited sequel to Handgun Stopping Power. It provides the latest results of real-life shootings in all of the major handgun calibers, plus more than 25 thought-provoking chapters that are vital to anyone interested in firearms, would ballistics, and combat shooting. This book also covers the street results of the hottest new caliber to hit the shooting world in years, the .40 Smith & Wesson. Updated street results of the latest exotic ammunition including Remington Golden Saber and CCI-Speer Gold Dot, plus the venerable offerings from MagSafe, Glaser, Cor-Bon and others. A fascinating look at the development of Hydra-Shok ammunition is included.

Understanding Ballistics, Revised 2nd Edition by Robert A. Rinker, Mulberry House Publishing Co., Corydon, IN, 2000. 430 pp., illus Paper covers. New, Revised and Expanded. 2nd Edition. $24.95
  Explains basic to advanced firearm ballistics in understandable terms.

Why Not Load Your Own?, by Col. T. Whelen, Gun Room Press, Highland Park, NJ 1996, 4th ed., rev. 237 pp., illus. $20.00
  A basic reference on handloading, describing each step, materials and equipment. Includes loads for popular cartridges.

Wildcat Cartridges Volumes 1 & 2 Combination, by the editors of Handloaders magazine, Wolfe Publishing Co., Prescott, AZ, 1997. 350 pp., illus. Paper covers. $39.95
  A profile of the most popular information on wildcat cartridges that appeared in the Handloader magazine.

COLLECTORS

A Glossary of the Construction, Decoration and Use of Arms and Armor in All Countries and in All Times. By George Cameron Stone., Dover Publishing, New York 1999. Softcover. $39.95
  An exhaustive study of arms and armor in all countries through recorded history - from the stone age up to the second world war. With over 4500 Black & White Illustrations. This Dover edition is an unabridged republication of the work originally published in 1934 by the Southworth Press, Portland MA. A new Introduction has been specially prepared for this edition.

Accoutrements of the United States Infantry, Riflemen, and Dragoons 1834-1839. by R.T. Huntington, Historical Arms Series No. 20. Canada: Museum Restoration. 58 pp. illus. Softcover. $8.95
  Although the 1841 edition of the U.S. Ordnance Manual provides ample information on the equipment that was in use during the 1840s, it is evident that the patterns of equipment that it describes were not introduced until 1838 or 1839. This guide is intended to fill this gap in our knowledge by providing an overview of what we now know about the accoutrements that were issued to the regular infantryman, rifleman, and dragoon, in the 1830's with excursions into earlier and later years.

Age of the Gunfighter; Men and Weapons on the Frontier 1840-1900, by Joseph G. Rosa, University of Oklahoma Press, Norman, OK, 1999. 192 pp., illustrated. Paper covers. $21.95
  Stories of gunfighters and their encounters and detailed descriptions of virtually every firearm used in the old West.

Air Guns, by Eldon G. Wolff, Duckett's Publishing Co., Tempe, AZ, 1997. 204 pp., illus Paper covers. $35.00
  Historical reference covering many makers, European and American guns, canes and more.

THE ARMS LIBRARY

Allied and Enemy Aircraft: May 1918; Not to be Taken from the Front Lines, Historical Arms Series No. 27. Canada: Museum Restoration. Softcover. $8.95

The basis for this title is a very rare identification manual published by the French government in 1918 that illustrated 60 aircraft with three or more views: French, English American, German, Italian, and Belgian, which might have been seen over the trenches ofFrance. Each is describe in a text translated from the original French. This is probably the most complete collection of illustrations of WW1 aircraft which has survived.

American Beauty; The Prewar Colt National Match Government Model Pistol, by Timothy J. Mullin, Collector Grade Publications, Cobourg, Ontario, Canada. 72 pp., illustrated. $34.95

Includes over 150 serial numbers, and 20 spectacular color photos of factory engraved guns and other authenticated upgrades, including rare "double-carved" ivory grips.

The American Military Saddle, 1776-1945, by R. Stephen Dorsey & Kenneth L. McPheeters, Collector's Library, Eugene, OR, 1999. 400 pp., illustrated. $59.95

The most complete coverage of the subject ever writeen on the American Military Saddle. Nearly 1000 actual photos and official drawings, from the major public and private collections in the U.S. and Great Britain.

American Police Collectibles; Dark Lanterns and Other Curious Devices, by Matthew G. Forte, Turn of the Century Publishers, Upper Montclair, NJ, 1999. 248 pp., illustrated. $24.95

For collectors of police memorabilia (handcuffs, police dark lanterns, mechanical and chain nippers, rattles, billy clubs and nightsticks) and police historians.

Ammunition; Small Arms, Grenades, and Projected Munitions, by Greenhill Publishing. 144 pp., Illustrated. $22.95 The best concise guide to modern ammunition available today. Covers ammo for small arms, grenades, and projected munitions. 144 pp., Illustrated. As NEW – Hardcover.

r Single Shot Rifles, by Gerald O. Kelver, Brighton, CO, 1982. 163 pp., illus. Paper covers. $13.95

A listing of most of the famous makers of reloading tools, sights and telescopes with a brief description of the products they manufactured.

The Remington-Lee Rifle, by Eugene F. Myszkowski, Excalibur Publications, Latham, NY, 1995. 100 pp., illus. Paper covers. $22.50.

Features detailed descriptions, including serial number ranges, of each model from the first Lee Magazine Rifle produced for the U.S. Navy to the last Remington-Lee Small Bores shipped to the Cuban Rural Guard.

Revolvers of the British Services 1854-1954, by W.H.J. Chamberlain and A.W.F. Taylerson, Museum Restoration Service, Ottawa, Canada, 1989. 80 pp., illus. $27.50.

Covers the types issued among many of the United Kingdom's naval, land or air services.

Rhode Island Arms Makers & Gunsmiths, by William O. Archibald, Andrew Mowbray, Inc., Lincoln, RI, 1990. 108 pp., illus. $16.50.

A serious and informative study of an important area of American arms making.

Rifles of the World, by Oliver Achard, Chartwell Books, Inc., Edison, NJ, 141 pp., illus. $24.95.

A unique insight into the world of long guns, not just rifles, but also shotguns, carbines and all the usual multi-barreled guns that once were so popular with European hunters, especially in Germany and Austria.

The Rock Island '03, by C.S. Ferris, C.S. Ferris, Arvada, CO, 1993. 58 pp., illus. Paper covers. $12.50.

A monograph of interest to the collector or historian concentrating on the U.S. M1903 rifle made by the less publicized of our two producing facilities.

Round Ball to Rimfire, Vol. 1, by Dean Thomas, Thomas Publications, Gettysburg, PA, 1997. 144 pp., illus. $40.00.

The first of a two-volume set of the most complete history and guide for all small arms ammunition used in the Civil War. The information includes data from research and development to the arsenals that created it.

Ruger and his Guns, by R.L. Wilson, Simon & Schuster, New York, NY, 1996. 358 pp., illus. $65.00.

A history of the man, the company and their firearms.

Russell M. Catron and His Pistols, by Warren H. Buxton, Ucross Books, Los Alamos, NM, 1998. 224 pp., illustrated. Paper covers. $49.50.

An unknown American firearms inventor and manufacturer of the mid twentieth century. Military, commerical, ammunition.

The SAFN-49 and The FAL, by Joe Poyer and Dr. Richard Feirman, North Cape Publications, Tustin, CA, 1998. 160 pp., illus. Paper covers. $14.95.

The first complete overview of the SAFN-49 battle rifle, from its pre-World War 2 beginnings to its military service in countries as diverse as the Belgian Congo and Argentina. The FAL was "light" version of the SAFN-49 and it became the Free World's most adopted battle rifle.

Sam Colt's Own Record 1847, by John Parsons, Wolfe Publishing Co., Prescott, AZ, 1992. 167 pp., illus. $24.50.

Chronologically presented, the correspondence published here completes the account of the manufacture, in 1847, of the Walker Model Colt revolver.

J. P. Sauer & Sohn, Sauer "Dein Waffenkamerad" Volume 2, by Cate & Krause, Walsworth Publishing, Chattanooga, TN, 2000. 440 pp., illus. $79.00.

A historical study of Sauer automatic pistols. This new volume includes a great deal of new knowledge that has surfaced about the firm J.P. Sauer. You will find new photos, documentation, serial number ranges and historial facts which will expand the knowledge and interest in the oldest and best of the German firearms companies.

Scottish Firearms, by Claude Blair and Robert Woosnam-Savage, Museum Restoration Service, Bloomfield, Ont., Canada, 1995. 52 pp., illus. Paper covers. $8.95.

This revision of the first book devoted entirely to Scottish firearms is supplemented by a register of surviving Scottish long guns.

The Scottish Pistol, by Martin Kelvin. Fairleigh Dickinson University Press, Dist. By Associated University Presses, Cranbury, NJ, 1997. 256 pp., illus $49.50.

The Scottish pistol, its history, manufacture and design.

Sharps Firearms, by Frank Seller, Frank M. Seller, Denver, CO, 1998. 358 pp., illus. $55.00.

Traces the development of Sharps firearms with full range of guns made including all martial variations.

Simeon North: First Official Pistol Maker of the United States, by S. North and R. North, The Gun Room Press, Highland Park, NJ, 1972. 207 pp., illus. $15.95.

Reprint of the rare first edition.

The SKS Carbine, by Steve Kehaya and Joe Poyer, North Cape Publications, Tustin, CA, 1997. 150 pp., illus. Paper covers. $16.95.

The first comprehensive examination of a major historical firearm used through the Vietnam conflict to the diamond fields of Angola.

The SKS Type 45 Carbines, by Duncan Long, Desert Publications, El Dorado, AZ, 1992. 110 pp., illus. Paper covers. $19.95

Covers the history and practical aspects of operating, maintaining and modifying this abundantly available rifle.

Smith & Wesson 1857-1945, by Robert J. Neal and Roy G. Jinks, R&R Books, Livonia, NY, 1996. 434 pp., illus. $50.00.

The bible for all existing and aspiring Smith & Wesson collectors.

Sniper Variations of the German K98k Rifle, by Richard D. Law, Collector Grade Publications, Ontario, Canada, 1997. 240 pp., illus. $47.50.

Volume 2 of "Backbone of the Wehrmacht" the author's in-depth study of the German K98k rifle. This volume concentrates on the telescopic-sighted rifle of choice for most German snipers during World War 2.

Southern Derringers of the Mississippi Valley, by Turner Kirkland, Pioneer Press, Tenn., 1971. 80 pp., illus., paper covers. $4.00.

A guide for the collector, and a much-needed study.

Soviet Russian Postwar Military Pistols and Cartridges, by Fred A. Datig, Handgun Press, Glenview, IL, 1988. 152 pp., illus. $29.95.

Thoroughly researched, this definitive sourcebook covers the development and adoption of the Makarov, Stechkin and the new PSM pistols. Also included in this source book is coverage on Russian clandestine weapons and pistol cartridges.

Soviet Russian Tokarev "TT" Pistols and Cartridges 1929-1953, by Fred Datig, Graphic Publishers, Santa Ana, CA, 1993. 168 pp., illus. $39.95.

Details of rare arms and their accessories are shown in hundreds of photos. It also contains a complete bibliography and index.

Soviet Small-Arms and Ammunition, by David Bolotin, Handgun Press, Glenview, IL, 1996. 264 pp., illus. $49.95.

An authoritative and complete book on Soviet small arms.

Sporting Collectibles, by Jim and Vivian Karsnitz, Schiffer Publishing Ltd., West Chester, PA, 1992. 160 pp., illus. Paper covers. $29.95.

The fascinating world of hunting related collectibles presented in an informative text.

The Springfield 1903 Rifles, by Lt. Col. William S. Brophy, USAR, Ret., Stackpole Books Inc., Harrisburg, PA, 1985. 608 pp., illus. $75.00.

The illustrated, documented story of the design, development, and production of all the models, appendages, and accessories.

Springfield Armory Shoulder Weapons 1795-1968, by Robert W.D. Ball, Antique Trader Books, Dubuque, IA, 1998. 264 pp., illus. $34.95.

This book documents the 255 basic models of rifles, including test and trial rifles, produced by the Springfield Armory. It features the entire history of rifles and carbines manufactured at the Armory, the development of each weapon with specific operating characteristics and procedures.

Springfield Model 1903 Service Rifle Production and Alteration, 1905-1910, by C.S. Ferris and John Beard, Arvada, CO, 1995. 66 pp., illus. Paper covers. $12.50.

A highly recommended work for any serious student of the Springfield Model 1903 rifle.

Springfield Shoulder Arms 1795-1865, by Claud E. Fuller, S. & S. Firearms, Glendale, NY, 1996. 76 pp., illus. Paper covers. $17.95.

Exact reprint of the scarce 1930 edition of one of the most definitive works on Springfield flintlock and percussion muskets ever published.

THE ARMS LIBRARY

Standard Catalog of Firearms, 11th Edition, by Ned Schwing, Krause Publications, Iola, WI, 2001.1328 Pages, illustrated. 6,000+ b&w photos plus a 16-page color section. Paper covers. $32.95.
This is the largest, most comprehensive and best-selling firearm book of all time! And this year's edition is a blockbuster for both shooters and firearm collectors. More than 12,000 firearms are listed and priced in up to six grades of condition. That's almost 80,000 prices! Gun enthusiasts will love the new full-color section of photos highlighting the finest firearms sold at auction this past year –including the new record for an American historical firearm: $684,000!

Standard Catalog of Winchester, 1st Edition, edited by David D. Kowalski, Krause Publications, Iola, WI, 2000. 704 pp., illustrated with 2,000 B&W photos and 75 color photos. Paper covers. $39.95.
This book identifies and values more than 5,000 collectibles, including firearms, cartridges shotshells, fishing tackle, sporting goods and tools manufactured by Winchester Repeating Arms Co.

Steel Canvas: The Art of American Arms, by R.L. Wilson, Random House, NY, 1995, 384 pp., illus. $65.00.
Presented here for the first time is the breathtaking panorama of America's extraordinary engravers and embellishers of arms, from the 1700s to modern times.

Stevens Pistols & Pocket Rifles, by K.L. Cope, Museum Restoration Service, Alexandria Bay, NY, 1992. 114 pp., illus. $24.50.
This is the story of the guns and the man who designed them and the company which he founded to make them.

A Study of Colt Conversions and Other Percussion Revolvers, by R. Bruce McDowell, Krause Publications, Iola, WI, 1997. 464 pp., illus. $39.95.
The ultimate reference detailing Colt revolvers that have been converted from percussion to cartridge.

The Sumptuous Flaske, by Herbert G. Houze, Andrew Mowbray, Inc., Lincoln, RI, 1989. 158 pp., illus. Soft covers. $35.00.
Catalog of a recent show at the Buffalo Bill Historical Center bringing together some of the finest European and American powder flasks of the 16th to 19th centuries.

The Swedish Mauser Rifles, by Steve Kehaya and Joe Poyer, North Cape Publications, Tustin, CA, 1999. 267 pp., illustrated. Paper covers. $19.95.
Every known variation of the Swedish Mauser carbine and rifle is described including all match and target rifles and all sniper fersions. Includes serial number and production data.

Televisions Cowboys, Gunfighters & Cap Pistols, by Rudy A. D'Angelo, Antique Trader Books, Norfolk, VA, 1999. 287 pp., illustrated in color and black and white. Paper covers. $31.95.
Over 850 beautifully photographed color and black and white images of cap guns, actors, and the characters they portrayed in the "Golden Age of TV Westerns. With accurate descriptions and current values.

Thompson: The American Legend, by Tracie L. Hill, Collector Grade Publications, Ontario, Canada, 1996. 584 pp., illus. $85.00.
The story of the first American submachine gun. All models are featured and discussed.

Toys That Shoot and Other Neat Stuff, by James Dundas, Schiffer Books, Atglen, PA, 1999. 112 pp., illustrated. Paper covers. $24.95.
Shooting toys from the twentieth century, especially 1920's to 1960's, in over 420 color photographs of BB guns, cap shooters, marble shooters, squirt guns and more. Complete with a price guide.

The Trapdoor Springfield, by M.D. Waite and B.D. Ernst, The Gun Room Press, Highland Park, NJ, 1983. 250 pp., illus. $39.95.
The first comprehensive book on the famous standard military rifle of the 1873-92 period.

Treasures of the Moscow Kremlin: Arsenal of the Russian Tsars, A Royal Armories and the Moscow Kremlin exhibition. HM Tower of London 13, June 1998 to 11 September, 1998. BAS Printers, Over Wallop, Hampshire, England. xxii plus 192 pp. over 180 color illustrations. Text in English and Russian. $65.00.
For this exchibition catalog each of the 94 objects on display are photographed and described in detail to provide a most informative record of this important exhibition.

U.S. Breech-Loading Rifles and Carbines, Cal. 45, by Gen. John Pitman, Thomas Publications, Gettysburg, PA, 1992. 192 pp., illus. $29.95.
The third volume in the Pitman Notes on U.S. Martial Small Arms and Ammunition, 1776-1933. This book centers on the "Trapdoor Springfield" models.

U.S. Handguns of World War 2: The Secondary Pistols and Revolvers, by Charles W. Pate, Andrew Mowbray, Inc., Lincoln, RI, 1998. 515 pp., illus. $39.00.
This indispensable new book covers all of the American military handguns of World War 2 except for the M1911A1 Colt automatic.

United States Martial Flintlocks, by Robert M. Reilly, Mowbray Publishing Co., Lincoln, RI, 1997. 264 pp., illus. $40.00.
A comprehensive history of American flintlock longarms and handguns (mostly military) c. 1775 to c. 1840.

U.S. Martial Single Shot Pistols, by Daniel D. Hartzler and James B. Whisker, Old Bedford Village Pess, Bedford, PA, 1998. 128 pp., illus. $45.00.
A photographic chronicle of military and semi-martial pistols supplied to the U.S. Government and the several States.

U.S. Military Arms Dates of Manufacture from 1795, by George Madis, David Madis, Dallas, TX, 1989. 64 pp. Soft covers. $6.00.
Lists all U.S. military arms of collector interest alphabetically, covering about 250 models.

U.S. Military Small Arms 1816-1865, by Robert M. Reilly, The Gun Room Press, Highland Park, NJ, 1983. 270 pp., illus. $39.95.
Covers every known type of primary and secondary martial firearms used by Federal forces.

U.S. M1 Carbines: Wartime Production, by Craig Riesch, North Cape Publications, Tustin, CA, 1994. 72 pp., illus. Paper covers. $16.95.
Presents only verifiable and accurate information. Each part of the M1 Carbine is discussed fully in its own section; including markings and finishes.

U.S. Naval Handguns, 1808-1911, by Fredrick R. Winter, Andrew Mowbray Publishers, Lincoln, RI, 1990. 128 pp., illus. $26.00.
The story of U.S. Naval Handguns spans an entire century—included are sections on each of the important naval handguns within the period.

Walther: A German Legend, by Manfred Kersten, Safari Press, Inc., Huntington Beach, CA, 2000. 400 pp., illustrated. $85.00.
This comprehensive book covers, in rich detail, all aspects of the company and its guns, including an illustrious and rich history, the WW2 years, all the pistols (models 1 through 9), the P-38, P-88, the long guns, .22 rifles, centerfires, Wehrmacht guns, and even a gun that could shoot around a corner.

Walther Pistols: Models 1 Through P99, Factory Variations and Copies, by Dieter H. Marschall, Ucross Books, Los Alamos, NM. 2000. 140 pages, with 140 b & w illustrations, index. Paper Covers. $19.95.
This is the English translation, revised and updated, of the highly successful and widely acclaimed German language edition. This book provides the collector with a reference guide and overview of the entire line of the Walther military, police, and self-defense pistols from the very first to the very latest. Models 1-9, PP, PPK, MP, AP, HP, P.38, P1, P4, P38K, P5, P88, P99 and the Manurhin models. Variations, where issued, serial ranges, calibers, marks, proofs, logos, and design aspects in an astonishing quantity and variety are crammed into this very well researched and highly regarded work.

The Walther Handgun Story: A Collector's and Shooter's Guide, by Gene Gangarosa, Steiger Publications, 1999. 300., illustrated. Paper covers. $21.95.
Covers the entire history of the Walther empire. Illustrated with over 250 photos.

Walther P-38 Pistol, by Maj. George Nonte, Desert Publications, Cornville, AZ, 1982. 100 pp., illus. Paper covers. $11.95.
Complete volume on one of the most famous handguns to come out of WWII. All models covered.

Walther Models PP & PPK, 1929-1945 – Volume 1, by James L. Rankin, Coral Gables, FL, 1974. 142 pp., illus. $40.00
Complete coverage on the subject as to finish, proofmarks and Nazi Party inscriptions.

Walther Volume II, Engraved, Presentation and Standard Models, by James L. Rankin, J.L. Rankin, Coral Gables, FL, 1977. 112 pp., illus. $40.00.
The new Walther book on embellished versions and standard models. Has 88 photographs, including many color plates.

Walther, Volume III, 1908-1980, by James L. Rankin, Coral Gables, FL, 1981. 226 pp., illus. $40.00.
Covers all models of Walther handguns from 1908 to date, includes holsters, grips and magazines.

Winchester: An American Legend, by R.L. Wilson, Random House, New York, NY, 1991. 403 pp., illus. $65.00.
The official history of Winchester firearms from 1849 to the present.

Winchester Bolt Action Military & Sporting Rifles 1877 to 1937, by Herbert G. Houze, Andrew Mowbray Publishing, Lincoln, RI, 1998. 295 pp., illus. $45.00.
Winchester was the first American arms maker to commercially manufacture a bolt action repeating rifle, and this book tells the exciting story of these Winchester bolt actions.

The Winchester Book, by George Madis, David Madis Gun Book Distributor, Dallas, TX, 1986. 650 pp., illus. $49.50.
A new, revised 25th anniversary edition of this classic book on Winchester firearms. Complete serial ranges have been added.

Winchester Dates of Manufacture 1849-1984, by George Madis, Art & Reference House, Brownsboro, TX, 1984. 59 pp. illus. $9.95.
A most useful work, compiled from records of the Winchester factory.

Winchester Engraving, by R.L. Wilson, Beinfeld Books, Springs, CA, 1989. 500 pp., illus. $135.00.
A classic reference work of value to all arms collectors.

THE ARMS LIBRARY

The Winchester Handbook, by George Madis, Art & Reference House, Lancaster, TX, 1982. 287 pp., illus. $24.95.
The complete line of Winchester guns, with dates of manufacture, serial numbers, etc.

The Winchester-Lee Rifle, by Eugene Myszkowski, Excalibur Publications, Tucson, AZ 2000. 96 pp., illustrated. Paper Covers. $22.95
The development of the Lee Straight Pull, the cartridge and the approval for military use. Covers details of the inventor and memorabilia of Winchester-Lee related material.

Winchester Lever Action Repeating Firearms, Vol. 1, The Models of 1866, 1873 and 1876, by Arthur Pirkle, North Cape Publications, Tustin, CA, 1995. 112 pp., illus. Paper covers. $19.95.
Complete, part-by-part description, including dimensions, finishes, markings and variations throughout the production run of these fine, collectible guns.

Winchester Lever Action Repeating Rifles, Vol. 2, The Models of 1886 and 1892, by Arthur Pirkle, North Cape Publications, Tustin, CA, 1996. 150 pp., illus. Paper covers. $19.95.
Describes each model on a part-by-part basis by serial number range complete with finishes, markings and changes.

Winchester Lever Action Repeating Rifles, Volume 3, The Model of 1894, by Arthur Pirkle, North Cape Publications, Tustin, CA, 1998. 150 pp., illus. Paper covers. $19.95.
The first book ever to provide a detailed description of the Model 1894 rifle and carbine.

The Winchester Lever Legacy, by Clyde "Snooky" Williamson, Buffalo Press, Zachary, LA, 1988. 664 pp., illustrated. $75.00
A book on reloading for the different calibers of the Winchester lever action rifle.

The Winchester Model 94: The First 100 Years, by Robert C. Renneberg, Krause Publications, Iola, WI, 1991. 208 pp., illus. $34.95.
Covers the design and evolution from the early years up to the many different editions that exist today.

Winchester Rarities, by Webster, Krause Publications, Iola, WI, 2000. 208 pp., with over 800 color photos, illus. $49.95.
This book details the rarest of the rare; the one-of-a-kind items and the advertising pieces from years gone by. With nearly 800 full color photos and detailed pricing provided by experts in the field, this book gives collectors and enthusiasts everything they need.

Winchester Shotguns and Shotshells, by Ronald W. Stadt, Krause Publications, Iola, WI, 1995. 256 pp., illus. $34.95.
The definitive book on collectible Winchester shotguns and shotshells manufactured through 1961.

The Winchester Single-Shot- Volume 1; A History and Analysis, by John Campbell, Andrew Mowbray, Inc., Lincoln RI, 1995. 272 pp., illus. $55.00.
Covers every important aspect of this highly-collectible firearm.

The Winchester Single-Shot- Volume 2; Old Secrets and New Discoveries, by John Campbell, Andrew Mowbray, Inc., Lincoln RI, 2000. 280 pp., illus. $55.00.
An exciting follow-up to the classic first volume.

Winchester Slide-Action Rifles, Volume 1: Model 1890 & 1906, by Ned Schwing, Krause Publications, Iola, WI, 1992. 352 pp., illus. $39.95.
First book length treatment of models 1890 & 1906 with over 50 charts and tables showing significant new information about caliber style and rarity.

Winchester Slide-Action Rifles, Volume 2: Model 61 & Model 62, by Ned Schwing, Krause Publications, Iola, WI, 1993. 256 pp., illus. $34.95.
A complete historic look into the Model 61 and the Model 62. These favorite slide-action guns receive a thorough presentation which takes you to the factory to explore receivers, barrels, markings, stocks, stampings and engraving in complete detail.

Winchester's North West Mounted Police Carbines and other Model 1876 Data, by Lewis E. Yearout, The author, Great Falls, MT, 1999. 224 pp., illustrated. Paper covers. $38.00
An impressive accumulation of the facts on the Model 1876, with particular empasis on those purchased for the North West Mounted Police.

Worldwide Webley and the Harrington and Richardson Connection, by Stephen Cuthbertson, Ballista Publishing and Distributing Ltd., Gabriola Island, Canada, 1999. 259 pp., illus. $50.00.
A masterpiece of scholarship. Over 350 photographs plus 75 original documents, patent drawings, and advertisements accompany the text.

GENERAL

Action Shooting: Cowboy Style, by John Taffin, Krause Publications, Iola, WI, 1999. 320 pp., illustrated. $39.95.
Details on the guns and ammunition. Explanations of the rules used for many events. The essential cowboy wardrobe.

Advanced Muzzleloader's Guide, by Toby Bridges, Stoeger Publishing Co., So. Hackensack, NJ, 1985. 256 pp., illus. Paper covers. $14.95.
The complete guide to muzzle-loading rifles, pistols and shotguns—flintlock and percussion.

Aids to Musketry for Officers & NCOs, by Capt. B.J. Friend, Excalibur Publications, Latham, NY, 1996. 40 pp., illus. Paper covers. $7.95.
A facsimile edition of a pre-WWI British manual filled with useful information for training the common soldier.

Air Gun Digest, 3rd Edition, by J.I. Galan, DBI Books, a division of Krause Publications, Iola, WI, 1995. 258 pp., illus. Paper covers. $19.95
Everything from A to Z on air gun history, trends and technology.

American and Imported Arms, Ammunition and Shooting Accessories, Catalog No. 18 of the Shooter's Bible, Stoeger, Inc., reprinted by Fayette Arsenal, Fayetteville, NC, 1988. 142 pp., illus. Paper covers. $10.95.
A facsimile reprint of the 1932 Stoeger's Shooter's Bible.

America's Great Gunmakers, by Wayne van Zwoll, Stoeger Publishing Co., So. Hackensack, NJ, 1992. 288 pp., illus. Paper covers. $16.95.
This book traces in great detail the evolution of guns and ammunition in America and the men who formed the companies that produced them.

Ammunition: Small Arms, Grenades and Projected Munitions, by Ian V. Hogg, Greenhill Books, London, England, 1998. 144 pp., illustrated. $22.95.
The best concise guide to modern ammunition. Wide-ranging and international coverage. Detailed specifications and illustrations.

Armed and Female, by Paxton Quigley, E.P. Dutton, New York, NY, 1989. 237 pp., illus. $16.95.
The first complete book on one of the hottest subjects in the media today, the arming of the American woman.

Arming the Glorious Cause: Weapons of the Second War for Independence, by James B. Whisker, Daniel D. Hartzler and Larry W. Yantz, R & R Books, Livonia, NY, 1998. 175 pp., illustrated. $45.00.
A photographic study of Confederate weapons.

Arms and Armour in Antiquity and the Middle Ages, by Charles Boutell, Stackpole Books, Mechanicsburg, PA, 1996. 352 pp., illus. $22.95.
Detailed descriptions of arms and armor, the development of tactics and the outcome of specific battles.

Arms & Armor in the Art Institute of Chicago, by Walter J. Karcheski, Jr., Bulfinch Press, Boston, MA, 1995. 128 pp., illus. $35.00.
Now, for the first time, the Art Institute of Chicago's arms and armor collection is presented in the visual delight of 103 color illustrations.

Arms for the Nation: Springfield Longarms, edited by David C. Clark, Scott A. Duff, Export, PA, 1994. 73 pp., illus. Paper covers. $9.95.
A brief history of the Springfield Armory and the arms made there.

Arsenal of Freedom, The Springfield Armory, 1890-1948: A Year-by-Year Account Drawn from Official Records, compiled and edited by Lt. Col. William S. Brophy, USAR Ret., Andrew Mowbray, Inc., Lincoln, RI, 1991. 400 pp., illus. Soft covers. $29.95.
A "must buy" for all students of American military weapons, equipment and accoutrements.

Assault Pistols, Rifles and Submachine Guns, by Duncan Long, Paladin Press, Boulder, CO, 1997, 8 1/2 x 11, soft cover, photos, illus. 152 pp. $21.95
This book offers up-to-date, practical information on how to operate and field-strip modern military, police and civilian combat weapons. Covers new developments and trends such as the use of fiber optics, liquid-recoil systems and lessening of barrel length are covered. Troubleshooting procedures, ballistic tables and a list of manufacturers and distributors are also included.

Assault Weapons, 5th Edition, The Gun Digest Book of, edited by Jack Lewis and David E. Steele, DBI Books, a division of Krause Publications, Iola, WI, 2000. 256 pp., illustrated. Paper covers. $21.95.
This is the latest word on true assault weaponry in use today by international military and law enforcement organizations.

The Belgian Rattlesnake: The Lewis Automatic Machine Gun, by William M. Easterly, Collector Grade Publications, Inc., Cobourg, Ont. Canada, 1998. 542 pp., illus. $79.95.
A social and technical biography of the Lewis automatic machine gun and its inventors.

The Big Guns: Civil War Siege, Seacoast, and Naval Cannon, by Edwin Olmstead, Wayne E. Stark and Spencer C. Tucker, Museum Restoration Service, Bloomfield, Ontario, Canada, 1997. 360 pp., illus. $80.00.
This book is designed to identify and record the heavy guns available to both sides during the Civil War.

Blackpowder Loading Manual, 3rd Edition, by Sam Fadala, DBI Books, a division of Krause Publications, Iola, WI, 1995. 368 pp., illus. Paper covers. $20.95.
Revised and expanded edition of this landmark blackpowder loading book. Covers hundreds of loads for most of the popular blackpowder rifles, handguns and shotguns.

Bolt Action Rifles, 3rd Edition, by Frank de Haas, DBI Books, a division of Krause Publications, Iola, WI, 1995. 528 pp., illus. Paper covers. $24.95.
A revised edition of the most definitive work on all major bolt-action rifle designs.

The Book of the Crossbow, by Sir Ralph Payne-Gallwey, Dover Publications, Mineola, NY, 1996. 416 pp., illus. Paper covers. $14.95.
Unabridged republication of the scarce 1907 London edition of the book on one of the most devastating hand weapons of the Middle Ages.

THE ARMS LIBRARY

Bows and Arrows of the Native Americans, by Jim Hamm, Lyons & Burford Publishers, New York, NY, 1991. 156 pp., illus. $19.95.
A complete step-by-step guide to wooden bows, sinew-backed bows, composite bows, strings, arrows and quivers.

British Small Arms of World War 2, by Ian D. Skennerton, I.D.S.A. Books, Piqua, OH, 1988. 110 pp., 37 illus. $25.00.

"Carbine," the Story of David Marshall Williams, by Ross E. Beard, Jr. Phillips Publications, Williamstown, NJ, 1999. 225 pp., illus. $29.95.
The story of the firearms genius, David Marshall "Carbine" Williams. From prison to the pinnacles of fame, the tale of this North Carolinian is inspiring. The author details many of Williams' firearms inventions and developments.

Combat Handgunnery, 4th Edition, The Gun Digest Book of, by Chuck Taylor, DBI Books, a division of Krause Publications, Iola, WI, 1997. 256 pp., illus. Paper covers. $18.95.
This edition looks at real world combat handgunnery from three different perspectives—military, police and civilian.

The Complete Blackpowder Handbook, 3rd Edition, by Sam Fadala, DBI Books, a division of Krause Publications, Iola, WI, 1997. 400 pp., illus. Paper covers. $21.95.
Expanded and completely rewritten edition of the definitive book on the subject of blackpowder.

The Complete Guide to Game Care and Cookery, 3rd Edition, by Sam Fadala, DBI Books, a division of Krause Publications, Iola, WI, 1994. 320 pp., illus. Paper covers. $18.95.
Over 500 photos illustrating the care of wild game in the field and at home with a separate recipe section providing over 400 tested recipes.

The Complete .50-caliber Sniper Course, by Dean Michaelis, Paladin Press, Boulder, CO, 2000. 576 pp, illustrated, $60.00
The history from German Mauser T-Gewehr of World War 1 to the Soviet PTRD and beyond. Includes the author's Program of Instruction for Special Operations Hard-Target Interdiction Course.

Complete Guide to Guns & Shooting, by John Malloy, DBI Books, a division of Krause Publications, Iola, WI, 1995. 256 pp., illus. Paper covers. $18.95.
What every shooter and gun owner should know about firearms, ammunition, shooting techniques, safety, collecting and much more.

Cowboy Action Shooting, by Charly Gullett, Wolfe Publishing Co., Prescott, AZ, 1995. 400 pp., illus. Paper covers. $24.50.
The fast growing of the shooting sports is comprehensively covered in this text—the guns, loads, tactics and the fun and flavor of this Old West era competition.

Crossbows, edited by Roger Combs, DBI Books, a division of Krause Publications, Iola, WI, 1986. 192 pp., illus. Paper covers. $15.95.
Complete, up-to-date coverage of the hottest bow going—and the most controversial.

Custom Firearms Engraving, by Tom Turpin, Krause Publications, Iola, WI, 1999. 208 pp., illustrated. $49.95.
Provides a broad and comprehensive look at the world of firearms engraving. The exquisite styles of more than 75 master engravers are shown on beautiful examples of handguns, rifles, shotguns, and other firearms, as well as knives.

Dead On, by Tony Noblitt and Warren Gabrilska, Paladin Press, Boulder, CO, 1998. 176 pp., illustrated. Paper covers. $22.00
The long-range marksman's guide to extreme accuracy.

Death from Above: The German FG42 Paratrooper Rifle, by Thomas B. Dugelby and R. Blake Stevens, Collector Grade Publications, Toronto, Canada, 1990. 147 pp., illus. $39.95.
The first comprehensive study of all seven models of the FG42.

Early American Flintlocks, by Daniel D. Hartzler and James B. Whisker, Bedford Valley Press, Bedford, PA 2000. 192 pp., Illustrated.
Covers early Colonial Guns, New England Guns, Pennsylvania Guns and Souther Guns.

Encyclopedia of Modern Firearms, Vol. 1, compiled and publ. by Bob Brownell, Montezuma, IA, 1959. 1057 pp. plus index, illus. $70.00. Dist. By Bob Brownell, Montezuma, IA 50171.
Massive accumulation of basic information of nearly all modern arms pertaining to "parts and assembly." Replete with arms photographs, exploded drawings, manufacturers' lists of parts, etc.

Encyclopedia of Native American Bows, Arrows and Quivers, by Steve Alley and Jim Hamm, The Lyons Press, N.Y., 1999. 160 pp., illustrated. $29.95.
A landmark book for anyone interested in archery history, or Native Americans.

The Exercise of Armes, by Jacob de Gheyn, edited and with an introduction by Bas Kist, Dover Publications, Inc., Mineola, NY, 1999. 144 pp., illustrated. Paper covers. $12.95.
Republications of all 117 engravings from the 1607 classic military manual. A meticulously accurate portrait of uniforms and weapons of the 17th century Netherlands.

Exploded Long Gun Drawings, The Gun Digest Book of, edited by Harold A. Murtz, DBI Books, a division of Krause Publications, Iola, WI, 512 pp., illus. Paper covers. $20.95.
Containing almost 500 rifle and shotgun exploded drawings.

Fighting Iron; A Metals Handbook for Arms Collectors, by Art Gogan, Mowbray Publishers, Inc., Lincoln, RI, 1999. 176 pp., illustrated. $28.00.
A guide that is easy to use, explains things in simple English and covers all of the different historical periods that we are interested in.

The Fighting Submachine Gun, Machine Pistol, and Shotgun, a Hands-On Evaluation, by Timothy J. Mullin, Paladin Press, Boulder, CO, 1999. 224 pp., illustrated. Paper covers. $35.00.
An invaluable reference for military, police and civilian shooters who may someday need to know how a specific weapon actually performs when the targets are shooting back and the margin of errors is measured in lives lost.

Fireworks: A Gunsight Anthology, by Jeff Cooper, Paladin Press, Boulder, CO, 1998. 192 pp., illus. Paper cover. $27.00
A collection of wild, hilarious, shocking and always meaningful tales from the remarkable life of an American firearms legend.

Frank Pachmayr: The Story of America's Master Gunsmith and his Guns, by John Lachuk, Safari Press, Huntington Beach, CA, 1996. 254 pp., illus. First edition, limited, signed and slipcased. $85.00; Second printing trade edition. $50.00.
The colorful and historically significant biography of Frank A. Pachmayr, America's own gunsmith emeritus.

From a Stranger's Doorstep to the Kremlin Gate, by Mikhail Kalashnikov, Ironside International Publishers, Inc., Alexandria, VA, 1999. 460 pp., illustrated. $34.95.
A biography of the most influential rifle designer of the 20th century. His AK-47 assault rifle has become the most widely used (and copied) assault rifle of this century.

The Frontier Rifleman, by H.B. LaCrosse Jr., Pioneer Press, Union City, TN, 1989. 183 pp., illus. Soft covers. $17.50.
The Frontier rifleman's clothing and equipment during the era of the American Revolution, 1760-1800.

The Gatling Gun: 19th Century Machine Gun to 21st Century Vulcan, by Joseph Berk, Paladin Press, Boulder, CO, 1991. 136 pp., illus. $34.95.
Here is the fascinating on-going story of a truly timeless weapon, from its beginnings during the Civil War to its current role as a state-of-the-art modern combat system.

German Artillery of World War Two, by Ian V. Hogg, Stackpole Books, Mechanicsburg, PA, 1997. 304 pp., illus. $44.95.
Complete details of German artillery use in WWII.

Grand Old Lady of No Man's Land: The Vickers Machine Gun, by Dolf L. Goldsmith, Collector Grade Publications, Cobourg, Canada, 1994. 600 pp., illus. $79.95.
Goldsmith brings his years of experience as a U.S. Army armourer, machine gun collector and shooter to bear on the Vickers, in a book sure to become a classic in its field.

The Grenade Recognition Manual, Volume 1, U.S. Grenades & Accessories, by Darryl W. Lynn, Service Publications, Ottawa, Canada, 1998. 112 pp., illus. Paper covers. $29.95.
This new book examines the hand grenades of the United States beginning with the hand grenades of the U.S. Civil War and continues through to the present.

The Grenade Recognition Manual, Vol. 2, British and Commonwealth Grenades and Accessories, by Darryl W. Lynn, Printed by the Author, Ottawa, Canada, 2001. 201 pp., illustrated with over 200 photos and drawings. Paper covers. $29.95.
Covers British, Australian, and Canadian Grenades. It has the complete British Numbered series, most of the L series as well as the Australian and Canadian grenades in use. Also covers Launchers, fuzes and lighters, launching cartridges, fillings, and markings.

Gun Digest Treasury, 7th Edition, edited by Harold A. Murtz, DBI Books, a division of Krause Publications, Iola, WI, 1994. 320 pp., illus. Paper covers. $17.95.
A collection of some of the most interesting articles which have appeared in Gun Digest over its first 45 years.

Gun Digest 2002, 56th Edition, edited by Ken Ramage, DBI Books a division of Krause Publications, Iola, WI, 2001. 544 pp., illustrated. Paper covers. $24.95.
This all new 56th edition continues the editorial excellence, quality, content and comprehensive cataloguing that firearms enthusiasts have come to know and expect. The most read gun book in the world for the last half century.

Gun Engraving, by C. Austyn, Safari Press Publication, Huntington Beach, CA, 1998. 128 pp., plus 24 pages of color photos. $50.00.
A well-illustrated book on fine English and European gun engravers. Includes a fantastic pictorial section that lists types of engravings and prices.

THE ARMS LIBRARY

Gun Notes, Volume 1, by Elmer Keith, Safari Press, Huntington Beach, CA, 1995. 219 pp., illustrated Limited Edition, Slipcased. $75.00
A collection of Elmer Keith's most interesting columns and feature stories that appeared in "Guns & Ammo" magazine from 1961 to the late 1970's.

Gun Notes, Volume 2, by Elmer Keith, Safari Press, Huntington Beach, CA, 1997. 292 pp., illus. Limited 1st edition, numbered and signed by Keith's son. Slipcased. $75.00. Trade edition. $35.00.
Covers articles from Keith's monthly column in "Guns & Ammo" magazine during the period from 1971 through Keith's passing in 1982.

Gun Talk, edited by Dave Moreton, Winchester Press, Piscataway, NJ, 1973. 256 pp., illus. $9.95.
A treasury of original writing by the top gun writers and editors in America. Practical advice about every aspect of the shooting sports.

The Gun That Made the Twenties Roar, by Wm. J. Helmer, rev. and enlarged by George C. Nonte, Jr., The Gun Room Press, Highland Park, NJ, 1977. Over 300 pp., illus. $24.95.
Historical account of John T. Thompson and his invention, the infamous "Tommy Gun."

Gun Trader's Guide, 23rd Edition, published by Stoeger Publishing Co., Wayne, NJ, 1999. 592 pp., illus. Paper covers. $23.95.
Complete specifications and current prices for used guns. Prices of over 5,000 handguns, rifles and shotguns both foreign and domestic.

Gun Writers of Yesteryear, compiled by James Foral, Wolfe Publishing Co., Prescott, AZ, 1993. 449 pp. $35.00.
Here, from the pre-American rifleman days of 1898-1920, are collected some 80 articles by 34 writers from eight magazines.

The Gunfighter, Man or Myth? by Joseph G. Rosa, Oklahoma Press, Norman, OK, 1969. 229 pp., illus. (including weapons). Paper covers. $14.95.
A well-documented work on gunfights and gunfighters of the West and elsewhere. Great treat for all gunfighter buffs.

Gunfitting: The Quest for Perfection, by Michael Yardley, Safari Press, Huntington Beach, CA, 1995. 128 pp., illus. $24.95.
The author, a very experienced shooting instructor, examines gun stocks and gunfitting in depth.

Guns Illustrated 2002, 3rd Edition, edited by Ken Ramage, DBI Books a division of Krause Publications, Iola, WI, 1999. 352 pp., illustrated. Paper covers. $22.95.
Highly informative, technical articles on a wide range of shooting topics by some of the top writers in the industry. A catalog section lists more than 3,000 firearms currently manufactured in or imported to the U.S.

Guns & Shooting: A Selected Bibliography, by Ray Riling, Ray Riling Arms Books Co., Phila., PA, 1982. 434 pp., illus. Limited, numbered edition. $75.
A limited edition of this superb bibliographical work, the only modern listing of books devoted to guns and shooting.

Guns, Bullets, and Gunfighters, by Jim Cirillo, Paladin Press, Boulder, CO, 1996. 119 pp., illus. Paper covers. $16.00.
Lessons and tales from a modern-day gunfighter.

Guns, Loads, and Hunting Tips, by Bob Hagel, Wolfe Publishing Co., Prescott, AZ, 1986. 509 pp., illus. $19.95.
A large hardcover book packed with shooting, hunting and handloading wisdom.

Handgun Digest, 3rd Edition, edited by Chris Christian, DBI Books, a division of Krause Publications, Iola, WI, 1995. 256 pp., illus. Paper covers. $18.95.
Full coverage of all aspects of handguns and handgunning from a highly readable and knowledgeable author.

Hidden in Plain Sight, "A Practical Guide to Concealed Handgun Carry" (Revised 2nd Edition), by Trey Bloodworth and Mike Raley, Paladin Press, Boulder, CO, 1997, 5 1/2 x 8 1/2, softcover, photos, 176 pp. $20.00
Concerned with how to comfortably, discreetly and safely exercise the privileges granted by a CCW permit? This invaluable guide offers the latest advice on what to look for when choosing a CCW, how to dress for comfortable, effective concealed carry, traditional and more unconventional carry modes, accessory holsters, customized clothing and accessories, accessibility data based on draw-time comparisons and new holsters on the market. Includes 40 new manufacturer listings.

HK Assault Rifle Systems, by Duncan Long, Paladin Press, Boulder, CO, 1995. 110 pp., illus. Paper covers. $27.95.
The little known history behind this fascinating family of weapons tracing its beginnings from the ashes of World War Two to the present time.

The Hunter's Table, by Terry Libby/Recipes of Chef Richard Blondin, Countrysport Press, Selma, AL, 1999. 230 pp. $30.00.
The Countrysport book of wild game cuisine.

I Remember Skeeter, compiled by Sally Jim Skelton, Wolfe Publishing Co., Prescott, AZ, 1998. 401 pp., illus. Paper covers. $19.95.
A collection of some of the beloved storyteller's famous works interspersed with anecdotes and tales from the people who knew best.

In The Line of Fire, "A Working Cop's Guide to Pistol Craft," by Michael E. Conti, Paladin Press, Boulder, CO, 1997, soft cover, photos, illus., 184 pp. $30.00
As a working cop, you want to end your patrol in the same condition you began: alive and uninjured. Improve your odds by reading and mastering the information in this book on pistol selection, stopping power, combat reloading, stoppages, carrying devices, stances, grips and Conti's "secrets" to accurate shooting.

Joe Rychertinik Reflects on Guns, Hunting, and Days Gone By, by Joe Rychertinik, Precision Shooting, Inc., Manchester, CT, 1999. 281 pp., illustrated. Paper covers. $16.95.
Thirty articles by a master story-teller.

Kill or Get Killed, by Col. Rex Applegate, Paladin Press, Boulder, CO, 1996. 400 pp., illus. $39.95.
The best and longest-selling book on close combat in history.

Larrey: Surgeon to Napoleon's Imperial Guard, by Robert G. Richardson, Quiller Press, London, 2000. 269 pp., illus. B & W photos, maps and drawings. $23.95
Not a book for the squeamish, but one full of interest, splendidly researched, bringing both the character of the Napoleonic wars and Larrey himself vividly to life. Authenticity of detail is preserved throughout.

The Long-Range War: Sniping in Vietnam, by Peter R. Senich, Paladin Press, Boulder, CO, 1994. 280 pp., illus. $49.95.
The most complete report on Vietnam-era sniping ever documented.

Manual for H&R Reising Submachine Gun and Semi-Auto Rifle, edited by George P. Dillman, Desert Publications, El Dorado, AZ, 1994. 81 pp., illus. Paper covers. $12.95.
A reprint of the Harrington & Richardson 1943 factory manual and the rare military manual on the H&R submachine gun and semi-auto rifle.

The Manufacture of Gunflints, by Sydney B.J. Skertchly, facsimile reprint with new introduction by Seymour de Lotbiniere, Museum Restoration Service, Ontario, Canada, 1984. 90 pp., illus. $24.50.
Limited edition reprinting of the very scarce London edition of 1879.

Master Tips, by J. Winokur, Potshot Press, Pacific Palisades, CA, 1985. 96 pp., illus. Paper covers. $11.95.
Basics of practical shooting.

The Military and Police Sniper, by Mike R. Lau, Precision Shooting, Inc., Manchester, CT, 1998. 352 pp., illustrated. Paper covers. $44.95.
Advanced precision shooting for combat and law enforcement.

Military Rifle & Machine Gun Cartridges, by Jean Huon, Paladin Press, Boulder, CO, 1990. 392 pp., illus. $34.95.
Describes the primary types of military cartridges and their principal loadings, as well as their characteristics, origin and use.

Military Small Arms of the 20th Century, 7th Edition, by Ian V. Hogg and John Weeks, DBI Books, a division of Krause Publications, Iola, WI, 2000. 416 pp., illustrated. Paper covers. $24.95.
Cover small arms of 46 countries. Over 800 photographs and illustrations.

Modern Custom Guns, Walnut, Steel, and Uncommon Artistry, by Tom Turpin, Krause Publications, Iola, WI, 1997. 206 pp., illus. $49.95.
From exquisite engraving to breathtaking exotic woods, the mystique of today's custom guns is expertly detailed in word and awe-inspiring color photos of rifles, shotguns and handguns.

Modern Guns Identification & Values, 13th Edition, by Russell & Steve Quertermous, Collector Books, Paducah, KY, 1999. 516 pp., illus. Paper covers. $12.95.
A standard reference for over 20 years. Over 1,800 illustrations of over 2,500 models with their current values.

Modern Law Enforcement Weapons & Tactics, 2nd Edition, by Tom Ferguson, DBI Books, a division of Krause Publications, Iola, WI, 1991. 256 pp., illus. Paper covers. $18.95.
An in-depth look at the weapons and equipment used by law enforcement agencies of today.

Modern Machine Guns, by John Walter, Stackpole Books, Inc. Mechanicsburg, PA, 2000. 144 pp., with 146 illustrations. $22.95.
A compact and authoritative guide to post-war machine-guns. A gun-by-gun directory identifying individual variants and types including detailed evaluations and technical data.

Modern Sporting Guns, by Christopher Austyn, Safari Press, Huntington Beach, CA, 1994. 128 pp., illus. $40.00.
A discussion of the "best" English guns; round action, over-and-under, boxlocks, hammer guns, bolt action and double rifles as well as accessories.

The More Complete Cannoneer, by M.C. Switlik, Museum & Collectors Specialties Co., Monroe, MI, 1990. 199 pp., illus. $19.95.
Compiled agreeably to the regulations for the U.S. War Department, 1861, and containing current observations on the use of antique cannons.

The MP-40 Machine Gun, Desert Publications, El Dorado, AZ, 1995. 32 pp., illus. Paper covers. $11.95.
A reprint of the hard-to-find operating and maintenance manual for one of the most famous machine guns of World War II.

Naval Percussion Locks and Primers, by Lt. J. A. Dahlgren, Museum Restoration Service, Bloomfield, Canada, 1996. 140 pp., illus. $35.00
First published as an Ordnance Memoranda in 1853, this is the finest existing study of percussion locks and primers origin and development.

THE ARMS LIBRARY

The Official Soviet AKM Manual, translated by Maj. James F. Gebhardt (Ret.), Paladin Press, Boulder, CO, 1999. 120 pp., illustrated. Paper covers. $18.00.

This official military manual, available in English for the first time, was originally published by the Soviet Ministry of Defence. Covers the history, function, maintenance, assembly and disassembly, etc. of the 7.62mm AKM assault rifle.

The One-Round War: U.S.M.C. Scout-Snipers in Vietnam, by Peter Senich, Paladin Press, Boulder, CO, 1996. 384 pp., illus. Paper covers $59.95.

Sniping in Vietnam focusing specifically on the Marine Corps program.

Pin Shooting: A Complete Guide, by Mitchell A. Ota, Wolfe Publishing Co., Prescott, AZ, 1992. 145 pp., illus. Paper covers. $14.95.

Traces the sport from its humble origins to today's thoroughly enjoyable social event, including the mammoth eight-day Second Chance Pin Shoot in Michigan.

Powder and Ball Small Arms, by Martin Pegler, Windrow & Greene Publishing, London, 1998. 128 pp., illustrated with 200 color photos. $39.95.

Part of the new "Live Firing Classic Weapons" series. Full-color photos of experienced shooters dressed in authentic costumes handling, loading and firing historic weapons.

Principles of Personal Defense, by Jeff Cooper, Paladin Press, Boulder, CO, 1999. 56 pp., illustrated. Paper covers. $14.00.

This revised edition of Jeff Cooper's classic on personal defense offers great new illustrations and a new preface while retaining the timeliness theory of individual defense behavior presented in the original book.

E.C. Prudhomme, Master Gun Engraver, A Retrospective Exhibition: 1946-1973, intro. by John T. Amber, The R. W. Norton Art Gallery, Shreveport, LA, 1973. 32 pp., illus. Paper covers. $9.95.

Examples of master gun engravings by Jack Prudhomme.

The Quotable Hunter, edited by Jay Cassell and Peter Fiduccia, The lyons Press, N.Y., 1999. 224 pp., illustrated. $20.00.

This collection of more than three hundred memorable quotes from hunters through the ages captures the essence of the sport, with all its joys idiosyncrasies, and challenges.

A Rifleman Went to War, by H. W. McBride, Lancer Militaria, Mt. Ida, AR, 1987. 398 pp., illus. $29.95.

The classic account of practical marksmanship on the battlefields of World War I.

Sharpshooting for Sport and War, by W.W. Greener, Wolfe Publishing Co., Prescott, AZ, 1995. 192 pp., illus. $30.00.

This classic reprint explores the *first* expanding bullet; service rifles; shooting positions; trajectories; recoil; external ballistics; and other valuable information.

The Shooter's Bible 2002, No. 93, edited by William S. Jarrett, Stoeger Publishing Co., Wayne, NJ, 2001. 576 pp., illustrated. Paper covers. $23.95.

Over 3,000 firearms currently offered by major American and foreign gunmakers. Represented are handguns, rifles, shotguns and black powder arms with complete specifications and retail prices.

Shooting To Live, by Capt. W. E. Fairbairn & Capt. E. A. Sykes, Paladin Press, Boulder, CO, 1997, 4 1/2 x 7, soft cover, illus., 112 pp. $14.00

Shooting to Live is the product of Fairbairn's and Sykes' practical experience with the handgun. Hundreds of incidents provided the basis for the first true book on life-or-death shootouts with the pistol. Shooting to Live teaches all concepts, considerations and applications of combat pistol craft.

Shooting Sixguns of the Old West, by Mike Venturino, MLV Enterprises, Livingston, MT, 1997. 221 pp., illus. Paper covers. $26.50.

A comprehensive look at the guns of the early West: Colts, Smith & Wesson and Remingtons, plus blackpowder and reloading specs.

Sniper Training, FM 23-10, Reprint of the U.S. Army field manual of August, 1994, Paladin Press, Boulder, CO, 1995. 352pp., illus. Paper covers. $30.00

The most up-to-date U.S. military sniping information and doctrine.

Sniping in France, by Major H. Hesketh-Prichard, Lancer Militaria, Mt. Ida, AR, 1993. 224 pp., illus. $24.95.

The author was a well-known British adventurer and big game hunter. He was called upon in the early days of "The Great War" to develop a program to offset an initial German advantage in sniping. How the British forces came to overcome this advantage.

Special Warfare: Special Weapons, by Kevin Dockery, Emperor's Press, Chicago, IL, 1997. 192 pp., illus. $29.95.

The arms and equipment of the UDT and SEALS from 1943 to the present.

Sporting Collectibles, by Dr. Stephen R. Irwin, Stoeger Publishing Co., Wayne, NJ, 1997. 256 pp., illus. Paper covers. $19.95.

A must book for serious collectors and admirers of sporting collectibles.

The Sporting Craftsmen: A Complete Guide to Contemporary Makers of Custom-Built Sporting Equipment, by Art Carter, Countrysport Press, Traverse City, MI, 1994. 240 pp., illus. $35.00.

Profiles leading makers of centerfire rifles; muzzleloading rifles; bamboo fly rods; fly reels; flies; waterfowl calls; decoys; handmade knives; and traditional longbows and recurves.

Sporting Rifle Takedown & Reassembly Guide, 2nd Edition, by J.B. Wood, DBI Books, a division of Krause Publications, Iola, WI, 1997. 480 pp., illus. $19.95.

An updated edition of the reference guide for anyone who wants to properly care for their sporting rifle. (Available September 1997)

2001 Standard Catalog of Firearms, the Collector's Price & Reference Guide, 11th Edition, by Ned Schwing, Krause Publications, Iola, WI, 2000. 1,248 pp., illus. Paper covers. $32.95.

Packed with more than 80,000 real world prices with more than 5,000 photos. Easy to use master index listing every firearm model.

The Street Smart Gun Book, by John Farnam, Police Bookshelf, Concord, NH, 1986. 45 pp., illus. Paper covers. $11.95.

Weapon selection, defensive shooting techniques, and gunfight-winning tactics from one of the world's leading authorities.

Stress Fire, Vol. 1: Stress Fighting for Police, by Massad Ayoob, Police Bookshelf, Concord, NH, 1984. 149 pp., illus. Paper covers. $9.95.

Gunfighting for police, advanced tactics and techniques.

Survival Guns, by Mel Tappan, Desert Publications, El Dorado, AZ, 1993. 456 pp., illus. Paper covers. $21.95.

Discusses in a frank and forthright manner which handguns, rifles and shotguns to buy for personal defense and securing food, and the ones to avoid.

The Tactical Advantage, by Gabriel Suarez, Paladin Press, Boulder, CO, 1998. 216 pp., illustrated. Paper covers. $22.00.

Learn combat tactics that have been tested in the world's toughest schools.

Tactical Marksman, by Dave M. Lauch, Paladin Press, Boulder, CO, 1996. 165 pp., illus. Paper covers. $35.00.

A complete training manual for police and practical shooters.

Thompson Guns 1921-1945, Anubis Press, Houston, TX, 1980. 215 pp., illus. Paper covers. $15.95.

Facsimile reprinting of five complete manuals on the Thompson submachine gun.

To Ride, Shoot Straight, and Speak the Truth, by Jeff Cooper, Paladin Press, Boulder, CO, 1997, 5 1/2 x 8 1/2, soft-cover, illus., 384 pp. $32.00

Combat mind-set, proper sighting, tactical residential architecture, nuclear war - these are some of the many subjects explored by Jeff Cooper in this illustrated anthology. The author discusses various arms, fighting skills and the importance of knowing how to defend oneself, and one's honor, in our rapidly changing world.

Trailriders Guide to Cowboy Action Shooting, by James W. Barnard, Pioneer Press, Union City, TN, 1998. 134 pp., plus 91 photos, drawings and charts. Paper covers. $24.95.

Covers the complete spectrum of this shooting discipline, from how to dress to authentic leather goods, which guns are legal, calibers, loads and ballistics.

The Ultimate Sniper, by Major John L. Plaster, Paladin Press, Boulder, CO, 1994. 464 pp., illus. Paper covers. $42.95.

An advanced training manual for military and police snipers.

Unrepentant Sinner, by Col. Charles Askins, Paladin Press, Boulder, CO, 2000. 322 pp., illustrated. $29.95.

The autobiography of Colonel Charles Askins.

U.S. Marine Corp Rifle and Pistol Marksmanship, 1935, reprinting of a government publication, Lancer Militaria, Mt. Ida, AR, 1991. 99 pp., illus. Paper covers. $11.95.

The old corps method of precision shooting.

U.S. Marine Corps Scout/Sniper Training Manual, Lancer Militaria, Mt. Ida, AR, 1989. Soft covers. $19.95.

Reprint of the original sniper training manual used by the Marksmanship Training Unit of the Marine Corps Development and Education Command in Quantico, Virginia.

U.S. Marine Corps Scout-Sniper, World War II and Korea, by Peter R. Senich, Paladin Press, Boulder, CO, 1994. 236 pp., illus. $44.95.

The most thorough and accurate account ever printed on the training, equipment and combat experiences of the U.S. Marine Corps Scout-Snipers.

U.S. Marine Corps Sniping, Lancer Militaria, Mt. Ida, AR, 1989. Irregular pagination. Soft covers. $17.95.

A reprint of the official Marine Corps FMFM1-3B.

Weapons of the Waffen-SS, by Bruce Quarrie, Sterling Publishing Co., Inc., 1991. 168 pp., illus. $24.95.

An in-depth look at the weapons that made Hitler's Waffen-SS the fearsome fighting machine it was.

THE ARMS LIBRARY

Weatherby: The Man, The Gun, The Legend, by Grits and Tom Gresham, Cane River Publishing Co., Natchitoches, LA, 1992. 290 pp., illus. $24.95.
  A fascinating look at the life of the man who changed the course of firearms development in America.

The Winchester Era, by David Madis, Art & Reference House, Brownsville, TX, 1984. 100 pp., illus. $19.95.
  Story of the Winchester company, management, employees, etc.

Winchester Repeating Arms Company by Herbert Houze, Krause Publications, Iola, WI. 512 pp., illus. $50.00.

With British Snipers to the Reich, by Capt. C. Shore, Lander Militaria, Mt. Ida, AR, 1988. 420 pp., illus. $29.95.
  One of the greatest books ever written on the art of combat sniping.

The World's Machine Pistols and Submachine Guns - Vol. 2a 1964 to 1980, by Nelson & Musgrave, Ironside International, Alexandria, VA, 2000. 673 pages, illustrated. $59.95
  Containing data, history and photographs of over 200 weapons. With a special section covering shoulder stocked automatic pistols, 100 additional photos.

The World's Submachine Guns - Vol. 1 1918 to 1963, by Nelson & Musgrave, Ironside International, Alexandria, VA, 2001. 673 pages, illustrated. $59.95.
  A revised edition covering much new material that has come to light since the book was originally printed in 1963.

The World's Sniping Rifles, by Ian V. Hogg, Paladin Press, Boulder, CO, 1998. 144 pp., illustrated. $22.95.
  A detailed manual with descriptions and illustrations of more than 50 high-precision rifles from 14 countries and a complete analysis of sights and systems.

GUNSMITHING

Accurizing the Factory Rifle, by M.L. McPherson, Precision Shooting, Inc., Manchester, CT, 1999. 335 pp., illustrated. Paper covers. $44.95.
  A long-awaiting book, which bridges the gap between the rudimentary (mounting sling swivels, scope blocks and that general level of accomplishment) and the advanced (precision chambering, barrel fluting, and that general level of accomplishment) books that are currently available today.

Advanced Rebarreling of the Sporting Rifle, by Willis H. Fowler, Jr., Willis H. Fowler, Jr., Anchorage, AK, 1994. 127 pp., illus. Paper covers. $32.50.
  A manual outlining a superior method of fitting barrels and doing chamber work on the sporting rifle.

The Art of Engraving, by James B. Meek, F. Brownell & Son, Montezuma, IA, 1973. 196 pp., illus. $38.95.
  A complete, authoritative, imaginative and detailed study in training for gun engraving. The first book of its kind—and a great one.

Artistry in Arms, The R. W. Norton Gallery, Shreveport, LA, 1970. 42 pp., illus. Paper covers. $9.95.
  The art of gunsmithing and engraving.

Barrels & Actions, by Harold Hoffman, H&P Publishers, San Angelo, TX, 1990. 309 pp., illus. Spiral bound. $29.95.
  A manual on barrel making.

Black Powder Hobby Gunsmithing, by Sam Fadala and Dale Storey, DBI Books, a division of Krause Publications, Iola, WI., 1994. 256 pp., illus. Paper covers. $18.95.
  A how-to guide for gunsmithing blackpowder pistols, rifles and shotguns from two men at the top of their respective fields.

Checkering and Carving of Gun Stocks, by Monte Kennedy, Stackpole Books, Harrisburg, PA, 1962. 175 pp., illus. $39.95.
  Revised, enlarged cloth-bound edition of a much sought-after, dependable work.

The Complete Metal Finishing Book, by Harold Hoffman, H&P Publishers, San Angelo, TX, 1992. 364 pp., illus. Paper covers. $29.95.
  Instructions for the different metal finishing operations that the normal craftsman or shop will use. Primarily firearm related.

Exploded Handgun Drawings, The Gun Digest Book of, edited by Harold A. Murtz, DBI Books, a division of Krause Publications, Iola, WI. 1992. 512 pp., illus. Paper covers. $20.95.
  Exploded or isometric drawings for 494 of the most popular handguns.

Exploded Long Gun Drawings, The Gun Digest Book of, edited by Harold A. Murtz, DBI Books, a division of Krause Publications, Iola, WI. 512 pp., illus. Paper covers. $20.95.
  Containing almost 500 rifle and shotgun exploded drawings. An invaluable aid to both professionals and hobbyists.

The Finishing of Gun Stocks, by Harold Hoffman, H&P Publishers, San Angelo, TX, 1994. 98 pp., illus. Paper covers. $17.95.
  Covers different types of finishing methods and finishes.

Firearms Assembly/Disassembly, Part I: Automatic Pistols, 2nd Revised Edition, The Gun Digest Book of, by J.B. Wood, DBI Books, a division of Krause Publications, Iola, WI, 1999. 480 pp., illus. Paper covers. $24.95.
  Covers 58 popular autoloading pistols plus nearly 200 variants of those models integrated into the text and completely cross-referenced in the index.

Firearms Assembly/Disassembly Part II: Revolvers, Revised Edition, The Gun Digest Book of, by J.B. Wood, DBI Books, a division of Krause Publications, Iola, WI, 1990. 480 pp., illus. Paper covers. $19.95.
  Covers 49 popular revolvers plus 130 variants. The most comprehensive and professional presentation available to either hobbyist or gunsmith.

Firearms Assembly/Disassembly Part III: Rimfire Rifles, Revised Edition, The Gun Digest Book of, by J. B. Wood, DBI Books, a division of Krause Publications, Iola, WI., 1994. 480 pp., illus. Paper covers. $19.95.
  Greatly expanded edition covering 65 popular rimfire rifles plus over 100 variants all completely cross-referenced in the index.

Firearms Assembly/Disassembly Part IV: Centerfire Rifles, Revised Edition, The Gun Digest Book of, by J.B. Wood, DBI Books, a division of Krause Publications, Iola, WI, 1991. 480 pp., illus. Paper covers. $19.95.
  Covers 54 popular centerfire rifles plus 300 variants. The most comprehensive and professional presentation available to either hobbyist or gunsmith.

Firearms Assembly/Disassembly, Part V: Shotguns, Revised Edition, The Gun Digest Book of, by J.B. Wood, DBI Books, a division of Krause Publications, Iola, WI, 1992. 480 pp., illus. Paper covers. $19.95.
  Covers 46 popular shotguns plus over 250 variants with step-by-step instructions on how to dismantle and reassemble each. The most comprehensive and professional presentation available to either hobbyist or gunsmith.

Firearms Assembly/Disassembly Part VI: Law Enforcement Weapons, The Gun Digest Book of, by J.B. Wood, DBI Books, a division of Krause Publications, Iola, WI, 1981. 288 pp., illus. Paper covers. $16.95.
  Step-by-step instructions on how to completely dismantle and reassemble the most commonly used firearms found in law enforcement arsenals.

Firearms Assembly 3: The NRA Guide to Rifle and Shotguns, NRA Books, Wash., DC, 1980. 264 pp., illus. Paper covers. $13.95.
  Text and illustrations explaining the takedown of 125 rifles and shotguns, domestic and foreign.

Firearms Assembly 4: The NRA Guide to Pistols and Revolvers, NRA Books, Wash., DC, 1980. 253 pp., illus. Paper covers. $13.95.
  Text and illustrations explaining the takedown of 124 pistol and revolver models, domestic and foreign.

Firearms Bluing and Browning, By R.H. Angier, Stackpole Books, Harrisburg, PA. 151 pp., illus. $19.95.
  A world master gunsmith reveals his secrets of building, repairing and renewing a gun, quite literally, lock, stock and barrel. A useful, concise text on chemical coloring methods for the gunsmith and mechanic.

Firearms Disassembly—With Exploded Views, by John A. Karns & John E. Traister, Stoeger Publishing Co., S. Hackensack, NJ, 1995. 320 pp., illus. Paper covers. $19.95.
  Provides the do's and don'ts of firearms disassembly. Enables owners and gunsmiths to disassemble firearms in a professional manner.

Guns and Gunmaking Tools of Southern Appalachia, by John Rice Irwin, Schiffer Publishing Ltd., 1983. 118 pp., illus. Paper covers. $9.95.
  The story of the Kentucky rifle.

Gunsmithing: Pistols & Revolvers, by Patrick Sweeney, DBI Books, a division of Krause Publications, Iola, WI, 1998. 352 pp., illus. Paper covers. $24.95.
  Do-it-Yourself projects, diagnosis and repair for pistols and revolvers.

Gunsmithing: Rifles, by Patrick Sweeney, Krause Publications, Iola, WI, 1999. 352 pp., illustrated. Paper covers. $24.95.
  Tips for lever-action rifles. Building a custom Ruger 10/22. Building a better hunting rifle.

Gunsmithing Tips and Projects, a collection of the best articles from the *Handloader* and *Rifle* magazines, by various authors, Wolfe Publishing Co., Prescott, AZ, 1992. 443 pp., illus. Paper covers. $25.00.
  Includes such subjects as shop, stocks, actions, tuning, triggers, barrels, customizing, etc.

Gunsmith Kinks, by F.R. (Bob) Brownell, F. Brownell & Son, Montezuma, IA, 1st ed., 1969. 496 pp., well illus. $22.98.
  A widely useful accumulation of shop kinks, short cuts, techniques and pertinent comments by practicing gunsmiths from all over the world.

Gunsmith Kinks 2, by Bob Brownell, F. Brownell & Son, Publishers, Montezuma, IA, 1983. 496 pp., illus. $22.95.
  A collection of gunsmithing knowledge, shop kinks, new and old techniques, shortcuts and general know-how straight from those who do them best—the gunsmiths.

Gunsmith Kinks 3, edited by Frank Brownell, Brownells Inc., Montezuma, IA, 1993. 504 pp., illus. $24.95.
  Tricks, knacks and "kinks" by professional gunsmiths and gun tinkerers. Hundreds of valuable ideas are given in this volume.

Gunsmith Kinks 4, edited by Frank Brownell, Brownells Inc., Montezuma, IA, 2001. 564 pp., illus. $27.75
  332 detailed illustrations. 560+ pages with 706 separate subject headings and over 5000 cross-indexed entries. An incredible gold mine of information.

Gunsmithing, by Roy F. Dunlap, Stackpole Books, Harrisburg, PA, 1990. 742 pp., illus. $34.95.
  A manual of firearm design, construction, alteration and remodeling. For amateur and professional gunsmiths and users of modern firearms.

Handgun Hunting

THE ARMS LIBRARY

Gunsmithing at Home: Lock, Stock and Barrel, by John Traister, Stoeger Publishing Co., Wayne, NJ, 1997. 320 pp., illus. Paper covers. $19.95.
A complete step-by-step fully illustrated guide to the art of gunsmithing.

The Gunsmith's Manual, by J.P. Stelle and Wm. B. Harrison, The Gun Room Press, Highland Park, NJ, 1982. 376 pp., illus. $19.95.
For the gunsmith in all branches of the trade.

Home Gunsmithing the Colt Single Action Revolvers, by Loren W. Smith, Ray Riling Arms Books, Co., Phila., PA, 2001. 119 pp., illus. $29.95.
Affords the Colt Single Action owner detailed, pertinent information on the operating and servicing of this famous and historic handgun.

How to Convert Military Rifles, Williams Gun Sight Co., Davision, MI, new and enlarged seventh edition, 1997. 76 pp., illus. Paper covers. $13.95.
This latest edition updated the changes that have occured over the past thirty years. Tips, instructions and illustratons on how to convert popular military rifles as the Enfield, Mauser 96 nad SKS just to name a few are presented.

Mauser M98 & M96, by R.A. Walsh, Wolfe Publishing Co., Prescott, AR, 1998. 123 pp., illustrated. Paper covers. $32.50.
How to build your own favorite custom Mauser rifle from two of the best bolt action rifle designs ever produced—the military Mauser Model 1898 and Model 1896 bolt rifles.

Mr. Single Shot's Gunsmithing-Idea-Book, by Frank de Haas, Mark de Haas, Orange City, IA, 1996. 168 pp., illus. Paper covers. $21.50.
Offers easy to follow, step-by-step instructions for a wide variety of gunsmithing procedures all reinforced by plenty of photos.

Pistolsmithing, by George C. Nonte, Jr., Stackpole Books, Harrisburg, PA, 1974. 560 pp., illus. $34.95.
A single source reference to handgun maintenance, repair, and modification at home, unequaled in value.

Practical Gunsmithing, by the editors of American Gunsmith, DBI Books, a division of Krause Publications, Iola, WI, 1996. 256 pp., illus. Paper covers. $19.95.
A book intended primarily for home gunsmithing, but one that will be extremely helpful to professionals as well.

Professional Stockmaking, by D. Wesbrook, Wolfe Publishing Co., Prescott AZ, 1995. 308 pp., illus. $54.00.
A step-by-step how-to with complete photographic support for every detail of the art of working wood into riflestocks.

Recreating the American Longrifle, by William Buchele, et al, George Shumway Publisher, York, Pa, 5th edition, 1999. 175 pp., illustrated. $40.00.
Includes full size plans for building a Kentucky rifle.

Riflesmithing, The Gun Digest Book of, by Jack Mitchell, DBI Books, a division of Krause Publications, Iola, WI, 1982. 256 pp., illus. Paper covers. $16.95.
The art and science of rifle gunsmithing. Covers tools, techniques, designs, finishing wood and metal, custom alterations.

Shotgun Gunsmithing, The Gun Digest Book of, by Ralph Walker, DBI Books, a division of Krause Publications, Iola, WI, 1983. 256 pp., illus. Paper covers. $16.95.
The principles and practices of repairing, individualizing and accurizing modern shotguns by one of the world's premier shotgun gunsmiths.

Sporting Rifle Take Down & Reassembly Guide, 2nd Edition, by J.B. Wood, Krause Publications, Iola, WI, 1997. 480 pp., illus. Paper covers. $19.95.
Hunters and shooting enthusiasts must have this reference featuring 52 of the most popular and widely used sporting centerfire and rimfire rifles.

The Story of Pope's Barrels, by Ray M. Smith, R&R Books, Livonia, NY, 1993. 203 pp., illus. $39.00.
A reissue of a 1960 book whose author knew Pope personally. It will be of special interest to Schuetzen rifle fans, since Pope's greatest days were at the height of the Schuetzen-era before WWI.

Survival Gunsmithing, by J.B. Wood, Desert Publications, Cornville, AZ, 1986. 92 pp., illus. Paper covers. $11.95.
A guide to repair and maintenance of the most popular rifles, shotguns and handguns.

The Tactical 1911, by Dave Lauck, Paladin Press, Boulder, CO, 1998. 137 pp., illus. Paper covers. $20.00.
Here is the only book you will ever need to teach you how to select, modify, employ and maintain your Colt.

HUNTING

NORTH AMERICA

Advanced Black Powder Hunting, by Toby Bridges, Stoeger Publishing Co., Wayne, NJ, 1998. 288 pp., illus. Paper covers. $21.95.
The first modern day publication to be filled from cover to cover with guns, loads, projectiles, accessories and the techniques to get the most from today's front loading guns.

Advanced Strategies for Trophy Whitetails, by David Morris, Safari Press, Inc., Huntington Beach, CA, 1999. 399 pp., illustrated. $29.95.
This book is a must-have for any serious trophy hunter.

After the Hunt With Lovett Williams, by Lovett Williams, Krause Publications, Iola, WI, 1996. 256 pp., illus. Paper covers. $15.95.
The author carefully instructs you on how to prepare your trophy turkey for a trip to the taxidermist. Plus help on planning a grand slam hunt.

Aggressive Whitetail Hunting, by Greg Miller, Krause Publications, Iola, WI, 1995. 208 pp., illus. Paper covers. $14.95.
Learn how to hunt trophy bucks in public forests, private farmlands and exclusive hunting grounds from one of America's foremost hunters.

All About Bears, by Duncan Gilchrist, Stoneydale Press Publishing Co., Stevensville, MT, 1989. 176 pp., illus. $19.95.
Covers all kinds of bears—black, grizzly, Alaskan brown, polar and leans on a lifetime of hunting and guiding experiences to explore proper hunting techniques.

American Duck Shooting, by George Bird Grinnell, Stackpole Books, Harrisburg, PA, 1991. 640 pp., illus. Paper covers. $19.95.
First published in 1901 at the height of the author's career. Describes 50 species of waterfowl, and discusses hunting methods common at the turn of the century.

American Hunting and Fishing Books, 1800-1970, Volume 1, by Morris Heller, Nimrod and Piscator Press, Mesilla, NM, 1997. 220 pp., illus. A limited, numbered edition. $125.00.
An up-to-date, profusely illustrated, annotated bibliography on American hunting and fishing books and booklets.

The American Wild Turkey, Hunting Tactics and Techniques, by John McDaniel, The Lyons Press, New York, NY, 2000. 240 pp., illustrated. $29.95.
Loaded with turkey hunting anectdotes gleaned from a lifetime of experience.

American Wingshooting: A Twentieth Century Pictorial Saga, by Ben O. Williams, Willow Creek Press, Minocqua, WI, 2000. 160 pp., illustrated with 180 color photographs. $35.00.
A beautifully photographed celebration of upland bird hunting now and how as it once existed.

The Art of Super-Accurate Hunting with Scoped Rifles, by Don Judd, Wolfe Publishing Co., Prescott, AZ, 1996. 99 pp., illus. Paper covers. $14.95.
The philosophy of super-accurate hunting and the rewards of making your shot a trophy.

As I Look Back; Musings of a Birdhunter, by Robert Branen, Safari Press, Inc., Huntington Beach, CA, 1999. Limited, signed and numbered edition. $60.00.
The author shares his recollections of bird hunting around the world.

Autumn Passages, Compiled by the editors of Ducks Unlimited Magazine, Willow Creek Press, Minocqua, WI, 1997. 320 pp. $27.50.
An exceptional collection of duck hunting stories.

Awesome Antlers of North America, by Odie Sudbeck, HTW Publications, Seneca, KS, 1993. 150 pp., illus. $35.00.
500 world-class bucks in color and black and white. This book starts up where the Boone & Crockett recordbook leaves off.

Backtracking, by I.T. Taylor, Safari Press, Inc., Huntington Beach, CA, 1998. 201 pp., illustrated. $24.95.
Reminiscences of a hunter's life in rural America.

Bare November Days, by George Bird Evans et al, Countrysport Press, Traverse City, MI, 1992. 136 pp., illus. $39.50.
A new, original anthology, a tribute to ruffed grouse, king of upland birds.

Bear Attacks, by K. Etling, Safari Press, Long Beach, CA, 1998. 574 pp., illus. In 2 volumes. $75.00.
Classic tales of dangerous North American bears.

The Bear Hunter's Century, by Paul Schullery, Stackpole Books, Harrisburg, PA, 1989. 240 pp., illus. $19.95.
Thrilling tales of the bygone days of wilderness hunting.

The Best of Babcock, by Havilah Babcock, selected and with an introduction by Hugh Grey, The Gunnerman Press, Auburn Hills, MI, 1985. 262 pp., illus. $19.95.
A treasury of memorable pieces, 21 of which have never before appeared in book form.

The Best of Nash Buckingham, by Nash Buckingham, selected, edited and annotated by George Bird Evans, Winchester Press, Piscataway, NJ, 1973. 320 pp., illus. $35.00.
Thirty pieces that represent the very cream of Nash's output on his whole range of outdoor interests—upland shooting, duck hunting, even fishing.

Better on a Rising Tide, by Tom Kelly, Lyons & Burford Publishers, New York, NY, 1995. 184 pp. $22.95.
Tales of wild turkeys, turkey hunting and Southern folk.

Big Bucks the Benoit Way, by Bryce Towsley, Krause Publications Iola, WI, 1998. 208 pp., illus. $24.95.
Secrets from America's first family of whitetail hunting.

THE ARMS LIBRARY

Big December Canvasbacks, by Worth Mathewson, Sand Lake Press, Amity, OR, 1997. 171 pp., illus. By David Hagenbaumer. Limited, signed and numbered edition. $29.95.
Duck hunting stories.

Big Game Hunting, by Duncan Gilchrist, Outdoor Expeditions, books and videos, Corvallis, MT, 1999. 192 pp., illustrated. $14.95
Designed to be a warehouse of hunting information covering the major North American big game species.

Big Woods, by William Faulkner, wilderness adventures, Gallatin Gateway, MT, 1998. 208 pp., illus. Slipcased. $60.00.
A collection of Faulkner's best hunting stories that belongs in the library of every sportsman.

Birdhunter, by Richard S. Grozik, Safari Press, Huntington Beach, CA, 1998. 180 pp., illus. Limited, numbered and signed edition. Slipcased. $60.00.
An entertaining salute to the closeness between man and his dog, man and his gun, and man and the great outdoors.

Bird Dog Days, Wingshooting Ways, by Archibald Rutledge, edited by Jim Casada, Wilderness Adventure Press, Gallatin Gateway, MT, 1998. 200 pp., illus. $35.00.
One of the most popular and enduring outdoor writers of this century, the poet laureate of South Carolina.

Birds on the Horizon, by Stuart Williams, Countrysport Press, Traverse City, MI, 1993. 288 pp., illus. $49.50.
Wingshooting adventures around the world.

Blacktail Trophy Tactics, by Boyd Iverson, Stoneydale Press, Stevensville, MI, 1992. 166 pp., illus. Paper covers. $14.95.
A comprehensive analysis of blacktail deer habits, describing a deer's and man's use of scents, still hunting, tree techniques, etc.

Boone & Crockett Club's 23rd Big Game Awards, 1995-1997, Boone & Crockett Club, Missoula, MT, 1999. 600 pp., illustrated with black & white photographs plus a 16 page color section. $39.95.
A complete listing of the 3,511 trophies accepted in the 23rd Awards Entry Period.

Bowhunter's Handbook, Expert Strategies and Techniques, by M.R. James with Fred Asbell, Dave Holt, Dwight Schuh & Dave Samuel, DBI Books, a division of Krause Publications, Iola, WI, 1997. 256 pp., illus. Paper covers. $19.95.
Tips from the top on taking your bowhunting skills to the next level.

The Buffalo Harvest, by Frank Mayer as told to Charles Roth, Pioneer Press, Union City, TN, 1995. 96 pp., illus. Paper covers. $8.50.
The story of a hide hunter during his buffalo hunting days on the plains.

Bugling for Elk, by Dwight Schuh, Stoneydale Press Publishing Co., Stevensville, MT, 1983. 162 pp., illus. $18.95.
A complete guide to early season elk hunting.

Call of the Quail: A Tribute to the Gentleman Game Bird, by Michael McIntosh, et al., Countrysport Press, Traverse City, MI, 1990. 175 pp., illus. $35.00.
A new anthology on quail hunting.

Calling All Elk, by Jim Zumbo, Cody, WY, 1989. 169 pp., illus. Paper covers. $14.95.
The only book on the subject of elk hunting that covers every aspect of elk vocalization.

Campfires and Game Trails: Hunting North American Big Game, by Craig Boddington, Winchester Press, Piscataway, NJ, 1985. 295 pp., illus. $23.95.
How to hunt North America's big game species.

Come October, by Gene Hill et al, Countrysport Press, Inc., Traverse City, MI, 1991. 176 pp., illus. $39.50.
A new and all-original anthology on the woodcock and woodcock hunting.

The Complete Book of Grouse Hunting, by Frank Woolner, The Lyons Press, New York, NY, 2000. 192 pp., illustrated Paper covers. $24.95.
The history, habits, and habitat of one of America's great game birds—and the methods used to hunt it.

The Complete Book of Mule Deer Hunting, by Walt Prothero, The Lyons Press, New York, NY, 2000. 192 pp., illustrated. Paper covers. $24.95.
Field-tested practical advice on how to bag the trophy buck of a lifetime.

The Complete Book of Wild Turkey Hunting, by John Trout Jr., The Lyons Press, New York, NY, 2000. 192 pp., illustrated. Paper covers. $24.95.
An illustrated guide to hunting for one of America's most popular game birds.

The Complete Book of Woodcock Hunting, by Frank Woolner, The Lyons Press, New York, NY, 2000. 192 pp., illustrated. Paper covers. $24.95.
A thorough, practical guide to the American woodcock and to woodcock hunting.

The Complete Guide to Bird Dog Training, by John R. Falk, Lyons & Burford, New York, NY, 1994. 288 pp., illus. $22.95.
The latest on live-game field training techniques using released quail and recall pens. A new chapter on the services available for entering field trials and other bird dog competitions.

The Complete Guide to Game Care & Cookery, 3rd Edition, by Sam Fadala, DBI Books, a division of Krause Publications, Iola, WI, 1994. 320 pp., illus. Paper covers. $18.95.
Over 500 photos illustrating the care of wild game in the field and at home with a separate recipe section providing over 400 tested recipes.

The Complete Smoothbore Hunter, by Brook Elliot, Winchester Press, Piscataway, NJ, 1986. 240 pp., illus. $16.95.
Advice and information on guns and gunning for all varieties of game.

The Complete Venison Cookbook from Field to Table, by Jim & Ann Casada, Krause Publications, Iola, WI, 1996. 208 pp., Comb-bound. $12.95.
More than 200 kitchen tested recipes make this book the answer to a table full of hungry hunters or guests.

Coveys and Singles: The Handbook of Quail Hunting, by Robert Gooch, A.S. Barnes, San Diego, CA, 1981. 196 pp., illus. $11.95.
The story of the quail in North America.

Coyote Hunting, by Phil Simonski, Stoneydale Press, Stevensville, MT, 1994. 126 pp., illus. Paper covers. $12.95.
Probably the most thorough "How-to-do-it" book on coyote hunting ever written.

Dabblers & Divers: A Duck Hunter's Book, compiled by the editors of Ducks Unlimited Magazine, Willow Creek Press, Minocqua, WI, 1997. 160 pp., illus. $39.95.
A word-and-photographic portrayal of waterfowl hunter's singular intimacy with, and passion for, watery haunts and wildfowl.

Dancers in the Sunset Sky, by Robert F. Jones, The Lyons Press, New York, NY, 1997. 192 pp., illus. $22.95.
The musings of a bird hunter.

Deer & Deer Hunting, by Al Hofacker, Krause Publications, Iola, WI, 1993. 208 pp., illus. $34.95.
Coffee-table volume packed full of how-to-information that will guide hunts for years to come.

Deer and Deer Hunting: The Serious Hunter's Guide, by Dr. Robert Wegner, Stackpole Books, Harrisburg, PA, 1984. 384 pp., illus. Paper covers. $18.95.
In-depth information from the editor of "Deer & Deer Hunting" magazine. Major bibliography of English language books on deer and deer hunting from 1838-1984.

Deer and Deer Hunting Book 2, by Dr. Robert Wegner, Stackpole Books, Harrisburg, PA, 1987. 400 pp., illus. Paper covers. $18.95.
Strategies and tactics for the advanced hunter.

Deer and Deer Hunting, Book 3, by Dr. Robert Wegner, Stackpole Books, Harrisburg, PA, 1990. 368 pp., illus. $18.95.
This comprehensive volume covers natural history, deer hunting lore, profiles of deer hunters, and discussion of important issues facing deer hunters today.

The Deer Hunters: The Tactics, Lore, Legacy and Allure of American Deer Hunting, Edited by Patrick Durkin, Krause Publications, Iola, WI, 1997. 208 pp., illus. $29.95.
More than twenty years of research from America's top whitetail hunters, researchers, and photographers have gone in to the making of this book.

Deer Hunting, by R. Smith, Stackpole Books, Harrisburg, PA, 1978. 224 pp., illus. Paper covers. $14.95.
A professional guide leads the hunt for North America's most popular big game animal.

Doves and Dove Shooting, by Byron W. Dalrymple, New Win Publishing, Inc., Hampton, NJ, 1992. 256 pp., illus. $17.95.
The author reveals in this classic book his penchant for observing, hunting, and photographing this elegantly fashioned bird.

Dove Hunting, by Charley Dickey, Galahad Books, NY, 1976. 112 pp., illus. $10.00.
This indispensable guide for hunters deals with equipment, techniques, types of dove shooting, hunting dogs, etc.

Dreaming the Lion, by Thomas McIntyre, Countrysport Press, Traverse City, MI, 1994. 309 pp., illus. $35.00.
Reflections on hunting, fishing and a search for the wild. Twenty-three stories by *Sports Afield* editor, Tom McIntyre.

Duck Decoys and How to Rig Them, by Ralf Coykendall, revised by Ralf Coykendall, Jr., Nick Lyons Books, New York, NY, 1990. 137 pp., illus. Paper covers. $14.95.
Sage and practical advice on the art of decoying ducks and geese.

The Duck Hunter's Handbook, by Bob Hinman, revised, expanded, updated edition, Winchester Press, Piscataway, NJ, 1985. 288 pp., illus. $15.95.
The duck hunting book that has it all.

Eastern Upland Shooting, by Dr. Charles C. Norris, Countrysport Press, Traverse City, MI, 1990. 424 pp., illus. $49.00.
A new printing of this 1946 classic with a new, original Foreword by the author's friend and hunting companion, renowned author George Bird Evans.

Elk and Elk Hunting, by Hart Wixom, Stackpole Books, Harrisburg, PA, 1986. 288 pp., illus. $34.95.
Your practical guide to fundamentals and fine points of elk hunting.

Handgun Hunting

THE ARMS LIBRARY

Elk Hunting in the Northern Rockies, by Ed. Wolff, Stoneydale Press, Stevensville, MT, 1984. 162 pp., illus. $18.95.
Helpful information about hunting the premier elk country of the northern Rocky Mountain states—Wyoming, Montana and Idaho.

Elk Hunting with the Experts, by Bob Robb, Stoneydale Press, Stevensville, MT, 1992. 176 pp., illus. Paper covers. $15.95.
A complete guide to elk hunting in North America by America's top elk hunting expert.

Elk Rifles, Cartridges and Hunting Tactics, by Wayne van Zwoll, Larsen's Outdoor Publishing, Lakeland, FL, 1992. 414 pp., illus. Paper covers. $24.95.
The definitive work on which rifles and cartridges are proper for hunting elk plus the tactics for hunting them.

Encyclopedia of Deer, by G. Kenneth Whitehead, Safari Press, Huntington, CA, 1993. 704 pp., illus. $130.00.
This massive tome will be the reference work on deer for well into the next century.

A Fall of Woodcock, by Tom Huggler, Countrysport Press, Selman, AL, 1997. 256 pp., illus. $39.00.
A book devoted to the woodcock and to those who await his return to their favorite converts each autumn.

Firelight, by Burton L. Spiller, Gunnerman Press, Auburn Hills, MI, 1990. 196 pp., illus. $19.95.
Enjoyable tales of the outdoors and stalwart companions.

Following the Flight, by Charles S. Potter, Countrysport Books, Selma, AL, 1999. 130 pp., illustrated. $25.00.
The great waterfowl passage and the experiences of a young man who has lived their migration come to life in the pages of this book.

Fresh Looks at Deer Hunting, by Byron W. Dalrymple, New Win Publishing, Inc., Hampton, NJ, 1993. 288 pp., illus. $24.95.
Tips and techniques abound throughout the pages of this latest work by Mr. Dalrymple whose name is synonymous with hunting proficiency.

From the Peace to the Fraser, by Prentis N. Gray, Boone and Crockett Club, Missoula, MT, 1995. 400 pp., illus. $49.95.
Newly discovered North American hunting and exploration journals from 1900 to 1930.

Fur Trapping In North America, by Steven Geary, Winchester Press, Piscataway, NJ, 1985. 160 pp., illus. Paper covers. $19.95.
A comprehensive guide to techniques and equipment, together with fascinating facts about fur bearers.

Getting the Most Out of Modern Waterfowling, by John O. Cartier, St. Martin's Press, NY, 1974. 396 pp., illus. $29.95.
The most comprehensive, up-to-date book on waterfowling imaginable.

Getting a Stand, by Miles Gilbert, Pioneer Press, Union City, TN, 1993. 204 pp., illus. Paper covers. $13.95.
An anthology of 18 short personal experiences by buffalo hunters of the late 1800s, specifically from 1870-1882.

The Gordon MacQuarrie Sporting Treasury. Introduction and commentary by Zack Taylor. Countrysport Press, Selman, AL, 1999. $29.50.
Hunting and fishing masterpieces you can read over and over.

Gordon MacQuarrie Trilogy: Stories of the Old Duck Hunters, by Gordon MacQuarrie, Willow Creek Press, Minocqua, WI, 1994. $49.00.
A slip-cased three volume set of masterpieces by one of America's finest outdoor writers.

The Grand Passage: A Chronicle of North American Waterfowling, by Gene Hill, et al., Countrysport Press, Traverse City, MI, 1990. 175 pp., illus. $35.00.
A new original anthology by renowned sporting authors on our world of waterfowling.

Greatest Elk; The Complete Historical and Illustrated Record of North America's Biggest Elk, by R. Selner, Safari Press, Huntington Beach, CA, 2000. 209 pages, profuse color illus. $39.95
Here is the book all elk hunters have been waiting for! This oversized book holds the stories and statistics of the biggest bulls ever killed in North America. Stunning, full-color photographs highlight over 40 world-class heads, including the old world records!

Grouse and Woodcock, A Gunner's Guide, by Don Johnson, Krause Publications, Iola, WI, 1995. 256 pp., illus. Paper covers. $14.95.
Find out what you need in guns, ammo, equipment, dogs and terrain.

Grouse of North America, by Tom Huggler, NorthWord Press, Inc., Minocqua, WI, 1990. 160 pp., illus. $29.95.
A cross-continental hunting guide.

Grouse Hunter's Guide, by Dennis Walrod, Stackpole Books, Harrisburg, PA, 1985. 192 pp., illus. $19.95.
Solid facts, observations, and insights on how to hunt the ruffed grouse.

Gunning for Sea Ducks, by George Howard Gillelan, Tidewater Publishers, Centreville, MD, 1988. 144 pp., illus. $14.95.
A book that introduces you to a practically untouched arena of waterfowling.

Heartland Trophy Whitetails, by Odie Sudbeck, HTW Publications, Seneca, KS, 1992. 130 pp., illus. $35.00.
A completely revised and expanded edition which includes over 500 photos of Boone & Crockett class whitetail, major mulies and unusual racks.

The Heck with Moose Hunting, by Jim Zumbo, Wapiti Valley Publishing Co., Cody, WY, 1996. 199 pp., illus. $17.95.
Jim's hunts around the continent including encounters with moose, caribou, sheep, antelope and mountain goats.

High Pressure Elk Hunting, by Mike Lapinski, Stoneydale Press Publishing Co., Stevensville, MT, 1996. 192 pp., illus. $19.95.
The secrets of hunting educated elk revealed.

Hill Country, by Gene Hill, Countrysport Press, Traverse City, MI, 1996. 180 pp., illus. $25.00.
Stories about hunting, fishing, dogs and guns.

Home from the Hill, by Fred Webb, Safari Press, Huntington Beach, CA, 1997. 283 pp., illus. Limited edition, signed and numbered. In a slipcase. $50.00.
The story of a big-game guide in the Canadian wilderness.

Horns in the High Country, by Andy Russell, Alfred A. Knopf, NY, 1973. 259 pp., illus. Paper covers. $12.95.
A many-sided view of wild sheep and their natural world.

How to Hunt, by Dave Bowring, Winchester Press, Piscataway, NJ, 1982. 208 pp., illus. Hardcover $15.00.
A basic guide to hunting big game, small game, upland birds, and waterfowl.

Hunt Alaska Now: Self-Guiding for Trophy Moose & Caribou, by Dennis W. Confer, Wily Ventures, Anchorage, AK, 1997. 309 pp., illus. Paper covers. $26.95.
How to plan affordable, successfull, safe hunts you can do yourself.

The Hunters and the Hunted, by George Laycock, Outdoor Life Books, New York, NY, 1990. 280 pp., illus. $34.95.
The pursuit of game in America from Indian times to the present.

A Hunter's Fireside Book, by Gene Hill, Winchester Press, Piscataway, NJ, 1972. 192 pp., illus. $17.95.
An outdoor book that will appeal to every person who spends time in the field— or who wishes he could.

A Hunter's Road, by Jim Fergus, Henry Holt & Co., NY, 1992. 290 pp. $22.50
A journey with gun and dog across the American uplands.

Hunt High for Rocky Mountain Goats, Bighorn Sheep, Chamois & Tahr, by Duncan Gilchrist, Stoneydale Press, Stevensville, MT, 1992. 192 pp., illus. Paper covers. $19.95.
The source book for hunting mountain goats.

The Hunter's Shooting Guide, by Jack O'Connor, Outdoor Life Books, New York, NY, 1982. 176 pp., illus. Paper covers. $9.95.
A classic covering rifles, cartridges, shooting techniques for shotguns/rifles/handguns.

The Hunter's World, by Charles F. Waterman, Winchester Press, Piscataway, NJ, 1983. 250 pp., illus. $29.95.
A classic. One of the most beautiful hunting books that has ever been produced.

Hunting Adventure of Me and Joe, by Walt Prothero, Safari Press, Huntington Beach, CA, 1995. 220 pp., illus. $22.50.
A collection of the author's best and favorite stories.

Hunting America's Game Animals and Birds, by Robert Elman and George Peper, Winchester Press, Piscataway, NJ, 1975. 368 pp., illus. $16.95.
A how-to, where-to, when-to guide—by 40 top experts—covering the continent's big, small, upland game and waterfowl.

Hunting Ducks and Geese, by Steven Smith, Stackpole Books, Harrisburg, PA, 1984. 160 pp., illus. $19.95.
Hard facts, good bets, and serious advice from a duck hunter you can trust.

Hunting for Handgunners, by Larry Kelly and J.D. Jones, DBI Books, a division of Krause Publications, Iola, WI, 1990. 256 pp., illus. Soft covers. $16.95.
A definitive work on an increasingly popular sport.

Hunting in Many Lands, edited by Theodore Roosevelt and George Bird Grinnell, et al., Boone & Crockett Club, Dumphries, VA, 1990. 447 pp., illus. $40.00.
A limited edition reprinting of the original Boone & Crockett Club 1895 printing.

Hunting Mature Bucks, by Larry L. Weishuhn, Krause Publications, Iola, WI, 1995. 256 pp., illus. Paper covers. $14.95.
One of North America's top white-tailed deer authorities shares his expertise on hunting those big, smart and elusive bucks.

Hunting Open-Country Mule Deer, by Dwight Schuh, Sage Press, Nampa, ID, 1989. 180 pp., illus. $18.95.
A guide taking Western bucks with rifle and bow.

The Arms Library

Hunting Predators for Hides and Profits, by Wilf E. Pyle, Stoeger Publishing Co., So. Hackensack, NJ, 1985. 224 pp., illus. Paper covers. $11.95.
The author takes the hunter through every step of the hunting/marketing process.

Hunting the American Wild Turkey, by Dave Harbour, Stackpole Books, Harrisburg, PA, 1975. 256 pp., illus. $24.95.
The techniques and tactics of hunting North America's largest, and most popular, woodland game bird.

Hunting the Rockies, Home of the Giants, by Kirk Darner, Marceline, MO, 1996. 291 pp., illus. $25.00.
Understand how and where to hunt Western game in the Rockies.

Hunting the Sun, by Ted Nelson Lundrigan, Countrysport Press, Selma, AL, 1997. 240 pp., illus. $30.00.
One of the best books on grouse and woodcock ever published.

Hunting Trips in North America, by F.C. Selous, Wolfe Publishing Co., Prescott, AZ, 1988. 395 pp., illus. $52.00.
A limited edition reprint. Coverage of caribou, moose and other big game hunting in virgin wilds.

Hunting Trophy Deer, by John Wootters, The Lyons Press, New York, NY, 1997. 272 pp., illus. $24.95.
A revised edition of the definitive manual for identifying, scouting, and successfully hunting a deer of a lifetime.

Hunting Trophy Whitetails, by David Morris, Stoneydale Press, Stevensville, MT, 1993. 483 pp., illus. $29.95.
This is one of the best whitetail books published in the last two decades. The author is the former editor of *North American Whitetail* magazine.

Hunting Upland Birds, by Charles F. Waterman, Countrysport Press, Selma, AL, 1997. 220 pp., illus. $30.00.
Originally published a quarter of a century ago, this classic has been newly updated with the latest information for today's wingshooter.

Hunting Western Deer, by Jim and Wes Brown, Stoneydale Press, Stevensville, MT, 1994. 174 pp., illus. Paper covers. $14.95.
A pair of expert Oregon hunters provide insight into hunting mule deer and blacktail deer in the western states.

Hunting Wild Turkeys in the West, by John Higley, Stoneydale Press, Stevensville, MT, 1992. 154 pp., illus. Paper covers. $12.95.
Covers the basics of calling, locating and hunting turkeys in the western states.

Hunting with the Twenty-two, by Charles Singer Landis, R&R Books, Livonia, NY, 1994. 429 pp., illus. $35.00.
A miscellany of articles touching on the hunting and shooting of small game.

I Don't Want to Shoot an Elephant, by Havilah Babcock, The Gunnerman Press, Auburn Hills, MI, 1985. 184 pp., illus. $19.95.
Eighteen delightful stories that will enthrall the upland gunner for many pleasureable hours.

In Search of the Buffalo, by Charles G. Anderson, Pioneer Press, Union City, TN, 1996. 144 pp., illus. Paper covers. $13.95.
The primary study of the life of J. Wright Mooar, one of the few hunters fortunate enough to kill a white buffalo.

In Search of the Wild Turkey, by Bob Gooch, Great Lakes Living Press, Ltd., Waukegan, IL, 1978. 182 pp., illus. $9.95.
A state-by-state guide to wild turkey hot spots, with tips on gear and methods for bagging your bird.

In the Turkey Woods, by Jerome B. Robinson, The Lyons Press, N.Y., 1998. 207 pp., illustrated. $24.95.
Practical expert advice on all aspects of turkey hunting—from calls to decoys to guns.

Indian Hunts and Indian Hunters of the Old West, by Dr. Frank C. Hibben, Safari Press, Long Beach, CA, 1989. 228 pp., illus. $24.95.
Tales of some of the most famous American Indian hunters of the Old West as told to the author by an old Navajo hunter.

Jack O'Connor's Gun Book, by Jack O'Connor, Wolfe Publishing Company, Prescott, AZ, 1992. 208 pp. Hardcover. $26.00.
Jack O'Connor imparts a cross-section of his knowledge on guns and hunting. Brings back some of his writings that have here-to-fore been lost.

Jaybirds Go to Hell on Friday, by Havilah Babcock, The Gunnerman Press, Auburn Hills, MI, 1985. 149 pp., illus. $19.95.
Sixteen jewels that reestablish the lost art of good old-fashioned yarn telling.

Last Casts and Stolen Hunts, edited by Jim Casada and Chuck Wechsler, Countrysport Press, Traverse City, MI, 1994. 270 pp., illus. $29.95.
The world's best hunting and fishing stories by writers such as Zane Grey, Jim Corbett, Jack O'Connor, Archibald Rutledge and others.

A Listening Walk...and Other Stories, by Gene Hill, Winchester Press, Piscataway, NJ, 1985. 208 pp., illus. $17.95.
Vintage Hill. Over 60 stories.

Longbows in the Far North, by E. Donnall Thomas, Jr. Stackpole Books, Mechanicsburg, PA, 1994. 200 pp., illus. $18.95.
An archer's adventures in Alaska and Siberia.

Mammoth Monarchs of North America, by Odie Sudbeck, HTW Publications, Seneca, KA, 1995. 288 pp., illus. $35.00.
This book reveals eye-opening big buck secrets.

Matching the Gun to the Game, by Clair Rees, Winchester Press, Piscataway, NJ, 1982. 272 pp., illus. $17.95.
Covers selection and use of handguns, blackpowder firearms for hunting, matching rifle type to the hunter, calibers for multiple use, tailoring factory loads to the game.

Measuring and Scoring North American Big Game Trophies, 2nd Edition, by Wm. H. Nesbitt and Philip L. Wright, The Boone & Crockett Club, Missoula, MT, 1999. 150 pp., illustrated. $34.95.
The definitive manual for anyone wanting to learn the Club's world-famous big game measuring system.

Meditation on Hunting, by Jose Ortego y Gasset, Wilderness Adventures Press, Bozeman, MT, 1996. 140 pp., illus. In a slipcase. $60.00.
The classic work on the philosophy of hunting.

Montana—Land of Giant Rams, by Duncan Gilchrist, Stoneydale Press Publishing Co., Stevensville, MT, 1990. 208 pp., illus. $19.95.
Latest information on Montana bighorn sheep and why so many Montana bighorn rams are growing to trophy size.

Montana—Land of Giant Rams, Volume 2, by Duncan Gilchrist, Outdoor Expeditions and Books, Corvallis, MT, 1992. 208 pp., illus. $34.95.
The reader will find stories of how many of the top-scoring trophies were taken.

Montana—Land of Giant Rams, Volume 3, by Duncan Gilchrist, Outdoor Expeditions, books and videos, Corvallis, MT, 1999. 224 pp. Paper covers. $19.95.
All new sheep information including over 70 photos. Learn about how Montana became the "Land of Giant Rams" and what the prospects of the future as we enter a new millenium.

More Grouse Feathers, by Burton L. Spiller, Crown Publ., NY, 1972. 238 pp., illus. $25.00.
Facsimile of the original Derrydale Press issue of 1938. Guns and dogs, the habits and shooting of grouse, woodcock, ducks, etc. Illus. by Lynn Bogue Hunt.

More Tracks: 78 Years of Mountains, People & Happiness, by Howard Copenhaver, Stoneydale Press, Stevensville, MT, 1992. 150 pp., illus. $18.95.
A collection of stories by one of the back country's best storytellers about the people who shared with Howard his great adventure in the high places and wild Montana country.

Moss, Mallards and Mules, by Robert Brister, Countrysport Books, Selma, AL, 1998. 216 pp., illustrated by David Maass. $30.00.
Twenty-seven short stories on hunting and fishing on the Gulf Coast.

Mostly Huntin', by Bill Jordan, Everett Publishing Co., Bossier City, LA, 1987. 254 pp., illus. $21.95.
Jordan's hunting adventures in North America, Africa, Australia, South America and Mexico.

Mostly Tailfeathers, by Gene Hill, Winchester Press, Piscataway, NJ, 1975. 192 pp., illus. $17.95.
An interesting, general book about bird hunting.

"Mr. Buck": The Autobiography of Nash Buckingham, by Nash Buckingham, Countrysport Press, Traverse City, MI, 1990. 288 pp., illus. $40.00.
A lifetime of shooting, hunting, dogs, guns, and Nash's reflections on the sporting life, along with previously unknown pictures and stories written especially for this book.

Mule Deer: Hunting Today's Trophies, by Tom Carpenter and Jim Van Norman, Krause Publications, Iola, WI, 1998. 256 pp., illustrated. Paper covers. $19.95.
A tribute to both the deer and the people who hunt them. Includes info on where to look for big deer, prime mule deer habitat and effective weapons for the hunt.

Murry Burnham's Hunting Secrets, by Murry Burnham with Russell Tinsley, Winchester Press, Piscataway, NJ, 1984. 244 pp., illus. $17.95.
One of the great hunters of our time gives the reasons for his success in the field.

My Health is Better in November, by Havilah Babcock, University of S. Carolina Press, Columbia, SC, 1985. 284 pp., illus. $24.95.
Adventures in the field set in the plantation country and backwater streams of SC.

North American Big Game Animals, by Byron W. Dalrymple and Erwin Bauer, Outdoor Life Books/Stackpole Books, Harrisburg, PA, 1985. 258 pp., illus. $29.95.
Complete illustrated natural histories. Habitat, movements, breeding, birth and development, signs, and hunting.

North American Elk: Ecology and Management, edited by Jack Ward Thomas and Dale E. Toweill, Stackpole Books, Harrisburg, PA, 1982. 576 pp., illus. $39.95.
The definitive, exhaustive, classic work on the North American elk.

The North American Waterfowler, by Paul S. Bernsen, Superior Publ. Co., Seattle, WA, 1972. 206 pp. Paper covers. $9.95.
The complete inside and outside story of duck and goose shooting. Big and colorful, illustrations by Les Kouba.

THE ARMS LIBRARY

Of Bears and Man, by Mike Cramond, University of Oklahoma Press, Norman, OK, 1986. 433 pp., illus. $29.95.
The author's lifetime association with bears of North America. Interviews with survivors of bear attacks.

The Old Man and the Boy, by Robert Ruark, Henry Holt & Co., New York, NY, 303 pp., illus. $24.95.
A timeless classic, telling the story of a remarkable friendship between a young boy and his grandfather as they hunt and fish together.

The Old Man's Boy Grows Older, by Robert Ruark, Henry Holt & Co., Inc., New York, NY, 1993. 300 pp., illus. $24.95.
The heartwarming sequel to the best-selling *The Old Man and the Boy*.

Old Wildfowling Tales, Volume 2, edited by Worth Mathewson, Sand Lake Press, Amity, OR, 1996. 240 pp. $21.95.
A collection of duck and geese hunting stories based around accounts from the past.

One Man, One Rifle, One Land; Hunting all Species of Big Game in North America, by J.Y. Jones, Safari Press, Huntington Beach, CA, 2000. 400 pp., illustrated. $59.95.
Journey with J.Y. Jones as he hunts each of the big-game animals of North America—from the polar bear of the high Artic to the jaguar of the low-lands of Mexico—with just one rifle.

161 Waterfowling Secrets, edited by Matt Young, Willow Creek Press, Minocqua, WI, 1997. 78 pp., Paper covers. $10.95.
Time-honored, field-tested waterfowling tips and advice.

The Only Good Bear is a Dead Bear, by Jeanette Hortick Prodgers, Falcon Press, Helena, MT, 1986. 204 pp. Paper covers. $12.50.
A collection of the West's best bear stories.

Outdoor Pastimes of an American Hunter, by Theodore Roosevelt, Stackpole Books, Mechanicsburg, PA, 1994. 480 pp., illus. Paper covers. $18.95.
Stories of hunting big game in the West and notes about animals pursued and observed.

The Outlaw Gunner, by Harry M. Walsh, Tidewater Publishers, Cambridge, MD, 1973. 178 pp., illus. $22.95.
A colorful story of market gunning in both its legal and illegal phases.

Passing a Good Time, by Gene Hill, Countrysport Press, Traverse City, MI, 1996. 200 pp., illus. $25.00.
Filled with insights and observations of guns, dogs and fly rods that make Gene Hill a master essayist.

Pear Flat Philosophies, by Larry Weishuhn, Safari Press, Huntington Beach, CA, 1995. 234 pp., illus. $24.95.
The author describes his more lighthearted adventures and funny anecdotes while out hunting.

Pheasant Days, by Chris Dorsey, Voyageur Press, Stillwater, MN, 1992. 233 pp., illus. $24.95.
The definitive resource on ringnecks. Includes everything from basic hunting techniques to the life cycle of the bird.

Pheasant Hunter's Harvest, by Steve Grooms, Lyons & Burford Publishers, New York, NY, 1990. 180 pp. $22.95.
A celebration of pheasant, pheasant dogs and pheasant hunting. Practical advice from a passionate hunter.

Pheasant Tales, by Gene Hill et al, Countrysport Press, Traverse City, MI, 1996. 202 pp., illus. $39.00.
Charley Waterman, Michael McIntosh and Phil Bourjaily join the author to tell some of the stories that illustrate why the pheasant is America's favorite game bird.

Pheasants of the Mind, by Datus Proper, Wilderness Adventures Press, Bozeman, MT, 1994. 154 pp., illus. $25.00.
No single title sums up the life of the solitary pheasant hunter like this masterful work.

Portraits of Elk Hunting, by Jim Zumbo, Safari Press, Huntington Beach, CA, 2001. 222 pp. illustrated. $39.95
Zumbo has captured in photos as well as in words the essence, charisma, and wonderful components of elk hunting: back-country wilderness camps, sweaty guides, happy hunters, favorite companions, elk woods, and, of course, the majestic elk. Join Zumbo in the uniqueness of the pursuit of the magnificent and noble elk.

Predator Calling with Gerry Blair, by Gerry Blair, Krause Publications, Iola, WI, 1996. 208 pp., illus. Paper covers. $14.95.
Time-tested secrets lure predators closer to your camera or gun.

Proven Whitetail Tactics, by Greg Miller, Krause Publications, Iola, WI, 1997. 224 pp., illus. Paper covers. $19.95.
Proven tactics for scouting, calling and still-hunting whitetail.

Quail Hunting in America, by Tom Huggler, Stackpole Books, Harrisburg, PA, 1987. 288 pp., illus. $22.95.
Tactics for finding and taking bobwhite, valleys, Gambel's Mountain, scaled-blue, and Mearn's quail by season and habitat.

Quest for Dall Rams, by Duncan Gilchrist, Duncan Gilchrist Outdoor Expeditions and Books, Corvallis, MT, 1997. 224 pp., illus. Limited numbered edition. $34.95.
The most complete book of Dall sheep ever written. Covers information on Alaska and provinces with Dall sheep and explains hunting techniques, equipment, etc.

Quest for Giant Bighorns, by Duncan Gilchrist, Outdoor Expeditions and Books, Corvallis, MT, 1994. 224 pp., illus. Paper covers. $19.95.
How some of the most successful sheep hunters hunt and how some of the best bighorns were taken.

Radical Elk Hunting Strategies, by Mike Lapinski, Stoneydale Press Publishing Co., Stevensville, MT, 1988. 161 pp., illus. $18.95.
Secrets of calling elk in close.

Rattling, Calling & Decoying Whitetails, by Gary Clancy, Edited by Patrick Durkin, Krause Publications, Iola, WI, 2000. 208 pp., illustrated. Paper covers. $19.95.
How to consistently coax big bucks into range.

Records of North American Big Game 11th Edition, with hunting chapters by Craig Boddington, Tom McIntyre and Jim Zumbo, The Boone and Crockett Club, Missoula, MT, 1999. 700 pp., featuring a 32 page color section. $49.95.
Listing over 17,150, of the top trophy big game animals ever recorded. Over 4,000 new listings are featured in this latest edition.

Records of North American Big Game 1932, by Prentis N. Grey, Boone and Crockett Club, Dumfries, VA, 1988. 178 pp., illus. $79.95.
A reprint of the book that started the Club's record keeping for native North American big game.

Records of North American Caribou and Moose, Craig Boddington et al, The Boone & Crockett Club, Missoula, MT, 1997. 250 pp., illus. $24.95.
More than 1,800 caribou listings and more than 1,500 moose listings, organized by the state or Canadian province where they were taken.

Records of North American Elk and Mule Deer, 2nd Edition, edited by Jack and Susan Reneau, Boone & Crockett Club, Missoula, MT, 1996. 360 pp., illus. Paper cover, $18.95; hardcover, $24.95.
Updated and expanded edition featuring more than 150 trophy, field and historical photos of the finest elk and mule deer trophies ever recorded.

Records of North American Sheep, Rocky Mountain Goats and Pronghorn edited by Jack and Susan Reneau, Boone & Crockett Club, Missoula, MT, 1996. 400 pp., illus. Paper cover, $18.95; hardcover, $24.95.
The first B&C Club records book featuring all 3941 accepted wild sheep, Rocky Mountain goats and pronghorn trophies.

Return of Royalty; Wild Sheep of North America, by Dr. Dale E. Toweill and Dr. Valerius Geist, Boone and Crockett Club, Missoula, MT, 1999. 224 pp., illustrated. $59.95.
A celebration of the return of the wild sheep to many of its historical ranges.

The Rifles, the Cartridges, and the Game, by Clay Harvey, Stackpole Books, Harrisburg, PA, 1991. 254 pp., illus. $32.95.
Engaging reading combines with exciting photos to present the hunt with an intense level of awareness and respect.

Ringneck; A Tribute to Pheasants and Pheasant Hunting, by Steve Grooms, Russ Sewell and Dave Nomsen, The Lyons Press, New York, NY, 2000. 120 pp., illustrated. $40.00.
A glorious full-color coffee-table tribute to the pheasant and those who hunt them.

Ringneck! Pheasants & Pheasant Hunting, by Ted Janes, Crown Publ., NY, 1975. 120 pp., illus. $15.95.
A thorough study of one of our more popular game birds.

Rub-Line Secrets, by Greg Miller, edited by Patrick Durkin, Krause Publications, Iola, WI, 1999. 208 pp., illustrated. Paper covers. $19.95.
Based on nearly 30 years experience. Proven tactics for finding, analyzing and hunting big bucks' rub-lines.

Ruffed Grouse, edited by Sally Atwater and Judith Schnell, Stackpole Books, Harrisburg, PA, 1989. 370 pp., illus. $59.95.
Everything you ever wanted to know about the ruffed grouse. More than 25 wildlife professionals provided in-depth information on every aspect of this popular game bird's life. Lavishly illustrated with over 300 full-color photos.

The Russell Annabel Adventure Series, by Russell Annabel, Safari Press, Huntington Beach, CA: Vol. 2, Adventure is My Business, 1951-1955. $35.00, Vol. 3, Adventure is in My Blood, 1957-1964. $35.00, Vol. 4, High Road to Adventure, 1964-1970. $35.00, Vol. 5, The Way We Were, 1970-1979. $35.00.
A complete collection of previously unpublished magazine articles in book form by this gifted outdoor writer.

The Season, by Tom Kelly, Lyons & Burford, New York, NY, 1997. 160 pp., illus. $22.95.
The delight and challenges of a turkey hunter's Spring season.

Secret Strategies from North America's Top Whitetail Hunters, compiled by Nick Sisley, Krause Publications, Iola, WI, 1995. 256 pp., illus. Paper covers. $14.95.
Bow and gun hunters share their success stories.

Secrets of the Turkey Pros, by Glenn Sapir, North American Hunting Club, Minnetonka, MN, 1999. 176 pp., illustrated. $19.95.
This work written by a seasoned turkey hunter draws on the collective knowledge and experience on some of the most renowned names in the world of wild turkey.

THE ARMS LIBRARY

Sheep Hunting in Alaska—The Dall Sheep Hunter's Guide, by Tony Russ, Outdoor Expeditions and Books, Corvallis, MT, 1994. 160 pp., illus. Paper covers. $19.95.
A how-to guide for the Dall sheep hunter.

Shorebirds: The Birds, The Hunters, The Decoys, by John M. Levinson & Somers G. Headley, Tidewater Publishers, Centreville, MD, 1991. 160 pp., illus. $49.95.
A thorough study of shorebirds and the decoys used to hunt them. Photographs of more than 200 of the decoys created by prominent carvers are shown.

Shots at Big Game, by Craig Boddington, Stackpole Books, Harrisburg, PA, 1989. 198 pp., illus. $24.95.
How to shoot a rifle accurately under hunting conditions.

Some Bears Kill!: True-Life Tales of Terror, by Larry Kanuit, Safari Press, Huntington Beach, CA, 1997. 313 pp., illus. $24.95.
A collection of 38 stories as told by the victims, and in the case of fatality, recounted by the author from institutional records, episodes involve all three species of North American bears.

Southern Deer & Deer Hunting, by Larry Weishuhn and Bill Bynum, Krause Publications, Iola, WI, 1995. 256 pp., illus. Paper covers. $14.95.
Mount a trophy southern whitetail on your wall with this firsthand account of stalking big bucks below the Mason-Dixon line.

Spring Gobbler Fever, by Michael Hanback, Krause Publications, Iola, WI, 1996. 256 pp., illus. Paper covers. $15.95.
Your complete guide to spring turkey hunting.

Spirit of the Wilderness, Compiled by Theodore J. Holsten, Jr., Susan C. Reneau and Jack Reneau, the Boone & Crockett Club, Missoula, MT, 1997 300 pp., illus. $29.95.
Stalking wild sheep, tracking a trophy cougar, hiking the back country of British Columbia, fishing for striped bass and coming face-to-face with a grizzly bear are some of the adventures found in this book.

Stand Hunting for Whitetails, by Richard P. Smith, Krause Publications, Iola, WI, 1996. 256 pp., illus. Paper covers. $14.95.
The author explains the tricks and strategies for successful stand hunting.

The Sultan of Spring: A Hunter's Odyssey Through the World of the Wild Turkey, by Bob Saile, The Lyons Press, New York, NY, 1998. 176 pp., illus. $22.95.
A literary salute to the magic and mysticism of spring turkey hunting.

Taking Big Bucks, by Ed Wolff, Stoneydale Press, Stevensville, MT, 1987. 169 pp., illus. $18.95.
Solving the whitetail riddle.

Taking More Birds, by Dan Carlisle and Dolph Adams, Lyons & Burford Publishers, New York, NY, 1993. 160 pp., illus. Paper covers. $15.95.
A practical handbook for success at Sporting Clays and wing shooting.

Tales of Quails 'n Such, by Havilah Babcock, University of S. Carolina Press, Columbia, SC, 1985. 237 pp. $19.95.
A group of hunting stories, told in informal style, on field experiences in the South in quest of small game.

Tears and Laughter, by Gene Hill, Countrysport Press, Traverse City, MI, 1996. 176 pp., illus. $25.00.
In twenty-six stories, Gene Hill explores the ancient and honored bond between man and dog.

Tenth Legion, by Tom Kelly, the Lyons Press, New York, NY, 1998. 128 pp., illus. $21.95.
The classic work on that frustrating, yet wonderful sport of turkey hunting.

They Left Their Tracks, by Howard Coperhaver, Stoneydale Press Publishing Co., Stevensville, MT, 1990. 190 pp., illus. $18.95.
Recollections of 60 years as an outfitter in the Bob Marshall Wilderness.

Timberdoodle, by Frank Woolner, Nick Lyons Books, N. Y., NY, 1987. 168 pp., illus. $18.95.
The classic guide to woodcock and woodcock hunting.

Timberdoodle Tales: Adventures of a Minnesota Woodcock Hunter, by T. Waters, Safari Press, Huntington Beach, CA, 1997. 220 pp., illus. $35.00.
The life history and hunt of the American woodcock by the author. A fresh appreciation of this captivating bird and the ethics of its hunt.

To Heck with Moose Hunting, by Jim Zumbo, Wapiti Publishing Co., Cody, WY, 1996. 199 pp., illus. $17.95.
Jim's hunts around the continent and even an African adventure.

Trail and Campfire, edited by George Bird Grinnel and Theodore Roosevelt, The Boone and Crockett Club, Dumfries, VA, 1989. 357 pp., illus. $39.50.
Reprint of the Boone and Crockett Club's 3rd book published in 1897.

Trailing a Bear, by Robert S. Munger, The Munger Foundation, Albion, MI, 1997. 352 pp., illus. Paper covers. $19.95.
An exciting and humorous account of hunting with legendary archer Fred Bear.

The Trickiest Thing in Feathers, by Corey Ford; compiled and edited by Laurie Morrow and illustrated by Christopher Smith, Wilderness Adventures, Gallatin Gateway, MT, 1998. 208 pp., illus. $29.95.
Here is a collection of Corey Ford's best wing-shooting stories, many of them previously unpublished.

Trophy Mule Deer: Finding & Evaluating Your Trophy, by Lance Stapleton, Outdoor Experiences Unlimited, Salem, OR, 1993. 290 pp., illus. Paper covers. $24.95.
The most comprehensive reference book on mule deer.

Turkey Hunter's Digest, Revised Edition, by Dwain Bland, DBI Books, a division of Krause Publications, Iola, WI, 1994. 256 pp., illus. Paper covers. $17.95.
A no-nonsense approach to hunting all five sub-species of the North American wild turkey that make up the Royal Grand Slam.

The Upland Equation: A Modern Bird-Hunter's Code, by Charles Fergus, Lyons & Burford Publishers, New York, NY, 1996. 86 pp. $18.00
A book that deserves space in every sportsman's library. Observations based on firsthand experience.

Upland Tales, by Worth Mathewson (Ed.), Sand Lake Press, Amity, OR, 1996. 271 pp., illus. $29.95.
A collection of articles on grouse, snipe and quail.

A Varmint Hunter's Odyssey, by Steve Hanson with a guest chapter by Mike Johnson, Precision Shooting, Inc. Manchester, CT, 1999. 279 pp., illustrated. Paper covers. $37.95.
A new classic by a writer who eats, drinks and sleeps varmint hunting and varmint rifles.

Varmint and Small Game Rifles and Cartridges, by various authors, Wolfe Publishing Co., Prescott, AZ, 1993. 228 pp., illus. Paper covers. $26.00.
This is a collection of reprints of articles originally appearing in Wolfe's *Rifle* and *Handloader* magazines from 1966 through 1990.

Waterfowler's World, by Bill Buckley, Ducks Unlimited, Inc., Memphis, TN, 1999. 192 pp., illustrated in color. $37.50.
An unprecedented pictorial book on waterfowl and waterfowlers.

Waterfowling Horizons: Shooting Ducks and Geese in the 21st Century, by Chris and Jason Smith, Wilderness Adventures, Gallatin Gateway, MT, 1998. 320 pp., illus. $49.95.
A compendium of the very latest in everything for the duck and goose hunter today.

Waterfowling These Past 50 Years, Especially Brant, by David Hagerbaumer, Sand Lake Press, Amity, OR, 1999. 182 pp., illustrated. $35.00.
This is the compilation of David Hagerbaumer's experiences as a waterfowler since the end of WW2.

Wegner's Bibliography on Dear and Deer Hunting, by Robert Wegner, St. Hubert's Press, Deforest, WI, 1993. 333 pp., 16 full-page illustrations. $45.00.
A comprehensive annotated compilation of books in English pertaining to deer and their hunting 1413-1991.

Western Hunting Guide, by Mike Lapinski, Stoneydale Press Publishing Co., Stevensville, MT, 1989. 168 pp., illus. $18.95.
A complete where-to-go and how-to-do-it guide to Western hunting.

When the Duck Were Plenty, by Ed Muderlak, Safari Press, Inc., Huntington Beach, CA, 2000. 300 pp., illustrated. Limited edition, numbered, signed, slipcased. $49.95.
The golden age of waterfowling and duck hunting from 1840 till 1920. An anthology.

Whispering Wings of Autumn, by Gene Hill and Steve Smith, Wilderness Adventures Press, Bozeman, MT, 1994. 150 pp., illus. $29.00.
Hill and Smith, masters of hunting literature, treat the reader to the best stories of grouse and woodcock hunting.

Whitetail: Behavior Through the Seasons, by Charles J. Alsheimer, Krause Publications, Iola, WI, 1996. 208 pp., illus. $34.95.
In-depth coverage of whitetail behavior presented through striking portraits of the whitetail in every season.

Whitetail: The Ultimate Challenge, by Charles J. Alsheimer, Krause Publications, Iola, WI, 1995. 228 pp., illus. Paper covers. $14.95.
Learn deer hunting's most intriguing secrets—fooling deer using decoys, scents and calls—from America's premier authority.

Whitetails by the Moon, by Charles J. Alsheimer, edited by Patrick Durkin, Krause Publications, Iola, WI, 1999. 208 pp., illustrated. Paper covers. $19.95.
Predict peak times to hunt whitetails. Learn what triggers the rut.

Wildfowler's Season, by Chris Dorsey, Lyons & Burford Publishers, New York, NY, 1998. 224 pp., illus. $37.95.
Modern methods for a classic sport.

Wildfowling Tales, by William C. Hazelton, Wilderness Adventures Press, Belgrade, MT, 1999. 117 pp., illustrated with etchings by Brett Smith. In a slipcase. $50.00.
Tales from the great ducking resorts of the Continent.

Wildfowling Tales 1888-1913, Volume One, edited by Worth Mathewson, Sand Lake Press, Amity, OR, 1998. 186 pp., illustrated by David Hagerbaumer. $22.50.
A collection of some of the best accounts from our literary heritage.

THE ARMS LIBRARY

Windward Crossings: A Treasury of Original Waterfowling Tales, by Chuck Petrie et al, Willow Creek Press, Minocqua, WI, 1999. 144 pp., 48 color art and etching reproductions. $35.00.

An illustrated, modern anthology of previously unpublished waterfowl hunting (fiction and creative non fiction) stories by America's finest outdoor journalists.

Wings of Thunder: New Grouse Hunting Revisited, by Steven Mulak, Countrysport Books, Selma, AL, 1998. 168 pp. illustrated. $30.00.

The author examines every aspect of New England grouse hunting as it is today - the bird and its habits, the hunter and his dog, guns and loads, shooting and hunting techniques, practice on clay targets, clothing and equipment.

Wings for the Heart, by Jerry A. Lewis, West River Press, Corvallis, MT, 1991. 324 pp., illus. Paper covers. $14.95.

A delightful book on hunting Montana's upland birds and waterfowl.

Wisconsin Hunting, by Brian Lovett, Krause Publications, Iola, WI, 1997. 208 pp., illus. Paper covers. $16.95.

A comprehensive guide to Wisconsin's public hunting lands.

The Woodchuck Hunter, by Paul C. Estey, R&R Books, Livonia, NY, 1994. 135 pp., illus. $25.00.

This book contains information on woodchuck equipment, the rifle, telescopic sights and includes interesting stories.

Woodcock Shooting, by Steve Smith, Stackpole Books, Inc., Harrisburg, PA, 1988. 142 pp., illus. $16.95.

A definitive book on woodcock hunting and the characteristics of a good woodcock dog.

World Record Whitetails, by Gordon Whittington, Safari Press, Inc., Huntington Beach, CA, 1998. 246 pp. with over 100 photos in color and black-and-white. $32.95.

The first and only complete chronicle of all the bucks that have ever held the title "World record whitetail."

The Working Retrievers, Tom Quinn, The Lyons Press, New York, NY, 1998. 257 pp., illus. $40.00.

The author covers every aspect of the training of dogs for hunting and field trials - from the beginning to the most advanced levels - for Labradors, Chesapeakes, Goldens and others.

World Record Whitetails, by Gordon Whittington, Safari Press Books, Inc., Huntington Beach, CA, 1998. 246 pp., illustrated. $39.95.

The first and only complete chronicle of all the bucks that have ever held the title "World Record Whitetail." Covers the greatest trophies ever recorded in their categories, typical, non-typical, gun, bow, and muzzleloader.

AFRICA/ASIA/ELSEWHERE

A Hunter's Wanderings in Africa, by Frederick Courteney Selous, Wolfe Publishing Co., Prescott, Arizona, 1986. 504 pp., illustrated plus folding map. $29.95.

A reprinting of the 1920 London edition. A narrative of nine years spent amongst the game of the far interior of South Africa.

The Adventurous Life of a Vagabond Hunter, by Sten Cedergren, Safari Press, Inc., Huntington Beach, CA, 2000. 300 pp., illustrated. Limited edition, numbered, signed, and slipcased. $70.00.

An unusual story in the safari business by a remarkable character.

Africa's Greatest Hunter; The Lost Writings of Frederick C. Selous, edited by Dr. james A. Casada, Safari Press, Huntington Beach, CA, 1999. $50.00.

All the stories in this volume relate to the continent that fascinated Selous his entire life. With many previously unpublished photos.

African Adventures, by J.F. Burger, Safari Press, Huntington Beach, CA, 1993. 222 pp., illus. $35.00.

The reader shares adventures on the trail of the lion, the elephant and buffalo.

The African Adventures: A Return to the Silent Places, by Peter Hathaway Capstick, St. Martin's Press, New York, NY, 1992. 220 pp., illus. $22.95.

This book brings to life four turn-of-the-century adventurers and the savage frontier they braved. Frederick Selous, Constatine "Iodine" Ionides, Johnny Boyes and Jim Sutherland.

African Camp-fire Nights, by J.E. Burger, Safari Press, Huntington Beach, CA, 1993. 192 pp., illus. $32.50.

In this book the author writes of the men who made hunting their life's profession.

African Game Trails, by Theodore Roosevelt, Peter Capstick, Series Editor, St. Martin's Press, New York, NY 1988. 583 pp., illustrated. $24.95.

The famed safari of the noted sportsman, conservationist, and President.

African Hunter, by James Mellon, Safari Press, Huntington Beach, CA, 1996. 522 pp., illus. Paper Covers, $75.00.

Regarded as the most comprehensive title ever published on African hunting.

African Hunting and Adventure, by William Charles Baldwin, Books of Zimbabwe, Bulawayo, 1981. 451 pp., illus. $75.00.

Facsimile reprint of the scarce 1863 London edition. African hunting and adventure from Natal to the Zambezi.

African Jungle Memories, by J.F. Burger, Safari Press, Huntington Beach, CA, 1993. 192 pp., illus. $32.50.

A book of reminiscences in which the reader is taken on many exciting adventures on the trail of the buffalo, lion, elephant and leopard.

African Rifles & Cartridges, by John Taylor, The Gun Room Press, Highland Park, NJ, 1977. 431 pp., illus. $35.00.

Experiences and opinions of a professional ivory hunter in Africa describing his knowledge of numerous arms and cartridges for big game. A reprint.

African Safaris, by Major G.H. Anderson, Safari Press, Long Beach, CA, 1997. 173 pp., illus. $35.00.

A reprinting of one of the rarest books on African hunting, with a foreword by Tony Sanchez.

African Twilight, by Robert F. Jones, Wilderness Adventure Press, Bozeman, MT, 1994. 208 pp., illus. $36.00.

Details the hunt, danger and changing face of Africa over a span of three decades.

A Man Called Lion: The Life and Times of John Howard "Pondoro" Taylor, by P.H. Capstick, Safari Press, Huntington Beach, CA, 1994. 240 pp., illus. $24.95.

With the help of Brian Marsh, an old Taylor acquaintance, Peter Capstick has accumulated over ten years of research into the life of this mysterious man.

An Annotated Bibliography of African Big Game Hunting Books, 1785 to 1950, by Kenneth P. Czech, Land's Edge Press, St. Cloud, MN 2000. $50.00

This bibliography features over 600 big game hunting titles describing the regions the authors hunted, species of game bagged, and physical descriptions of the books (pages, maps, plates, bindings, etc.) It also features a suite of 16 colored plates depicting decorated bindings from some of the books. Limited to 700 numbered, signed copies.

Argali: High-Mountain Hunting, by Ricardo Medem, Safari Press, Huntington Beach, CA, 1995. 304 pp., illus. Limited, signed edition. $150.00.

Medem describes hunting seven different countries in the pursuit of sheep and other mountain game.

Baron in Africa; The Remarkable Adventures of Werner von Alvensleben, by Brian Marsh, Safari Press, Huntington Beach, CA, 2001. 288 pp., illus. $35.00

Follow his career as he hunts lion, goes after large kudu, kills a full-grown buffalo with a spear, and hunts for elephant and ivory in some of the densest brush in Africa. The adventure and the experience were what counted to this fascinating character, not the money or fame; indeed, in the end he left Mozambique with barely more than the clothes on his back. This is a must-read adventure story on one of the most interesting characters to have come out of Africa after World War II. Foreword by Ian Player.

The Big Five; Hunting Adventures in Today's Africa, by Dr. S. Lloyd Newberry, Safari Press, Huntington Beach, CA, 2001. 214 pp., illus. Limited edition, numbered, signed and slipcased. $70.00.

Many books have been written about the old Africa and its fabled Big Five, but almost nothing exits in print that describes hunting the Big Five as its exists today.

Big Game and Big Game Rifles, by John "Pondoro" Taylor, Safari Press, Huntington Beach, CA, 1999. 215 pp., illus. $24.95.

Covers rifles and calibers for elephant, rhino, hippo, buffalo, and lion.

Big Game Hunting Around the World, by Bert Klineburger and Vernon W. Hurst, Exposition Press, Jericho, NY, 1969. 376 pp., illus. $30.00.

The first book that takes you on a safari all over the world.

Big Game Hunting in North-Eastern Rhodesia, by Owen Letcher, St. Martin's Press, New York, NY, 1986. 272 pp., illus. $24.95.

A classic reprint and one of the very few books to concentrate on this fascinating area, a region that today is still very much safari country.

Big Game Shooting in Cooch Behar, the Duars and Assam, by The Maharajah of Cooch Behar, Wolfe Publishing Co., Prescott, AZ, 1993. 461 pp., illus. $49.50.

A reprinting of the book that has become legendary. This is the Maharajah's personal diary of killing 365 tigers.

Buffalo, Elephant, and Bongo, by Dr. Reinald von Meurers, Safari Press, Huntington Beach, CA, 1999. Limited edition signed and in a slipcase. $75.00.

Alone in the Savannas and Rain Forests of the Cameroon.

Campfire Lies of a Canadian Guide, by Fred Webb, Safari Press, Inc., Huntington Beach, CA, 2000. 250 pp., illustrated. Limited edition, numbered, signed and slipcased. $50.00.

Forty years in the life of a guide in the North Country.

THE ARMS LIBRARY

Cottar: The Exception was the Rule, by Pat Cottar, Trophy Room Books, Agoura, CA, 1999. 350 pp., illustrated. Limited, numbered and signed edition. $135.00
   The remarkable big game hunting stories of one of Kenya's most remarkable pioneers.

A Country Boy in Africa, by George Hoffman, Trophy Room Books, Agoura, CA, 1998. 267 pp., illustrated with over 100 photos. Limited, numbered edition signed by the author. $85.00
   In addition to the author's long and successful hunting career, he is known for developing a most effective big game cartridge, the .416 Hoffman.

Death and Double Rifles, by Mark Sullivan, Nitro Express Safaris, Phoenix, AZ, 2000. 295 pages, illus. $85.00
   Sullivan has captured every thrilling detail of hunting dangerous game in this lavishly illustrated book. Full of color pictures of African hunts & rifles.

Death in a Lonely Land, by Peter Capstick, St. Martin's Press, New York, NY, 1990. 284 pp., illus. $22.95
   Twenty-three stories of hunting as only the master can tell them.

Death in the Dark Continent, by Peter Capstick, St. Martin's Press, New York, NY, 1983. 238 pp., illus. $22.95
   A book that brings to life the suspense, fear and exhilaration of stalking ferocious killers under primitive, savage conditions, with the ever present threat of death.

Death in the Long Grass, by Peter Hathaway Capstick, St. Martin's Press, New York, NY, 1977. 297 pp., illus. $22.95
   A big game hunter's adventures in the African bush.

Death in the Silent Places, by Peter Capstick, St. Martin's Press, New York, NY, 1981. 243 pp., illus. $23.95
   The author recalls the extraordinary careers of legendary hunters such as Corbett, Karamojo Bell, Stigand and others.

Duck Hunting in Australia, by Dick Eussen, Australia Outdoor Publishers Pty Ltd., Victoria, Australia, 1994. 106 pp., illus. Paper covers. $17.95
   Covers the many aspects of duck hunting from hides to hunting methods.

East Africa and its Big Game, by Captain Sir John C. Willowghby, Wolfe Publishing Co., Prescott, AZ, 1990. 312 pp., illus. $52.00
   A deluxe limited edition reprint of the very scarce 1889 edition of a narrative of a sporting trip from Zanzibar to the borders of the Masai.

Elephant Hunting in East Equatorial Africa, by A. Neumann, St. Martin's Press, New York, NY, 1994. 455 pp., illus. $26.95
   This is a reprint of one of the rarest elephant hunting titles ever.

Elephants of Africa, by Dr. Anthony Hall-Martin, New Holland Publishers, London, England, 1987. 120 pp., illus. $45.00
   A superbly illustrated overview of the African elephant with reproductions of paintings by the internationally acclaimed wildlife artist Paul Bosman.

Encounters with Lions, by Jan Hemsing, Trophy Room books, Agoura, CA, 1995. 302 pp., illus. $75.00
   Some stories fierce, fatal, frightening and even humorous of when man and lion meet.

Fourteen Years in the African Bush, by A. Marsh, Safari Press Publication, Huntington Beach, CA, 1998. 312 pp., illus. Limited signed, numbered, slipcased. $70.00
   An account of a Kenyan game warden. A graphic and well-written story.

From Sailor to Professional Hunter: The Autobiography of John Northcote, Trophy Room Books, Agoura, CA, 1997. 400 pp., illus. Limited edition, signed and numbered. $125.00
   Only a handfull of men can boast of having a fifty-year professional hunting career throughout Africa as John Northcote has had.

Gone are the Days; Jungle Hunting for Tiger and other Game in India and Nepal 1953-1969, by Peter Byrne, Safari Press, Inc., Huntington Beach, CA, 2001. 225 pp., illus. Limited signed, numbered, slipcased. $70.00

Great Hunters: Their Trophy Rooms and Collections, Volume 1, compiled and published by Safari Press, Inc., Huntington Beach, CA, 1997. 172 pp., illustrated in color. $60.00
   A rare glimpse into the trophy rooms of top international hunters. A few of these trophy rooms are museums.

Great Hunters: Their Trophy Rooms & Collections, Volume 2, compiled and published by Safari Press, Inc., Huntington Beach, CA, 1998. 224 pp., illustrated with 260 full-color photographs. $60.00
   Volume two of the world's finest, best produced series of books on trophy rooms and game collections. 46 sportsmen sharing sights you'll never forget on this guided tour.

Great Hunters: Their Trophy Rooms & Collections, Volume 3, compiled and published by Safari Press, Inc., Huntington Beach, CA, 2000. 204 pp., illustrated with 260 full-color photographs. $60.00
   At last, the long-awaited third volume in the best photographic series ever published of trophy room collections is finally available. Unbelievable as it may sound, this book tops all previous volumes. Besides some of the greatest North American trophy rooms ever seen, an extra effort was made to include European collections. Believe it or not, volume 3 includes the Sandringham Castle big-game collection, home of Queen Elizabeth II! Also included is the complete Don Cox African and Asian collection as displayed at his alma mater. This stupendous gallery contains the trophy collections of Prince D' Arenberg, Umberto D'Entreves, George and Edward Keller, Paul Roberts, Joe Bishop, and James Clark to name but a few. Whether it be castles, palaces, mansions, or museums, the finest of the finest in trophy room designs and collection unequaled anywhere will be found in this book. As before, each trophy room is accompanied by an informative text explaining the collection and giving you insights into the hunters who went to such great efforts to create their trophy rooms. All professionally photographed in the highest quality possible.

Heart of an African Hunter, by Peter F. Flack, Safari Press, Inc., Huntington Beach, CA, 1999. Limited, numbered, slipcased edition. $70.00
   Stories on the Big Five and Tiny Ten.

Horned Death, by John F. Burger, Safari Press, Huntington Beach, CA, 1992. 343 pp.illus. $35.00
   The classic work on hunting the African buffalo.

Horn of the Hunter, by Robert Ruark, Safari Press, Long Beach, CA, 1987. 315 pp., illus. $35.00
   Ruark's most sought-after title on African hunting, here in reprint.

Horned Giants, by Capt. John Brandt, Safari Press, Inc., Huntington Beach, CA, 1999. 288 pp., illustrated. Limited edition, numbered, signed and slipcased. $80.00
   Hunting Eurasian wild cattle.

Hunter, by J.A. Hunter, Safari Press Publications, Huntington Beach, CA, 1999. 263 pp., illus. $24.95
   Hunter's best known book on African big-game hunting. Internationally recognized as being one of the all-time African hunting classics.

A Hunter's Africa, by Gordon Cundill, Trophy Room Books, Agoura, CA, 1998. 298 pp., over 125 photographic illustrations. Limited numbered edition signed by the author. $125.00
   A good look by the author at the African safari experience - elephant, lion, spiral-horned antelope, firearms, people and events, as well as the clients that make it worthwhile.

A Hunter's Wanderings in Africa, by Frederick Courteney Selous, Wolfe Publishing Co., Prescott, Arizona, 1986. 504 pp., illustrated plus folding map. $29.95
   A reprinting of the 1920 London edition. A narrative of nine years spent amongst the game of the far interior of South Africa.

Hunter's Tracks, by J.A. Hunter, Safari Press Publications, Huntington Beach, CA, 1999. 240 pp., illustrated. $24.95
   This is the exciting story of John Hunter's efforts to capture the shady headman of a gang of ivory poachers and smugglers. The story is interwoven with the tale of one of East Africa's most grandiose safaris taken with an Indian maharaja.

Hunting Adventures Worldwide, by Jack Atcheson, Jack Atcheson & Sons, Butte, MT, 1995. 256 pp., illus. $29.95
   The author chronicles the richest adventures of a lifetime spent in quest of big game across the world – including Africa, North America and Asia.

Hunting in Ethiopia, An Anthology, by Tony Sanchez-Arino, Safari Press, Huntington Beach, CA, 1996. 350 pp., illus. Limited, signed and numbered edition. $135.00
   The finest selection of hunting stories ever compiled on hunting in this great game country.

The Hunting Instinct, by Phillip D. Rowter, Safari Press, Inc., Huntington Beach, CA, 1999. Limited edition signed and numbered and in a slipcase. $50.00
   Safari chronicles from the Republic of South Africa and Namibia 1990-1998.

Hunting in Kenya, by Tony Sanchez-Arino, Safari Press, Inc., Huntington Beach, CA, 2000. 350 pp., illustrated. Limited, signed and numbered edition in a slipcase. $135.00
   The finest selection of hunting stories ever compiled on hunting in this great game country make up this anthology.

Hunting in Many Lands, by Theodore Roosevelt and George Bird Grinnel, The Boone and Crockett Club, Dumfries, VA, 1987. 447 pp., illus. $40.00
   Limited edition reprint of this 1895 classic work on hunting in Africa, India, Mongolia, etc.

Hunting in the Sudan, An Anthology, compiled by Tony Sanchez-Arino, Safari Press, Huntington Beach, CA, 1992. 350 pp., illus. Limited, signed and numbered edition in a slipcase. $125.00
   The finest selection of hunting stories ever compiled on hunting in this great game country.

Hunting, Settling and Remembering, by Philip H. Percival, Trophy Room Books, Agoura, CA, 1997. 230 pp., illus. Limited, numbered and signed edition. $85.00
   If Philip Percival is to come alive again, it will be through this, the first edition of his easy, intricate and magical book illustrated with some of the best historical big game hunting photos ever taken.

Hunting the Dangerous Game of Africa, by John Kingsley-Heath, Sycamore Island Books, Boulder, CO, 1998. 477 pp., illustrated. $95.00
   Written by one of the most respected, successful, and ethical P.H.'s to trek the sunlit plains of Botswana, Kenya, Uganda, Tanganyika, Somaliland, Eritrea, Ethiopia, and Mozambique. Filled with some of the most gripping and terrifying tales ever to come out of Africa.

THE ARMS LIBRARY

In the Salt, by Lou Hallamore, Trophy Room Books, Agoura, CA, 1999. 227 pp., illustrated in black & white and full color. Limited, numbered and signed edition. $125.00
 A book about people, animals and the big game hunt, about being outwitted and out maneuvered. It is about knowing that sooner or later your luck will change and your trophy will be "in the salt."

International Hunter 1945-1999, Hunting's Greatest Era, by Bert klineburger, Sportsmen on Film, Kerrville, TX, 1999. 400 pp., illustrated. A limited, numbered and signed edition. $125.00
 The most important book of the greatest hunting era by the world's preeminent International hunter.

Jaguar Hunting in the Mato Grosso and Bolivia, by T. Almedia, Safari Press, Long Beach, CA, 1989. 256 pp., illus. $35.00
 Not since Sacha Siemel has there been a book on jaguar hunting like this one.

Jim Corbett, Master of the Jungle, by Tim Werling, Safari Press, Huntington Beach, CA, 1998. 215 pp., illus. $30.00
 A biography of India's most famous hunter of man-eating tigers and leopards.

King of the Wa-Kikuyu, by John Boyes, St. Martin Press, New York, NY, 1993. 240 pp., illus. $19.95
 In the 19th and 20th centuries, Africa drew to it a large number of great hunters, explorers, adventurers and rogues. Many have become legendary, but John Boyes (1874-1951) was the most legendary of them all.

Last Horizons: Hunting, Fishing and Shooting on Five Continents, by Peter Capstick, St. Martin's Press, New York, NY, 1989. 288 pp., illus. $19.95
 The first in a two volume collection of hunting, fishing and shooting tales from the selected pages of The American Hunter, Guns & Ammo and Outdoor Life.

Last of the Few: Forty-Two Years of African Hunting, by Tony Sanchez-Arino, Safari Press, Huntington Beach, CA, 1996. 250 pp., illus. $39.95
 The story of the author's career with all the highlights that come from pursuing the unusual and dangerous animals that are native to Africa.

Last of the Ivory Hunters, by John Taylor, Safari Press, Long Beach, CA, 1990. 354 pp., illus. $29.95
 Reprint of the classic book "Pondoro" by one of the most famous elephant hunters of all time.

Legends of the Field: More Early Hunters in Africa, by W.R. Foran, Trophy Room Press, Agoura, CA, 1997. 319 pp., illus. Limited edition. $100.00
 This book contains the biographies of some very famous hunters: William Cotton Oswell, F.C. Selous, Sir Samuel Baker, Arthur Neumann, Jim Sutherland, W.D.M. Bell and others.

The Lost Classics, by Robert Ruark, Safari Press, Huntington Beach, CA, 1996. 260 pp., illus. $35.00
 The magazine stories that Ruark wrote in the 1950s and 1960s finally in print in book form.

The Lost Wilderness; True Accounts of Hunters and Animals in East Africa, by Mohamed Ismail & Alice Pianfetti, Safari Press, Inc., Huntington Beach, CA, 2000. 216 pp, photos, illustrated. Limited edition signed and numbered and slipcased. $60.00

The Magic of Big Games, by Terry Wieland, Countrysport Books, Selma, AL, 1998. 200 pp., illus. $39.00
 Original essays on hunting big game around the world.

Mahonhboh, by Ron Thomson, Hartbeesport, South Africa, 1997. 312 pp., illustrated. Limited signed and numbered edition. $50.00
 Elephants and elephant hunting in South Central Africa.

The Man-Eaters of Tsavo, by Lt. Colonel J.H. Patterson, Peter Capstick, series editor, St. Martin's Press, New York, NY, 1986, 5th printing. 346 pp., illus. $22.95
 The classic man-eating story of the lions that halted construction of a railway line and reportedly killed one hundred people, told by the man who risked his life to successfully shoot them.

McElroy Hunts Asia, by C.J. McElroy, Safari Press, Inc., Huntington Beach, CA, 1989. 272 pp., illustrated. $50.00
 From the founder of SCI comes a book on hunting the great continent of Asia for big game: tiger, bear, sheep and ibex. Includes the story of the all-time record Altai Argali as well as several markhor hunts in Pakistan.

Memoirs of an African Hunter, by Terry Irwin, Safari Press Publications, Huntington Beach, CA, 1998. 421 pp., illustrated. Limited numbered, signed and slipcased. $125.00
 A narrative of a professional hunter's experiences in Africa.

Memoirs of a Sheep Hunter, by Rashid Jamsheed, Safari Press, Inc., Huntington Beach, CA, 1996. 330 pp., illustrated. $70.00
 The author reveals his exciting accounts of obtaining world-record heads from his native Iran, and his eventual move to the U.S. where he procured a grand-slam of North American sheep.

Months of the Sun; Forty Years of Elephant Hunting in the Zambezi Valley, by Ian Nyschens, Safari Press, Huntington Beach, CA, 1998. 420 pp., illus. $60.00
 The author has shot equally as many elephants as Walter Bell, and under much more difficult circumstances. His book will rank, or surpass, the best elephant-ivory hunting books published this century.

Mundjamba: The Life Story of an African Hunter, by Hugo Seia, Trophy Room Books, Agoura, CA, 1996. 400 pp., illus. Limited, numbered and signed by the author. $125.00
 An autobiography of one of the most respected and appreciated professional African hunters.

My Last Kambaku, by Leo Kroger, Safari Press, Huntington Beach, CA, 1997. 272 pp., illus. Limited edition signed and numbered and slipcased. $60.00
 One of the most engaging hunting memoirs ever published.

The Nature of the Game, by Ben Hoskyns, Quiller Press, Ltd., London, England, 1994. 160 pp., illus. $37.50
 The first complete guide to British, European and North American game.

On Target, by Christian Le Noel, Trophy Room Books, Agoura, CA, 1999. 275 pp., illustrated. Limited, numbered and signed edition. $85.00
 History and hunting in Central Africa.

One Long Safari, by Peter Hay, Trophy Room Books, Agoura, CA, 1998. 350 pp., with over 200 photographic illustrations and 7 maps. Limited numbered edition signed by the author. $100.00
 Contains hunts for leopards, sitatunga, hippo, rhino, snakes and, of course, the general African big game bag.

Optics for the Hunter, by John Barsness, Safari Press, Inc., Huntington Beach, CA, 1999. 236 pp., illustrated. $24.95
 An evaluation of binoculars, scopes, range finders, spotting scopes for use in the field.

Out in the Midday Shade, by William York, Safari Press, Inc., Huntington Beach, CA, 1999. Limited, signed and numbered edition in a slipcase. $70.00
 Memoirs of an African Hunter 1949-1968.

The Path of a Hunter, by Gilles Tre-Hardy, Trophy Room Books, Agoura, CA, 1997. 318 pp., illus. Limited Edition, signed and numbered. $85.00
 A most unusual hunting autobiography with much about elephant hunting in Africa.

The Perfect Shot; Shot Placement for African Big Game, by Kevin "Doctari" Robertson, Safari Press, Inc., Huntington Beach, CA, 1999. 230 pp., illustrated. $65.00
 The most comprehensive work ever undertaken to show the anatomical features for all classes of African game. Includes caliber and bullet selection, rifle selection, trophy handling.

Peter Capstick's Africa: A Return to the Long Grass, by Peter Hathaway Capstick, St. Martin's Press, N. Y., NY, 1987. 213 pp., illus. $35.00
 A first-person adventure in which the author returns to the long grass for his own dangerous and very personal excursion.

Pondoro, by John Taylor, Safari Press, Inc., Huntington Beach, CA, 1999. 354 pp., illustrated. $29.95
 The author is considered one of the best storytellers in the hunting book world, and Pondoro is highly entertaining. A classic African big-game hunting title.

The Quotable Hunter, by Jay Cassell and Peter Fiduccia, The Lyons Press, N.Y., 1999. 288 pp., illustrated. $20.00
 This collection of more than three hundred quotes from hunters through the ages captures the essence of the sport, with all its joys, idosyncrasies, and challenges.

The Recollections of an Elephant Hunter 1864-1875, by William Finaughty, Books of Zimbabwe, Bulawayo, Zimbabwe, 1980. 244 pp., illus. $85.00
 Reprint of the scarce 1916 privately published edition. The early game hunting exploits of William Finaughty in Matabeleland and Nashonaland.

Records of Big Game, XXV (25th) Edition, Rowland Ward, distributed by Safari Press, Inc., Huntington Beach, CA, 1999. 1,000 pp., illustrated. Limited edition. $150.00
 Covers big game records of Africa, Asia, Europe, and the America's.

Robert Ruark's Africa, by Robert Ruark, edited by Michael McIntosh, Countrysport Press, Selma, AL, 1999. 256 pp illustrated with 19 original etchings by Bruce Langton. $32.00
 These previously uncollected works of Robert Ruark make this a classic big-game hunting book.

Safari: A Chronicle of Adventure, by Bartle Bull, Viking/Penguin, London, England, 1989. 383 pp., illus. $40.00
 The thrilling history of the African safari, highlighting some of Africa's best-known personalities.

Safari: A Dangerous Affair, by Walt Prothero, Safari Press, Huntington Beach, CA, 2000. 275 pp., illustrated. Limited edition, numbered, signed and slipcased. $60.00
 True accounts of hunters and animals of Africa.

The Arms Library

Safari Rifles: Double, Magazine Rifles and Cartridges for African Hunting, by Craig Boddington, Safari Press, Huntington Beach, CA, 1990. 416 pp., illus. $37.50
A wealth of knowledge on the safari rifle. Historical and present double-rifle makers, ballistics for the large bores, and much, much more.

Safari: The Last Adventure, by Peter Capstick, St. Martin's Press, New York, NY, 1984. 291 pp., illus. $22.95
A modern comprehensive guide to the African Safari.

Safari Guide - A Guide To Planning Your Hunting Safari, by Richard Conrad, Safari Press, Huntington Beach, CA, 314pp, photos, illustrated. $29.95
Dozens of books have been published in the last decade on tales of African hunting. But few, if any, give a comprehensive country-by-country and animal-by-animal comparison or a guide on how to plan your (first) safari.

Sands of Silence, by Peter H. Capstick, Saint Martin's Press, New York, NY, 1991. 224 pp., illus. $35.00
Join the author on safari in Nambia for his latest big-game hunting adventures.

Shoot Straight And Stay Alive: A Lifetime of Hunting Experiences, by Fred Bartlett, Safari Press, Huntington Beach, CA, 2000. 256 pp., illus. $35.00
Bartlett grew up on a remote farm in Kenya where he started hunting at an early age. After serving in WWII, he returned to Kenya to farm. After a few years, he decided to join the Kenya Game Department as a game control officer, which required him to shoot buffalo and elephant at very close range. He had a fine reputation as a buffalo hunter and was considered to be one of the quickest shots with a double rifle.

Solo Safari, by T. Cacek, Safari Press, Huntington Beach, CA, 1995. 270 pp., illus. $30.00
Here is the story of Terry Cacek who hunted elephant, buffalo, leopard and plains game in Zimbabwe and Botswana on his own.

Spiral-Horn Dreams, by Terry Wieland, Trophy Room Books, Agoura, CA, 1996. 362 pp., illus. Limited, numbered and signed by the author. $85.00
Everyone who goes to hunt in Africa is looking for something; this is for those who go to hunt the spiral-horned antelope—the bongo, myala, mountain nyala, greater and lesser kudu, etc.

Sport Hunting on Six Continents, by Ken Wilson, Sportsmen of Film, Kerrville, TX, 1999. 300 pp., illustrated. $69.95
Hunting around the world....from Alaska to Australia...from the Americas, to Africa, Asia, and Europe.

Tales of the African Frontier, by J.A. Hunter, Safari Press Publications, Huntington Beach, CA, 1999. 308 pp., illus. $24.95
The early days of East Africa is the subject of this powerful John Hunter book.

Trophy Hunter in Africa, by Elgin Gates, Safari Press, Huntington Beach, CA, 1994. 315 pp., illus. $40.00
This is the story of one man's adventure in Africa's wildlife paradise.

Uganda Safaris, by Brian Herne, Winchester Press, Piscataway, NJ, 1979. 236 pp., illus. $24.95
The chronicle of a professional hunter's adventures in Africa.

Under the African Sun, by Dr. Frank Hibben, Safari Press, Inc., Huntington Beach, CA, 1999. Limited edition signed, numbered and in a slipcase. $85.00
Forty-eight years of hunting the African continent.

Under the Shadow of Man Eaters, by Jerry Jaleel, The Jim Corbett Foundation, Edmonton, Alberta, Canada, 1997. 152 pp., illus. A limited, numbered and signed edition. Paper covers. $35.00
The life and legend of Jim Corbett of Kumaon.

Use Enough Gun, by Robert Ruark, Safari Press, Huntington Beach, CA, 1997. 333 pp., illus. $35.00
Robert Ruark on big game hunting.

Warrior: The Legend of Col. Richard Meinertzhagen, by Peter H. Capstick, St. Martins Press, New York, NY, 1998. 320 pp., illus. $23.95
A stirring and vivid biography of the famous British colonial officer Richard Meinertzhagen, whose exploits earned him fame and notoriety as one of the most daring and ruthless men to serve during the glory days of the British Empire.

The Waterfowler's World, by Bill Buckley, Willow Creek Press, Minocqua, WI, 1999. 176 pp., 225 color photographs. $37.50
Waterfowl hunting from Canadian prairies, across the U.S. heartland, to the wilds of Mexico, from the Atlantic to the Pacific coasts and the Gulf of Mexico.

Where Lions Roar: Ten More Years of African Hunting, by Craig Boddington, Safari Press, Huntington Beach, CA, 1997. 250 pp $35.00
The story of Boddington's hunts in the Dark Continent during the last ten years.

White Hunter, by J.A. Hunter, Safari Press Publications, Huntington Beach, CA, 1999. 282 pp., illustrated. $24.95
This book is a seldom-seen account of John Hunter's adventures in pre-WW2 Africa.

A White Hunters Life, by Angus MacLagan, an African Heritage Book, published by Amwell Press, Clinton, NJ, 1983. 283 pp., illus. Limited, signed, and numbered deluxe edition, in slipcase. $100.00
True to life, a sometimes harsh yet intriguing story.

Wild Sports of Southern Africa, by William Cornwallis Harris, New Holland Press, London, England, 1987. 376 pp., illus. $36.00
Originally published in 1863, describes the author's travels in Southern Africa.

Wind, Dust and Snow, by Robert M. Anderson, Safari Press, Inc., Huntington Beach, CA, 1997. 240 pp., illustrated. $65.00
A complete chronology of modern exploratory and pioneering Asian sheep-hunting expeditions from 1960 until 1996, with wonderful background history and previously untold stories.

With a Gun in Good Country, by Ian Manning, Trophy Room Books, Agoura, CA, 1996. Limited, numbered and signed by the author. $85.00
A book written about that splendid period before the poaching onslaught which almost closed Zambia and continues to the granting of her independence. It then goes on to recount Manning's experiences in Botswana, Congo, and briefly in South Africa.

RIFLES

The Accurate Rifle, by Warren Page, Claymore Publishing, Ohio, 1997. 254 pages, illustrated. Revised edition. Paper Covers. $17.95
Provides hunters & shooter alike with detailed practical information on the whole range of subjects affecting rifle accuracy, he explains techniques in ammo, sights & shooting methods. With a 1996 equipment update from Dave Brennan.

The Accurate Varmint Rifle, by Boyd Mace, Precision Shooting, Inc., Whitehall, NY, 1991. 184 pp., illus. $15.00
A long overdue and long needed work on what factors go into the selection of components for and the subsequent assembly of...the accurate varmint rifle.

The AK-47 Assault Rifle, Desert Publications, Cornville, AZ, 1981. 150 pp., illus. Paper covers. $13.95
Complete and practical technical information on the only weapon in history to be produced in an estimated 30,000,000 units.

American Hunting Rifles: Their Application in the Field for Practical Shooting, by Craig Boddington, Safari Press, Huntington Beach, CA, 1996. 446 pp., illus. First edition, limited, signed and slipcased. $85.00. Second printing trade edition. $35.00
Covers all the hunting rifles and calibers that are needed for North America's diverse game.

The AR-15/M16, A Practical Guide, by Duncan Long. Paladin Press, Boulder, CO, 1985. 168 pp., illus. Paper covers. $22.00
The definitive book on the rifle that has been the inspiration for so many modern assault rifles.

The Art of Shooting With the Rifle, by Col. Sir H. St. John Halford, Excalibur Publications, Latham, NY, 1996. 96 pp., illus. Paper covers. $12.95
A facsimile edition of the 1888 book by a respected rifleman providing a wealth of detailed information.

The Art of the Rifle, by Jeff Cooper, Paladin Press, Boulder, CO, 1997. 104 pp., illus. $29.95
Everything you need to know about the rifle whether you use it for security, meat or target shooting.

Australian Military Rifles & Bayonets, 200 Years of, by Ian Skennerton, I.D.S.A. Books, Piqua, OH, 1988. 124 pp., 198 illus. Paper covers. $19.50

Australian Service Machine Guns, 100 Years of, by Ian Skennerton, I.D.S.A. Books, Piqua, OH, 1989. 122 pp., 150 illus. Paper covers. $19.50

The Big Game Rifle, by Jack O'Connor, Safari Press, Huntington Beach, CA, 1998. 370 pp., illus. $37.50
An outstanding description of every detail of construction, purpose and use of the big game rifle.

Big Game Rifles and Cartridges, by Elmer Keith, reprint edition by The Gun Room Press, Highland Park, NJ, 1984. 161 pp., illus. $17.95
Reprint of Elmer Keith's first book, a most original and accurate work on big game rifles and cartridges.

Black Magic: The Ultra Accurate AR-15, by John Feamster, Precision Shooting, Manchester, CT, 1998. 300 pp., illustrated. $29.95
The author has compiled his experiences pushing the accuracy envelope of the AR-15 to its maximum potential. A wealth of advice on AR-15 loads, modifications and accessories for everything from NRA Highpower and Service Rifle competitions to benchrest and varmint shooting.

The Black Rifle, M16 Retrospective, R. Blake Stevens and Edward C. Ezell, Collector Grade Publications, Toronto, Canada, 1987. 400 pp., illus. $59.95
The complete story of the M16 rifle and its development.

Bolt Action Rifles, 3rd Edition, by Frank de Haas, DBI Books, a division of Krause Publications, Iola, WI, 1995. 528 pp., illus. Paper covers. $24.95
A revised edition of the most definitive work on all major bolt-action rifle designs.

The Book of the Garand, by Maj. Gen. J.S. Hatcher, The Gun Room Press, Highland Park, NJ, 1977. 292 pp., illus. $26.95
A new printing of the standard reference work on the U.S. Army M1 rifle.

THE ARMS LIBRARY

The Book of the Twenty-Two: The All American Caliber, by Sam Fadala, Stoeger Publishing Co., So. Hackensack, NJ, 1989. 288 pp., illus. Soft covers. $16.95

The All American Caliber from BB caps up to the powerful 226 Barnes. It's about ammo history, plinking, target shooting, and the quest for the one-hole group.

British Military Martini, Treatise on the, Vol. 1, by B.A. Temple and Ian Skennerton, I.D.S.A. Books, Piqua, OH, 1983. 256 pp., 114 illus. $40.00

British Military Martini, Treatise on the, Vol. 2, by B.A. Temple and Ian Skennerton, I.D.S.A. Books, Piqua, OH, 1989. 213 pp., 135 illus. $40.00

British .22RF Training Rifles, by Dennis Lewis and Robert Washburn, Excaliber Publications, Latham, NY, 1993. 64 pp., illus. Paper covers. $10.95

The story of Britain's training rifles from the early Aiming Tube models to the post-WWII trainers.

Classic Sporting Rifles, by Christopher Austyn, Safari Press, Huntington Beach, CA, 1997. 128 pp., illus. $50.00

As the head of the gun department at Christie's Auction House the author examines the "best" rifles built over the last 150 years.

The Complete AR15/M16 Sourcebook, by Duncan Long, Paladin Press, Boulder, CO, 1993. 232 pp., illus. Paper covers. $35.00

The latest development of the AR15/M16 and the many spin-offs now available, selective-fire conversion systems for the 1990s, the vast selection of new accessories.

The Competitive AR15: The Mouse That Roared, by Glenn Zediker, Zediker Publishing, Oxford, MS, 1999. 286 pp., illustrated. Paper covers. $29.95

A thorough and detailed study of the newest precision rifle sensation.

Complete Book of U.S. Sniping, by Peter R. Senich, Paladin Press, Boulder, CO, 1997, 8 1/2 x 11, hardcover, photos, 288 pp. $52.95

Trace American sniping materiel from its infancy to today's sophisticated systems with this volume, compiled from Senich's early books, Limited War Sniping and The Pictorial History of U.S. Sniping. Almost 400 photos, plus information gleaned from official documents and military archives, pack this informative work.

Complete Guide To The M1 Garand and The M1 Carbine, by Bruce Canfield, Andrew Mowbray, Inc., Lincoln, RI, 1999. 296 pp., illustrated. $39.50

Covers all of the manufacturers of components, parts, variations and markings. Learn which parts are proper for which guns. The total story behind these guns, from their invention through WWII, Korea, Vietnam and beyond! 300+ photos show you features, markings, overall views and action shots. Thirty-three tables and charts give instant reference to serial numbers, markings, dates of issue and proper configurations. Special sections on Sniper guns, National Match Rifles, exotic variations, and more!

The Complete M1 Garand, by Jim Thompson, Paladin Press, Boulder, CO, 1998. 160 pp., illustrated. Paper cover. $25.00

A guide for the shooter and collector, heavily illustrated.

Exploded Long Gun Drawings, The Gun Digest Book of, edited by Harold A. Murtz, DBI Books, a division of Krause Publications, Iola, WI, 512 pp., illus. Paper covers. $20.95

Containing almost 500 rifle and shotgun exploded drawings. An invaluable aid to both professionals and hobbyists.

The FAL Rifle, by R. Blake Stevens and Jean van Rutten, Collector Grade Publications, Cobourg, Canada, 1993. 848 pp., illus. $129.95

Originally published in three volumes, this classic edition covers North American, UK and Commonwealth and the metric FAL's.

The Fighting Rifle, by Chuck Taylor, Paladin Press, Boulder, CO, 1983. 184 pp., illus. Paper covers. $25.00

The difference between assault and battle rifles and auto and light machine guns.

Firearms Assembly/Disassembly Part III: Rimfire Rifles, Revised Edition, The Gun Digest Book of, by J. B. Wood, DBI Books, a division of Krause Publications, Iola, WI., 1994. 480 pp., illus. Paper covers. $19.95

Covers 65 popular rimfires plus over 100 variants, all cross-referenced in the index.

Firearms Assembly/Disassembly Part IV: Centerfire Rifles, Revised Edition, The Gun Digest Book of, by J.B. Wood, DBI Books, a division of Krause Publications, Iola, WI, 1991. 480 pp., illus. Paper covers. $19.95

Covers 54 popular centerfire rifles plus 300 variants. The most comprehensive and professional presentation available to either hobbyist or gunsmith.

The FN-FAL Rifle, et al, by Duncan Long, Delta Press, El Dorado, AR, 1998. 148 pp., illustrated. Paper covers. $18.95

A comprehensive study of one of the classic assault weapons of all times. Detailed descriptions of the basic models plus the myriad of variants that evolved as a result of its universal acceptance.

Forty Years with the .45-70, second edition, revised and expanded, by Paul A. Matthews, Wolfe Publishing Co., Prescott, AZ, 1997. 184 pp., illus. Paper covers. $14.95

This book is pure gun lore-lore of the .45-70. It not only contains a history of the cartridge, but also years of the author's personal experiences.

F.N.-F.A.L. Auto Rifles, Desert Publications, Cornville, AZ, 1981. 130 pp., illus. Paper covers. $16.95

A definitive study of one of the free world's finest combat rifles.

German Sniper 1914-1945, by Peter R. Senich, Paladin Press, Boulder, CO, 1997 8 1/2 x 11, hardcover, photos, 468 pp. $69.95

The complete story of Germany's sniping arms development through both World Wars. Presents more than 600 photos of Mauser 98's, Selbstladegewehr 41s and 43s, optical sights by Goerz, Zeiss, etc., plus German snipers in action. An exceptional hardcover collector's edition for serious military historians everywhere.

Hints and Advice on Rifle-Shooting, by Private R. McVittie with new introductory material by W.S. Curtis, W.S. Curtis Publishers, Ltd., Clwyd, England, 1993. 32 pp. Paper covers. $10.00

A reprint of the original 1886 London edition.

How-To's for the Black Powder Cartridge Rifle Shooter, by Paul A. Matthews, Wolfe Publishing Co., Prescott, AZ, 1996. 136 pp., illus. Paper covers. $22.50

Practices and procedures used in the reloading and shooting of blackpowder cartridges.

Hunting with the .22, by C.S. Landis, R&R Books, Livonia, NY, 1995. 429 pp., illus. $35.00

A reprinting of the classical work on .22 rifles.

The Hunting Rifle, by Townsend Whelen, Wolfe Publishing Co., Prescott, Arizona, 1984. 463 pp., illustrated. $24.95

A thoroughly dependable coverage on the materiel and marksmanhip with relation to the sportsman's rifle for big game.

Illustrated Handbook of Rifle Shooting, by A.L. Russell, Museum Restoration Service, Alexandria Bay, NY, 1992. 194 pp., illus. $24.50

A new printing of the 1869 edition by one of the leading military marksman of the day.

Know Your M1 Garand, by E. J. Hoffschmidt, Blacksmith Corp., Southport, CT, 1975, 84 pp., illus. Paper covers. $15.95

Facts about America's most famous infantry weapon. Covers test and experimental models, Japanese and Italian copies, National Match models.

Know Your Ruger 10/22 Carbine, by William E. Workman, Blacksmith Corp., Chino Valley, AZ, 1991. 96 pp., illus. Paper covers. $12.95

The story and facts about the most popular 22 autoloader ever made.

The Lee Enfield No. 1 Rifles, by Alan M. Petrillo, Excaliber Publications, Latham, NY, 1992. 64 pp., illus. Paper covers. $10.95

Highlights the SMLE rifles from the Mark 1-VI.

The Lee Enfield Number 4 Rifles, by Alan M. Petrillo, Excalibur Publications, Latham, NY, 1992. 64 pp., illus. Paper covers. $10.95

A pocket-sized, bare-bones reference devoted entirely to the .303 World War II and Korean War vintage service rifle.

Legendary Sporting Rifles, by Sam Fadala, Stoeger Publishing Co., So. Hackensack, NJ, 1992. 288 pp., illus. Paper covers. $16.95

Covers a vast span of time and technology beginning with the Kentucky Long-rifle.

The Li'l M1 .30 Cal. Carbine, by Duncan Long, Desert Publications, El Dorado, AZ, 1995. 203 pp., illus. Paper covers. $14.95

Traces the history of this little giant from its original creation.

Make It Accurate: Get the Maximum Performance from Your Hunting Rifle, by Craig Boddington, Safari Press Publications, Huntington Beach, CA, 1999. 224 pp., illustrated. $24.95

Tips on how to select the rifle, cartridge, and scope best suited to your needs. A must-have for any hunter who wants to improve his shot.

Mauser Smallbore Sporting, Target and Training Rifles, by Jon Speed, Collector Grade Publications, Inc., Cobourg, Ont., Canada, 1998. 372 pp., illustrated. $67.50

The history of all the smallbore sporting, target and training rifles produced by the legendary Mauser-Werke of Obendorf am Neckar.

Mauser: Original-Oberndorf Sporting Rifles, by Jon Speed, Collector Grade Publications, Inc., Cobourg, Ont., Canada, 1997. 508 pp., illustrated. $89.95

The most exhaustive study ever published of the design origins and manufacturing history of the original Oberndorf Mauser Sporter.

M14/M14A1 Rifles and Rifle Markmanship, Desert Publications, El Dorado, AZ, 1995. 236 pp., illus. Paper covers. $18.95

Contains a detailed description of the M14 and M14A1 rifles and their general characteristics, procedures for disassembly and assembly, operating and functioning of the rifles, etc.

The M14 Owner's Guide and Match Conditioning Instructions, by Scott A. Duff and John M. Miller, Scott A. Duff Publications, Export, PA, 1996. 180 pp., illus. Paper covers. $19.95

Traces the history and development from the T44 through the adoption and production of the M14 rifle.

The M-14 Rifle, facsimile reprint of FM 23-8, Desert Publications, Cornville, AZ, 50 pp., illus. Paper $11.95

Well illustrated and informative reprint covering the M-14 and M-14E2.

THE ARMS LIBRARY

The M14-Type Rifle: A Shooter's and Collector's Guide, by Joe Poyer, North Cape Publications, Tustin, CA, 1997. 82 pp., illus. Paper covers. $18.95
Covers the history and development, commercial copies, cleaning and maintenance instructions, and targeting and shooting.

The M16/AR15 Rifle, by Joe Poyer, North Cape Publications, Tustin, CA, 1998. 150 pp., illustrated. Paper covers. $19.95
From its inception as the first American assault battle rifle to the firing lines of the National Matches, the M16/AR15 rifle in all its various models and guises has made a significant impact on the American rifleman.

Military Bolt Action Rifles, 1841-1918, by Donald B. Webster, Museum Restoration Service, Alexander Bay, NY, 1993. 150 pp., illus. $34.50
A photographic survey of the principal rifles and carbines of the European and Asiatic powers of the last half of the 19th century and the first years of the 20th century.

The Mini-14, by Duncan Long, Paladin Press, Boulder, CO, 1987. 120 pp., illus. Paper covers. $17.00
History of the Mini-14, the factory-produced models, specifications, accessories, suppliers, and much more.

Mr. Single Shot's Book of Rifle Plans, by Frank de Haas, Mark de Haas, Orange City, IA, 1996. 85 pp., illus. Paper covers. $22.50
Contains complete and detailed drawings, plans and instructions on how to build four different and unique breech-loading single shot rifles of the author's own proven design.

M1 Carbine Owner's Manual, M1, M2 & M3 .30 Caliber Carbines, Firepower Publications, Cornville, AZ, 1984. 102 pp., illus. Paper covers. $16.95
The complete book for the owner of an M1 Carbine.

The M1 Garand Serial Numbers & Data Sheets, by Scott A. Duff, Scott A. Duff, Export, PA, 1995. 101 pp. Paper covers. $11.95
This pocket reference book includes serial number tables and data sheets on the Springfield Armory, Gas Trap Rifles, Gas Port Rifles, Winchester Repeating Arms, International Harvester and H&R Arms Co. and more.

The M1 Garand: Post World War, by Scott A. Duff, Scott A. Duff, Export, PA, 1990. 139 pp., illus. Soft covers. $19.95
A detailed account of the activities at Springfield Armory through this period. International Harvester, H&R, Korean War production and quantities delivered. Serial numbers.

The M1 Garand: World War 2, by Scott A. Duff, Scott A. Duff, Export, PA, 1993. 210 pp., illus. Paper covers. $39.95
The most comprehensive study available to the collector and historian on the M1 Garand of World War II.

Modern Sniper Rifles, by Duncan Long, Paladin Press, Boulder, CO, 1997, 8 1/2 x 11, soft cover, photos, illus., 120 pp. $20.00
Noted weapons expert Duncan Long describes the .22 LR, single-shot, bolt-action, semiautomatic and large-caliber rifles that can be used for sniping purposes, including the U.S. M21, Ruger Mini-14, AUG and HK-94SG1. These and other models are evaluated on the basis of their features, accuracy, reliability and handiness in the field. The author also looks at the best scopes, ammunition and accessories.

More Single Shot Rifles and Actions, by Frank de Haas, Mark de Haas, Orange City, IA, 1996. 146 pp., illus. Paper covers. $22.50
Covers 45 different single shot rifles. Includes the history plus photos, drawings and personal comments.

The Muzzle-Loading Rifle...Then and Now, by Walter M. Cline, National Muzzle Loading Rifle Association, Friendship, IN, 1991. 161 pp., illus. $32.00
This extensive compilation of the muzzleloading rifle exhibits accumulative preserved data concerning the development of the "hallowed old arms of the Southern highlands."

The No. 4 (T) Sniper Rifle: An Armourer's Perspective, by Peter Laidler with Ian Skennerton, I.D.S.A. Books, Piqua, OH, 1993. 125 pp., 75 illus. Paper covers. $19.95

Notes on Rifle-Shooting, by Henry William Heaton, reprinted with a new introduction by W.S. Curtis, W.S. Curtis Publishers, Ltd., Clwyd, England, 1993. 89 pp. $19.95
A reprint of the 1864 London edition. Captain Heaton was one of the great rifle shots from the earliest days of the Volunteer Movement.

The Official SKS Manual, Translation by Major James F. Gebhardt (Ret.), Paladin Press, Boulder, CO, 1997. 96 pp., illus. Paper covers. $16.00
This Soviet military manual covering the widely distributed SKS is now available in English.

The Pennsylvania Rifle, by Samuel E. Dyke, Sutter House, Lititz, PA, 1975. 61 pp., illus. Paper covers. $10.00
History and development, from the hunting rifle of the Germans who settled the area. Contains a full listing of all known Lancaster, PA, gunsmiths from 1729 through 1815.

Police Rifles, by Richard Fairburn, Paladin Press, Boulder, CO, 1994. 248 pp., illus. Paper covers. $35.00
Selecting the right rifle for street patrol and special tactical situations.

The Poor Man's Sniper Rifle, by D. Boone, Paladin Press, Boulder, CO, 1995. 152 pp., illus. Paper covers. $18.95
Here is a complete plan for converting readily available surplus military rifles to high-performance sniper weapons.

A Potpourri of Single Shot Rifles and Actions, by Frank de Haas, Mark de Haas, Ridgeway, MO, 1993. 153 pp., illus. Paper covers. $22.50
The author's 6th book on non-bolt-action single shots. Covers more than 40 single-shot rifles in historical and technical detail.

Precision Shooting with the M1 Garand, by Roy Baumgardner, Precision Shooting, Inc., Manchester, CT, 1999. 142 pp., illustrated. Paper covers. $12.95
Starts off with the ever popular ten-article series on accurinzing the M1 that originally appeared in Precision Shooting in the 1993-95 era. There follows nine more Baumgardner authored articles on the M1 Garand and finally a 1999 updating chapter.

Purdey Gun and Rifle Makers: The Definitive History, by Donald Dallas, Quiller Press, London, 2000. 245 pp., illus. Color throughout. $100.00
A limited edition of 3,000 copies. Signed and Numbered. With a PURDEY book plate.

The Remington 700, by John F. Lacy, Taylor Publishing Co., Dallas, TX, 1990. 208 pp., illus. $44.95
Covers the different models, limited editions, chamberings, proofmarks, serial numbers, military models, and much more.

The Revolving Rifles, by Edsall James, Pioneer Press, Union City, TN, 1975. 23 pp., illus. Paper covers. $5.00
Valuable information on revolving cylinder rifles, from the earliest matchlock forms to the latest models of Colt and Remington.

Rifle Guide, by Sam Fadala, Stoeger Publishing Co., S. Hackensack, NJ, 1993. 288 pp., illus. Paper covers. $16.95
This comprehensive, fact-filled book beckons to both the seasoned rifleman as well as the novice shooter.

The Rifle: Its Development for Big-Game Hunting, by S.R. Truesdell, Safari Press, Huntington Beach, CA, 1992. 274 pp., illus. $35.00
The full story of the development of the big-game rifle from 1834-1946.

Riflesmithing, The Gun Digest Book of, by Jack Mitchell, DBI Books, a division of Krause Publications, Iola, WI, 1982. 256 pp., illus. Paper covers. $16.95
Covers tools, techniques, designs, finishing wood and metal, custom alterations.

Rifles of the World, 2nd Edition, edited by John Walter, DBI Books, a division of Krause Publications, Iola, WI, 1998. 384 pp., illus. $24.95
The definitive guide to the world's centerfire and rimfire rifles.

Ned H. Roberts and the Schuetzen Rifle, edited by Gerald O. Kelver, Brighton, CO, 1982. 99 pp., illus. $13.95
A compilation of the writings of Major Ned H. Roberts which appeared in various gun magazines.

Schuetzen Rifles, History and Loading, by Gerald O. Kelver, Gerald O. Kelver, Publisher, Brighton, CO, 1972. Illus. $13.95
Reference work on these rifles, their bullets, loading, telescopic sights, accuracy, etc. A limited, numbered ed.

Shooting the Blackpowder Cartridge Rifle, by Paul A. Matthews, Wolfe Publishing Co., Prescott, AZ, 1994. 129 pp., illus. Paper covers. $22.50
A general discourse on shooting the blackpowder cartridge rifle and the procedure required to make a particular rifle perform.

Shooting Lever Guns of the Old West, by Mike Venturino, MLV Enterprises, Livingston, MT, 1999. 300 pp., illustrated. Paper covers. $27.95
Shooting the lever action type repeating rifles of our American west.

Single Shot Rifles and Actions, by Frank de Haas, Orange City, IA, 1990. 352 pp., illus. Soft covers. $27.00
The definitive book on over 60 single shot rifles and actions.

Sixty Years of Rifles, by Paul A. Matthews, Wolfe Publishing Co., Prescott, AZ, 1991. 224 pp., illus. $19.50
About rifles and the author's experience and love affair with shooting and hunting.

S.L.R.—Australia's F.N. F.A.L. by Ian Skennerton and David Balmer, I.D.S.A. Books, Piqua, OH, 1989. 124 pp., 100 illus. Paper covers. $19.50

Small Arms Identification Series, No. 2—.303 Rifle, No. 4 Marks I, & I*, Marks 1/2, 1/3 & 2, by Ian Skennerton, I.D.S.A. Books, Piqua, OH, 1994. 48 pp. $9.50

Small Arms Identification Series, No. 3—9mm Austen Mk I & 9mm Owen Mk I Sub-Machine Guns, by Ian Skennerton, I.D.S.A. Books, Piqua, OH, 1994. 48 pp. $9.50

Small Arms Identification Series, No. 4—.303 Rifle, No. 5 Mk I, by Ian Skennerton, I.D.S.A. Books, Piqua, OH, 1994. 48 pp. $9.50

Small Arms Identification Series, No. 5—.303-in. Bren Light Machine Gun, by Ian Skennerton, I.D.S.A. Books, Piqua, OH, 1994. 48 pp. $9.50

Small Arms Series, No. 1 DeLisle's Commando Carbine, by Ian Skennerton, I.D.S.A. Books, Piqua, OH, 1981. 32 pp., 24 illus. $9.00

Small Arms Identification Series, No. 1—.303 Rifle, No. 1 S.M.L.E. Marks III and III*, by Ian Skennerton, I.D.S.A. Books, Piqua, OH, 1981. 48 pp. $9.50

Sporting Rifle Takedown & Reassembly Guide, 2nd Edition, by J.B. Wood, DBI Books, a division of Krause Publications, Iola, WI, 1997. 480 pp., illus. $19.95
An updated edition of the reference guide for anyone who wants to properly care for their sporting rifle. (Available September 1997)

THE ARMS LIBRARY

The Springfield Rifle M1903, M1903A1, M1903A3, M1903A4, Desert Publications, Cornville, AZ, 1982. 100 pp., illus. Paper covers. $12.00
Covers every aspect of disassembly and assembly, inspection, repair and maintenance.

Still More Single Shot Rifles, by James J. Grant, Pioneer Press, Union City, TN, 1995. 211 pp., illus. $29.95
This is Volume Four in a series of Single-Shot Rifles by America's foremost authority. It gives more in-depth information on those single-shot rifles which were presented in the first three books.

The Sturm, Ruger 10/22 Rifle and .44 Magnum Carbine, by Duncan Long, Paladin Press, Boulder, CO, 1988. 108 pp., illus. Paper covers. $15.00
An in-depth look at both weapons detailing the elegant simplicity of the Ruger design. Offers specifications, troubleshooting procedures and ammunition recommendations.

The Tactical Rifle, by Gabriel Suarez, Paladin Press, Boulder, CO, 1999. 264 pp., illustrated. Paper covers. $25.00
The precision tool for urban police operations.

Target Rifle in Australia, by J.E. Corcoran, R&R, Livonia, NY, 1996. 160 pp., illus. $40.00
A most interesting study of the evolution of these rifles from 1860 - 1900. British rifles from the percussion period through the early smokeless era are discussed.

To the Dreams of Youth: The .22 Caliber Single Shot Winchester Rifle, by Herbert Houze, Krause Publications, Iola, WI, 1993. 192 pp., illus. $34.95
A thoroughly researched history of the 22-caliber Winchester single shot rifle, including interesting photographs.

The Ultimate in Rifle Accuracy, by Glenn Newick, Stoeger Publishing Co., Wayne, N.J., 1999. 205 pp., illustrated. Paper covers. $11.95
This handbook contains the information you need to extract the best performance from your rifle.

U.S. Marine Corps AR15/M16 A2 Manual, reprinted by Desert Publications, El Dorado, AZ, 1993. 262 pp., illus. Paper covers. $16.95
A reprint of TM05538C-23&P/2, August, 1987. The A-2 manual for the Colt AR15/M16.

U.S. Rifle M14—From John Garand to the M21, by R. Blake Stevens, Collector Grade Publications, Inc., Toronto, Canada, revised second edition, 1991. 350 pp., illus. $49.50
A classic, in-depth examination of the development, manufacture and fielding of the last wood-and-metal ("lock, stock, and barrel") battle rifle to be issued to U.S. troops.

War Baby!: The U.S. Caliber 30 Carbine, Volume I, by Larry Ruth, Collector Grade Publications, Toronto, Canada, 1992. 512 pp., illus. $69.95
Volume 1 of the in-depth story of the phenomenally popular U.S. caliber 30 carbine. Concentrates on design and production of the military 30 carbine during World War II.

War Baby Comes Home: The U.S. Caliber 30 Carbine, Volume 2, by Larry Ruth, Collector Grade Publications, Toronto, Canada, 1993. 386 pp., illus. $49.95
The triumphant competion of Larry Ruth's two-volume in-depth series on the most popular U.S. military small arm in history.

The Winchester Model 52, Perfection in Design, by Herbert G. Houze, Krause Publications, Iola, WI, 1997. 192 pp., illus. $34.95
This book covers the complete story of this technically superior gun.

The Winchester Model 94: The First 100 Years, by Robert C. Renneberg, Krause Publications, Iola, WI, 1991. 208 pp., illus. $34.95
Covers the design and evolution from the early years up to today.

Winchester Slide-Action Rifles, Volume I: Model 1890 and Model 1906 by Ned Schwing, Krause Publications, Iola, WI. 352 pp., illus. $39.95
Traces the history through word and picture in this chronolgy of the Model 1890 and 1906.

Winchester Slide-Action Rifles, Volume II: Model 61 & Model 62 by Ned Schwing, Krause Publications, Iola, WI. 256 pp., illus. $34.95
Historical look complete with markings, stampings and engraving.

SHOTGUNS

Advanced Combat Shotgun: The Stress Fire Concept, by Massad Ayoob, Police Bookshelf, Concord, NH, 1993. 197 pp., illus. Paper covers. $9.95
Advanced combat shotgun fighting for police.

Best Guns, by Michael McIntosh, Countrysport Press, Selma, AL, 1999, revised edition. 418 pp. $39.00
Combines the best shotguns ever made in America with information on British and Continental makers.

The Better Shot, by Ken Davies, Quiller Press, London, England, 1992. 136 pp., illus. $39.95
Step-by-step shotgun technique with Holland and Holland.

The Big Shots; Edwardian Shooting Parties, by Jonathan Ruffer, Quiller Press, London, England, 1997 160pp. B & W illus. $24.95
A book about Edwardian shooting parties, now a former pastime and enjoyed by the selected few, who recall the hunting of pheasants. Foreword by HRH The Prince of Wales.

The British Shotgun, Volume 1, 1850-1870, by I.M. Crudington and D.J. Baker, Barrie & Jenkins, London, England, 1979. 256 pp., illus. $65.00
An attempt to trace, as accurately as is now possible, the evolution of the shotgun during its formative years in Great Britain.

Boothroyd on British Shotguns, by Geoffrey Boothroyd, Sand Lake Press, Amity, OR, 1996. 221 pp., illus. plus a 32 page reproduction of the 1914 Webley & Scott catalog. A limited, numbered edition. $34.95
Based on articles by the author that appeared in the British Publication *Shooting Times & Country Magazine.*

Boss & Co. Builders of the Best Guns Only, by Donald Dallas, Quiller Press, London, 1995. 262 pp., illustrated. $79.95
Large four colour plates, b/w photos, bibliography. The definitive history authorized by Boss & Co.

The British Over-and-Under Shotgun, by Geoffrey and Susan Boothroyd, Sand Lake Press, Amity, OR, 1996. 137 pp., illus. $34.95
Historical outline of the development of the O/U shotgun with individual chapters devoted to the twenty-two British makers.

The Browning Superposed: John M. Browning's Last Legacy, by Ned Schwing, Krause Publications, Iola, WI, 1996. 496 pp., illus. $49.95
An exclusive story of the man, the company and the best-selling over-and-under shotgun in North America.

Clay Target Handbook, by Jerry Meyer, Lyons & Buford, Publisher, New York, NY, 1993. 182 pp., illus. $22.95
Contains in-depth, how-to-do-it information on trap, skeet, sporting clays, international trap, international skeet and clay target games played around the country.

Clay Target Shooting, by Paul Bentley, A&C Black, London, England, 1987. 144 pp., illus. $25.00
Practical book on clay target shooting written by a very successful international competitor, providing valuable professional advice and instruction for shooters of all disciplines.

Cogswell & Harrison; Two Centuries of Gunmaking, by G. Cooley & J. Newton, Safari Press, Long Beach, CA, 2000. 128pp, 30 color photos, 100 b&w photos. $39.95
The authors have gathered a wealth of fascinating historical and technical material that will make the book indispensable, not only to many thousands of "Coggie" owners worldwide, but also to anyone interested in the general history of British gunmaking.

A Collector's Guide to United States Combat Shotguns, by Bruce N. Canfield, Andrew Mowbray Inc., Publishers, Lincoln, RI, 1993. 184 pp., illus. Paper covers. $24.00
Full coverage of the combat shotgun, from the earliest examples to the Gulf War and beyond.

Combat Shotgun and Submachine Gun, "A Special Weapons Analysis" by Chuck Taylor, Paladin Press, Boulder, CO, 1997, soft cover, photos, 176 pp. $25.00
From one of America's top shooting instructors comes an analysis of two controversial, misunderstood and misemployed small arms. Hundreds of photos detail field-testing of both, basic and advanced training drills, tactical rules, gun accessories and modifications. Loading procedures, carrying and fighting positions and malfunction clearance drills are included to promote weapon effectiveness.

Cradock on Shotguns, by Chris Cradock, Banford Press, London, England, 1989. 200 pp., illus. $45.00
A definitive work on the shotgun by a British expert on shotguns.

The Defensive Shotgun, by Louis Awerbuck, S.W.A.T. Publications, Cornville, AZ, 1989. 77 pp., illus. Soft covers. $14.95
Cuts through the myths concerning the shotgun and its attendant ballistic effects.

The Double Shotgun, by Don Zutz, Winchester Press, Piscataway, NJ, 1985. 304 pp., illus. $22.95
Revised, updated, expanded edition of the history and development of the world's classic sporting firearms.

The Ducks Unlimited Guide to Shotgunning, by Don Zutz, Willow Creek Press, Minocqua, WI, 2000. 166 pg. Illustrated. $24.50
This book covers everything from the grand old guns of yesterday to todays best shotguns and loads, from the basic shotgun fit and function to expert advice on ballistics, chocks, and shooting techniques.

Finding the Extra Target, by Coach John R. Linn & Stephen A. Blumenthal, Shotgun Sports, Inc., Auburn, CA, 1989. 126 pp., illus. Paper covers. $14.95
The ultimate training guide for all the clay target sports.

Fine Gunmaking: Double Shotguns, by Steven Dodd Hughes, Krause Publications Iola, WI, 1998. 167 pp., illustrated. $34.95
An in-depth look at the creation of fine shotguns.

Firearms Assembly/Disassembly, Part V: Shotguns, Revised Edition, The Gun Digest Book of, by J.B. Wood, DBI Books, a division of Krause Publications, Iola, WI, 1992. 480 pp., illus. Paper covers. $19.95
Covers 46 popular shotguns plus over 250 variants. The most comprehensive and professional presentation available to either hobbyist or gunsmith.

THE ARMS LIBRARY

A.H. Fox "The Finest Gun in the World", revised and enlarged edition, by Michael McIntosh, Countrysport, Inc., New Albany, OH, 1995. 408 pp., illus. $49.00
The first detailed history of one of America's finest shotguns.

Game Shooting, by Robert Churchill, Countrysport Press, Selma, AL, 1998. 258 pp., illus. $30.00
The basis for every shotgun instructional technique devised and the foundation for all wingshooting and the game of sporting clays.

The Golden Age of Shotgunning, by Bob Hinman, Wolfe Publishing Co., Inc., Prescott, AZ, 1982. $22.50
A valuable history of the late 1800s detailing that fabulous period of development in shotguns, shotshells and shotgunning.

The Greener Story, by Graham Greener, Safari Press, Long Beach, CA, 2000. 231pp, color and b&w illustrations. $69.95
The history of the Greener Gunmakers and their guns

Grand Old Shotguns, by Don Zutz, Shotgun Sports Magazine, Auburn, CA, 1995. 136 pp., illus. Paper covers. $19.95
A study of the great smoothbores, their history and how and why they were discontinued. Find out the most sought-after and which were the best shooters.

Gun Digest Book of Sporting Clays, 2nd Edition, edited by Harold A. Murtz, Krause Publications, Iola, WI, 1999. 256 pp., illus. Paper covers. $21.95
A concise Gun Digest book that covers guns, ammo, chokes, targets and course layouts so you'll stay a step ahead.

The Gun Review Book, by Michael McIntosh, Countrysport Press, Selman, AL, 1999. Paper covers. $19.95
Compiled here for the first time are McIntosh's popular gun reviews from *Shooting Sportsman; The Magazine of Wingshooting* and *Fine Shotguns*. The author traces the history of gunmakes, then examines, analyzes, and critique the fine shotguns of England, Continental Europe and the United States.

Hartman on Skeet, by Barney Hartman, Stackpole Books, Harrisburg, PA, 1973. 143 pp., illus. $19.95
A definitive book on Skeet shooting by a pro.

The Heyday of the Shotgun, by David Baker, Safari Press, Inc., Huntington Beach, CA, 2000. 160 pp., illustrated. $39.95
The art of the gunmaker at the turn of the last century when British craftsmen brought forth the finest guns ever made.

The Italian Gun, by Steve Smith & Laurie Morrow, wilderness Adventures, Gallatin Gateway, MT, 1997. 325 pp., illus. $49.95
The first book ever written entirely in English for American enthusiasts who own, aspire to own, or simply admire Italian guns.

The Ithaca Featherlight Repeater; the Best Gun Going, by Walter C. Snyder, Southern Pines, NC, 1998. 300 pp., illus. $89.95
Describes the complete history of each model of the legendary Ithaca Model 37 and Model 87 Repeaters from their conception in 1930 throught 1997.

The Ithaca Gun Company from the Beginning, by Walter C. Snyder, Cook & Uline Publishing Co., Southern Pines, NC, 2nd Edition, 1999. 384 pp., illustrated in color and black and white. $90.00
The entire family of Ithaca Gun Company products is described along with new historical information and the serial number/date of manufacturing listing has been improved.

L.C. Smith Shotguns, by Lt. Col. William S. Brophy, The Gun Room Press, Highland Park, NJ, 1979. 244 pp., illus. $35.00
The first work on this very important American gun and manufacturing company.

The Little Trapshooting Book, by Frank Little, Shotgun Sports Magazine, Auburn, CA, 1994. 168 pp., illus. Paper covers. $19.95
Packed with know-how from one of the greatest trapshooters of all time.

Lock, Stock, and Barrel, by C. Adams & R. Braden, Safari Press, Huntington Beach, CA, 1996. 254 pp., illus. $24.95
The process of making a best grade English gun from a lump of steel and a walnut tree trunk to the ultimate product plus practical advise on consistent field shooting with a double gun.

Mental Training for the Shotgun Sports, by Michael J. Keyes, Shotgun Sports, Auburn, CA, 1996. 160 pp., illus. Paper covers. $24.95
The most comprehensive book ever published on what it takes to shoot winning scores at trap, Skeet and Sporting Clays.

The Model 12, 1912-1964, by Dave Riffle, Dave Riffle, Ft. Meyers, FL, 1995. 274 pp., illus. $49.95
The story of the greatest hammerless repeating shotgun ever built.

More Shotguns and Shooting, by Michael McIntosh, Countrysport Books, Selma, AL, 1998. 256 pp., illustrated. $30.00
From specifics of shotguns to shooting your way out of a slump, it's McIntosh at his best.

Mossberg: More Gun for the Money, by Victor & Cheryl Havlin, Blue Book Publications, Minneapolis, MN, 1995. 204 pages, illustrated. $24.95
The History of O.F. Mossberg & Sons, Inc.

Mossberg's Shotguns, by Duncan Long, Delta Press, El Dorado, AR, 2000. 120 pp., illustrated. $24.95
This book contains a brief history of the company and it's founder, full coverage of the pump and semiautomatic shotguns, rare products and a care and maintenance section.

The Mysteries of Shotgun Patterns, by George G. Oberfell and Charles E. Thompson, Oklahoma State University Press, Stillwater, OK, 1982. 164 pp., illus. Paper covers. $25.00
Shotgun ballistics for the hunter in non-technical language.

The Parker Gun, by Larry Baer, Gun Room Press, Highland Park, NJ, 1993. 195 pages, illustrated with B & W and Color photos. $35.00
Covers in detail, production of all models on this classic gun. Many fine specimens from great collections are illustrated.

Parker Guns "The Old Reliable", by Ed Muderiak, Safari Press, Inc., Huntington Beach, CA, 1997. 325 pp., illus. $40.00
A look at the small beginnings, the golden years, and the ultimate decline of the most famous of all American shotgun manufacturers.

The Parker Story; Volumes 1 & 2, by Bill Mullins, "etal". The Double Gun Journal, East Jordan, MI, 2000. 1,025 pages of text and 1,500 color and monochrome illustrations. Hardbound in a gold-embossed cover. $295.00
The most complete and attractive "last word" on America's preeminent double gun maker. Includes tables showing the number of guns made by gauge, barrel length and special features for each grade.

Positive Shooting, by Michael Yardley, Safari Press, Huntington Beach, CA, 1995. 160 pp., illus. $30.00
This book will provide the shooter with a sound foundation from which to develop an effective, personal technique that can dramatically improve shooting performance.

Purdey Gun and Rifle Makers: The Definitive History, by Donald Dallas, Quiller Press, London 2000. 245 pages, illus. $100.00
245 Colour plates, b/w photos, ills, bibliography. The definitive history. A limited edition of 3,000 copies. Signed and Numbered. With a PURDEY book plate.

Recognizing Side by Side Shotguns, by Charles Carder, Anvil Onze Publishing, 2000. 25 pp., illus. Paper Covers. $5.95
A graphic description of the visible features of side by side breech loading shotguns.

Reloading for Shotgunners, 4th Edition, by Kurt D. Fackler and M.L. McPherson, DBI Books, a division of Krause Publications, Iola, WI, 1997. 320 pp., illus. Paper covers. $19.95
Expanded reloading tables with over 11,000 loads. Bushing charts for every major press and component maker. All new presentation on all aspects of shotshell reloading by two of the top experts in the field. (Available October 1997.)

Remington Double Shotguns, by Charles G. Semer, Denver, CO, 1997. 617 pp., illus. $60.00
This book deals with the entire production and all grades of double shotguns made by Remington during the period of their production 1873-1910.

75 Years with the Shotgun, by C.T. (Buck) Buckman, Valley Publ., Fresno, CA, 1974. 141 pp., illus. $10.00
An expert hunter and trapshooter shares experiences of a lifetime.

The Shotgun in Combat, by Tony Lesce, Desert Publications, Cornville, AZ, 1979. 148 pp., illus. Paper covers. $14.00
A history of the shotgun and its use in combat.

Shotgun Digest, 4th Edition, edited by Jack Lewis, DBI Books, a division of Krause Publications, Iola, WI, 1993. 256 pp., illus. Paper covers. $17.95
A look at what's happening with shotguns and shotgunning today.

The Shotgun Encyclopedia, by John Taylor, Safari Press, Inc., Huntington Beach, CA, 2000. 260 pp., illustrated. $34.95
A comprehensive reference work on all aspects of shotguns and shotgun shooting.

Shotgun Gunsmithing, The Gun Digest Book of, by Ralph Walker, DBI Books, a division of Krause Publications, Iola, WI, 1983. 256 pp., illus. Paper covers. $16.95
The principles and practices of repairing, individualizing and accurizing modern shotguns by one of the world's premier shotgun gunsmiths.

The Shotgun: History and Development, by Geoffrey Boothroyd, Safari Press, Huntington Beach, CA, 1995. 240 pp., illus. $35.00
The first volume in a series that traces the development of the British shotgun from the 17th century onward.

The Shotgun Handbook, by Mike George, The Croswood Press, London, England, 1999. 128 pp., illus. $35.00
For all shotgun enthusiasts, this detailed guide ranges from design and selection of a gun to adjustment, cleaning, and maintenance.

Shotgun Stuff, by Don Zutz, Shotgun Sports, Inc., Auburn, CA, 1991. 172 pp., illus. Paper covers. $19.95
This book gives shotgunners all the "stuff" they need to achieve better performance and get more enjoyment from their favorite smoothbore.

Shotgunner's Notebook: The Advice and Reflections of a Wingshooter, by Gene Hill, Countrysport Press, Traverse City, MI, 1990. 192 pp., illus. $25.00
Covers the shooting, the guns and the miscellany of the sport.

THE ARMS LIBRARY

Shotgunning: The Art and the Science, by Bob Brister, Winchester Press, Piscataway, NJ, 1976. 321 pp., illus. $18.95

Hundreds of specific tips and truly novel techniques to improve the field and target shooting of every shotgunner.

Shotgunning Trends in Transition, by Don Zutz, Wolfe Publishing Co., Prescott, AZ, 1990. 314 pp., illus. $29.50

This book updates American shotgunning from post WWII to present.

Shotguns and Cartridges for Game and Clays, by Gough Thomas, edited by Nigel Brown, A & C Black, Ltd., Cambs, England, 1989. 256 pp., illus. Soft covers. $24.95

Gough Thomas' well-known and respected book for game and clay pigeon shooters in a thoroughly up-dated edition.

Shotguns and Gunsmiths: The Vintage Years, by Geoffrey Boothroyd, Safari Press, Huntington Beach, CA, 1995. 240 pp., illus. $35.00

A fascinating insight into the lives and skilled work of gunsmiths who helped develop the British shotgun during the Victorian and Edwardian eras.

Shotguns and Shooting, by Michael McIntosh, Countrysport Press, New Albany, OH, 1995. 258 pp., illus. $30.00

The art of guns and gunmaking, this book is a celebration no lover of fine doubles should miss.

Shotguns for Wingshooting, by John Barsness, DBI Books, a division of Krause Publications, Inc., Iola, WI, 1999. 208 pp., illustrated. $49.95

Detailed information on all styles of shotgun. How to select the correct ammunition for specific hunting applications.

Side by Sides of the World for Y2K, by Charles Carder, Anvil Onze Publishing, 2000. 221 pp., illus. Paper Covers. $25.95

This book lists more than 1600 names & features side by sides shotguns from all over the world, in alphabetical order. 500 + illustrations.

Sidelocks & Boxlocks, by Geoffrey Boothroyd, Sand Lake Press, Amity, OR, 1991. 271 pp., illus. $24.95

The story of the classic British shotgun.

Spanish Best: The Fine Shotguns of Spain, by Terry Wieland, Countrysport, Inc., Traverse City, MI, 1994. 264 pp., illus. $45.00

A practical source of information for owners of Spanish shotguns and a guide for those considering buying a used shotgun.

The Sporting Clay Handbook, by Jerry Meyer, Lyons and Burford Publishers, New York, NY, 1990. 140 pp., illus. Soft covers. $17.95

Introduction to the fastest growing, and most exciting, gun game in America.

Streetsweepers, "The Complete Book of Combat Shotguns", by Duncan Long, Paladin Press, Boulder, CO, 1997, soft cover, 63 photos, illus., appendices, 160 pp. $24.95

Streetsweepers is the newest, most comprehensive book out on combat shotguns, covering single- and double-barreled, slide-action, semi-auto and rotary cylinder shotguns, plus a chapter on grenade launchers you can mount on your weapon and info about shotgun models not yet on the market. Noted gun writer Duncan Long also advises on which ammo to use, accessories and combat shotgun tactics.

The Tactical Shotgun, by Gabriel Suzrez, Paladin Press, Boulder, CO, 1996. 232 pp., illus. Paper covers. $25.00

The best techniques and tactics for employing the shotgun in personal combat.

Taking More Birds, by Dan Carlisle & Dolph Adams, Lyons & Burford, New York, NY, 1993. 120 pp., illus. $19.95

A practical guide to greater success at sporting clays and wing shooting.

Tip Up Shotguns from Hopkins and Allen, by Charles Carder, Anvil Onze Publishing, 2000. 81 pp., illus. Paper Covers. $13.95

All the descriptive material and graphics used in this book have been reproduced from original Hopkins & Allen Arms Company catalogs, except the patent drawings.

Trap & Skeet Shooting, 3rd Edition, by Chris Christian, DBI Books, a division of Krause Publications, Iola, WI, 1994. 288 pp., illus. Paper covers. $17.95

A detailed look at the contemporary world of Trap, Skeet and Sporting Clays.

Trapshooting is a Game of Opposites, by Dick Bennett, Shotgun Sports, Inc., Auburn, CA, 1996. 129 pp., illus. Paper covers. $19.95

Discover everything you need to know about shooting trap like the pros.

Turkey Hunter's Digest, Revised Edition, by Dwain Bland, DBI Books, a division of Krause Publications, Iola, WI, 1994. 256 pp., illus. Paper covers. $17.95

Presents no-nonsense approach to hunting all five sub-species of the North American wild turkey.

U.S. Shotguns, All Types, reprint of TM9-285, Desert Publications, Cornville, AZ, 1987. 257 pp., illus. Paper covers. $9.95

Covers operation, assembly and disassembly of nine shotguns used by the U.S. armed forces.

U.S. Winchester Trench and Riot Guns and Other U.S. Military Combat Shotguns, by Joe Poyer, North Cape Publications, Tustin, CA, 1992. 124 pp., illus. Paper covers. $15.95

A detailed history of the use of military shotguns, and the acquisition procedures used by the U.S. Army's Ordnance Department in both World Wars.

The Winchester Model Twelve, by George Madis, David Madis, Dallas, TX, 1984. 176 pp., illus. $24.95.

A definitive work on this famous American shotgun.

The Winchester Model 42, by Ned Schwing, Krause Pub., Iola, WI, 1990. 160 pp., illus. $34.95

Behind-the-scenes story of the model 42's invention and its early development. Production totals and manufacturing dates; reference work.

Winchester Shotguns and Shotshells, by Ron Stadt, Krause Pub., Iola, WI. 288 pp., illus. $34.95.

Must-have for Winchester collectors of shotguns manufactured through 1961.

Winchester's Finest, the Model 21, by Ned Schwing, Krause Publications, Iola, WI, 1990. 360 pp., illus. $49.95

The classic beauty and the interesting history of the Model 21 Winchester shotgun.

The World's Fighting Shotguns, by Thomas F. Swearengen, T.B.N. Enterprises, Alexandria, VA, 1979. 500 pp., illus. $39.95

The complete military and police reference work from the shotgun's inception to date, with up-to-date developments.

INDEX

A

Alpine ibex, 167
Anschutz Exemplar, 26, 32
aoudad sheep, 89
argali sheep, 154
axis deer, 93, 179

B

banteng, 142, 144-47
Bausch & Lomb, 27, 36, 53, 58, 74, 85, 98, 102, 182
bears, 11, 152
Black Hills Ammunition, 37, 184
black springbuck, 100
black wildebeest, 123
blackbuck antelope, 94, 179
Blesbok, 123
blue duiker, 97, 103
blue sheep, 165
blue wildebeest, 107, 123
bobcats, 38
bongo, 125
bontebok, 123
brocket deer, 173, 175
Buckmark, 26
Burris, 26, 27, 36, 46, 58, 59, 182
bushbuck, 111, 124, 128
Bushnell, 53, 155, 183
bushpig, 106, 110

C

Cape buffalo, 126, 127
cape grysbok, 102-03
caracal, 104
CCI ammo, 26
civet, 104
common reedbuck, 98
common springbuck, 102, 103
Contender, 25, 38, 42, 53, 57, 59
Cor-Bon, 67, 74, 144, 147
corsican sheep, 94
coyotes, 32, 38
crocodile, 141
crows, 38

D

dik-dik, 104
duiker, 107

E

Eastern tur, 21, 160
eland, 94, 105, 109, 110, 125
elephant, 126, 129, 130, 132, 133, 135, 152
Encore, 12, 124, 125
Encore, 13, 46, 59
Europe, 166

F

fallow deer, 93
Federal, 184
feral goat, 179
feral hogs, 179
Fox Ridge Outfitters, 59
fox, 37-38
Freedom Arms, 11, 61, 62

G

Garrett Cartridges, 67
gaur, 152
gemsbok, 122
genet, 104
Gredos Ibex, 170
groundhogs, 32, 37, 38

H

Handgun Hunters International, 22
hartebeest, 123
hippo, 137, 141
hog deer, 151
Hornady XTP, 15
Hornady, 46, 67, 69, 74, 77, 78, 82, 92, 102, 108, 122, 127, 128, 135, 150, 175, 181, 184
Hornady's V-Max, 32, 37
H-S Precision Pro-Series 2000, 34, 90
H-S Precision, 12, 14, 46, 59

I

Ibex, 94, 154-160, 164, 165
impala, 105, 107, 109, 112, 123, 128, 140

K

Klipspringer, 101
kudu, 101, 108-111, 125, 128, 135

L

leopard, 126, 137-141
Leupold, 26, 27, 36, 56, 58, 59, 107, 154, 175, 182
Linebaugh, 142
lion, 126, 135-137
Lone Eagle, 14, 35, 46, 59

M

Mag-Na-Port International, 41, 61, 130
Magnum Research, 14, 35, 181
Marco Polo sheep, 164-65
McMillan, 14, 46, 59
Mediterranean Sea, 170
moose, 11
mouflon sheep, 179
Mouflon, 91
mountain reedbuck, 101, 103
M.O.A. Maximum, 34

N

National Rifle Association, 22
Nikon, 27, 182
nilgai, 91-92
Nosler Ballistic Tips, 32
Nosler, 32, 33, 37, 46-48, 53, 58-59, 67, 81, 90, 93, 98, 100, 123, 165
nyala, 124

O

oribi, 97, 100

P

pelts, 37
prairie dogs, 32, 37-38
Predator, 41, 61, 74
puma, 173, 175-76

R

red deer, 94
red duiker, 102
red stag, 173, 179
Redhawk, 178
Redhawk, 41
Remington XP-100, 14
rhino, 126, 128, 129, 134-35, 152
roan, 125
Ruger Blackhawk, 26
Ruger Super Blackhawk, 41
Ruger, 11, 67, 73, 74, 107, 110-11, 130, 178, 181
Ruger Mark II, 26
rusa deer, 150

S

sable, 108, 112, 122, 128
Safari Club International, 22, 51
sambar, 142, 150, 151
Savage Striker, 26, 34
scimitar-horned oryx, 94
serval, 104
Sharpe grysbok, 96
Sierra, 67
sika deer, 93-94
Simmons, 27, 182
sind ibex, 165
sitatunga, 125
Smith & Wesson, 41
Smith & Wesson_s Model 41, 26
snow leopard, 152
southern bush duiker, 102
Spanish ibex, 169
Speer, 67, 69, 108-110, 112
SSK Industries, 12, 13, 32, 47, 59, 74, 183
steenbok, 102, 107
Striker, 12, 14, 18
suni, 102, 104
Super Blackhawk, 67, 130
Super Redhawk, 41
Swarovski, 45, 158
Swift, 144, 146

T

Tasco, 27, 182
Taurus, 11

The Hunting Consortium, 153
tiger, 152
tsessebe, 125
tur, 160-162

V

vaal rhebuck, 98-99

W

warthogs, 106-107, 109, 111-112, 128
water buffalo, 94, 142, 147, 152, 173,
waterbuck, 106
white springbuck, 102
white-lipped peccary, 177
wild boar, 142
Winchester, 68, 73, 102, 154, 157, 175, 178, 184
Winchester's Partition Gold, 15

X

XP-100, 32-33, 46

Z

zebra, 107

Numbers

17 Remington, 34
22 Hornet, 32, 35
22 Magnum, 26, 32,
22 rimfire, 97, 182, 185
221 Remington, 32
22-250, 14, 34
223 Remington, 32
223 Winchester, 102
223, 34
250 Savage, 33-34, 53,
257 JDJ, 33, 53
284 Winchester, 46, 59
300 Savage, 46, 58, 93-94
30-06, 13
30-30 Winchester, 12, 46
308 Winchester, 18, 58, 59, 68, 125, 154, 157, 173
309 JDJ, 12, 46-47, 59, 78, 98, 100
338 Woodswalker, 93
35 Remington, 14, 33, 68
357 Magnum, 64
358 JDJ, 105-106, 109, 142, 151,
375 JDJ, 12, 56, 58, 66, 68, 75, 77, 82-83, 90, 92, 96, 101-2, 105, 108-109, 122, 128-129, 132, 134-5, 137, 140-142, 144, 147, 173
375 Winchester, 66, 68
375/06 JDJ, 13, 85, 128
44 Magnum, 41-42, 51, 52, 56, 107, 110, 178, 181
450 Marlin, 181
454 Casull, 41-42, 61-62, 66-68, 75, 77, 97, 128, 134, 142, 181
45-70, 33, 46, 66, 74-75, 77, 105-106, 108, 110, 112, 127-128, 134, 142, 181
6mm BR, 33
6mm TCU, 33
629 Stealth Hunter, 41
6.5 JDJ, 12, 33, 46, 53, 58-59, 91, 100, 123
6.5 X 284, 59
6.5mm BR, 33
7 JDJ, 150
7mm BR, 33-34
7mm TCU, 33
7mmBR, 14
7mm-08 Remington, 13-14, 34-35, 46, 53, 58, 59, 68
7X30 Waters, 12,
7-30 Waters, 46
.22 rimfire, 32
.22-250, 34-36
.223 Winchester, 12, 33-35
.243 Winchester, 13, 35
.250 Savage, 12
.270 Winchester, 13
.284 Winchester, 14
.308 Winchester, 13-14, 34, 46-47, 66
.309 JDJ, 53
.338 Woodswalker, 150
.35 Remington, 46, 66
.357 Magnum, 9, 42
.41 Magnum, 10, 41
.410, 29
.44 Magnum, 10, 15, 67-68, 75
.454 Casull, 11, 125
.45-70, 12, 68
.480 Ruger, 11, 125

Enjoy Success on All Outdoors Adventures

Whitetail Behavior Through the Seasons
by Charles J. Alsheimer
More than 160 striking action shots reveal a rarely seen side of North America's most impressive game animal. In-the-field observations will help you better understand all aspects of the whitetail deer, from breeding to bedding. Nature lovers and hunters will love this stunning book.
Hardcover • 9 x 11-1/2 • 208 pages
166 color photos
Item# WHIT • $34.95

The Complete Guide to Hunting Knives
by Durwood Hollis
Once you bring your game home, the next part of the hunt (utilization) begins. Knowing which knife to use to get the job done quickly and safely is a paramount concern. This text details information on construction, materials, characteristics, handles, sheaths, and blades as well as care and maintenance. Knives for big game, small game, upland and waterfowl, camping and filleting are covered.
Softcover • 8-1/2 x 11 • 224 pages
225 b&w photos • 16-page color section
Item# BHKN • $19.95

Elk: Strategies for the Hunter
by Durwood Hollis
If you want to bag a trophy elk, author Durwood Hollis provides a detailed map to success. He'll guide you through the complicated process of applying for a license and hiring a guide and show you exactly what you need to succeed at elk camp. If you're serious about the most majestic animal in North America, this book is for you.
Softcover • 8-1/2 x 11 • 208 pages
125 b&w photos
Item# ELK • $19.95

Whitetail
Fundamentals and Fine Points For the Hunter
by George Mattis
Revisit an era of deer hunting when hunters donned wool jackets, congregated in deer camps, and still-hunting was considered a skill. This hardcover reprint is the third *Deer & Deer Hunting* classic showcasing whitetails and offering valuable insight into the secretive world of white-tailed deer. Learn hunting strategies that were taught decades ago but are still considered essential techniques today, including stalking, using the land's contour to travel, and reading the weather to predict whitetail behavior.
Hardcover • 8-1/4 x 10-7/8 • 240 pages
200 b&w sketches
Item# WHFUN • $34.95

The Complete Book Of Outdoor Survival
by J. Wayne Fears
Be prepared for the unexpected-and survive. Full of technical tips, useful skills, and real life examples, the practical information covered in this comprehensive guide benefits all outdoor enthusiasts from scouts and hikers to hunters and adventurers. Topics include edible plants, edible animals, smoking meat, making solar stills, and many more.
Softcover • 8-1/2 x 11 • 368 pages
550 b&w photos
Item# OTSUR • $24.95

Hunting North American Big Game
by Durwood Hollis
Plan the hunt of a lifetime and learn where and how to hunt North America's most popular big game species. You'll get inside information on four types of deer, three types of bear, and elk, pronghorn, moose, caribou, bighorn sheep, mountain goats, bison, musk ox, wild boar, and javelinas. Additional chapters focus on guns, ammunition, and other gear, plus field dressing animals, caring for meat, and preparing trophies for taxidermy.
Softcover • 8-1/2 x 11 • 320 pages
300 b&w photos • 16-page color section
Item# NABG • $24.95

Legendary Deer Camps
by Robert Wegner
Travel back in time to experience deer camps of famous Americans such as William Faulkner, Aldo Leopold and Oliver Hazard Perry. Rediscover classic hunting traditions such as freedom, solitude, camaraderie, rites of initiation, storytelling and venison cuisine through a series of famous deer camp biographies and rare historical paintings and photographs. This is the second book in the *Deer and Deer Hunting* Classics Series.
Hardcover • 8-1/4 x 10-7/8 • 208 pages
125 b&w photos • 75 color photos
Item# DERCP • $34.95

Camping Digest
by Janet Groene
Before reserving your campsites, consult this reference for the latest camping gear designed to outfit you with everything needed for an enjoyable outdoors experience. National and state parks, leading campgrounds, and U.S. travel organizations are listed with contact information to assist you in making your camping plans. Feature articles offer advice on choosing proper equipment, finding the right campground, setting up, enjoying the great outdoors, and more.
Softcover • 8-1/2 x 11 • 352 pages
200 b&w photos
Item# CRV1 • $24.95

To order call **800-258-0929** Offer OTB2
M-F 7am - 8pm • Sat 8am - 2pm, CST
Krause Publications, Offer OTB2
P.O. Box 5009, Iola WI 54945-5009 • **www.krausebooks.com**

Shipping & Handling: $4.00 first book, $2.25 each additional. Non-US addresses $20.95 first book, $5.95 each additional.
Sales Tax: CA, IA, IL, NJ, PA, TN, VA, WI residents please add appropriate sales tax.
Satisfaction Guarantee: If for any reason you are not completely satisfied with your purchase, simply return it within 14 days of receipt and receive a full refund, less shipping charges.